Lotte Reiniger

Lotte Reiniger
Pioneer of Film Animation

WHITNEY GRACE

McFarland & Company, Inc., Publishers
Jefferson, North Carolina

Frontispiece: Lotte Reiniger's Animal Alphabet (n.d.). These are fine examples of Reiniger's silhouette illustrations intended for an unfinished German alphabet book. Her attention to detail extended to human as well as animal forms (courtesy the Tübingen Stadtmuseum).

LIBRARY OF CONGRESS CATALOGUING-IN-PUBLICATION DATA

Names: Grace, Whitney, author.
Title: Lotte Reiniger : pioneer of film animation / Whitney Grace.
Description: Jefferson, North Carolina : McFarland & Company, Inc., Publishers. 2017 | Includes bibliographical references and index.
Identifiers: LCCN 2017029900 | ISBN 9781476662060 (softcover : acid free paper) ∞
Subjects: LCSH: Reiniger, Lotte. | Animators—Germany—Biography. | Women animators—Germany—Biography. | Animated films—Germany—History and criticism.
Classification: LCC NC1766.G32 R4535 2017 | DDC 741.5/8092 [B] —dc23
LC record available at https://lccn.loc.gov/2017029900

BRITISH LIBRARY CATALOGUING DATA ARE AVAILABLE

ISBN (print) 978-1-4766-6206-0
ISBN (ebook) 978-1-4766-2873-8

© 2017 Whitney Grace. All rights reserved

No part of this book may be reproduced or transmitted in any form or by any means, electronic or mechanical, including photocopying or recording, or by any information storage and retrieval system, without permission in writing from the publisher.

Front cover: Still from the 1926 film *The Adventures of Prince Achmed* (courtesy of Paul Gelder, © Primrose Productions)

Printed in the United States of America

McFarland & Company, Inc., Publishers
Box 611, Jefferson, North Carolina 28640
www.mcfarlandpub.com

For Will
And for the one outside looking in

Table of Contents

Acknowledgments	ix
A propos de Lotte Reiniger	xi
Introduction	1
1. Paper Fairytales	3
2. Lengthening Shadows	13
3. Defining the Art of Puppetry and Animation	21
4. *The Adventures of Prince Achmed*	49
5. Sound Cartoons and Miscredited Ideas	90
6. Fanboy Hitler and the Short Life of Hansi and Schnuff	114
7. Animated Women and Lost Love	146
8. The Fine Line Between Animation and Puppetry	183
9. Fine Art and Resurgent Praise	201
10. Lotte's Legacy	229
11. Influence and Adaptation	240
Afterword	249
Appendix I: Filmography	251
Appendix II: Works Written by Reiniger	253
Chapter Notes	254
Bibliography	258
Index	267

Acknowledgments

Throughout the writing of this book, I learned that Lotte Reiniger has a bigger fanbase than I imagined. Whenever I brought her up in a conversation, people were ecstatic she was the subject of my book and were happy to contribute. The following people donated their time and resources to help me (in no particular order) and I thank all of them!

Jez Stewart of the British Film Institute was a constant source of information and humor. He unearthed several files for me that revealed facts about Lotte's time in England. Evamarie Blattner of the Stadtmuseum Tübingen, who provided rare photos and blessing to write about the first lady of German animation. Carolin Beinroth of the Deutsches Filminstitut helped me with information related to composer Wolfgang Zeller. I owe a lot to shadow puppeteer and German Lotte biographer Alfred Happ, who had the most thorough account of Lotte's life. My best to the fine folk at the National Film Board of Canada for digging into their archives and sharing details about Lotte's time in North America and production of *Aucassin and Nicolette*. Former head of the NFB Gordon Martin gave his constant support and Academy Award winning animator Co Hoedeman supplied me with lovely stories. Photographer Lois Segal was kind enough to supply lovely photos of Lotte. Lois also discovered a brilliant, never before heard, audio interview with Lotte! British journalist Paul Gelder and former Lott biographer was a huge supporter in the completion of this project. He supplied me with many lovely articles, original silhouettes, and photos of Lotte that he collected when he sought to write his own Lotte Reiniger biography.

I owe Kevin Kern of Walt Disney Company Archives a debt of gratitude for scouring the Disney vaults for any fact that Walt and Lotte had met once upon a time. Also humbling me by requesting a copy of *Lotte Reiniger: Pioneer of Film Animation* to add to the archive library. Henson Company archivist Karen Falk proved to be an invaluable contact for my research. Not only was she able to supply me with key contacts and facts. I thank the Museum of Modern Art Archives for their historical records and being one of the first fine art institutes to recognize animation as a serious art medium. Columbia University Archives was also helpful for housing the Cecile Starr papers. The University of Texas at Austin's Harry Ransom Center houses Eric Walter White's papers and Ariel Evans was a vigilant contact there.

I also thank Lois White of the Getty Research Institute for scanning some rare silhouette figures and books related to Lotte for my research. The Center for Puppetry Arts in Atlanta, GA provided me with some wonderful articles about the puppetry aspect of Lotte's career. The Harvard University Archives cleared up a few mysteries about the film rights to *Die Abenteuer des Prinzen Achmed*. Thank you Cindy Keefer, Director of the Center for Visual Music in Los Angeles, CA for telling me more about Cecile Starr. I also thank the University of California, Los Angeles Archives for sharing Jean Renoir's papers. The U.S. Library of Congress was a huge help as I researched *Prinzen Achmed's* restoration.

I owe a huge debut to the Women In Animation organization and their wonderful leadership for their support in writing this book. Tracey Miller-Zarneke and Fumi Kitahara were especially helpful by connecting me with Lotte fans that currently work in the industry and supplying me with printed resources. Fairytale expert Jack Zipes gave me encouragement and resources I am grateful for. Ulrich Marzolph was my partner in Arabian Nights investigation, so thank you for helping me track down the clues. Thank you Maureen Furniss for narrowing down my thoughts.

As for the Lotte Reiniger fans, I individually thank William Joyce, Brenda Chapman, Rebecca Sugar, Michel Ocelot, Nora Twomey, Henry Selick, and Jorge R. Gutiérrez. I am eternally grateful for Richard Bradshaw, Janibeth Johnson, and Mara Alper, who knew Lotte personally, for their insights and sharing their photos with me.

My thanks to Dave and Vicky for allowing me to stay in their home. I am much obliged and grateful to finding Paul Gelder, who shared his experiences traveling with his "aunt."

Lastly, I thank the parents and siblings for their support, library cards, and not making a big deal when I ate the last of the dessert.

A propos de Lotte Reiniger

I first met Lotte Reiniger as the echoes of the First World War still resounded in the distance. It was at the entrance to the Théâtre Marigny in Paris, where her film distributors had presented "Prince Achmed" (July, 1926). The few steps I had taken had not broken the film's spell for admirers had said to me, "She has fairy hands.' It was true.

We spent the rest of the evening talking to each other. What can you say when you find yourself in the presence of Mozart, especially if this Mozart is a charming woman, slightly plump, who chats like a magpie?

Carl Koch, Lotte's husband and collaborator, wanted to put me at my ease so we all went to café nearby. A sentence came to my lips but I did not dare to pronounce it. The sentence was: "You have fairy hands." It was not flattery, it was a statement of fact.

We were a small group and we spoke about all sorts of things, except for Lotte herself. We expected Lotte to give us her definitive opinions in *ombres chinoises* (shadow plays). Instead, she had only one thought in her head ... to go to the Folies Bergère cabaret! Shows with artistic aspirations bored Lotte to death, it seems.

The group were surprised, so I suggested that instead we might all go to Montparnasse to hear Georgious (George Guibourg), one of the most popular singers in Paris. Koch was not interested. Our conversation exhausted all sorts of banalities. The day had been a continuation of almost uninterrupted interviews. We discussed war memories, etc. Koch and I discovered to our great amusement that he had served in 1916 as captain of a German anti-aircraft artillery battery in the Rheims sector. It seems their biggest target was the airfield I was flying from as part of a reconnaissance squadron. So Koch and I had made war together. Now the exchange of "projectiles" ended with an exchange of friendly souvenirs around a Paris café table. It was an overwhelming moment for us.

Suddenly, I noticed Lotte was exhausted and wanted to go to bed. We took her to her hotel and a friend, who accompanied us, said to me after Lotte disappeared: "Surely she creates wonders." Certainly Prince Achmed is a *chef d'oeuvre* (masterpiece). But modest Lotte never claimed the full credit she deserved. She simply felt lucky to have been born with fairy hands.—Jean Renoir, 29 April 1977

Film director Renoir was a cinematic pioneer and a dear friend to Lotte Reiniger and Carl Koch. In the 1970s, journalist Paul Gelder wrote a biography of Reiniger and approached Renoir to write a preface. The book was never published. When Renoir died in 1979, the preface was among his papers—now housed at the University of California, Los Angeles—and Gelder kept a copy. He graciously provided access to his Reiniger archive for this book and permission to use Renoir's preface, appearing here for the first time.

Introduction

If you were to ask anyone what the first feature-length animated movie was, they might respond with Walt Disney's 1937 classic *Snow White and the Seven Dwarfs*. It is such a common misconception it has been taken as fact, along with other Disney lore such as: Tinkerbell was modeled after Marilyn Monroe (it was actually Margaret Kerry), that there are sexual references in *Aladdin*, *The Lion King* and *The Little Mermaid*, and that good old Walt had himself put on ice. None of these are true, but they circulate among the masses like urban legends.

A quick search on IMDb or Wikipedia proves that *Snow White* wasn't the first animated film. That distinction goes to Argentine animator Quirino Cristiani's film *El Apóstel* (*The Apostle*), followed by his *Sin dejar rastros* (*Without a Trace*). The latter film's title proved prophetic: both features were lost in a fire that consumed Cristiani's body of work.

The oldest *surviving* feature-length animated film was created by a German woman named Lotte Reiniger.

Reiniger fell in love with silhouettes and film at a young age. She was highly skilled in the German folk craft *Scherenschnitte* or "paper cuts," and used her skill with scissors to create shadow puppets. She used a stop-motion animation process to animate the puppets on film, making a number of shorts before she completed the feature-length *Die Abenteuer des Prinzen Achmed* (*The Adventures of Prince Achmed*). It was released in 1926, 11 years before *Snow White*. Reiniger's story was inspired by the Middle Eastern fairytale saga *1001 Arabian Nights*, drawing on German storytelling elements that have become universal in part due to the Brothers Grimm.

Reiniger had a stellar career. While her talents spoke for themselves and earned her modest respect among her peers, what is even more amazing is that she was able to pioneer a new art style in the early twentieth century as a woman. While Europe has arguably been considered to be more enlightened on matters of social progress than the United States, Europe was still a male-centric society.

With the support of her husband-partner, Reiniger created a groundbreaking film during a time when any woman who stepped outside the home and accomplished a goal in a male-dominated field was a rarity. Yet very few people outside of the animation and puppetry fields recognize her name and most who do think of her as a footnote in animation history, puppetry and German cinema books.

Much of the recorded history and archived works about Reiniger, housed at the Tübingen Stadtmuseum, Düsseldorf Stadtmuseum and the Deutsches Filminstitut in Germany, have not been translated into English. The British Film Institute has a fair amount of information on her, given that she became a British citizen and emigrated there after World War II, but it is still limited. Her contributions to animation, puppetry, storytelling and film have been overlooked for unspecified reasons.

Over the years, the few publications on her have slipped into out-of-print status. Each usually offered a biography on Reiniger, praise for her work, and some form of poetic expression about her importance. Rachel Palfreyman mentioned this lack of appreciation and documentation in her essay "Life and Death in the Shadows: Lotte Reiniger's *Die Abenteuer des Prinzen Achmed.*" But instead of slipping into an easy theme of praise and rant about Reiniger's neglect, Palfreyman noted:

> [D]ifficult though it may be, we need to go beyond a sense of wonder at Reiniger's achievements and engage with her work: brief, if extravagant, praise might, after all, amount to another form of neglect. Less admiration and more critique are needed. For somehow she remains in canonical limbo, on a kind of pedestal with her "unique" silhouette technique, not easily contextualised or located within a tradition, and therefore isolated by the very perception of her astonishing uniqueness, her unparalleled technique.
>
> Is it, then, wrong to suggest that she is unique? No—it is absolutely fair to say that her silhouette animations are unparalleled. She did reach unimaginable heights in technique, and other animators have not followed her particular lead.... There are not great numbers of filmmakers where you can see a direct influence..., but there is by no means a great Reiniger "school." However, focusing entirely on her uniqueness says more about the academy than it does about her. For it is not true that she has no connection to aesthetic movements and traditions [and the actual animation industry]. The issue is more that she is connected to so many ... that the academy appears not to negotiate very well, though audiences respond much more readily to such a challenge [2011, 9–10].

What is astonishing is that given our modern mentalities, instant access to information, and hunger for stories packed with rare facts that break histories' traditional trappings, no one has touched Reiniger. Why?

Maybe it's due to her lack of an overly dramatic World War II story having to flee the Nazis? Maybe being German was a primary factor? Maybe because of her gender, no one bothered to record her? Maybe her focus on silhouette animation and shadow puppetry was considered too old-fashioned? Maybe it's due to the undervalued and consigned to children mediums of animation and puppetry? Maybe a mouse clad in red shorts had more appeal to audiences? Maybe it's because she was only recognized for one feature-length film in her lifetime? Or maybe she slipped through history's cracks to be regaled in quiet solemnity?

Reiniger pioneered many techniques and art forms that even today still ring with originality and grace often lacking in many modern animated films. She has more than earned a place in animation and puppetry history. While I intend to enthrall with Reiniger's story, I do suspend my awe long enough to accept the challenge by writing a critical approach relating her to animation history and the industry as a whole, her importance as a puppeteer, and discussing the informal Lotte Reiniger school that has sprung up among modern animators. It's time to remember and be amazed by her work.

As many of her stories begin, "Once upon a time..."

Author's Note: One of the perils of writing about people and events of long ago (and in non–English-speaking countries) is alternate spellings. Lotte Reiniger and her husband Carl Koch were ethnic Germans and British citizens at the time of their deaths. They were friends with many people around the world who spoke multiple languages, which contributed to more alternate spellings of events, people and items. For consistency, I refer to films by their original titles in their original languages. When I use direct quotes within the text, I maintain the author's spellings as they appeared in their original publications. Mistakes in direct quotes have been noted by me and addressed where necessary.

1

Paper Fairytales

> I just want to tell stories, spin a yarn, dream. I never expect my audience to split their sides laughing. I try, instead, to tempt them to smile.—Lotte Reiniger

Frank Johnston and Ollie Thomas were two of Walt Disney's Nine Old Men, the animators who were integral to developing the core of the company's animation department. Together they wrote one of the most important books documenting animation and its process, 1981's *Disney Animation: The Illusion of Life*. It is still one of the most sought-after references for professional and student animators. With the book's title, Thomas and Johnston coined the term "the illusion of life" to describe what animation is.

Animation, in a sense, is the younger sibling of puppetry—one of the first illusions of life (others being paintings and tapestries). Puppetry is an ancient practice used to entertain the masses and provide social commentary. British history cannot be told without referring to the infamous Punch and Judy shows, just as Italy is proud of its marionettes epitomized by the wooden boy Pinocchio. Crossing over hemispheres into Asia offers a rich history of unique puppetry arts foreign to western imaginations.

Animation drew on many of the techniques common to puppetry; Johnston and Thomas touched on them in their book, showing how similar art forms are. In the Atlanta Center for Puppetry Arts, there used to be an exhibit entitled "Puppets: The Power of Wonder" curated by Michael Malkin, and within the exhibit was a small informative plaque that read:

> Animation: The illusion of life becomes life through movement, sculpture, light and shadow. Audiences infer life and spirit from movement as well movement and spirit from life. Animation of an object works on two square levels. The first is intellectual and activates the audience's tendency to think symbolically. The second level engages a spiritual or aesthetic level of appreciation in which our memories, intuitions and emotions are activated. Puppetry has to appeal to both levels of consciousness [Smith email to author, February 17, 2016].

Animation, as well, must appeal to both consciousnesses, otherwise you just have renderings on a screen that don't go anywhere, emotionally or physically.

Nowadays it's easier to merge animation and puppetry principles into one medium, mostly due to technological improvements. Stop-motion or stop frame animation relies on puppets and stages moved in small increments and filmed frame by frame, so that when all the pieces are placed together it simulates cohesive movement. There are digital puppetry studios that capture a puppeteer's movements and translate them to a digital character. For decades, videogames have used motion capture to make movements more lifelike and in many ways transform the person wearing the skintight suit with glued-on ping-pong balls into a puppet themselves. Animation studios are using these same techniques to animate their characters.

Lotte Reiniger had none of our twenty-first century conveniences and like many pioneers she had to do everything by hand and literally due to her chosen medium. How did a young German woman of the early twentieth century create a groundbreaking animation technique? She first drew on aspects of puppetry and her talent for scherenschnitte, not to mention her desire to be a storyteller.

Before answering the question of how, it's important to answer the question: Who was Lotte Reiniger? She was born Charlotte Elizabeth Eleonare Reiniger to Eleanor née Raquette and Karl Reiniger on June 2, 1899, at 11 Knesebeckstraßein, now the Charlottenburg borough of Berlin. Karl's family was Austrian and lived in Mariánské Lázně (Marienbad) in what is now Czechoslovakia. Her mother Eleanor came from Silesia, although her ancestry was French. Her parents enrolled her in the Charlottenburger Waldschule with a curriculum set in reform pedagogical ideas (Wiegmann & Blattner, 2010, 110) Among her favorite activities were listening to her grandfather's stories and developing her scherenschnitte skills (Happ, 2004, 7). In her winter years, Reiniger said that as a child she aimed to please her family and friends, and by cutting silhouettes she pleased everyone ("Lotte Reiniger Recording," 1976). Scherenschnitte is the art of paper cutting with precise scissor cuts. Paper cutting is a craft traditionally practiced in various cultures around the globe, beginning in China with the invention of paper. It became a popular folk art in Switzerland and Germany. Reiniger was skilled at paper cutting and especially at making silhouettes (which had fallen in and out of vogue in Europe). Alfred Happ, the one person to have written a biography on Reiniger, said that while she was growing up, she was inspired by art nouveau artist Karl Wilhelm Diefenbach's black-inked silhouette postcard set "Per Aspera Ad Astra" (Happ, 2004, 9).

Fairytales played a critical role in her childhood and she loved retelling and reinventing the stories. Reiniger's exposure to fairytales was not any different from other German child's. The Grimm Brothers' *Children's and Household Tales* (*Kinder- und Hausmärchen*) was a primary part of German children's education since the 1870s (Zipes, 2002, 48). Fairytales were used to teach morals and society rules, and serve as cautionary stories. Germany as a whole was struggling with its collective identity as a single country and many educated Germans saw fairytales as a tool to unite the country under one cultural umbrella. This belief increased the popularity of fairytales and "by the beginning of the twentieth century, *Children's and Household Tales* was second only to the Bible as a best-seller in Germany..." (Zipes, 2002, 48).

The young girl wasn't entirely occupied by fairytales and scherenschnitte. "When I was a child, I had the uncanny ability to cut silhouettes. But I didn't like for them to remain motionless, I was always playing with them and at 12 years old I had a primitive shadow theater" (Happ, 2004, 9). By playing with her silhouettes, Reiniger stumbled upon shadow puppetry and built her own theater to perform for her family and friends. There is even a recollection of her using silhouettes during a school performance of Shakespeare's *The Tempest*, *Romeo and Juliet* and *Twelfth Night* (Wiegmann & Blattner, 2010, 7 & 110; Happ, 2004, 130; "Lotte Reiniger Recording," 1976). For *Romeo and Juliet*, Reiniger used her primitive shadow theater to depict the famous balcony scene between the two lovers ("Lotte Reiniger Recording," 1976). During her class' *Tempest* production,

Reiniger was enthralled with the savage mooncalf Caliban and decided that none of her classmates "were fit to occupy" the role, so she used a silhouette to perform him instead (Happ, 2004, 130). The performance was so wonderfully grim and horrific (apt for Caliban's character) that Reiniger fell in love with performing (Happ, 2004, 130).

These shadow theater performances taught Reiniger storytelling elements and entertainment practices that would echo throughout her later work. Her love for shadow puppetry was only equaled by a fascination with cinema. Young Lotte was "absolutely crazy about films" and her grandmother would take her to see them at a local theater. Reiniger recalled one outing:

> My poor grandma would have to take me to the cinema in its early days around 1907. One time I went to a cinema on Berlin's Kant Street, they were showing *Sleeping Beauty*, and I was keen to see it as I was a fairytale "fan," right? When we got there it was no longer being screened. I started crying so awfully that the old ladies running the cinema demanded that the film be reordered. They had the projectionist come in the morning, and had the film screened especially for me. I was very proud indeed [qt. in Marschall *et al.*, 2012].

Reiniger was 17 in 1916 and her love for film peaked when she attended a lecture given by Paul Wegener. Wegener was a movie and stage actor renowned for his work during the German Expressionist film era; at the time he gave his lecture. his most famous roles were in 1913's *Der Student von Prag* (*The Student of Prague*) and 1915's *Der Golem*. In 1916, he spoke about animation's potential in film with Reiniger in the audience. His words inspired her to speak with her parents about attending the Max Reinhardt School, a drama school associated with the theater of the same name, to pursue becoming an actress. Eleanor and Karl Reiniger were quite upset about their daughter's decision, mostly due to their unfamiliarity with theater. They were concerned for her virtue (although they did support progressive education). Reiniger said, "I persuaded my parents to let me go to this school.... [M]y father had a sleepless night before he signed the paper. He said that he felt like a chicken who had hatched a duck, but later they both calmed down" (qt. in Happ, 2004, 11). Wegener taught at the Max Reinhardt School and used it as a base for his acting troupe and to work on his projects. She longed for the chance to work for Wegener; one of her reasons for attending the school was to get the opportunity. She would later say that attending the acting school was the cleverest thing she had done in her life as it made her more extroverted—and that marrying her husband was the second wisest thing she did (qt. in Ashoff, 1981).

As a student, Reiniger wasn't allowed to attend the theater's rehearsals. But students and alumni were allowed to get acting experience by being extras in Wegener's stage shows and movie productions. Patience is a requirement for any actor, due to the long stretches between scene changes and movie takes. These can take hours and entertaining oneself in a quiet manner is a must, lest you be booted from the production. Even though she wanted to be an actress, Reiniger didn't abandon her childhood pastimes and she believed her scherenschnitte skills would capture Wegener's attention. It was also the perfect hobby for an extra: What was quieter than cutting paper while the camera rolled or the actors were on stage? She created silhouette portraits of the performers and sold them for tuition (Moritz, 1996a, 40). Her silhouettes became so admired that she got her wish: She *was* noticed by Wegener, who "noticed not only the quality of the silhouettes she made, but also her incredible dexterity in cutting: holding the scissors nearly still in her right hand and moving the paper deftly in the swift gestures that uncannily formulated a complex profile" (Moritz, 1996a, 41). Among the many actors she constructed into

From *Sleeping Beauty*, the prince is overwhelmed by Princess Aurora's beauty in the cursed castle (©Primrose Productions).

silhouettes were Emil Jannings and Ernst Lubitsch, who encouraged her to cut more (Gelder, 1981). Her silhouettes of the actors were gathered into a book published in 1916 or 1917, *Schauspieler Silhouetten* (*Silhouettes of Actors*). It received the approval of the theater's namesake Max Reinhardt (Bendazzi, 1999, 31; Wiegmann & Blattner, 2010, 110).

Reiniger mentioned that she was so inspired to be involved with acting and filmmaking that every time Wegener was in his office, she pestered him to look at her new drawings. Later in life, she realized that she probably annoyed him, but he was always kind and she was grateful for his encouragement ("Lotte Reiniger Recording," 1976). Wegener decided to use Reiniger's talents in the 1916 silent film *Rübezahl's Hochzeit* (*Rumpelstiltskin's Wedding*), a film he co-directed with Rochus Gliese. Silent movies relied entirely on the audience's interpretations of actions on screen to understand the story. Music and sometimes an in-house interpreter were used to convey certain moods and narrate the story, but intertitles were soon spliced into the films. Intertitles are comparable to the ancient Greek chorus that commented on action, narrated scenes, and provided key dialogue for the characters (the latter reserved for silent films). Rather than having people wear masks and appear on the screen, the intertitles were graphical representations inserted between scenes. If a silent movie reel was laid and was blown up to be comfortably read by the human eye, it would resemble a graphic novel. The intertitles allowed movie production teams to be creative and add a level of static art to the film. Intertitles could be decorated with different motifs and the text could be changed to enhance the movie's theme. Wegener used Reiniger's silhouettes for *Rübezahls Hochzeits* intertitles. He played Rumplestiltskin and his third wife Lyda Salmonova played the lady elf, the love interest. Salmonova acted opposite Wegener in many of his famous films, including the *Golem* series and *Der Student von Prag*.

Rübezahls Hochzeits opens with an intertitle of Rumpelstiltskin atop a mountain, peering through a telescope at his lady love. The other intertitles Reiniger cut were of a single dancing elf and another of a group of elves dancing (Happ, 2004, 12).

Wegener apparently had a knack for finding raw talent and nurturing it, because both Gliese and Reiniger thrived under his tutelage and worked on several recognized projects. She collaborated with Gliese on two films, *Die schöne Prinzessin von China* (*The Beautiful Chinese Princess*) and *Apokalypse* (*Apocalypse*). Gliese was a theatrical set designer who, like Reiniger, caught Wegener's attention. Wegener hired Gliese to design the sets for the 1915 classic *Der Golem*, often cited as Wegener's most notable work. Gliese stepped into the director's role for a string of collaborations with Wegener, including *Der Yoghi, Hans Trutz im Schlaraffenland, Der fremde Fürst* (*The Foreign Prince*, in which Reiniger had a minor role) and *The Golem and the Dancing Girl*, a comedic parody of *Der Golem*.

The German studio UFA was beginning to take form around the time these films were made. Wegener's work served to set the precedent for much of the German film industry. Klaus Kreimeier, author of *The Ufa Story*, described Wegener's influence: "With *The Student of Prague* (1913) and *The Golem* (1914) [sic] Wegener had introduced ambitious artistic goals and a conception of film work not unlike today's auteur moviemakers, and he had won over members of the literary intelligentsia to the new medium" (1999, 45). Kreimeier said that in the 1916 speech Reiniger heard, Wegener foresaw film's future as an art form: "His early recognition that the camera had to be 'the real poet of film' and his vision of 'kinetic lyricism'...anticipated the aesthetics of animated films and the abstract films of the 1920s" (1999, 45). This solidifies Wegener's ambition to support budding artists and his desire to see what they would create with film. Gliese and Reiniger were two star students showcasing their talents for their master and they were given free rein to experiment. On the *Die schöne Prinzessin von China* (1916), while Gliese directed, Reiniger shifted away from her silhouettes. She designed costumes, special effects, sets and more (Schönfeld, 2006, 174). Her paper cutouts, however, arguably inspired the short film, because its actors appeared as live action silhouettes on a screen. During 1917, Reiniger was asked to make silhouettes of Wegener as the farmer Hans Trutz and Ernst Lubitsch as Satan for *Hans Trutz im Schlaraffenland* (*Hans Trutz on the Big Rock Candy Mountain*) (Happ, 2004, 12). Wegener joined Reiniger and Gliese once more for the anti–war film *Apokalypse* (1918) as a writer and cast member. Reiniger provided silhouettes that depicted atrocities committed during war and among them was one of the Four Horsemen (Moritz, 1996a; Happ, 2004, 12).

That same year, Wegener hired Reiniger for her first stab at animation with the film *Der Rattenfänger von Hameln* (*The Pied Piper of Hamelin*), based on the old story of how the city of Hamelin was overrun by rats. A piper was hired to lure the rats out of town, but when he demanded payment, the townsfolk refused. As revenge, the piper lured all Hamelin's children out of town with his music and disappeared with them. The tale alludes to the many children's deaths during the Middle Ages in Germany, mostly associated with either plague or the Children's Crusades.

Reiniger once more provided intertitles for a film, this time depicting the film's main characters and key scenes: "The Pied Piper," "The Mouse Plague," "The Minstrel," "The Wizard," "The High Court" and "Revenge" (Happ, 2004, 12). She also did something even more amazing; Wegener and his crew attempted to use real rats during production, but they proved to be too difficult to train. While modern filmmaking has demonstrated that rodents are very intelligent and capable of being trained for film, it is doubtful that Wegener had an animal trainer on staff. Wegener resorted to something that many of today's filmmakers can't do without: the special effects department. Reiniger was *Der Rattenfänger von Hameln*'s entire special effects team and she created animated rat models that followed the piper out of the town.

Reiniger described the humorous attempts Wegener and his crew made to use live rats on set in her book *Shadow Theaters and Shadow Films:*

> It was Wegener's idea to have the movement of the rats done with wooden rats, using "stop-motion." ... The producing company thought quite rightly that this would take up an enormous amount of time and labour and so it was decided to do the scene with real rats.
>
> A quaint little medieval street was chosen and all of the members of the unit (including me) were given a basketful of rats and were hidden in the cellars of the street. Early in the morning the street was cleared of traffic and Wegener in his Pied Piper costume passed along it, piping enticingly. Then a revolver shot was fired ... whereupon we all opened our baskets and let the rats escape through the cellar windows. And escape they did! None of them thought of following the Pied Piper. They whisked across the road and vanished in an instant.... In spite of the fact that the Pied Piper, so far from freeing the town of Hamelin from a plague of rats, had infected the town ... with another....
>
> Now we took guinea pigs instead. These poor guinea pigs were painted grey and were adorned with long tails, and again each of us took a basketful into his cellar. The same scene was repeated.... But unlike the rats, the guinea pigs did not escape. They, unaware of the script, sat cheerfully down in the middle of the street, played with each other, lost their tails, and amused themselves as best they could. But none followed the Pied Piped.
>
> So it had to be wooden rats and stop-motion [1970a, 82–83].

After filming *Der Rattenfänger von Hameln* in 1918, Reiniger was probably struck with the idea to use her talents to make a film entirely with silhouettes. During this time, animation was still in its infancy with small interested sects dedicated to the art popping up all over the globe. Notable animation legends Ub Iwerks, Max Fleischer and Walt Disney were just filling their inkwells to draw the first line on what would be careers still revered today (Beckerman, 2004). Those are just the United States animators; all over Europe and the future animation powerhouse Japan, there were fledging artists, such as Junichi Kouichi, Kitayama Seitaro and Shimokawa Oten, eager to test out the new medium, although it wouldn't be until after World War II that Japanese animation would take off under Osamu Tezuka's guidance. Reiniger was to become one of the leading, unacknowledged animators in Germany, but to get there she had to start.

Whenever a creative individual is asked to define the exact moment he or she knew they were embarking on a groundbreaking career, the answer is always the same: It's a series of events and experiences rather than a singular instance in time that leads up to inspiration. Lightning doesn't strike for every original idea, sometimes they just happen, which is more than likely what happened to Reiniger. She was using her paper cutting skills in films and received high praise from not only her peers, but also from one of Germany's most reputable actors. The next logical move was to do something even grander than intertitles and special effects.

In the aftermath of *Der Rattenfänger von Hameln*'s success, Reiniger was encouraged to further pursue silhouette animation. Wegener pulled another string to advance the experimentation stage of her career by bringing her to the attention of the brand new Institute for Cultural Research or Discovery (Institut für Kulturforschung), a studio that produced educational films.

Most resources that mention Reiniger's student years always point to *Der Rattenfänger von Hameln* as her first major project, glancing over the other short films and chalking up her childhood to little more than one typical of a budding entertainer. What these accounts fail to mention, other than Alfred Happ's biography, are how her prior experiences shaped her to be up for the challenge of feature film.

Her earliest influences were fairytales, which remained an inspiration throughout her life. Reiniger was born in Germany, arguably the birthplace of collected märchen due to the Brothers Grimm. It serves to illustrate that her early education centered on fairytales given their historical and cultural significance in her country. Jack Zipes in *The Brothers Grimm* eloquently explains Germans and their importance to Germany's national identity:

> In Germany, the obsession with the Grimms is actually an obsession with the fairytale as a vital and dynamic literary institution that offers writers and non-literate storytellers a means to participate in a dialogue and discourse about specific social conditions. Germans depend on this institution more than people in other Western countries because its development occurred exactly at a time when the nation was forming itself and when the bourgeoisie was achieving self-consciousness [2002, 120].

While Germany had become an official country consisting of smaller kingdoms and principalities when Reiniger was born, it was still struggling to place itself in a world that was rapidly moving away from feudal governments and agrarian economies to industrialization, democracy, communism and socialism. Reiniger's younger years were spent in relative peace, allowing her to approach fairytales with the awe and wonder reserved for the innocent. Although their more nationalistic overtones were pervasive, those didn't come much into play for Reiniger. The fairytale, indeed, was a cultural institution as Zipes claims, but it wasn't until the heavy losses in World War I, the Treaty of Versailles and the disastrous League of Nations were flames fanned to make it a political institute. The rising Nazi party appropriated the fairytales as a propaganda tool and from there we all know the results.

Reiniger's approach to fairytales was gentle and romantic, comparable to Disney, she took the stories and made them her own. Wegener was also a big fairytale fan and enamored with the world created on the screen. Kreimeier said, "Wegener continued his efforts to let 'the fantasy world of past centuries flow together with contemporary life.' He wanted to 'kill off' in the viewer the everyday, common urban dweller and make him a child again, marveling at a pre-rational fairytale world" (1999, 45). Like Reiniger, Wegener wanted to retain the innocence in fairytales and give the audience a whole new form of escapism, which would be needed to cope with both World Wars.

Reiniger's films are bookended between two dark periods in Germany's history and innocent films were lost in the chaos, leading to one of the reasons why she was overlooked by most historians.

Despite harsh realities, Reiniger's views on fairytales as fantastical stories are more commonly held today than the radical ideas projected onto them. Fairytales are the most popular stories to tell children in their developing years to shape their early perceptions about life and teach them the components of communication. They are also used to educate children by teaching them how to read and even basic storytelling principles. Fairytales frequently cross cultural barriers just as puppetry, one of the oldest forms of entertainment, did. Reiniger absorbed these "fairy" lessons to create her own magic on film.

Albert Einstein, also German born, was impacted by fairytales. While many of his quotes are taken out of context of their true meaning, Einstein did have this to say about märchen: "If you want your children to be intelligent, read them fairytales. If you want them to be more intelligent, read them more fairytales" (qt. in Heiner, 2007). Many would argue that Einstein's meaning in this quote was that he believed imagination was and is more important than hard facts. Doing so actually negates not only his point, but also Einstein's entire body of work. As a theoretical physicist, he sought to connect proven science with theoretical science, e.g., ideas that possibly exist based on assembled evidence or scientific fairytales. He's really arguing that reality and fantasy are interwoven together, thus children need the fairytale magic to expand their minds to discover "magic" in the real world. This assertion is ratified by another Einstein quote: "When I examine myself and my methods of thought, I come to the conclusion that the gift of fantasy has meant more to me than any talent for abstract, positive thinking" (qt. in Heiner, 2007).

Artists use imagination to create new ideas and then work within reality's confines to make them happen, similar to how scientists test theories. From the very start, fairytales were a huge inspiration to Reiniger, not only for their stories and educational components, but the fact they allowed her to see potential in animation.

Without scherenschnitte (paper cutting), Reiniger wouldn't even have a footnote in animation books. By being taught this old folk craft, she managed to breathe new life into what was regarded as a lowbrow hobby. Scherenschnitte history, however, started out as a noble pastime before it was co-opted by lower classes.

Scherenschnitte had been in practice in Europe for centuries, but the history of paper cutting is rooted in China and the invention of paper in the second century. While paper served an obvious practical use, it soon transformed into art mastered by royalty and peasants. The paper cutouts were made for adornment and were also used to depict stories, a practice continued by other cultures as the craft traveled across the world.

China was a cultural bastion for Asian countries and a huge trading partner for Persia and Turkey. Merchants carried paper cuttings over the Silk Road as early as the eighth century. Along the way, new techniques and names were given to the art, as well as different purposes. When paper cutting arrived in Europe around the fifteenth century, there were many drastic changes. In Europe, it was predominantly practiced by nobility and religious orders, due to the high cost of paper (it was still being handmade). Nuns and monks mastered the craft, creating intricate decoration for religious texts as well as devotionals (*klosterarbeiten*) with imitation lace patterns sold as pilgrimage souvenirs, and prayer papers that were handed out as gifts.

The earliest European paper cutting is the magnificent *The Book of Passion* from 1500, made for England's Henry VII. Cutouts were included on each vellum page and entire Latin passages were trimmed from paper. The impressive book is quite small despite its grandeur: 7.5 × 5.5 inches.

Eventually paper cutting was embraced by the masses and became the popular German scherenschnitte folk art in the seventeenth century. Cutters varied their techniques with layered, folded and paper laid flat. "Most scherenschnitte was cut from black and white paper and depended on contour rather than color for its effect" (Rich, 1993, 12). It was used to decorate legal documents, letters and cards, including the German valentine, and illustrate fairytales, making paper-cut embellishments common, useful and highly sought after. Reiniger was inherently influenced by these uses when she made her intertitles and eventually her animated films.

Reiniger's favored paper cutting, the silhouette, didn't emerge until the eighteenth century when it became a popular and cheaper alternative to a full-blown portrait. The silhouette is named after the French Minister of Finance Étienne de Silhouette, who served during Louis XV's reign. For lack of a better term, he was a cheapskate. During the Seven Years War with the United States, Silhouette attempted to control government spending. His name was pulled into the French vernacular to be associated with any items or services done cheaply. It became associated with portraiture due to the fact that a solid black form on white paper cost much less to produce than a painted miniature portrait.

Silhouettes embellished all walks of life, from fashion accessories to book illustrations to formal portraits hung on walls. They remained in fashion until photography replaced them. The silhouette had established a place for itself in folk art, although it was regarded as kitsch when Reiniger was young.

Discussing how paper cuttings were viewed when Reiniger started incorporating them in her films, Noga Wizansky notes that the silhouette's fall from consideration as true art was due to its adoption by the lower classes (2004, 86). She goes on to say that paper historians Max Von Bohn and E. Nevill Jackson "linked the emergence of formal impurities in silhouette practice such as the addition of white and color, to the concomitant departure of the silhouette from the ranks of 'good society,' its rising popularity among the middle class, inclusion in curriculums of young ladies' schools, and practiced by unskilled artists. They also pointed to the silhouette's dispersion into mass and popular forms of display and distribution," collected like stamps, printed on snuff boxes, and in porcelain factories (2004, 86).

Reiniger was employing silhouettes at a time when the noble art form had been relegated to lowly crafts meant to occupy children and the elderly. While she might have received compliments from her fellow actors and filmmakers, it appeared she would have a difficult time convincing the public to watch moving silhouettes on a screen.

The scenario might sound familiar to anyone upon the advent of a new medium: Change is bad and it will never be accepted. In *Moving Innovation*, Tom Sito explains how especially in the entertainment industry, the old school always resented the new innovators. Old Hollywood was built on a nepotism system and woe be to anyone who attempted to change the established "creative assembly line [that] chugged on for years, picture by picture" from the 1930s and onwards (Sito, 2013, 6). Some examples of the system at its best were Louis B. Mayer hiring family members to fill key positions. Backstage workers were so unionized they were able to pass down their jobs to sons (Sito, 2013, 6). By the 1960s, the once bold and impressive Hollywood machine was showing its age; Sito uses an apt metaphor to describe the next decade: "By the 1970s the studio production system had ossified into something resembling the protocol of the Manchu Court in the Forbidden City" (Sito, 2013, 7).

Animation and puppetry have more than their share of critics, doubters and people incapable of viewing it through a different lens other than their preconceived notions. The best-known stories include Disney's critics saying audiences would never sit through an hour-long cartoon with *Snow White and the Seven Dwarfs*. Pixar's John Lasseter and other CGI pioneers encountered resistance from Frank Thomas and Ollie Johnston with the adoption of computer animation (though early CGI film tests were really rough even by the 1980s standards). "[Thomas and Johnston] initially dismissed CG. Thomas said, 'Well, to be an animator, you had to be a really solid draftsman. With a computer, you don't have to be able to draw your ass.' Johnston said, 'What you could not put in the 3D animation was the charm and magic achieved through graphic cheats that are only possible in 2D drawing.' It seemed foolish to them to spend so much on technology just to recreate what they could do with a humble pencil. [Johnston continued,] 'Old-fashioned animation has more control and more freedom, and also offers a greater range of expression'" (qt. in Sito, 2013, 222).

Thomas continued with his anti-computer animation idea with his 1984 article "Can Classic Disney Animation Be Duplicated on the Computer?" He began by writing that computer engineers don't understand the concepts behind animation and that there wasn't an "electronic process that produces anything close to '*Snow White* quality' and there is little reason to believe there ever will be" (1984, 20). In the 1980s, computer animation was still in the homo habilis phase of evolution compared to modern marvels and were still beyond the greater range of "subtle pantomime, believable dialogue … and most of all that personal artistic statement may be beyond our reach in the mechanical area of electronic circuitry" (Thomas, 1984, 25).

Drifting over into puppetry, Jim Henson had a hard time convincing U.S. TV studios that puppets could be a valid medium for adult entertainment. Brit Lew Grade was the only one who took a chance on *The Muppet Show*.

Reiniger put Einstein's quote into practice by taking the old and revisualizing it. While Germany was still recovering from World War I, its film industry was about to have as much success as the Disney Renaissance in the 1990s to early 2000s. In 1919, the same year that Reiniger released her first silhouette film, the Weimar Republic was established and it would serve as Germany's governing body until 1933. Reiniger had started her film career at a pivotal time; cultural perspectives were changing, new technology was emerging, and the world was desperate for change to forget the Great War. "The years of the Weimar Republic have played a key role in the writing of German history and contributed greatly to the recognition of film as an essential part of twentieth-century German culture" (Hake, 2002, 26). Reiniger was hard at work to get her own piece of the silver screen by developing new animation techniques. She was contributing not only to German culture, but to something much grander.

2

Lengthening Shadows

There is a difference between this type of film to the normal animation is [sic] that it's made with scissors, you see. So it all moves in profile, this is so-called profile art. And you must compose your pictures so that it can all be done in a profile action, very direct towards each other and so on. But the benefit is that you can work all by yourself, you don't have to divide this work to so many people who do the drawings. And so you can really work like an artist paints his pictures. That's what I like about this style. That makes it easier.—Lotte Reiniger, 1981

The 1920s are portrayed as a glimmering decade that propelled humanity into the modern era. With the advances in technology, social convention changes, economic boom and the euphoria from the Great War, life had a genuine "newness" and wonder that was best captured in the period films. The movie industry was still young and the moviemakers were as enchanted with the process of creating films as the audience was in viewing them. This light-hearted approach to the budding entertainment medium was conveyed through the movies, which bore a simplistic fairytale quality, with messages of hope and endless possibilities.

Animation's progress paralleled the film industry's. The two mediums fueled each other as one's developments advanced the other's. The moment that directed Reiniger's animation career was Paul Wegener's lecture "Neue Kinoziele" ("New Goals of Cinema"), delivered in April 1916. As a film star and director, his words inspired Reiniger as much as film helped inspire the animated medium. His words foreshadowed how animation would grow in Europe and how Reiniger would later be a pivotal part of it:

You have all seen films in which suddenly a line appears, curves and changes its form. Out of it grow faces and the line disappears. To me the impressions seems highly remarkable. But such things are always shown as an intermezzo and nobody has ever thought of the colossal possibilities of this technique. I think the film as art should be based—as in the case of music—on tones, on rhythm. In these changeable planes, events unreel which are partly identified with natural pattern, yet partly beyond real lines and forms. Imagine one of [Arnold] Böcklin's sea paintings with all the fabulous tritons and nereids. And imagine an artist duplicating this work in hundreds of copies but with each copy having small displacements so that all copies revealed in succession would result in continuous movement. Suddenly we would see before our very eyes a world of pure fantasy come to life. Such effects can also be achieved with specially constructed little models animated like marionettes…. We are entering a new pictorial fantasy world as we would enter a magic forest. We are setting foot in the field of pure kinetics—or optical [kinetic] lyric as I call it. This field will perhaps be of major importance and will open new beautiful sights. This eventually is the final objective of each art, and so cinema would gain an autonomous aesthetic domain for itself. A movie could be created which would become an experience of art—an optical vision, a great symphonic fantasy! That it will happen one day, I am sure—and beyond that, I am certain, later generations will look upon our early efforts as upon childish stutterings [qt. in Giesen & Storm, 2012, 3–4].

Henry Nicolella and John T. Soister wrote of Wegener's "Neue Kinoziele" speech, "Wegener was not reticent about criticizing the film industry for its lack of vision and its reliance on books and plays for movie material and his biting comments resulted in considerable controversy" (2013, 119). Ironically, Wegener's next film *Rübezahls Hochzeit* didn't have near the amount of spectacular special effects Wegener wanted (his effects man Guide Seeber was off fighting in World War I) and it paled compared to his *Der Student von Prag* (Nicolella & Soister, 2013, 119). But Lotte Reiniger would more than live up to Wegener's fantastic vision. By 1919, she had an impressive start on her film career by working on the special effects and animation for five films. She moved to the next stage with further help from Wegener and the Institut für Kulturforschung.

The institute was founded with this goal: the making of films that merged art and science. Prof. Eduard Hanslick, a Fine Arts professor and a respected music critic, created the Institut in Vienna and Cürlis took charge of the Berlin branch. Cürlis wrote an essay for *Das Kulturfilmbuch* (edited by Edgar Beyfuss and A. Kossowsky) describing his intent with the institute. Wizansky summarized it: "[T]he institute was not interested in merely displaying art in films as pedagogical material. It endeavored instead, through collaborations between scientists and artists, to fuse artistic principles with film's unique properties, and to create an entirely new expressive form that would serve a range of documentary topics" (2004, 84). Animation was the perfect medium for the institute to carry out their mission. It combined the principles and aesthetics of art and filmmaking science. Cürlis also "included Reiniger's early short fairy tale films in this project, discussing them as productions, which contributed to the study of cinema's motion and rhythm" (Wizansky, 2004, 85).

Carl Koch (born Charles Robert Koch on July 30, 1892, in Nübrecht, Germany) would be an integral part of Reiniger's career, as he would become her husband and creative partner. Between 1912 and 1920, he attended the universities in Munich, Bönn, Göttingen, Marburg and Berlin (Happ, 2004, 19). His studies were disrupted when he was drafted to fight in World War I, where he became an artillery captain and commanded an anti-aircraft battery in the Rheims. Koch's future colleague and director Jean Renoir were stationed in the same area. Renoir wrote: "'It was a good sector,' [Koch] told me. 'Nothing against it except the incessant attack of the French squadron opposite us.' As it happens, in 1916 I was flying in a reconnaissance squadron in the same sector, and we were the main target of a German battery which gave us a lot of trouble. Koch and I concluded that this was his battery: so we had made war together" (1974, 161).

After his army service, Koch returned to his studies, specializing in art history and philosophy. He used his knowledge and expertise to write art books about the Far East (Bendazzi, 1999, 31). He graduated in Berlin, where he met Paul Wegener and Dr. Cürlis and began working on multiple projects at the Institute for Cultural Research. He said, "I started working with educational and documentary films and then for later films I tried some animation methods" (Happ, 2004, 19).

The institute would be referred to as an experimental animation studio and its intentions towards animation fell in line with the visually striking effects Reiniger created for *Der Rattenfänger von Hameln*. Wegener, Koch and Cürlis were associates, and in the summer of 1919 Wegener made "formal introductions" on Reiniger's behalf. Reiniger remembered him saying with (presumably) semi-sarcasm, "For heaven's sake, help me get rid of this mad silhouette girl. She makes very good silhouettes which cry out for animation. Can't you let her make a film with those silhouettes as they make cartoons?" (qt. in Bendazzi, 1999, 31). While Wegener encouraged Reiniger to try her hand at animation, she was also motivated by her own determination. Up to this point, her silhouettes had only been used as intertitles, decoration and special effects, and she realized there were many possibilities in animation using shadow puppetry techniques combined with scherenschnitte. With Koch and Cürlis backing her, she decided to make her first silhouette cartoon.

Reiniger's scherenschnitte skills were also in demand for book illustration. She was tapped some time between 1918 and 1919 to cut silhouettes for a poetry book by Gustav Hochstetter. *Venus in Seide: ein neues Liebesbrevier* (*Venus in Silk: A Breviary on New Love*), published in 1919, contains poems about love in all its form complemented by Reiniger's silhouettes on the pages. Her silhouette illustrations are pure art nouveau inventions with delicate detail. As soon as she finished one book job, she was hired for another: Hellmuth Krüger's *Das Loch im Vorhang: Licht und Schattenbilder aus dem deutschen Theater* (*The Hole in the Curtain: Light and Shadow Images of the German Theater*) (1920). Similar to *Schauspieler Silhouetten*, it included poems, stories, and biographies about popular German theater actors with silhouettes Reiniger clipped of them.

Throughout the fall, Koch, Cürlis and Reiniger worked on the short animation and on December 12, 1919, they released an art nouveau-esque piece, *Das Ornament des verliebten Herzens*. This title has several translations, including *The Ornament of the Loving Heart* (Reiniger favored this title), *Enamored Heart, Amorous Heart, Heart in Love* and *Infatuated Heart*. It is about two dancing lovers whose emotions are reflected through an ornament as they court one another. In 1981, interviewer Alfio Bastiancich asked Reiniger to describe the expressionist, abstract film, and she said,

> It was a balletic duet: a man and a woman moved around a wreath, which was made up of figures expressing their feelings. At first the man and the woman are very sweet and gentle, then they quarrel, and the wreath quivers. The woman leaves and the man is very sad, and weeps, but she returns and the ornament is reconstituted in the shape of a heart [1992/1981, 9].

Audiences loved it; the film was 92 or 60 meters in length (accounts differ on its length) (Happ, 2004, 14; White, 1931, 14). Cürlis said it was so popular that it ran "for 40 weeks on the Ufa cinema circuit" (qt. in Jouvanceau, 2004, 35). After receiving the praise, Reiniger made a decision to continue working with silhouette animation and did so until her death. "Now I finally had the opportunity to put my shadows in motion.... Something new was born: the movement (the silhouettes) on the screen" (qt. in Happ, 2004, 14).

Prior to making *Das Ornament des verliebten Herzens*, Reiniger learned animation techniques from Berthold Bartosch. He studied architecture and fine arts in Vienna and he was also a student of Eduard Hanslick, who gave him the idea to make educational movies using animation (Russett & Starr, 1976, 83). Hanslick collaborated with Bartosch on educational movies before moving on to films with political overtones. Bartosch moved to Berlin in 1919, joining Reiniger, Koch and Cürlis (Bendazzi, 1999, 38).

Reiniger's talents were in high demand after her film's success and in 1920 she was commissioned to work on more cinematic projects. Rochus Gliese tasked her with creating visual effects for his film *Der verlorene Schatten*[1] (*The Lost Shadow*). The film is about musician Sebaldus (Paul Wegener) and how he trades his shadow to a demonic shadow player for a magical violin to woo his sweetheart Barbara. Reiniger downplayed the work she did on the film, but Happ recounts that she made prop silhouette portraits for the actors to use on screen, a special effect of a violin's shadow being played without the musician, the intertitles and a silhouette play depicting a happy ending (2004, 17). *Der verlorene Schatten* was the last collaboration between Wegener and Reiniger, but they would remain friends until his death in 1948.

Throughout the 1920s, Reiniger attended ballet performances and then cut out the scenes from memory as a hobby. She would also attend the cinema as much as possible, sometimes twice a day (Wiegmann & Blattner, 2010, 9; "Lotte Reiniger Recording," 1976).

Advertiser Julius Pinschewer was the next to hire Reiniger and her silhouettes to make promotional films for his agency. Pinschewer was one of the first animators in Germany and it was primarily due to him that animation gained notice during the Weimar years. Most of the films Reiniger made for him between 1919 and 1924 were lost, but *Das Geheimnis der Marquis* (*The Marquise's Secret*) and *Die Barcarole* (*The Barcarole*), both made some time in the 1920s, survive. Moritz eloquently described *Das Geheimnis der Marquis* as "an exquisite reverse silhouette film … in which elegant white figures of the eighteenth century nobility (urging you to use Nivea skin cream!) seem like cameo or Wedgewood images" (1996b, 40). In *Die Barcarole,* a four-minute advertisement for Mauxion chocolates with a Romeo and Juliet theme, the items that win Juliet's affections are Mauxion chocolates.

Funds from the Pinschewer films were poured into new creative scherenschnitte films for the institute. Koch and Reiniger discovered they worked well together and Koch proved a deft hand at mastering animation. Their *Amor und das standhafte Liebespaar* (*Cupid and the Steadfast Lovers*, 1920) combined Reiniger's silhouettes with a live actor (Moritz, 1996b, 40).

In 1921, another busy year for Koch and Reiniger, they made the film *Die fliegende Koffer* (*The Flying Suitcase*), based on Hans Christian Andersen's tale.[2] Reiniger reimagines it with an Oriental setting; the animation is rudimentary, but one can see how she experimented with new techniques. Reiniger's version tells the tale of a princess who cannot marry a mortal man, so the fisherman Yen lies and says he is the god of the butterflies. The princess' father approves the match, but when the butterflies discover Yen's deception they kidnap him and maroon him on a mountain. Koch and Reiniger also finished *Der Stern von Bethlehem* (*The Star of Bethlehem*), a recounting of the Nativity, "made in the modern style, very Expressionist" (qt. in Bastiancich, 1992/1981, 10).

On December 6, 1921, Koch and Reiniger were married in the Berlin-Schonberg registrar office. She brought an impish personality and creative talent to the marriage, but only a nightshirt in her trousseau (Gelder, 1981). Happ described their marriage as the "perfect unity of Lotte Reiniger's playful fantasy and Carl Koch's creative and technical ideas" (2004, 20). Christel Strobel wrote, "The two were very different in character. She was really the artist, she would patiently create animation films step by step, and he was the technician. She'd always say she wanted no part in the technical side, as technology scared her. This was why things worked so well between the two of them" (qt. in Marschall *et al.*, 2012). Walter Schobert's felt that, without Koch, Reiniger might not have been able to make her films:

> I believe Carl Koch was the constant emotive in her life. The star she followed who prepared her way. I don't think she could have started her career so easily if Carl Koch hadn't founded the institute and put all the technique at her disposal, helping her like this. This changed later when Carl Koch had his

2. Lengthening Shadows

Lotte Reiniger (right) and her husband Carl Koch (left) working and relaxing; date unknown (courtesy the Tübingen Stadtmuseum).

feature film ambitions and worked together with Renoir. That changed the relationship. But I think it was enormous luck for them. Two people so suited to each other being able to live and work together so closely [qt. in Raganelli, 1999].

In 1922, Reiniger adapted the Grimm fairy tales *Aschenputtel* (*Cinderella*) and *Dornröschen* (*Sleeping Beauty*). In the former, she hinted at how she animated the film with the lovely line, "What Cinderella suffered from the two sisters and her stepmother, how she grew into a fairy-princess here is seen, told by a pair of scissors on a screen." Reiniger considered herself blessed that she was able to work with her husband and that he augmented her work with his own film skills despite their different work processes. She said, "He mastered the technical things I was not very good with and he was also an excellent animator, so that we could share the work.... Sometimes I was appalled at how he forced figures into positions. It was completely unusual and sharply contrasted with my cautious handling..." (qt. in Happ, 2004, 20). Koch and Reiniger incorporated more people into their team; for example, on *Aschenputtel*, animator Toni Raboldt and comedic actor Alexander Kardan.

Reiniger never had a formal art education; she did attend evening classes at a private art school. "I noticed that what you could learn in art school ... was not the right thing for [animated films]. You had to have a kind of profile fantasy. You have to transform the anatomy into profile movements and then you have to study movements a great [deal]" ("Lotte Reiniger Recording," 1976). It would take decades for a dedicated animation curriculum to be installed at American universities, much less Europe. Animators had to make due with art classes and then apply what they learned to the process. Reiniger differed from Walt Disney in her disregard for the need for further art training. Disney enrolled all his animators in art classes provided by the studio to improve their craft and he believed it was the best way to replicate material in cartoons. While Reiniger didn't continue with art classes, she consistently trained herself by studying movement and cutting silhouette figures, and disciplined herself to achieve perfection. She first began studying human movement by watching actors in the theater's spotlight.

During the production of the famous UFA-Decla film *Die Nibelungen* (*The Nibelungs*), Fritz Lang wanted to create Kriemhild's dream (Kriemhild is the hero Siegfried's love interest). "In 1923, [Reiniger] made a short trick film of birds, including a superb eagle for Kriemhild's dream in *The Nibelungs*; but this was never used, and Fritz Lang finally substituted for it a 'Dream of Hawks' by Walther Ruttmann" (White, 1931, 15). Ruttmann, a well-regarded experimental film director, was acquainted with Reiniger. Siegfried Kracauer, however, dismissed the sequence as "nothing but an animated heraldic design involving two black hawks and a white dove in rhythmic movements" (1947, 94). Bendazzi, in contract, describes Ruttmann's work, demonstrating how differing perspectives view the same event and their significance: "[T]he sequence of Kriemhild's nightmare stands out, with flocks of menacing birds flying about in a darkly shaded sky, visiting the queen in her dreams" (1994, 28).

People in the 1920s, especially in Germany and the rest of Europe, viewed animation differently from the modern conception that animation is a "genre" meant for children. (Animated films that disprove that theory depict serious dramas, such as *Grave of the Fireflies*, *Persepolis*, *Arrugas* and *Waltz with Bashir*, while the exploits of *South Park: Bigger, Longer, and Uncut*, Ralph Bakshi's *Fritz the Cat* and *Sausage Party* point towards the lewd, more mature comical uses of animation.) Animation historian Jerry Beck noted that this is changing as people who have grown up with cartoons and introduce them to their children see them as more than a children's genre (Beck interview with author, April 1, 2015).

One must take into consideration that animation was brand new to most audiences and every screening of a cartoon presented itself as the first of its kind. In the 1920s, animation was in the hotbed of the German expressionist film movement and was a large part of German film history. The legendary UFA, Germany's most prominent and famous movie studio of the era, epitomized expressionism with its films, beginning with *Das Cabinet des Dr. Caligari* (*The Cabinet of Dr. Caligari*) and reaching the apex with Fritz Lang's *Metropolis*. Many filmmakers remembered for their experimental film work during this period also identified as animators: Ruttmann, Pinschewer, Hans Richter, Viking Eggeling, Oskar Fischinger. Why they are tied to experimental film and not animation relates to how "in the following years of Nazism, World War II and the postwar, the animators' importance steadily weakened and the public lost interest in the very same films it had applauded only a few years earlier" (Bendazzi, 1999, 26), paving the way for modern conceptions of animation.[3]

Bendazzi claims that, before the second World War, Germany was the friendliest creative landscape for animation, citing Bauhaus and expressionism principles as the reason (1994, 26). Bauhaus was an architecture design school that placed simplicity and functionality above all else, while artists used expressionism to convey experiences of internal emotional to the outer world. The combination of the two left a lot of room for avant garde exploration in film science, which is why Dr. Cürlis and Koch founded the Institute for Cultural Research and gave Reiniger the chance to make her first silhouette cartoon. Hake explains that while Weimar films were shifted "towards narrative and verisimilitude, formal experimentation continued to thrive in avant-garde practices [in] the abstract or absolute film[s that] cultivated the free play with movement, rhythm, light, contrast and form and maintained strong links to modern painting and photography" (2002, 38). This overarching belief coursing through the German film industry and the success of her silhouette films (plus an investment from a banker) inspired Reiniger and Koch to try something bigger than a short: a full-length animated film. Thus started production on *Die Abenteuer des Prinzen Achmed* (*The Adventures of Prince Achmed*) in 1923.

Film techniques were limited in the early twentieth century, evidenced by the difficulties Wegener and his crew had with rodents. Reiniger was aware of film's limitations and she viewed animation as a way to not only overcome them, but also present more creative possibilities than live action. In "Leben Schatten" from 1929 she wrote,

> This kind of work (that of silhouette films, see note) has the merit, that the moulding artist need not take any consideration in his drafts on the otherwise all-dominating laws of gravity, the coherence of the subject matter, in short, on every natural movement—determining law of nature. He can, with his forms and patterns, switch and prevail over what he wants. Just the full reversal of the laws of nature plays a main role, for example, in the superb American cartoons of Felix the Cat or Oswald the Lucky Rabbit. There an animal becomes, for example, longer, because his front legs go faster than his hind legs, a train becomes infinitely wide because the track gap widens, or infinitely narrow, because it otherwise couldn't go through a tunnel. The excessive fantasies are not restricted. Conversely, the largest effects can be achieved, when—like in my films—silhouettes move with the utmost faith to life, so that one totally loses the sensation, that there aren't any true actors [p. 8].

Filmmakers could be considered scientists as they experimented with techniques and processes. They made discoveries through trial and error, an essential part of the scientific method. As a film scientist, Reiniger was unique. The obvious factor was her gender, but also her general approach to animation: When given the challenge to make an animated film, she did it without having an overarching message to communicate to audiences. She just wanted to make a film and tell a good story. "The avant-garde artist and filmmaker Hans Richter, a lifelong friend, wrote of her that 'she belonged to the avant-garde as far as independent production and courage were concerned,' but that the spirit of her work harked back to an earlier, more innocent age" (qt. in Kemp, 2004). More proof of Reiniger's approach: a conversation[4] she and Ruttmann had while they were working on *Die Abenteuer des Prinzen Achmed*:

> "Lotte, why are you making a fairytale film like this?"
> "I don't know either," she replied.
> "What has it got to do with the year 1923?" he pursued.
> "Nothing at all. Any why should it? I'm here, living in the year 1923, and I have the chance to make this film, so naturally I'm going to do it. That's all it has to do with the year 1923."
> "That doesn't seem right to me," he insisted [qt. in Moritz, 1996b, 48].

Reiniger and Koch weren't apolitical and some of their films can be interpreted as allegories, but it wasn't their main driving force. Her main desire was to be part of the surreal magic that occupies the screen and her optimism that her skills were sufficient to discern solutions to animation's technical process made her stand out from her contemporaries, paving the way for the film that earns her a single sentence or footnote in most film and animation books.

While information about Reiniger is scarce, the rare article, interview and movie review were published, often with conflicting information about her. Thanks to the efforts of the Tübingen Stadtmuseum, the Düsseldorf Stadtmuseum, the British Film Institute and Alfred Happ's biography *Lotte Reiniger 1899–1981: Schöpferin einer neuen Silhouettenkunst*, facts about her life and career are finally pinned down. The Internet also plays a huge role when a curious animation or puppetry fan happens upon her films, but all these efforts haven't alleviated her obscurity, especially as they are limited to European and primarily German-speaking audiences.

I've considered many reasons for Reiniger's understated contributions to animation and puppetry history. K. Vivian Taylor observed, "The contributions of Reiniger to the development of film have historically been marginalized in film history and discourse due to a combination of her German national identity, gender and the genre [sic] in which she works" (2011, 4).[5] German people are plagued with both World Wars, women have been considered lesser beings until the modern era (and still in many cultures), and animation and puppetry aren't regarded as serious industries in the collective consciousness. While it is a combination of these factors that contribute to Reiniger's footnoted career, I've discovered other reasons that augment them and I will discuss throughout the chapters. One item that I can be sure of is that one factor cannot be singled above the rest for her marginalization; all have equal bearing.

3

Defining the Art of Puppetry and Animation

> Puppets are a lot like masks. Children—and adults—can perform without inhibitions and without being seen. That sort of helps to foster true expression.—Jim Henson

To gain an in-depth understanding of who Lotte Reiniger was involves discussing the "how" of her animation technique. Explaining the process requires more than transcribing a silhouette stop-motion instruction manual; one must clear up modern misconceptions of animation and puppetry. Much like the audiences in the early twentieth century, people are still confused about the actual concept of animation and its elder sibling, puppetry. As mentioned before, animation and puppetry tends to get lumped into the kiddie corral with consistent MPAA "G" ratings (PG on a dark day) from family-friendly plots, themes and characters. According to famous British puppeteers Ann Hogarth and Jan Bussell, "[P]uppetry conjures up pictures of children's hour television, and this modern sideline of employing puppets as something with which to keep the children quiet has achieved such momentum that many people accept the idea that this is all the art has to offer, and will scoff at the use of the word 'art' for such antics—and in this last they are, alas, quite right" (1985, 9). The general consensus among most parents: If cartoons or puppets are involved, then it's safe to sit their child in front of the TV.

Animators and puppeteers acknowledge that a large percentage of their audience are children, but many don't ascribe to being strictly children's entertainers. This has led to some demonstrating the mediums' versatilities by creating puppet shows and cartoons shifted towards the adult spectrum, veering into cursing, sex and other adult-ish topics. Even famous entertainers associated with children's media didn't want their skills limited to the "under ten" crowd. Jim Henson refused to call himself a puppeteer, partially because he didn't want his work to be regarded as strictly children's entertainment. The same can be said for his literal right hand man Frank Oz.

Henson said at an American Film Institute lecture in 1989, "I love the fact that we are doing work for children, but puppetry is capable of handling adult subject matter as well.... As a form, puppetry is capable of a very wide range of styles and looks. I find that fascinating" (Falk email to author, March 17, 2016). Former Henson creative director and executive vice-president Michael Firth said, "One of Jim's real goals with *The Muppet Show* was to demonstrate, again, that puppetry could be for everyone. And that it could exist on a sophisticated, albeit silly, level. And that it had a perfectly viable world in adult entertainment" (qt. in Henson, 1994).

Chuck Jones, father of many of the Looney Tunes characters, said about the cartoons he made during his Warner Brothers period, "Those cartoons were never made for children. Nor were they made for adults. They were made for me" (Beck, email to author, May 8, 2015). When critics pegged *Snow White and the Seven Dwarfs* as too intense for children, Walt Disney said, "But I didn't make the picture for children. I made it for adults—for the child that exists in all adults" (Barrier, 2007, 131). Stop-motion animation director and animator Henry Selick has a thoughtful view that ties the two mediums to the world of fine art:

> If the only paintings ever made were of kittens and puppies and baby ducks, you might conclude that paintings are just for children. Well, a lot of animation *is* made for children but animation can be as provocative and startling and adult as the work of Van Gogh, Picasso, Da Vinci, Hopper and Kahlo and a hundred other geniuses. Great animation can tell any kind of story for any kind of audience and be as timeless as the Mona Lisa [Selick email to author, March 29, 2016].

All these admired, creative people shared the same vision that their media could be a cross-generational entertainment, but Henson noted the biggest barrier: "It's difficult to convince adults that puppetry wasn't just kids' stuff" (B.J. Jones, 2013, 178). Even those who made huge profits from cartoons weren't convinced about animation's potential.

Warner Brothers head Jack Warner insulted his animators and the animation industry in 1953 when he said, "I don't even know where the hell the cartoon studio is. The only thing I know is that we make Mickey Mouse" (B. Thomas, 1990, 211–12). He was referring to Termite Terrace, a building in a faraway part of Warners' Sunset lot.[1]

A consistent challenge for animators and puppeteers is to define themselves not as a genre, but as versatile media to tell a variety of stories that appeal to children *and* adults together or separately. Many books have been written on this topic and with proper presentation and support it is an open-and-shut argument to win. One can even do a basic Internet search to locate movies, TV shows and plays that verify that animation and puppetry with mature themes do exist.

Puppetry is a term used to refer to inanimate objects brought to life via human manipulation. It's a blanket definition, which can be further simplified by breaking puppetry into its different types: marionettes, rod puppetry, shadow puppetry, bunraku, glove puppets, etc. While the same general principle of definition can be applied to animation, all animation usually gets filed under the word: cartoon. Why? Puppetry is puppetry no matter the type, but what few realize is that while all cartoons are animated, not all animation consists of cartoons. It's more appropriate to define animation by its process.

Cartoon is used as the blanket term to refer to animation, because that is the form of animation most people are exposed to—mostly large studios such as Walt Disney Company/Pixar, DreamWorks, Blue Sky, Studio Ghibli and others. If proper nouns can be used as synonyms, Disney is synonymous with animation in most people's heads. Disney is arguably the world's most recognized animation studio and for decades it was the only animation studio releasing animated films on a large commercial scale. This has led to the public believing that every animated film is made by the Mouse or, at least, is family-friendly entertainment. (A similar situation: Many people refer to all 3D animated films as "Pixar" films.)

The cause dates back to Walt Disney's early days as an animator. The popular cartoons of the day were Otto Messmer's *Felix the Cat* cartoons made by Pat Sullivan's studio and Max and Dave Fleischer's *Out of the Inkwell* starring Koko the Clown and Fritz the Dog. Cartoons, though, were more of a novelty than a valid film medium and it was "felt that by 1923 just about everything had been done that was possible" (Thomas & Johnston, 1981, 23). In the early 1920s, partners Disney and Ub Iwerks taught themselves animation and made films at night after working their day jobs. Eventually they created Oswald the Lucky Rabbit and gained a small following. "To an observer in 1928, Walt Disney would have seemed an unlikely choice as the man who would revolutionize both the art and the industry of animation. His films were good, but by no means extraordinary; Koko and Felix were far more popular than Disney's Oswald Rabbit" (Solomon, 1994, 37). By 1928, Disney and Iwerks combined their strengths to make Oswald a visually appealing cartoon with strong stories. Disney lost the rights to Oswald that same year and he then created the lovable Mickey Mouse. Iwerks made the first two Mickey Mouse cartoons *Plane Crazy* and *Gallopin' Gaucho*, but they were silent cartoons and audiences were mad about sound after the release of Warner Brothers' *The Jazz Singer*. Disney, always eager to embrace new technology, decided to make a Mickey Mouse cartoon with sound and on November 28, 1928, the premiere of *Steamboat Willie* ushered in a new era of animation.

When Disney and Iwerks started their animation careers, cartoons were being churned out on cheap budgets with quick turnaround. It didn't leave room for mastering the art of story or making a work of art. Veteran animator Richard "Dick" Huemer (his résumé includes work at the Fleischers, Charles Mintz and Disney Studios) described how animation was viewed: "There was a time when they were given away with features. It was a package deal. You got a feature, you got a newsreel, you got some other strange thing, then you got a cartoon. If the exhibitor hated cartoons, he didn't run them. That's how interested they were" (qt. in Newsom, 1980, 283).

Disney saw potential in what animation could be if given more money, time and better talent. With the success of *Steamboat Willie*, Disney was able to hire more skilled artists, negotiate contracts with higher budgets, and test more of his ideas. "In ten years the studio went from the raw vitality and crude, clumsy actions of *Steamboat Willie* to the surprising sophistication and glowing beauty of *Snow White*.... [Disney] continued to experiment with many approaches to filmmaking and different uses of animation, from 'stop-motion' with cutouts, limited movement, stylized design, puppets, and 3D, to the full cel animation" (Thomas & Johnston, 1981, 25). In 1936, ten years after animating her most well-known work *Die Abenteuer des Prinzen Achmed*, Reiniger wrote a short essay, "Moving Silhouettes," about her love for making silhouette films and experimenting with movement. "Moving Silhouettes" carries a semi-bitter tone about Disney's cel animation: "The genius of Disney and his followers has made the audience love this kind of fake motion, and by now has acquired a special place in the development of the cinema" (Reiniger, 1936a, 15). The ironic part about this quote is that Disney and his animators would continue to experiment in improving "fake movement" to become as close to lifelike as possible, while Reiniger continued to favor her animation process and would be regarded as old-fashioned by more than one industry professional. Disney's use of cel animation and his extraordinary popularity made the "Disney style" the best-known form of animation, forcing all others to the margins.

One of the official definitions of cartoon, according to the Oxford American English Dictionary and Thesaurus (2003), is "humorous drawing in a newspaper, magazine, etc."—

essentially a simple drawing intended to make viewers crack a smile. The definition continues with another meaning related to animation: "a filmed sequence of drawings using the technique of animation" (p. 214). It is better to refer to this as an animated cartoon, yet neither definition suggests that a cartoon makes up the entire world of animation. Turning to the actual definition of animation, a more all-encompassing meaning is given: "the technique of filming successive drawings or positions of puppets, etc., to create an illusion of movement when the film is shown in a sequence" (p. 53). Notice how an official definition of animation uses drawings and puppetry to convey its meaning, again not relying on just one form.

Philip Kelly Denslow discussed the evolution of an animation definition in his essay "What is Animation and Who Needs to Know?" He explains how different organizations (professional associations, academia, entertainment industry) create their own animation definitions and how it either remains static or constantly in flux to chronicle new technological advances. "Definitions of animation vary from one another for many reasons, including historical development, production and marketing requirements, and aesthetic preferences" (Denslow, 1997, 1).

Animation fans have written their own definitions of the word. The meaning varies from one individual to another based on their viewing preferences, age and fandom intensity, and usually includes a subjective insertion of what animation means to them. While animation fan definitions may lack the objectivity and brevity of an Oxford or Webster dictionary, they can carry an in-depth, all-encompassing meaning that conveys the true range and possibilities of the medium. Animation fans are quick to correct the improper usage of the word "cartoon" and "animation" and to assert that the medium is an art form. Animation fans eschew the term "cartoon" and prefer to use "animation" when referring to their hobby as the word "cartoon" continues to be associated with juvenile TV series and films.

A "true" animation definition has been the abstract of many scholarly writings, written from an anthropological angle of outsiders looking through the window of a substandard cinematic perspective or the more extreme approach as a subculture occupied by social pariahs also known as geeks, nerds, etc. More objective definition scholarship emerged after the Disney Renaissance, Nickelodeon's Golden Age and the early twenty-first century anime boom. An "official" definition still doesn't exist, but remains a popular discussion topic. Lotte Reiniger's collaborator at England's GPO under John Grierson was famous Scottish-born Canadian animator Norman McLaren, who worked at the National Film Board of Canada (NFB) and pioneered many animation and filmmaking techniques. While at the NFB, McLaren devised his own animation definition:

- Animation is not the art of *drawings-that-move* but the art of *movements-that-are-drawn*.
- What happens *between* each frame is much more important than what exists *on* each frame.
- Animation is therefore the art of manipulating the invisible interstices that lie between the frames [qt. in Small & Levinson, 1989, 68].

McLaren's take is less poetic than Thomas and Johnston's "illusion of life," but when combined together McLaren's adds a technique approach to the illusion of life, the science behind the Old Men's whimsical magic. Another popular approach to an animation definition comes from Edward S. Small and Eugene Levinson; they tried to create an animation definition in "Towards a Theory of Animation." The pair concluded, "[T]he most significant aspect of animation theory will be its location within the larger discipline of film theory and its potential for initiating revision within the larger discipline" (1989, 73).

"Towards a Theory of Animation" was published in 1989 before the Disney Renaissance and anime boom began, in the midst of Nickelodeon's Golden Age as well as network Saturday morning cartoons. Animation was just beginning to be sanctioned as a serious medium, but what makes Small and Levinsons' conclusion different is that it recognizes animation as another aspect of cinematic arts. Live action and animation grew up alongside each other in film's development. Often the belief is that they developed parallel to each other, never to meet, rather than perpendicular and met at many corners. The two are related and have more in common than they do differences, especially as the lines are blurred with CGI special effects. Animation is part of film's legacy and live action film theory can be applied to it; however, it is a separate medium that needs to be approached differently from live action. After all, it is a creation of human hands instead of recording humans on screen—think about René Magritte's *The Treachery of Images*, "This is not a pipe."

Robert Zemeckis was obsessed with motion capture technology for a time, beginning with his infamous Christmas classic *The Polar Express*, based on Chris Van Allsburg's picture book and starred Tom Hanks. There was speculation that *The Polar Express* would win the Oscar for best animated film, but it caused the animation community to once again focus on the animation definition idea. Instead of defining the entire medium, animator Gene Deitch and historian Jerry Beck both agreed that motion capture, "being basically the same as any live action film, that is action created in real time, is [not] consistent with the definition of cinematic animation" (2005). John Halas had asked Deitch to write an animation definition and he adhered to his technical definition of "cinematic animation: The recording of individually created phases of imagined action in such a way as to achieve the illusion of motion when shown at a constant, predetermined rate, exceeding that of human persistence of vision" (2005).

Deitch argues that it is important that the animation community understand the technical parts of animation and when he wrote his cinematic animation definition in 1978 for the International Association of Film Animation (ASIFA) it was intended to be timeless (Deitch, 2015). Continuing on his train of thought, Deitch employed a technical definition so we would be able to understand animation's rules. It reminds us that one must know all the rules and understand past accomplishments in order to break the rules and add the emotional expressions, which is why Deitch said he enjoyed Steven Millhauser's definition from his *Little Kingdoms*:

> [An] immobile world of inanimate drawings that had been granted the secret of motion, [a] deathworld with its hidden gift of life. But that life was a deeply ambiguous life, a conjurer's trick, a crafty illusion based on an accidental property of the retina, which retained an image for a fraction of a second after the image was no longer present. On this frail fact was erected the entire structure of the cinema, that colossal confidence game.
>
> The animated cartoon was a far more honest expression of the cinematic illusion than the so-called realistic (live-action) film, because the cartoon reveled in its own illusory nature, exulted in the impossible—indeed it claimed the impossible as its own, exalted it as its own highest end, found in impossibility, in the negation of the actual, its profoundest reason for being.
>
> The animated cartoon was nothing but the poetry of the impossible—therein lay its exhilaration and its secret melancholy. For this willful violation of the actual, while it was an intoxicating release from the constriction of things, was at the same time nothing but a delusion, an attempt to outwit

mortality. As such it was doomed to failure. And yet it was desperately important to smash through the constriction of the actual, to unhinge the universe and let the impossible stream in, because otherwise—well, otherwise, the world was nothing but an editorial cartoon [qt. in Deitch, 2015].

This is the type of animation definition that most animation fans cleave to as a description of their emotional connection and love for the art. But is Deitch correct in excluding in animation's arguable next evolution: live action animation? Live action animation appears to negate the basic principle, the illusion of life that humans as animators become the gods of an imaginary world that only exists in the imagination and is brought to life by technology. Without getting too philosophical (ghost in the machine, anyone?), live action animation breaks the illusory fourth wall that exists between reality and fiction. Deitch wrote, "In live-action, a camera records action taking place before its lens. In animation, only still images are recorded, and the 'illusion of action' only takes place at the moment of projecting it on a screen, or playing it back on a visual device" (2015). He continues that animation only exists in the dimension of time (the fourth dimension ironically), but tying it to the previous thoughts, it is time that brings animation to life, fueled by the imagination (Deitch, 2015). The barrier between CGI special effects blurs the line between animation and live action, except for the people who want the distinction.

Technical and emotional definitions aside, when anime is tossed into the equation it becomes even more complex. During the anime boom, I used to read a news site when people in the U.S. were struggling to understand anime. It underwent the same type of battles as broader animation (and other geeky trends) when mainstream consensus failed to comprehend the Japanese imports' appeal. The site's editor Luis Reyes created his own apt anime definition: "anime, everything under the sun and moon only drawn." When anime became popular, however, it opened a whole new range of understanding that the medium could be used beyond Disney, Pixar and children's entertainment. Anime had something western cartoons didn't: genre options. There were mature North American cartoons during the anime boom, but the range was primarily limited to lewd comedies. Anime introduced the idea to a wider audience that animation could cater to any genre and any age group.

Anime might have opened audiences' eyes to wider possibilities, but there is a distinct cultural and aesthetic difference between anime and western cartoons that keeps them separated. Like the rest of animation, however, anime has been lumped into the same niche and has added a new, complex level to the definition game. Anime is part of animation, a distinct group with its own genres and tropes, but it requires a certain understanding easily acquired from exposure. Charles Kenny wrote in "The Debate Over the Term 'Anime' Is Pointless": "I'd go so far to argue that the 'anime' is like good art: you know it when you see it. If some explanation is necessary, it will be asked for and given. The context of the particular conversation probably plays more of a role in how anime is defined than anything else. The same goes for animation in general" (2015). His opinion on establishing a universal animation definitions adds the needed humor to remain sane: "[G]etting the word out about a general consensus for a common term for animation is going to be a nightmare even within the industry, let alone the fans and general public!" (2015). With the addition of anime, we go full circle to the simple task of defining.

I return to the earlier question, "What is animation?" The technical and emotional aspects each contribute to a greater part, but it changes from person to animation type. Going back to Denslow, he concluded his essay by quoting the *Motion Pictures from the*

Library of Congress Paper Print Collection 1894–1912 catalog that is all inclusive for every film type, both live action and animation; "Before motion pictures got the name as such, they were called 'animated' picture" (qt. in 1997, 4). Charles Kenny included a quote from Tissa David about when she was hired at UPA, "[S]he was asked by Grim Natwick what animation was. Her answer was, animation is animation. Which is, realistically, about the best answer anyone could give" (2015). Is defining animation really that simple?

Reyes was on the right path when he wrote that anime is everything under the sun and moon, but it's limited to one part of the greater whole. Animation is animation in the sense that an individual makes of it what they desire and it can be anything based on the selected process. Dare I say, animation can be anything and everything within the universe only created from human imagination? To quote Deitch, "But don't conform! Do it your way!" (2015). In short, yes.

When Lotte Reiniger began animating, the "sophisticated" distinctions between animation, stop-motion and cartoons did not exist as they were being invented at that time. British animator John Halas and film scholar Roger Manvell agree that the silhouette film "played a considerable part in the pioneer stages of animation" (1976, 278). Rather than spending their time pondering what to call their individual techniques, Reiniger and other animators just made their films. In German, a cartoon or animated film is called "ein trickfilm." With a little critical thinking, an English speaker can discern that "trickfilm" refers to a type of film with a special purpose, gimmick or trick. Animation is a film trick on the eye, it is a series of drawings or puppet movements that are filmed frame by frame in a progressive order and fool the brain into thinking they are a complete sequence. For Reiniger, Wegener and other German animators and filmmakers, animation was a special effect trick to accomplish otherwise seemingly impossible acts on film.

Cartoons were imported from the U.S. and popular amongst German audiences, but along with Reiniger's short films, were referred to as trick films. Distinctions over different types of trick films were made by attaching adjectives as descriptors. Reiniger's films are not cartoons, they are animated films or, a better description, stop-motion silhouette films (Beck email to author, March 29, 2015). As trickfilm translates directly into cartoon in English, Reiniger, film reviewers and academics referred to her films as cartoons. It goes to show that even the experts can get the terms wrong, but for the general purpose of this book Reiniger's films are not cartoons.

This brings us back to Reiniger and the lack of research surrounding her work. One of the reasons why she was blotted out of animation and film history is due to the lack of understanding of how to define her work. While she was an animator, she is also a puppeteer. Animation and puppetry have more in common with each other than they do differences and the lines between animation and puppetry have been blurred as technology has advanced. In stop-motion animation, the models made for the films are called puppets. The two mediums, however, remain separate and distinct, so while an animator might use methods similar to a puppeteer and vice versa, the artists identify as either an animator or puppeteer, not both (unless they practice both types of art individually).

Reiniger relied on old-fashioned silhouette puppets and the new animation techniques she pioneered to make her films, but since she fell into both camps, she can't be pinned to just one category. Likewise, modern animators who use puppets fit succinctly under both titles. Puppetry scholarship, unlike many histories on animation, provides a bit more documentation on Reiniger's work. While there might be a few more paragraphs about her in puppetry books, they still lack a singular tie between puppetry and animation that distinguishes Reiniger as someone who married the two mediums.

A clear understanding of the type of animation Reiniger specialized in is imperative to comprehending the great lengths she went to create her films. Nowadays the type of animation Reiniger practiced is a subset of stop-motion or stop frame. In her 1970 book *Shadow Theatres and Shadow Films*, Reiniger explained the process of how to make a teapot[2] dance on a tea table:

> You light the field of action up properly, the lamp well out of focus, and place your film camera in front of it, bring it into focus and make one shot, in other words you move the film in your camera on for one frame.... So you boldly approach your tea-table and move the teapot forward an inch, and shoot it again. And so on, and so on, until your dancing teapot has done a whole circle round the table [pp. 84–85].

Stop-motion animation, an extremely slow process, requires patience, repetition and exact movements of the objects being animated to ensure continuity. Reiniger said that when she first started animating, stop-motion devices hadn't been invented and she had to crank a camera handle manually in such a way to only take one frame at a time (Reiniger, 1970a, 85).

Repetition is the key to this slow process. While modern technology has simplified stop-motion (or made it more complicated based on the amount of visual effects and high details of the puppets used), the same steps are still used by stop-motion animators. Eric Walter White in *Walking Shadows* described the importance of repetition more eloquently:

> [I]t becomes immediately obvious that one of [stop-motion animation's] most vital characteristics is repetition, whether repetition of certain movements in a single figure (such as a simple step forward) or parallel movements between similar figures, or movements reflected and reversed, and carried back to their original starting point. All these forms of repetition are necessary owing to the essential nature of animated cartoon films, for it is manifestly absurd for a producer to make any attempt to imitate the asymmetry of nature-that would involve herculean labours and call for monumental patience [1931, 11–12].[3]

Reiniger animated shadow puppets she designed, drew and cut herself. To her, the puppets were the most important part of production, because through their movements, actions and implied emotions, the story would be told. Many lucky individuals who saw her making the puppets, commented on her dexterity and ability to form exquisite shapes. She first started making the puppets out of lead sheets, but discovered that cardboard gave her better movement. White noted that she "cut some of the parts of her movable silhouettes out of soft metal sheets, since she finds that the extra weight makes them lie better on the trick table" (White, 1931, 16). In other words, a combination of metal and cardboard worked best for Reiniger. Any piece of cardboard Reiniger got her hands on was apt to be transformed into a puppet. Her puppets would include pieces of soapboxes and other scraps (Reiniger, 1970a, 95). Later, for her shadow plays, she would tape colored plastic (same material used in gel light filters) over an incision to use as an accent, such as in a belt or scarf (Bussell & Hogarth, 1985, 138). When viewing her puppets off screen, it's fun to see how an ordinary box would be recycled into movable art. The puppets also act as time capsules for packaging materials available at the various times Reiniger made her films. She generally used black cardboard. She relied on cheap scrap materials to construct her puppets in the early part of her career when Germany experienced high inflation (Reiniger, 1970b, 2). In 1978, Pat Martin, Reiniger's assistant on *Aucassin and*

Nicolette, revealed, "Some figures from her films were donated to the British Film Institute for a display. There was a figure of a giant and she had used a piece of a soap carton to make the giant [and part of it] read 'good for babies' nappies' or something like that. The British Film Institute insisted on coloring that black [for the display]" *(Reiniger with Starr and others)*.

While Reiniger was known to cut free hand, for her films she preferred to plan every detail in advance from the shape of a hand to the amount of frames used in each scene. White describes how Reiniger cut out her puppets:

> As a prelude to cutting, the figure is usually sketched out roughly in chalk or charcoal on the verso of the cardboard; but such sketches are merely intended to save errors in the proportions of the figure. The rhythm of the lines, expression of the features, and details of dress all possess the unmistakable quality that comes from the subtle and incisive cutting of a pair of scissors, and not from the random wanderings of a pencil or pen [1931, 16].

After cutting the silhouettes from their tracings, she used an awl and hammer to punch holes into the joints, where wire was inserted to create hinges for articulation. To flatten the characters, she used a roller to ensure they laid flat. For the leading characters, Reiniger made more than one size for different camera shots. "Close-ups are faked, i.e., the distance between the camera and the trick table remains the constant, but a larger figure is substituted and the setting modified accordingly" (White, 1931, 17). The puppets used for the most action scenes were nine inches in height and for wide shots or crowd scenes she made the figures five inches tall. The extreme close-ups only required a head with movable arms and hands (Reiniger, 1970, 98).

Not all of Reiniger's puppets were made equally: The amount of articulation each was given depended on the character's importance and action in the story (Isaacs, 1971):

> [She] said that the construction of the silhouettes is, of all the stages in the production of a film, the one that demands most time and care, she was including in this process both the design of the outlines themselves and the calculation of the joints. As well as the division into separate elements that is part and parcel of the jointing, and the necessary simplification of forms that results, silhouettes have to demonstrate, no matter their position, consistently correct proportions and permanent readability [Jouvanceau, 2004, 64].

The silhouette construction might have yielded simplified forms, but it made animating movements difficult for the untrained hand. As White described, silhouette construction

> makes only two positions possible: figures may face right, or they may face left, and once they face one direction, they must continue to move in that direction, unless the plot of the film makes it credible for them to move backwards. Sometimes figures at rest appear to have their bodies facing the camera, while their heads are turned in profile, a stance reminiscent of the conventionalised poses of early Egyptian pictorial art [1931, 20].

It was not only valuable to understand human form; Reiniger stressed the importance of researching animal bodies and movement in order to replicate them with silhouette puppets. She enjoyed studying animals and play-acted to understand them better. "I remember well, when I was studying at the zoo, how people looked at me astounded when I tried to imitate the animal's movements in front of the cage, trying to memorize its timing, and how my husband burst out laughing when he discovered me on all fours in the floor at home, to get the feeling of the animal's movement into my own bones (Reiniger, 1970a, 100–101).

While her films centered on her silhouette puppets, Reiniger also had to create a world for them to exist in. The puppets lived in a flat, two-dimensional world, but while it limited their movements and Reiniger didn't uphold cartoon physics, she noted in *Das Kulturfilmbuch*, "The Puppets lay flat on the surface. They are missing that centre of gravity which gives the marionette such a charming unreality.... But in exchange, they are masters of this surface, and there is no limit to their delicate mobility" (qt. in Cowan, 2013, 790). She noted how "purist shadow-players" abhorred scenery, but she learned that a pure white background scratched easily and picked up "rain" common on celluloid reels (Reiniger, 1970a, 101).

She cut the backgrounds with scissors from transparent tissue paper or black cardboard. The black cardboard was used to create opaque objects, such as houses, trees, etc., that had a direct connection with the characters. These were usually placed in the foreground over tissue paper layers that created a static background. The tissue paper was cut according to the film's need and could be layered for different effects on the glass animation plate. Sometimes more than one glass panel was used for different visual effects.

> For colored silhouette, backgrounds are formed using colored transparencies. Combining different colors allows for an almost infinite number of shades. The slides are then covered with a mat, transparent sheet to soften the contrasting colours and to ensure that the figures don't get caught in the background layers. Colored paper is glued to the puppets in color films [for more detail]. More overhead lighting is used to bring out the figures' colors. Lighting from below only creates black and white silhouettes on a coloured background [Isaacs, 1971].

White describes that, by this means, Reiniger gave "her scenes a feeling of depth, a matter of considerable importance in all her films, since her silhouettes are two-dimensional and move solely in a two-dimensional plane parallel to the camera, they are unable to demonstrate that they inhabit a three-dimensional space by moving backwards and forwards and obeying the laws of perspective" (1931, 17).

She always left three inches or more of ground for the characters to walk on at the bottom of a scene, because the camera was prone to cut off the bottom. The backgrounds were always cut to fit the size of the tricktisch's glass plate. She filmed scenes with longer backgrounds vertically to capture its entirety.

To animate her characters and backgrounds, Reiniger and Koch designed an animation rig she called her tricktisch (trick table). The tricktisch's modern-day equivalent is animation software. Unlike computers, which allow the animator to choose the camera angle, lighting, colors, textures and style within a single program, the tricktisch had to house the camera, lights and the scene to be animated and it all had to be adjusted manually and separately. While modern animation needs to be adjusted "manually" as well, it usually doesn't demand as much physical work from the animator. (On *Die Abenteuer des Prinzen Achmed*, Reiniger had several assistants to help her with the tricktisch's various aspects.)

Tissue paper layers and varying puppet sizes could only give so much of an illusion of depth. To trick the human eye into seeing more on the flat screen, she developed the multiplane camera for *Die Abenteuer des Prinzen Achmed*. The multiplane camera is a device where different components to a scene, including characters, backgrounds and props, are filmed at varying distances from the camera. To accomplish this, Reiniger and Koch built a mounting stand where glass panes could be placed at different levels replicating "distance" when the camera filmed through the panes. As the camera filmed, it would focus on the different objects creating a depth illusion, the equivalent of real life.

3. Defining the Art of Puppetry and Animation

Another beautiful example of Lotte Reiniger's background and set construction for her films, from *Aucassin and Nicolette*. Note the use of black silhouettes in the foreground versus the translucent tissue paper in the background (courtesy Janibeth Johnson).

Throughout her career, Reiniger had several tricktisches, each getting progressively more elaborate and more expensive as her skills grew. When she first started, she used the Institut für Kulturforschung's tricktisch that doubled as a hand-drawn animator's desk with an old camera mounted overhead. "The camera was held by steel supports fixed to wooden posts, and on these it could be moved up and down; for the table was also used for drawn animation which required animation-fields of different sizes" (qt. in Jouvanceau, 2004, 115). For *Prinzen Achmed*, with the provided funds she and Koch built a trick table that had more than one glass plate to experiment with different special effects. With later incarnations she had a movable camera and glass plates on metal poles. Reiniger worked on a wooden tricktisch in the early part of her career, but later had a metal one built and disliked it. She returned to her wooden tricktisch "because you can nail and pin things to it more easily" (qt. in Beckerman, 1974, 42). However the trick tables were designed, they had the same basic construction: a mounted camera on top of the rig, a table with a glass plate in the center, and a light box underneath the glass plate to light the animation.

Sitting at her tricktisch alone and sometimes with one or two assistants, Reiniger directed her silhouette films scene by scene in endless repetition required of stop-motion animation. British animator Richard Taylor noted that silhouette animation, or "cutout animation" as he referred to it in his book *The Encyclopedia of Animation Techniques*,

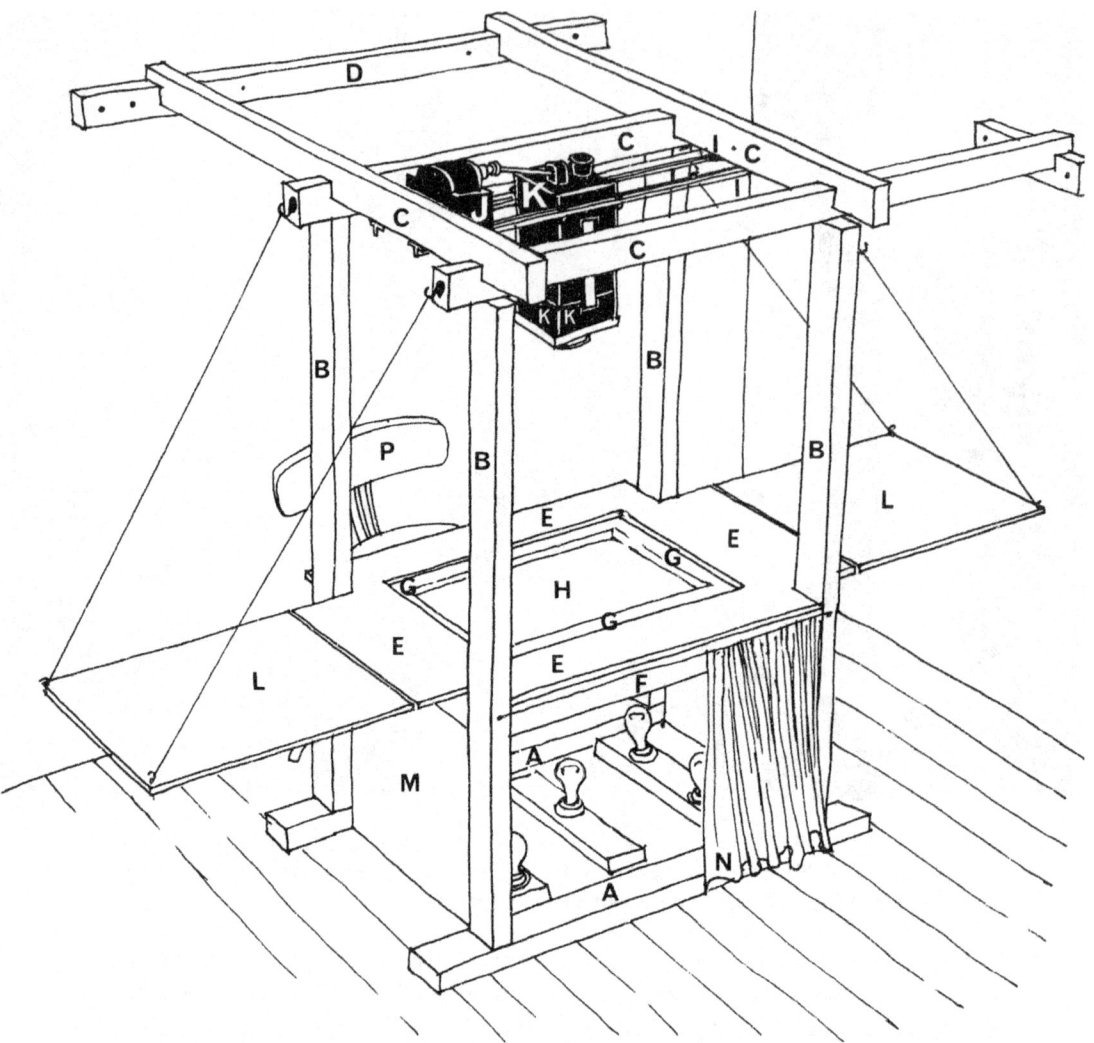

The blueprint for Reiniger's tricktisch.

isn't all that different from cel animation minus the inclusion of a glass plate to keep the puppets from curling from the lamp's heat conduction (which Reiniger no doubt experienced before she used lead and heavier paper stock) (1996, 62).[4] Reiniger and Richard Taylor stressed in their respective animation books that it was vital to only move the characters and objects required to move in a particular scene. Reiniger even suggested that perspective animators install a metal or wood bar along the "field of action" for an armrest (Reiniger, 1970a, 106). To manipulate the puppets, she would use her hands or a small, fine tool like tweezers or scissors.

Manipulating a shadow puppet (or *any* puppet) requires the puppeteer to convey emotion through the puppet, which is very difficult unless one has a firm grasp on acting, human movement, expressions, etc. "[E]ssentially a [puppet] must be conceived in such a way as to express different reactions and emotions when presented in different ways. Thus, held at one angle, it may appear to register apprehension, while, posed at another angle, even though no physical change has occurred, it may register satisfaction" (Finch, 1981, 49). Shadow puppets only show expression through body language and placement in the screen.

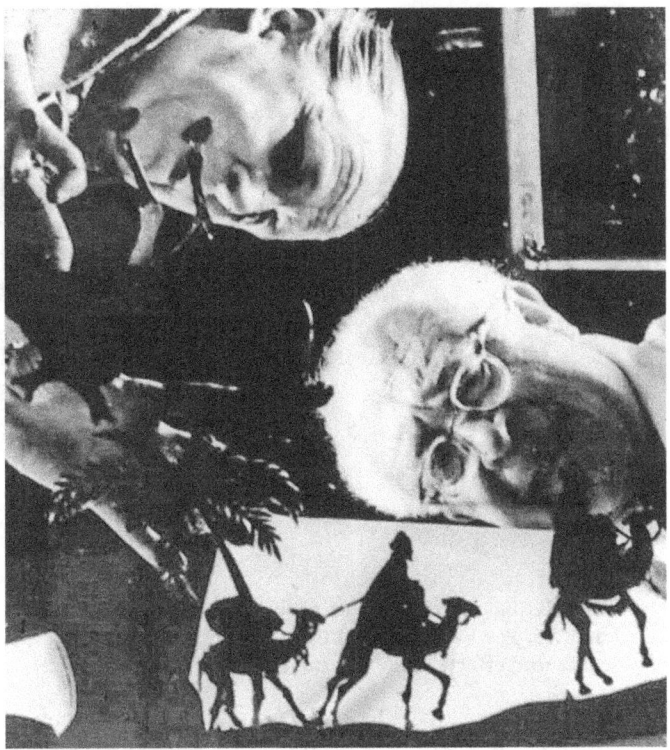

Lotte Reiniger and Carl Koch leaning over the tricktisch as they animate a scene from the 1956 *The Star of Bethlehem* (courtesy the Tübingen Stadtmuseum).

> "It's all in the way they move," noted animator [and] author John Canemaker. "That's always been the signifier of great character animation that defines itself by the way it moves, not by the way it sounds. If a silhouetted character's pose conveys the meaning of the action or the mood, that is considered a great animation pose. Here's Lotte Reiniger, whose film is completely silhouetted and has to depend on the power and the timing of her 'acting,' and it's just great" [qt. in Liebenson, 2001].

For the actual animation, Reiniger laid her characters and props flat on the glass panel. A second or third glass pane with silhouettes, placed directly above on a wooden platform, gave a scene the illusion of depth. "The impermeability of the glass planes prevented the puppets from being filmed while receding into space. This made it necessary to also contrast spatial recession artificially. The main characters and other selected figures were therefore constructed in up to 20 sizes" (Wizansky, 2004, 107). Reiniger made storyboards that mapped out the movie's plot, which is still a vital part of the animation process. She also kept a written record of a film's progression in a journal used to chronicle all the details related to the film; these included camera check, date, film in camera, intended scene length, loading waste, action information as to what happened in a particular scene, frames taken, music charts and camera shots (Reiniger, 1970a, 114). To achieve a single, fluid motion took 26 [sic, it's really 24] frames per second, and though the puppets "never completely lost [their jerkiness], the degree to which they did elicited delighted comments by critics about the transformation of tedious labor into an appearance of effortless grace" (Wizansky, 2004, 107). The number of frames Reiniger used in each of her films numbered in the thousands, even the hundred thousands for her longer pieces.

John Halas and Roger Manvell asked Reiniger and Koch to give them a "detailed description of their production process" for their book *The Technique of Film Animation*:

> 1. Once we have chosen our subject, which is frequently derived from some well-known opera or ballet, Lotte Reiniger starts drawing our first sketches. We explore imaginary scenes or situations conjured up by the general atmosphere of the characters

Lotte Reiniger's friends always commented she had a pair of scissors in hand and was cutting silhouettes. For her animated films, she made multiple puppets of the same character for different scenes and effects (courtesy the Tübingen Stadtmuseum).

and setting, as well as, of course, the music. These drawings are key moments from any part of what we shall eventually develop into our story-groupings, backgrounds, characters in various postures, comic situations, figure shapes, anything that excites us initially.

2. Parallel with making these sketches, we begin discussing how we shall contract the original score down to the ten or fifteen minutes that we need for our film. We select those phases of the music that suit best the story treatment we are devising and contain the airs likely to be most familiar to our audience.

3. Next, with the music in mind, we prepare a written script of our story, which is largely of our own invention-a kind of 'variation on the theme' of the full-length original.

4. After the script comes the preparation of the storyboard sketches, derived, of course, from our first scrap-book of initial sketches.

5. In collaboration with our director of music, who is responsible for arranging the contracted score, we record the music track for the film. The musical arrangement is normally scored for a very small orchestra, with the instruments chosen to suit the mood of the film as we have conceived it. The music must interact with our story and our characters.

6. Next we analyse every bar of the music track on a music chart, showing the exact length of the track in terms of bars and frames of animation. This chart acts as our guide to the detailed movement of the figures, since each beat of the music is now measured for us in the chart in terms of the given number of frames required on the picture track.

7. All this time we are also getting our principal characters ready. They emerge gradually from a multiplicity of sketches. As soon as we feel they are ready for experiment we draw on thin card, and cut them out and joint them. What we are looking

for now is movements of face and body which began to take on an inner life of their own that appeals to us. They must have postures and movements which reveal at once the distinctive, dramatic characterization that belongs naturally to this particular kind of flat, mobile figure. Our particular style of figure design is asserting itself, emphasizing flatness with a stylization very like that of the ancient Egyptian figures, their faces seen always in profile (in the case of principal characters), but with their bodies turned frontwards.

8. The proportions of each character are determined at the sketching and storyboard stages, though naturally we need to have each individual character designed and cut-out in many different sizes and versions according to the nature of the shots-long shot, medium shot or close up-and the expressions required in each scene. The basic sizes are, roughly speaking, five in number, varying from about 24 inches to as little as one inch. We also need segments of the figures for certain close-ups, for example a head or a hand, all elaborately jointed for detailed movement. The figures, cut out from thin card, are dressed by means of various kind of paper-translucent, filigree or opaque-and by other thin materials.

In addition to size, we have to allow for the different kinds of posture that our figures must assume in individual scenes-sitting, running, and so on. For each standard size of figure it is usually necessary to make a large range of different hands, feet and faces (with moveable eyes and mouths). If the film is in flat-figure animation (as distinct from silhouette), then the outlines and colours on the figure themselves become an added factor in their design. But the actual method of making the figures mobile through jointing remains, of course, the same for both the silhouettes and flat-figure animation.

The kind of life we are trying to achieve through these figures is, of course, an artificial one of its own; we are creating a special sort of world of character and setting and action. Our figures move within their own simplified limits, freed from the restrictions of actuality. They are the timeless creatures of fantasy with their own laws of movement and action-their own style or stylization, in fact.

9. Parallel with this work of designing and cutting out the figures comes the design of the sets. Like the performing figures these, too, are cut-outs. We use no painted backgrounds on sheets of paper as in normal animation. The sets are cut out in sections, and the figures can move in and out of these sections with the controlled timing necessary for the action. Some of our settings are made of translucent material (in particular, coloured gelatines) which lie on top of each other and give various coloured densities of light.

The lighting of silhouette films comes exclusively from beneath the table which the sets or figures are manipulated beneath the camera; the silhouette film registers its pictures in terms of various shades from black to white.

The lighting of coloured cut-out films comes both from behind and in front; the rear lighting gives a high degree of luminosity to the transparent or translucent elements in our settings (such as skies and clouds) and the frontal lighting accentuates the colour design of the characters and of the opaque elements in the sets. Also light from this double, and opposite, source eliminates any small unwanted shadows cast by the characters. The sense of distance, too, in this essentially flat world can be suggested in many ways through both the design and the makeup of the sets-including slight spacing of the various layers. For example, a moving sea can be suggested with a multiplicity of variable shadows of light sources placed at different angles behind a gelatine sheet are interrupted by a system of spirals made of either translucent or opaque materials. The different spirals are then turned individually with a timing which differs according to the impression of receding distance that we want to create.

10. The shooting stage is first reached when all the preparations are complete for photographing whatever sequence in the film we happen to have chosen which to initiate ourselves into the subject. We like to ease our way into a film in this manner, choosing the particular sequence which we think will act as the best guide to our work on the rest of the film. It becomes kind of a test of sequence.

For silhouette or flat figure animation there are the following main layers of material between the camera and the light source beneath the table:

(i) a clear plate of crystal glass which acts as the translucent surface on which the work is manipulated;

(ii) the transparent coloured backgrounds (such as sky, clouds, waves, and certain elements of landscape);

(iii) a sheet of translucent, non-slip plastic;

(iv) the non-transparent elements in the settings (houses, walls, furniture, etc.);

(v) the figures themselves which are always in the forefront when they have to move.

This is the basic lay-out, but there are certain additional effects which may be required and are installed between the crystal glass plate and the light source-such as mobile waves, mists, clouds, shadows and certain kinds of supernatural effects. Other forms of effect can be obtained in a different way, by means of mounted objects placed between the set-up and the camera-rain or foreground mist, for example, or supernatural forms.

We complete our shooting frame by frame, recording each exposure in a shooting book. The action is controlled by means of the original music chart, which acts as a guide to each frame-by-frame phase of the movements. We are thinking in terms of so many frames to each beat of music, and we adjust the limbs and the expressions of our characters in such a way that they respond to the music as subtly as we can make them.

This for us is the crucial part of the work in our medium, at once the root and the climax of its artistry. It is so because we have to be able to sense intuitively how we may create a living action in terms of our particular characters in the time dictated to use by the needs of the music. We rehearse the movements in sketch form as well as by manipulating the figures themselves. But the final result depends on our intuitive understanding of what our flat, jointed cut-out characters can perform most expressively. That for us is our art [1976, 279–286].

Stop-motion animator Henry Selick relayed how he planned his scenes for animation. Since Selick specializes in three-dimensional stop-motion, one would believe his process was more complicated that Reiniger's, but they are actually strikingly similar:

Well, there's a certain amount of planning that comes beforehand with exposure sheets that mark where you need a character to be at a given time and, if there's lip sync, exactly when they must move their mouth. And there may be rough tests to find the best poses and timing for movements. Mainly, I think that knowing how much to move a character comes from study and experience. Nothing is

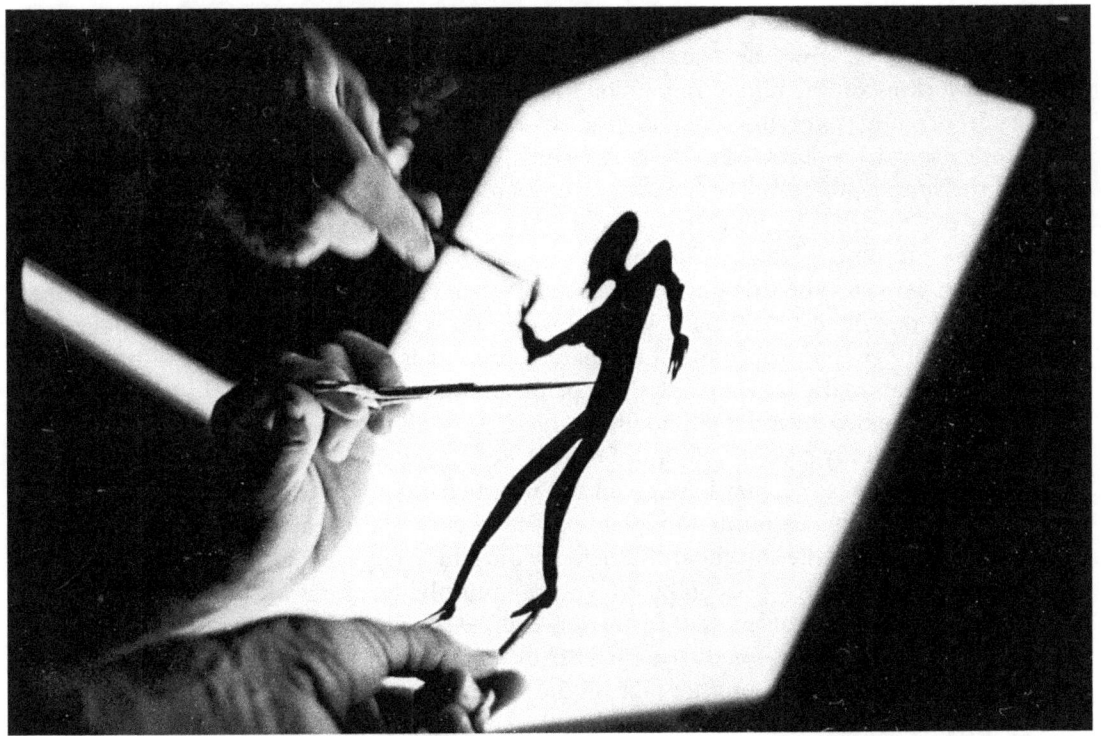

Reiniger and an assistant animate a silhouette (photo by Lois Segal).

harder than a great, individualized walk or a dance. Lotte Reiniger was a master of both and much more [Selick email to author, March 29, 2016].

Selick also mentioned that, despite Reiniger's characters being filmed on a two-dimensional plane and often described as flat, he finds that her illusion of life extends to dimensionality as well:

On one hand, Lotte didn't move things on the Z axis, toward or away from the viewer (at least as far as I know). And virtually everything in her films is cut out from flat paper. But she achieved illusions of depth at times, with what I think is a nod to classic Asian perspective rules. And, whenever I imagined what I couldn't see on her characters and worlds—the features on faces, clothing, leaves on trees—I imagined them as being dimensional, just as we do when we see a backlit object or person in real life [Selick email to author, March 29, 2016].

As with any animator or puppeteer, Reiniger feared making errors while filming. When she animated *Prinzen Achmed*, she "at first wanted the emperor to have a beard and Peri Banu would pull it, but Reiniger changed to the fairy taking his hat instead. In early scenes he has a beard, but later it disappears. The fear of a continuity error stuck with her for over 50 years" (Jouvanceau, 2004, 175). Jouvanceau believed that Reiniger didn't like to improvise during animation due to this one continuity error and this caused her to rely on "overdeveloped storyboards" (Jouvanceau, 2004, 175). Given Reiniger's strong adherence to realistic body movement, lifelike cutout silhouettes and her balletic expression with a strong reliance on music with a specific beat, she made the detailed storyboards as close to perfect as possible and it was her method of the animation process.

Storyboards are an integral tool in the animation process as well as with live action films. The storyboard is a "blueprint" for the film and it helps filmmakers "find out by drawing pictures how [they] are going to develop the action of the film." It also helps others working on the film to remain on the same page (R. Taylor, 1996, 19). Storyboards are part of a film's experimental phase: artists can work out the rough patches or visualize different scenarios that lead to the best result. "The storyboard at this stage is concerned with the simple projection of the idea or ideas of the film ... and the essential quality in all this early work is its fluidity—its adaptability to show the various purposes the animator has in mind" (Halas, 1976, 162).

Reiniger's storyboards might have been "overdeveloped," but this was the test phase where she imagined how long it would take to move from one action to the next. As described above, the stop-motion animation process is long and tedious, so having to redo a take and edit it seamlessly into prior action would lack the fluidity and grace Reiniger expressed with her silhouette puppets. As with the invention of the multiplane camera, mistakenly credited to Walt Disney, the Disney Studio also discovered the storyboard's usefulness. "It may have taken a year or two before the idea of telling a complete story through sketches pinned to a large piece of corkboard really took hold. But even in embryonic form, the storyboard's efficiency must have appealed to Walt Disney himself, at a time when the pressures on his time were multiplying, along with the budgets of his cartoons and the size of his staff" (Barrier, 2007, 92).

In a modern animated movie (3D, 2D or stop-motion) or even a puppetry film, it may be a tad easier to do another take on the same scene, but it still slows down the filmmaking process and requires reanimating the scene or reacting in the case of puppetry. Storyboards help prevent the "redos" from happening too much.

Animator Richard Williams was the lead animator and director on *The Thief and the Cobbler*, a film that took over 30 years to complete. Williams began working on his once magnum opus in 1964, but he was unable to secure funding until the late 1980s after investors saw his work on *Who Framed Roger Rabbit*. The film was forcibly removed from him after numerous delays. One of the reasons for the delays was that he didn't want to use storyboards. Kevin Schreck directed *Persistence of Vision*, a documentary that details Williams' process on the film. According to Schreck,

> *The Thief and the Cobbler* was being produced by Warner Bros. in 1990–92, Richard Williams did not have storyboards ready, until the studio demanded it so they could move the project along. Williams did do some storyboard work with Corny Cole in 1970–73 or so, often involving the then-lead character Nasrudin and a band of desert brigands. But as the film changed and expanded, Williams seemed to become less interested in that old-fashioned approach. Then-inbetweener Greg Duffell recalls seeing Williams and story development artist ... John Culhane running around with corkboards and pins and cutting out lavish images from art books in 1973 and 1974. These inspiration boards were their idea of "storyboarding," even though they didn't depict scenes or story from the movie they were making.
>
> Under pressure from Warner Bros. almost two decades later, Williams did eventually cobble together the storyboards for sequences that had not been animated yet (they're quite detailed and precise, and beautifully colored, even though he made them all in just a couple of weeks). The theory among the animators (who assumed he had the storyboards in private) was that he felt the process of storyboarding was too constricting when you had the script and you wanted the ideas to keep evolving. "It's all in my head, all up in here," Williams would say, gleefully and a bit naively [Schreck email to author, February 12, 2016].

Jouvanceau continued that little spontaneity leads to the "purging of happy innovation" and "can make shooting into a painstaking manual labor from which imagination is banished" (2004, 175). He concluded:

> Perhaps it is because of its undisciplined creativity and slightly sketchy look that *Prince Achmed* appears to be Reiniger's least polished film. Certainly the narrative is at times more muddled, but this very fact makes the film more open than some others.... It seems clear that without the presence of Ruttmann or Bartosch, without the director's fear of possibly boring viewers confronted with a feature-length silhouette film, *Prince Achmed* would also have been decidedly more standardised [Jouvanceau, 2004, 175].

Given that Reiniger later noted that *Prinzen Achmed* wasn't as polished her later films, it needs to be remembered that animation is painstaking manual labor, and imagination can be banished from the process with or without overdeveloped storyboards. Jouvanceau was making a value judgment about Reiniger's animation process without understanding the true nature of it and he appeared to be tied to the notion that animation is all fun and fancy free, as with the corporate image the Walt Disney Company projected in "making of documentaries." Rather it is an involved process requiring the teamwork of dozens to hundreds of people and in Reiniger's case (for most of her films) it was just her and her husband. She relied on storyboards to prevent errors that would have slowed production, resulting in a loss for her. She was a perfectionist, but it was necessary to make her silhouette films presentable and relatively error-free.

As for the assumption that Ruttmann and Bartosch were responsible for making the film less "boring," Jouvanceau cedes too much credit to them. Reiniger was *Prinzen Achmed*'s director and while she did have her doubts about making Europe's first animated feature film, Jouvanceau is negating the fact that Reiniger was doing an animated film of such great length for the first time. Ruttmann and Bartosch had a profound impact, but they were more interested in working on special effects and experimental films over developing an intricate fairytale story. Reiniger and Koch kept the movie on track, while she guided it as any director should.

Animation practices had achieved some standards, but nothing to the point of industry standardization we have today. Reiniger admitted later in her career that *Prinzen Achmed* had its faults, but was proud of the final product and only in hindsight and in relation to other animated films can it be labeled "standardized." As the first of its kind, there was nothing standard about *Prinzen Achmed*.

Reiniger called her projects shadow films. Feminine literary scholar and historian Marina Warner encapsulated Reiniger's career in a chapter of her book *Stranger Magic*, exploring the influences of the *1001 Arabian Nights* and Orientalism in western culture. The chapter devoted to Reiniger explored how *The Adventures of Prince Achmed* drew on stories from the literary classic and how silhouette animation was a fitting representation for the *1001 Arabian Nights*, but she disagrees over the term "shadow film" in reference to Reiniger's work:

> Although the term "ShadowFilm" is the one she used and it appears in the titles of her work, her films—and the medium itself—do not involve shadows strictly speaking. A shade, a shadow, or a reflection is not the same as a silhouette. While the latter is made from drawing a cast shadow, it acquires an independent existence as an artefact, and is no longer attached to the person or object it represents. Reiniger's silhouettes are neither ghosts nor shades, but have material presence and a certain solidarity, however two-dimensional [2011, 399–400].

Reiniger's films are the product of an animation process that has been improved and simplified since her first film premiered in 1919. While it's easy to glance back on early days of animation and feel superior with today's advances in the field, do not forget that what Reiniger and Koch were doing was groundbreaking. She said, "The cinema camera was still in its infancy then and we had the satisfying opportunity of doing things for the first time, things which are now a household word in animation" (Reiniger, 1970a, 87).

Modern filmmakers and insightful audiences who understand the rigorous animation process can look back and appreciate the amount of time and labor Reiniger invested in her films.

Warner says that Reiniger's work possesses a great ineffable quality that many people experience when viewing one of her films. They still emit an ethereal, fey charm that comes from the small paper cut details in each scene and the expressive motion of the puppets. Her films create their own worlds, existing between the camera lens and the glass pane on a tricktisch, but brought to life on a movie screen. They draw on the feeling we experience whenever we watch a movie: We suspend our disbelief to be transported to an instance in the characters' lives and we journey with them as the projector rolls. This cinematic sense of wonder has its origins in the puppet shows of old, where the characters were reflections of life and illusions of the imagination.

Another reason for the shortage of coverage of Reiniger could be the fact that she didn't belong to any huge artistic, philosophical and political movements during her career. It also relates how Weimar films depict all Germans as followers of the popular movements of the era. While animation and puppetry are shoved into the juvenile department, their history can be traced and categorized into neat boxes. Animation's history is less extensive than that of puppetry, but it has its own artistic taxonomy divided by country of origin, studios, famous animators and eras. Puppetry, on the other hand (pun intended), tends to be designated by type and country of origin. The grander spectrum of art has loftier terms for description, such as baroque, art deco, art nouveau, classicism, Renaissance, surrealism, impressionism, etc., and these are only a smattering of western art movements without even touching on the eastern portion or how the two intermingle. Reiniger said, "But we did not belong to the industry. We always had been outsiders and we had always done what we wanted to do" (1970b, 2). While Reiniger and Koch were "outside looking in" on the artistic and philosophical movements in the early twentieth century, the couple were involved with politics. Reiniger was less inclined to vocally express her political views, but Koch was very steadfast about his allegiances. In pre-war Germany, Koch had to be careful to keep his mouth shut, because he and his friends had some close calls with authorities. Reiniger even made an anti-war war silhouette film so laden with metaphors, she was able to sneak it under Goebbels' nose. Their anti–Nazi beliefs forced them to flee the country, lest they be killed like so many others in that period.

Politics aside, the husband-and-wife team appeared to pride themselves on being outside the circles of whatever popular movement appealed to the masses. "Despite inroads into well-funded, widely distributed, and thoroughly documented areas of early German films, Reiniger consciously decided to remain autonomous" (K.V. Taylor, 2011, 8). This might have been to their financial detriment, especially later in their lives, for while Reiniger's films were groundbreaking, they fell outside of the popular sphere and classifiable movements. She was not lauded as a "master of [insert movement here]," except later in her life and especially upon her death. Had Reiniger been associated with some movement, it might have been easier for her to secure funding for more of her films and maybe she would have made another feature-length film. One can only speculate what could have been for Reiniger and Koch had they aligned themselves with a bigger studio, popular movements, and even worked more closely with their contemporaries.

In Weimar Germany, arts and entertainment were overtaken by a wave of art movements: expressionism, surrealism, Dada, Bauhaus, new objectivity, constructivism, futurism, cubism and many other movements that fell under the avant-garde umbrella. "Members were often unified by shared and easily identifiable, perhaps oversimplified traits, values and goals" (K.V. Taylor, 2011, 8). These art movements had the biggest cultural impact on artists who pioneered the values and traits or expressed them via their work. In the U.S. and also in Europe, "[a] regular supply of [Disney cartoons] helped make Disney an icon of modernity in the eyes of the emerging avant-gardes in the 1920s and 30s" due to the detailed and advanced technological process (Smoodin, 2012, 12–13).

While the art movements inspired artists in the traditional sense, "modern artists were eyeing the motion picture as the medium that could add movement to their paintings and graphic designs" (Starr, 1987, 9). Animation was practically alluring as a brand new art form and Cecile Starr called this new experimentation "fine art animation." During the time, it was sometimes called "pure cinema" (Starr, 1987, 9). Many of Reiniger's contemporaries were "fine art animators": Oskar Fischinger, Hans Richter, Berthold Bartosch, Walter Ruttmann and Viking Eggeling. Other fine art animators garnered a positive reputation outside Germany: Norman McLaren, Mary Ellen Bute, Alexander Alexeieff, Len Lye and Claire Parker (Starr, 1987, 9).

But the average German citizen didn't adhere to the movements' principles as they went about their daily routines and their only exposure to them was through films, literature, newspapers, fashion and new construction for the architecture-related styles. Despite the limited exposure, Germans were aware of these new movements if only at a subconscious level. To assert that Reiniger was not was affected by cultural movements of her time and place in history would be misinterpreting her life story (making that claim for anyone would be a misbegotten idea). While Reiniger is not a dictionary definition of any of these art movements, her silhouette films do adhere to some of their traits.

Exactly which artistic movements Reiniger drew influences from is open to interpretation based on the individual, which actually represents one of the main values Dada brought to the modern art discussion. One of the most respected Dada artists, filmmakers and animators was Hans Richter and in his book *Dada: Art and Anti-Art* he wrote:

> the image of Dada is full of contradictions. This is not surprising. Dada invited, or rather defied, the world to misunderstand it, and foster every kind of confusion.... However this confusion was only a facade.... Our real motive force was not rowdiness for its own sake, or contradiction and revolt in themselves, but the question (basic then, as it is now), "where next?" Dada was not an artistic movement in the accepted sense.... It came without warning ... in which the stored-up energies released by Dada were evidenced in new forms, new materials, new ideas, new directions, new people—and in which they addressed themselves to new people. Dada had now unified formal characteristics as have other styles. But it did have a new artistic ethic from which, in unforeseen ways, new means of expression emerged [1997, 9].

The purpose of Dada was to rouse people out of their traditional thought patterns and rethink the world with new ideas that challenged accepted bourgeois social standards, cultural meanings and the very manner of humanity. Animation is a medium that fit nicely into the Dada category, although the prevalent Dada artists followed the traditional high art forms (sculpture, painting, etc.), so it is a contradiction within a contradiction. As an animator, Reiniger challenged audiences' notions of what an animation was capable of, how puppetry could be revitalized to fit into filmmaking, and how classic storytelling methods could literally be revisualized. The animated feature film was a brand new means of expression unseen by the world (sans Argentina) and Reiniger achieved an new artistic aesthetic combining the old with the new via a new modern medium which pointed animators down the road. Animation answered Richter's "where next?" question and modern animators are still challenging its final destination with technology.

Another Dada value was its use of anti–Dada, in effect a mockery of itself. The best known example is Marcel Duchamp's 1917 sculpture *Fountain*, which was just a urinal signed by "R. Mutt." Critiques and the public viewed it as obscene, but it makes a statement that art can be anything and everything.[5] It gave rise to modern notions that art can be interpreted in many ways, just as animation or puppetry can be utilized to tell any type of story in any manner.

This view on Dada feeds into my expressionist, surrealist and Bauhaus interpretations of Reiniger's silhouette films. Allow me to bring in Einstein's quote once again about a child's brain development: "If you want your children to be intelligent, read them fairy tales. If you want them to be more intelligent, read them more fairy tales" (qt. in Heiner, 2007). This quote strengthens Reiniger's ties to these art movements. Fairytales are as much a reflection of society as the art movements, but Reiniger merged them through experimental animation as a way for her to explore her own craft, entertain, express and teach audiences about her views. She challenged her audiences to become smarter by watching her take on *1001 Arabian Nights* and the Brothers Grimm's fairytales via a modern medium. When her films are tied to expressionism, surrealism, Dada and Bauhaus, she challenges their intelligence even more to rethink and revisualize the world.

Out of all the popular movements in Weimar Germany, Reiniger is most associated with expressionism. Expressionism was an inward reflection of the artist's creation and emotions, rather than representing the external world. How artists expressed their feelings outweighed a work's medium or composition. German expressionist films mark a significant period in film development, characterized by *Das Cabinet des Dr. Caligari* (*The Cabinet of Dr. Caligari,* 1920) and Fritz Lang's *Metropolis* (1927). Klaus Kreimeier wrote, "The term 'expressionism' applied to film is misleading if it suggests a tie to the Expressionism in the visual arts" (1999, 87). Kreimeier fails to make a connection that German cinematographers adapted visual art expressionism to fit their own interpretation built off post–World War I feelings and the desire to reinstill pride in the German people. Siegfried Kracauer also refutes this thought:

> The birth of the German film originated not only in the foundation of Ufa, but also in the intellectual excitement surging through Germany after the war. All Germans were then in a mood which can best be described as *Aufbruch*. In the pregnant sense in which it was used at the time, the term meant departure from the shattered world of yesterday towards a tomorrow built on the grounds of revolutionary conceptions. This explains why ... expressionist art became popular during that period [the 1920s]. People suddenly grasped the significance of avant-garde paintings and mirrored themselves in visionary dramas announcing to a suicidal mankind the gospel of a new age of brotherhood [1948, 38].

German film expressionism took on a singular meaning for the German people as a time to reinvent themselves after a time of turmoil, but were still haunted by old memories. Despite Kreimer not fully understanding that expressionism was an outward reflection of internal feelings, he still defined the true significance after reading Lotte Eisner's *Dämonische Leinwand,* "Lotte Eisner speaks of a 'gothic' style.... A gloomy bizarre fantasy of 'gothic tales,' a partiality to the irrational, to the psychological extremes, to the 'night side' of life, and to the central themes of Dark Romanticism.... [A]ll these elements harken back to the imaginary medieval era, to the relics of pre-industrial structures in the German (and European) psychic landscape" (1999, 87).

While German film expressionism was an awakening of the German consciousness, it summoned dark turmoil and medieval horrors. Expressionism is directly correlated to Romanticism, a period of affable enlightenment, emotional awakening and glorification of the past. German expressionism took these past ideals and trod over them with black postwar scars. Gothic is deemed as dark and elaborate explorations into the dark psyche and its horrors, not necessarily blood and gore. Residing within Germany's gothic thrills were shadows, a symbolic device with many meanings and one that Reiniger embodied with her silhouette animation.

Shadows are immaterial items, they're not even objects, but they come into existence when a solid object comes between light rays and a surface. Shadows are a dark reflection of life and silhouettes also are dark pictures made by human hands, thus capturing the lightless reflection in material form. Reiniger embraced the shadows, but instead of continuing the popular Gothic themes riddled with dark thoughts and depression, she animated fairytales. Any reader of the original fairytales knows these versions are dark, filled with blood, gore and death, and they would be deemed inappropriate for children by modern standards. Fairytales were created hundreds of years ago, many are even thousands of years old, inspired by mythology. Thanks to the Brothers Grimm and oral traditions, fairytales are embedded within the German national identity. Reiniger returned to a traditional form or "medieval" of German literature, but didn't retell the original, violent versions. By using silhouette animation, however, she did revert to the "dark side" of German film expressionism but, pulling on earlier romantic aspects she presented a lighter, happier take on fairytales although intense emotion is expressed via the puppets "acting."

J.P. Telotte offers a complimentary, albeit different approach to understanding Reiniger's films in comparison with German expressionism. Expressionism was an awakening of the German consciousness and it pushed against the boundaries instilled in old art movements and social conventions. German film pushed against the accepted boundaries to test their limits, but within the silhouette realm, unlike live action films that had infinite space with sound stages only limited by budgets, space was limited to one flat plane. Telotte wrote:

> [Esther] Leslie suggests that Reiniger's work essentially failed because its only connection "with modernism's logic" was through its "oscillation between a stark flatness and the exploration of depth through its fakery" (50)—that is, insofar as it made audiences aware of the limited efforts at constructing space. And indeed, these silhouette films, consonant with their theatrical origins, seem to carry a far greater weight of obvious artifice than other forms of animation, and thus a greater sense of the boundaries or limitations within which they worked. But Reiniger's ability to draw an unusual and even unexpected depth out of this sort of material, and even to explore how the world might, from a different perspective, produce its own curious and appealing patterns, also suggests its kinship to the expressionist cinema of the period and its potential for offering its own commentary on a modernist sense of space [2010, 36–37].

Reiniger may have been offering a commentary of space, but she was really pushing the boundaries for how much emotion could be conveyed through her puppets and gave an illusion of more than two dimensions. She expressed that with limited resources or a space for her characters to exist, she was capable of a wide creative range like her contemporaries in this period.

Reiniger's best-known film *Die Abenteuer des Prinzen Achmed* is an adaptation of *1001 Arabian Nights*, a succession of fables translated from Middle Eastern literature. Another huge aspect of expressionist films was Orientalism and exoticism, which is romanticizing foreign cultures by relying on stereotypes and false impressions of the cultures (K.V. Taylor, 2011, 33). After World War I, film audiences were obsessed with escapist fantasies centered around exotic locales in the Far East. Reiniger represents this ideal via *Prinzen Achmed*'s Asian and Middle Eastern settings, the characters' costumes, the *mise en scéne* and the paper cut designs.

Surrealism is an art movement that also shaped Weimar Germany and is conveyed through Reiniger's films. While expressionism was more popular with filmmakers, surrealism did leave an impact. Surrealism also has its roots in romanticism by focusing on imagination, but rather than relying on intuition it was believed revelations could be found on the street and in everyday life ("Surrealism," 2016). Austrian psychiatrist Sigmund Freud's book *The Interpretation of Dreams* and his other writings left a big impact of the surrealist movement. "Freud legitimized the importance of dreams and the unconscious as valid revelations of human emotion and desires; his exposure of the complex and repressed inner worlds of sexuality, desire and violence provided a theoretical basis for much of Surrealism" ("Surrealism," 2016).

Unconscious thought and dream imagery are the most recognized surrealism principles. Shadows and silhouettes have an ethereal aura as dark reflections of life or rather a dream-like quality that fades once the light wakes up a person. Freud wrote in his groundbreaking book, "In the waking state we commonly very soon forget a great many sensations and perceptions because they are too slight to remember, and because they are charged with only a slight amount of emotional feeling. This is true also of many dream-images; they are forgotten because they are too weak, while the stronger images in their neighbourhood are remembered" (1900). Shadows and silhouettes have a poetic and romantic association that makes them dream symbols. When Reiniger used shadow puppetry techniques within her silhouette animation process, she is giving life to dreams as a solid presence recorded on film. Shadows don't have a solid form until they are transferred to paper as a silhouette, thus shadows are weak and quickly forgotten. Yet silhouettes retain a stronger emotional intensity through perceived actions on film.

In one of the many dream interpretations discussed in the book, Freud recounts how dreams can be self-critical messengers and in particular one case: "In this series of dreams of a poet who, in his younger years, had been a journeyman tailor, it is hard to recognize the domination of the wish-fulfillment. All the delightful things occurred in his waking life, while the dream seemed to drag along with it the ghost-like shadow of an unhappy existence which had long been forgotten" (1900). Freud continued that dreams can remind us of times we would rather forget as well and when we sleep remind us, especially when life might be pleasant. Reiniger's use of shadows aren't critical messengers animated to snub the audience; rather their animated existence provides a respite from nightmares. While many might have "the conflict raging in other psychic strata between vanity and self-criticism had certainly determined the dream-content, but the more deeply-rooted wish for youth had alone made it possible as a dream. One often says to oneself even in the waking state: 'To be sure, things are going well with you today, and once you found life very hard; but, after all, life was sweet in those days, when you were still so young'" (1900). Reiniger's films embody the sweet innocence we had in earlier years and brings it to life for reflection and escapism.

The Bauhaus movement was started by the German architect Walter Gropius in 1919 as school of design that focused on arts and crafts and uniting art with functional design. Bauhaus stressed "intellectual and theoretical pursuits, and linked these to an emphasis on practical skills, crafts and techniques that was more reminiscent of the medieval guild system. Fine art and craft were brought together with the goal of problem solving for a modern industrial society. In so doing, the Bauhaus effectively leveled the old hierarchy of the arts, placing crafts on par with fine arts such as sculpture and painting, and paving the way for many of the ideas that have inspired artists in the late 20th century" ("Bauhaus," 2016). The movement rejuvenated handmade craft making and allowed artists to reclaim and explore mediums consigned to industrialization. Bauhaus artists were encouraged to approach their art from a practical method and experiment with new ways to manipulate their chosen medium, but functionalism called for simplified designs over useless adornments.

"The craftsmanship that Gropius valued was a fundamental trait of *Prince Achmed* [and Reiniger's other films], in which handmade construction and manual manipulation of figures and sets rely on craftsmanship. Since the figures were cut from paper and lead sheets and moved by hand for each shot, her films were literally handmade" (V.K. Taylor, 2011, 35). For her entire career, Reiniger would prefer handmaking all of her films as a way to keep total control over her creativity, but also it was the aesthetic that best suited her personal style.

While Reiniger's work can be interpreted to fit within the Bauhaus, expression, surrealism and Dada schools of thought, her artistic style should be defined as an example of post art nouveau. (J.P. Telotte agrees with me in his book *Animating Space* [2010, 26].) Art nouveau, or Jugendstil, as Reiniger would have known it, was an art movement that means "new art" or German "youth style" and was *en vogue* from the late nineteenth century to early twentieth as a predecessor to the prior described movements. "Artists drew inspiration from both organic and geometric forms, evolving elegant designs that united flowing, natural forms with more angular contours," but they focused on modernizing design without frivolous ornamentation or returning to past decorative trends ("Art Nouveau," 2016). Art nouveau artists believed "that the function of an object should dictate its form," which inspired artists to revisualize an item's use in an artistic manner ("Art Nouveau," 2016).

Art nouveau directly inspired early filmmakers' design aesthetics, Georges Méliès being the best example. Klaus-Jürgen Sembach described the early relationship between film and art nouveau:

> The 1890s gave the world two innovations: cinema and Art Nouveau. The two are not unconnected, since they started from the same premises, their aims were comparable and they shared the same yearnings. Motion pictures and stylistic animation [such as Reiniger's] both resulted in one way or another from the industrial age—directly, as one of its inventions, or indirectly, as a search for greater refinement [2002, 8].

Art nouveau and the cinema searched for the refinement of the arts in a modernistic sense. Michael Cowan and Olive Blackham describe Reiniger's art (especially her earliest films) as rococo, due to the ornate details, lighthearted stories and graceful lines (Cowan, 2013, 789; Blackham, 1960, 86). The rococo influences are seen in *Das Geheimnis der Marquise*, *Die Barcarole* and *Das Ornament des verliebten Herzens*. Art nouveau is a direct descendent of rococo, borrowing the flowing lines, curves, ornate (although less intense) details and focus on human figures, and even borrowing the fairytale association. Gabriele Fahr-Becker wrote, "Even Rococo was termed 'style moderne' by its contemporaries" in the eighteenth century (2004, 7). Reiniger grew up in the art nouveau's prime (1890–1910) and she probably absorbed the style via magazines and film. Reiniger's art style is much simpler than rococo with modernistic, smooth lines complemented by ornamentation that flows from characters' costumes to the background designs and adds to their functionality as a character rather than serving as mere decoration.

Reiniger's gender also cannot be ignored regarding her lack of association with the aforementioned movements. There were female artists during the Weimar period who rose to great status and gained more attention than Reiniger, especially in contemporary scholarship. Pursuing art and filmmaking was considered improper for a woman, who should have been occupied with housekeeping and child rearing. Her choice of artistic medium (silhouette animation) firmly placed her in feminine arts and thus unworthy of greater attention. But it did allow her to take full credit for her films and make them independently (Cowan, 2013, 787).

By the early twentieth century, silhouettes were regarded as feminine craft, kitschy and old-fashioned. Even though the Bauhaus school embraced fine craftsmanship and austere design, women students were encouraged to pursue "areas of ornamentation and decoration, such as textiles" as a direct contrast to functional, simplistic design and it was deemed better suited for female hands (Baumhoff qt. in Cowan, 2014, 790). Two words used to describe Reiniger's silhouettes are ornamentation and decoration (despite the art nouveau characteristics), which contrasted with not only the Bauhaus but also aspects of surrealism, expressionism—but not Dada as ornamentation and decoration was an "anti-art" in this light.

As Reiniger's work was called pure ornamentation and was simple, pure storytelling for the sake of telling a story (art for art's sake), she was ignored by her contemporaries. Animation was a charming, cinematic novelty, not meant to be taken too seriously either. Reiniger made silhouettes films employing the feminine scherenschnitte and the novelty animation process. Her choices were a blatant message to disregard her as a serious filmmaker. Cowan points out that Pinschewer was aware of the feminine power silhouettes possessed and it was one of the reasons he hired Reiniger to made advertising films: to advertise feminine products (2013, 790–791).

Despite her famous friendships, female artist Reiniger faced ridicule and her art was considered a trifle amongst the era's greater male filmmakers. Her gender discredited her as a "true" member of any of these movements, even though she chose to remain independent. In terms of animation and cinematic history, although she arguably made the larger contribution and inspired her contemporaries to pursue animation on their own, she is rendered negligible compared to Hans Richter, Walter Ruttmann, Viking Eggeling, Berthold Bartosch and Oskar Fischinger. The feminist argument that she was overlooked due to her gender applies to these male animators having more studies dedicated to their films, but an equal argument is that they were also more associated with the prevailing art movements of the 1920 and '30s. These men are deemed the innovators in experimental film for their reliance on abstract subjects. Fischinger was a pure expressionist; Richter and Eggeling exemplified Dada; Bartosch and Ruttmann dipped into whatever inspired them. "Weimar artists and intellectuals often belonged to several movements simultaneously" (K.V. Taylor, 2011, 34). All of them are considered the ideal avant-garde animators.

3. Defining the Art of Puppetry and Animation

Reiniger and Koch studying some silhouettes (courtesy Paul Gelder).

Evaluating a creative individual's work is as much based on historical interpretation as subjective criticism. When some film historians and critics tried to place Reiniger's work into an artistic niche and failed, their opinions can be construed as misunderstanding and/or condescending. Despite the narrow perspectives of some critics, in her own way Reiniger does uphold the principles of expressionism, surrealism, Dada and Bauhaus. Noga Wizansky explained how she fit within the boundaries, while also stepping outside them:

Unlike the explosive rhetoric of dada artists earlier in the decade, or functionalist discourses in the Bauhaus, the idea of modernization that emerges from most reviews of *Prince Achmed* entailed reconfiguring past practices and traditions by joining them with contemporary ones, thereby granting the past a crucial role in shaping the present. In doing so, reviews stressed that the outmoded, non-rationalized attributes of silhouettes and shadow puppets, manifested in their handcrafted laboriousness, artificiality and calming, familiar appeal to both viewers and practitioners, were crucial aspects of their contribution to modern film culture [2004, 89].

She is not the ultimate candidate to represent any of these movements, but she made films during the highpoint in the German film industry and worked alongside the big names in the profession. She could not help but be influenced by the times. Jouvanceau wrote

> Reiniger's strength was her base halfway between series animation, then widely distributed and appealing to mass audiences, and the German avant-garde cinema, born as the intellectual and visual response of local artists to the American model. It was the mid-way positioning that brought Reiniger her success—it was how, without working it out in advance, she was able to "reconcile" the upholders of a modern cinematography closely linked to visual innovation with the defenders of a narrative and figurative tradition which was doubtless favoured by far larger audiences. But it also brought isolation. Unclassifiable thanks to this apparently paradoxical duality of influence and also to her constancy in continuing to use a technique already deemed outdated—but admired for the same reasons—Reiniger found herself marginalised from mainstream cinema history, a strange and unusual personality who could not be labeled or classified within the important movements of the period [Jouvanceau, 2004, 41–42].

The defining feature of all these movements, especially within the film industry, was to be regarded as avant-garde. To be avant-garde was to cast off traditional ideations and social norms in favor of experimentation and innovation with new culture, technology and progressive social reforms. Hans Richter wrote that Reiniger "'belonged to the avant-garde as far as independent production and courage were concerned,' but the spirit of her work seemed Victorian" (qt. in Starr, 1998, 351). Reiniger and Koch were the definition of avant-garde given their pioneering efforts in animation and desire *not* to be associated with other collective filmmakers. They were the ultimate form of avant-garde; they didn't belong anywhere. Thus Reiniger and Koch were the avant-gardes of the avant-gardes.

4

The Adventures of Prince Achmed

I believe more in the truth of fairytales than I do newspapers.—Lotte Reiniger

Nineteen twenty-three was the year Lotte Reiniger began work on the film that would make her an animation legend: *Die Geschichte des Prinzen Achmed* or *Die Abenteuer des Prinzen Achmed* (*The Adventures of Prince Achmed*). It was at the beginning of the 1920s, a decade that has since attained the romantic status of an era that proffered limitless possibilities due to the technological advances in industry, travel, medicine and entertainment. People in western nations were imbued with a restless, ingenious spirit, but in a Germany still reeling from the effects of the Great War it was felt the strongest in its movie industry. As noted in Chapter 2, Weimar cinema was the hotbed of avantgarde and experimental cinema epitomized by the expressionist films, many of which came from UFA.

While the Weimar movie industry exploded into what would be later deemed its Golden Age (mirroring a term affixed to this period once the country achieved economic stability, the Golden Twenties), the German economy suffered from record-breaking inflation, immortalized by people pushing wheelbarrows of currency to stores to purchase daily essentials. Movies, however, made money and—very similar to how Americans turned to the theater for escapism during the 1930s Depression—Germans did the same.

For financiers, investing in the movie industry had low risks and potential for high returns. The Jewish banker Louis Hagen of Berlin was a patron of the arts, especially new and modern ideas, and one day he visited the Institute for Cultural Research and noticed Reiniger and Koch working on a silhouette film. He asked if they would be able to make a full-length silhouette animation film. Reiniger remembered, "We had to think twice. This was a never heard of thing. Animated films were supposed to make people roar with laughter, and nobody had dared entertain an audience with them for more than ten minutes" (Reiniger, 1970b, 2). She *had* dreamed of making a longer film, but she didn't have a way to cover the costs. When she expressed her desire and hesitations to Hagen, his reply was, "Let me work that out for you" (Raganelli, 1999). As a patron of the arts, Hagen was a patron of the arts, other accounts say he had invested in raw film stock to shelter his wealth from inflation. "The gamble had not paid off, and to him the film became worthless; but to Lotte Reiniger it was a gift that made her film possible" (Crafton, 1982, 243). Reiniger told Guy Coté a different story: "One banker, wiser than most, converted some of his rapidly diminishing assets into raw negative film stock, which he then presented to Miss Reiniger: 'There! Now make your film and come to see me when it's finished'" (1954, 17). Whether Hagen wanted to rid himself of the useless film stock or was curious about animation's potential, he didn't have anything to lose.

Reiniger wasn't the only animator who experienced doubt in the face of making a full-length animated film. Some of Walt Disney's work appeared in feature films long before thoughts of *Snow White* entered his head. He and actress Mary Pickford planned to shoot a live-action animated *Alice in Wonderland,* and Disney animation appeared in *My Lips Betray* (1933), *Sabotage* (1936), *Michael O'Halloran* (1937), *Sullivan's Travels* (1941), *Dillinger* (1945) and others (Kaufman, 1993, 158–71). Disney knew he needed to have a solid plan before venturing into a big film project; he said, "We've got to be sure of it before we start, because if it isn't good we will destroy it. If it is good, we shall make at least a million" (qt. in Kaufman, 1993, 172). Disney had much more at risk than Reiniger, who only had a small production team and her patron was invested in the project as much as to satisfy his curiosity as to use his film stock. If Disney failed with his first picture, it would have been a big loss for his entire studio and reputation.

"When the Disney artists began work on *Snow White* in 1934, they realized that they were embarking on an untrodden path. There were so many unanswered questions that, with the possible exception of Walt Disney himself, few felt that such a project would be anything but a folly. Would audiences sit in a theater for 80–90 minutes to watch a cartoon? Could the animators make the characters believable? …Would the tremendous cost of the project be justified?" (Smith, 1987, 37–39) Walt Disney's leading story man Bill Peet revealed, "They called *Snow White* Disney's Folly. The picture would be a box office flop! People would never sit through a full-length cartoon feature! Disney was getting too big for his britches!" (1989, 85) The media referred to the movie as Disney's Folly, because his focus on quality and detail forced him to go over budget.

Animation historian Michael Barrier paints a different picture in his Disney biography *The Animated Man.* When *Snow White* was made, its negative cost was almost $1.5 million, more than the studio's total 1937 revenue (Barrier, 2007, 130).

> Disney liked to talk as if he was flirting with disaster in the last months *Snow White* was in production.… Despite the scale of the borrowing required to finish the film, there was probably never any serious risk that the money would run out.… As the film opened … the answer was not in doubt. Critics as well as audiences adored *Snow White,* which was praised as much in intellectual journals as in the mainstream press. Disney had so thoroughly transformed animation in just a few years that sophisticates would have yawned at the old silent cartoons found themselves weeping with the dwarfs at *Snow White*'s bedside [Barrier, 2007, 130–131].

In 2015, Barrier expressed his thoughts in response to PBS's *American Experience* Disney biopic:

> I was so impolitic as to suggest, among other things … that the Disney studio was not in financial distress in the 1930s, and that *Snow White and the Seven Dwarfs* was not a daring gamble that many people believed would fail.… On the latter point, the interviewer rather triumphantly pointed out that Walt and Roy had put up their library of cartoons as collateral when they borrowed hundreds of thousands of dollars from the Bank of America to finish *Snow White.* Didn't that prove something? I was too flummoxed by the question to answer adequately, but of course that transaction proved, if anything, that the bank had a lot of confidence in Walt and in the value of his cartoons, the older shorts and the new feature alike. And there was certainly nothing strange about a bank's wanting collateral for a large loan [Barrier, 2015].

The 2015 documentary *Behind the Magic: Snow White,* a behind-the-scenes look at Disney's first feature-length film, features interviews with experts on animation, fairytales and Disney history. Among those interviewed were Jack Zipes, Jake Friedman, John Canemaker, Eric Goldberg, John Lasseter, Alan Menken and Maria Tartar. When the topic of Walt and Roy Disney's money "woes" came up, viewers were told that the brothers still needed another quarter million dollars with three months left until the premiere date. Before Bank of America loaned Disney more funds, they wanted to see how the movie was progressing. Walt didn't want anyone to see the film until its completion. The Disney brothers didn't have a choice if they wanted to keep artists drawing, so they arranged for a Saturday showing for banker Joe Rosenberg. Walt showed Rosenberg a patchwork reel with some completed scenes and others were pencil sketches, explaining his intentions with the story and animation. Rosenberg was silent during the entire screening. Afterwards, they went outside with Rosenberg making small talk without mentioning the loan. Finally the banker got into his car, rolled down the window, and told Walt, "So long Walt, you're going to make a pile of money on that picture." Rosenberg's words were the official approval for the loan and they proved prophetic when the box office yields were totaled (Lustberg & Crowell, 2015).

The Walt Disney Company has a flair for the dramatic when creating the image that its films, parks, etc., are imbued with magic and blessed with miracles. The Rosenberg and Walt Disney story has been Disneyfied, however; even if Rosenberg did have confidence that Disney's Folly would be a hit, Bank of America still needed collateral and that was where the cartoon shorts came into play. Barrier makes a rather poignant platform for Disney not doubting *Snow White and the Seven Dwarfs'* success. Reiniger was self-assured to a point with *Prinzen Achmed*'s own success; based on her accounts of the time, she was more concerned with finishing the film and would worry about the success upon completion.

Barrier negates very important factors in his stance that Disney wasn't afraid of his "folly" that apply to Reiniger as well: the human tendency towards self-doubt and the human tendency to dislike change or anything new. As discussed throughout this book, Reiniger and Disney were animation pioneers undertaking actions that no one (sans Cristiani) has done before and were paving the way for the future animation industry in the U.S. and Europe. These two wouldn't have been human if they didn't doubt themselves at some point during the production on their films. Reiniger was a young woman working in a male-dominated film industry and despite her supportive team and husband, there must have been many people who thought she was mad making a film or chalked it off as a girl playing with her paper dolls. Despite Mickey Mouse's success, Disney had failed in several of his prior ventures and had gone way over budget and must have been apprehensive that his longer cartoon would fail, especially when the media labeled it a folly.

As for the tendency for humans to dislike change or new innovations, this harks back to the basic instinct to like predictability and routine. Anything that disrupts that routine, such as a new form of entertainment, is viewed as bad or as generally an automatic failure. There are endless examples of people not liking change and Reiniger and Disney were just two more innovators out to prove their visions. Based on Barrier's argument, if the Disney Studio wasn't in the red and they used their cartoon library as collateral, Bank of America might have seen the loans for *Snow White* as an investment just as much as they saw the cartoon library as ample opportunity to make their money back if the movie failed. If *Snow White* did fail, then the bank owned all the Mickey Mouse shorts and the rights to show them at theaters or sell them at a high price based on the Mouse's popularity.[1]

The bank wasn't gambling anything, Roy and Walt Disney were, because even if they were self-assured, there still was the possibility of failure. The same can be said for Reiniger, although her patron Louis Hagen only had to lose film stock and she her reputation amongst her fellow artists.

In 1935, Walt was once more stressed and showed signs that resembled his nervous breakdown in 1931, so he went to Europe with his wife, brother and sister-in-law to recharge. While in France, he visited a theater that had combined several of Disney's shorter cartoons into one longer picture (Lustberg & Crowell, 2015). Perhaps the theater had been inspired to connect the movies after a *Prinzen Achmed* showing? The more likely truth, however, is that animation fans were inclined to appreciate a feature-length animated film if they already enjoyed a cartoon marathon. Once the idea to turn a "marathon" into a feature film left the novelty phase, audiences vocalized their doubts. Despite whether or not the odds were stacked against them, Reiniger and Disney knew audiences would watch a longer cartoon if the story was engrossing, the visuals stunning, and if it touched their imaginations. Reiniger's film was a plethora of trickfilm special effects, Disney had the glory of full color and sound, and both had stories that enraptured the audience in fantasy.[2]

In the course of research about *Prinzen Achmed*'s creation, I never came across any German film critics who expressed their doubt about Reiniger's full-length animated creation or any of her previous works on par with Disney's Folly. "While it was generally received as a new kind of film, as a number of reviewers as indicated, it was not the first time Weimar audiences had watched filmed silhouettes. A long-standing popular visual tradition in Germany, by the mid–1920s silhouettes had appeared in films as inter-titles, advertising films, shorts projected as main features, and as special effects in narrative films" (Wizansky, 2004, 82). Reiniger had all of these already on her résumé, but her doubts had to be withheld and forgotten until production was complete as she was in the thick of silhouette puppets, sand, tissue paper and *1001 Arabian Nights,* and she was stuffed into a small garage attic with five men in Potsdam.

Animation in the 1920s was valued as pre-show filler, but it wasn't seen as a lucrative medium beyond the occasional merchandising tie-ins. (*Felix the Cat* had a huge fan base in Germany and that black and white feline was the most popular and profitable cartoon character of his day.) Europeans, especially Germans, viewed the medium with higher regard, but while the critics might not have said anything, Reiniger discovered that "everybody to whom we talked in the industry was horrified" and it's not hard to imagine why (Reiniger, 1970b, 2). Germany's film industry was preoccupied with expressionism, surrealism and scripts that challenged the country's strongly held traditional values. Reiniger, Koch and their compatriots at the institute were doing something new and the general consensus for new ideas is "vulgar" to quote the silent movie actress Olga Mara in 1952's classic musical *Singin' in the Rain* about Hollywood's transition from silent pictures to talkies.

Hagen thought there was potential in the idea and Reiniger and Koch had the luxury of being free to explore, because "we did not belong to the industry. We had always been outsiders and we always had done what we wanted to do" (Reiniger, 1970b, 2). Animation wasn't considered a viable medium, much less an honorable profession. As it was viewed as filler, it was very much perceived as the dregs of the entertainment industry. Other animating pioneers began their careers doing the work themselves or forming their own studios and attaching themselves to larger distribution houses. The animators existed on the outskirts and had to fight to be taken seriously, because loosening a few laughs from audiences with comedic cartoon animals really was the furthest thing from seriousness on screen and in the industry's mindset. So the idea of making an entire movie using only animation was not only "vulgar" but absurd as well.

The animation process in the early twentieth century was monotonous and time-consuming, another reason why full-length animated films were few and far between. Quirino Cristiani animated the full-length movies *El Apóstel* (*The Apostle*) in 1917 and *Sin dejar rastros* (*Without a Trace*) in 1918 using the stop-motion technique in South America, but these weren't seen outside Argentina and are now lost films. Howard Moss animated dolls for the majority of a five-reel film called *The Dream Doll* he made for Essanay Films in 1917 (Kaufman, 2012, 32). The Fleischer brothers made *Einstein's Theory of Relativity* released in 1923 and *Darwin's Theory of Evolution* premiered in 1925, but they are shorter and only partially animated (Pidhajny, 2001). *Snow White and the Seven Dwarfs* wouldn't appear on screens until 1937, so Reiniger was creating something brand new to the world.

Belonging to the industry would have only hindered Reiniger, as she notes, just as it proved hindering to later animators as the medium garnered more attention and became more profitable. Hagen even separated Reiniger and Koch from the entertainment industry when they accepted his tempting offer, because he wasn't fond of the institute's experimental environment for the new feature-length film. He also didn't want the film to be associated with the institute, so he installed Reiniger and Koch in the room above his garage in his Potsdam country home near his fruit and vegetable gardens. Koch and Reiniger moved to Potsdam without much persuasion.

Hagen was not only interested in new art endeavors, but also in alternative education methods. He founded a private school in his neighborhood for his children and those belonging to friends and family. His son Louis Hagen, Jr., remembered that his father didn't want him or his siblings in a "stiff, Prussian military type of school atmosphere" (Raganelli, 1999). The school was run by a woman named Claire With and it had ten to twelve children enrolled (Happ, 2004, 21). During production, Koch would also teach at the school (geography and history) and Reiniger taught art; Eric Walter White, an English poet from Bristol, also was a teacher with them, and would become a very close friend (Happ, 2004, 23; Raganelli, 1999). White would become a prominent name in the arts, serving on the English Council for the Encouragement of Music and the Arts (now known as the Arts Council) from 1942 to 1971 (Cleverdon, 1985). Director Jean Renoir became friends with the husband-and-wife team after the film's Paris premiere and he later visited them in Germany. He made several humorous observations about Koch's teaching methods:

> To see this respectable gentleman down on his knees, helping his young pupils to build a clay fortress, was a surprising sight. He maintained that this game was more stimulating to the mind of a five-year-old child than any amount of manufactured toys. He explained the use of the moats and towers, and then, lying on his stomach, he launched an attack of toy soldiers. When the attack was defeated by rain he took advantage of the circumstance to declare his belief in the influence of weather on earthly affairs.
> On another occasion I watched him explaining the formation of valleys in mountainous country with the help of watering cans of which the contents were poured over a heap of sand. The sand heap played a large part in his method of teaching [1974, 163].

After the move to Potsdam, Koch and Reiniger also founded their production company Comenius Film following Hagen's advice. It was formed for the release of *Die Abenteuer des Prinzen Achmed* (Blattner & Weigmann, 2010, 7). Comenius Film would also be used to release Koch's travel film about Egypt and another about educational issues (Happ, 2004, 22). The pair selected the name Comenius after the Czech educator and philosopher John Amos Comenius (1592–1670). An educational reformer, Comenius introduced the concept of pictorial textbooks written in vernacular languages, supported lifelong learning, and promoted logical thinking over fact memorization. Hagen designed his school based around Comenius' teaching principles, which was another reason why they chose the name (Happ, 2004. p. 22).

By funding *Die Abenteuer des Prinzen Achmed*, Hagen became the film's producer. Due to the high inflation, while he wanted to remove the husband-and-wife team from the institute's influence, another reason they were moved to Potsdam was to secure his investment. Germans were concerned about the papiermark's fluctuating value, but it also made it fairly inexpensive to make the film. "As the making of those silhouette films did not require very expensive equipment nor a great personnel, and money in this time of inflation became less valuable from day to day, our conscience was not over-burdened in that direction" (Reiniger, 1970b, 2). The inflation also allowed Reiniger and Koch to hire a team of artists to assist them full-time animating the film. The biggest concern Reiniger faced during production was in 1924, when the Weimar government suddenly made money valuable again. The German Rentenmark was put into circulation and inflation ceased, but "they were only halfway through production. Despite the economic stabilization, the film's equipment and supplies were still cheap and the animation process was simple, although time-consuming and it used only 'wood and patience.' …[Hagen eventually] allowed them to carry on, and the production was finished in the spring of 1926" (Ratner, 2006, 47; Pidhajny Milestone Press Kit, 2001).

Considering everything that could have gone wrong during filming, in hindsight and given the technological limitations of the time, a momentary financial hiccup (swiftly resolved by a generous patron) being the only problem was a blessing.

Reiniger and Koch assembled an animation team that included two men who would later enter the history books as major players in the Golden Age of German cinema. When Reiniger described her team in her introduction to *Die Abenteuer des Prinzen Achmed*, it sounds like a recitation of band members at a rock concert:

> We, that was me, my husband Carl Koch, Walter Ruttmann, Bertold Bartosch, Alexander Kardan and Walter Turck. Koch was the producer and had control of the technical aspects, I cut out the figures and sets and animated them, assisted by Alexander Kardan and Walter Turck. Ruttmann invented and created wonderful movements for the magic events, fire, volcanoes, battles of good and evil spirits and Bartosch composed and cut out movement of waves for a sea storm, now a household word in animation but something quite new at this period [qt. in Pidhajny Milestone Press Kit, 2001].

She elaborated on their roles in her book *Shadow Theaters and Shadow Films*: her husband's control of the technical aspects meant he was the cameraman, Kardan was responsible for the stop-motion switch and he tracked the shot frames, and Tuerck's other duties were "perform[ing] some magic on the upper glass plate" (Reiniger, 1970a, 87). Another way Kardan and Türck's roles were explained was that both "were responsible for the décor and exposure sheets." Türck really manipulated the second glass level to animate backgrounds and other items (Moritz, 1996b, 41; Schönfeld, 2006, 175).

Out of the five-person team, Ruttmann and Bartosch are usually singled out for their contributions to *Die Abenteuer des Prinzen Achmed*. Their special effects work were monumental for the 1920s, but as Reiniger noted in the previous quote and later mentioned in her book, "[W]e had the satisfying opportunity of doing things for the first time, which are now a household word in animation" (Reiniger, 1970a, 87). The special effects she refers to might not be so much a household word now as a refined computer process that can be achieved through a few algorithms with several variations to suit the animators' needs. Christel Strobel reminds viewers that Reiniger was never Walt Disney and her team's origins were in the high art world: "Ruttmann created the magic battle, Bartosch did the movement of the waves. They all belonged to the avant-garde. So this was an epoch-making work. This was art that was not mass-market material. I always say Lotte Reiniger is not Disney. You have to recognize that" (qt. in Marschall *et al.*, 2012). Both men are noted German animators and their contributions to the field are still praised today.

It seems that Ruttmann and Reiniger had an antagonistic relationship, especially with his direct question about 1923, but they had respect for each other. Reiniger was a fan of Ruttmann's previous work *Lichtspiel Opus I*, and while she didn't like working on a fairytale film, it was a paying gig and options were limited in Germany.

In 1980, Reiniger recalled, "Mr. Ruttmann was much older than me. He was an established artist in these circles. I was this silly young girl and I didn't dare tell him what to do at all. I'd record my scenes in black and white, gave them to him, and let him get on with it" (qt. in Marschall *et al.*, 2012). Christiane Schönfeld commented on how Reiniger was aware of Ruttmann's talents and how they would enhance *Prinzen Achmed*'s dimensionality without using a multiplane camera: "Although much of Ruttmann's work for Reiniger's silhouette film is quite similar to the animation of abstract films from his *Opus* films, his backgrounds for *Prinzen Achmed* provide the silhouettes with an illusion of three-dimensional presence. Therefore, Ruttmann's transformations of abstract form enhance the realism of this particular visual representation." Ruttmann's signatures within the film are the changes of light and inverted images, seen in his other films (2006, 173). Schönfeld later concluded that a combination of Reiniger's silhouette mastery, "Ruttmann's talent for creating three-dimensional space through the movement of abstract forms," Reiniger's multiplane camera and "frame compositions that emphasize the effect of linear perspective, all add to a simulation of three-dimensional space" (2006, 173).

Walter Ruttmann (1887–1941) studied architecture in Zurich, Switzerland, and painting in Munich, but he was drafted, made a lieutenant, and sent to the Eastern front during the Great War. His military service later turned him into a pacifist and also made him spend a few bouts in a sanatorium (Bock, 2009, 405). Prior to the war and after, Ruttmann experimented with abstract painting, leading to abstract cinema or "painting with time" (Bendazzi, 1999, 28). Between 1919 and 1921 he made his first cartoon, *Lichtspiel Opus I*, which premiered on April 27, 1921. It consisted of over 10,000 colored pictures and featured music composed by Max Butting. Well-received by audiences and critics, it is cited as the "first 'proper' cartoon produced in Germany" (Bendazzi, 1999, 28–29; Bock, 2009, 405). He made three more *Opus* cartoons and replaced Reiniger on Kriemhild's nightmare sequence in Fritz Lang's *Die Nibelungen*. "He created another nightmare sequence for Paul Wegener's *Lebende Buddha* (*Living Buddha*)"; subsequently he was introduced to Reiniger and her crew through Wegener. Ruttmann didn't enjoy working on *Die Abenteuer des Prinzen Achmed* and he no longer wanted to work on abstractionism. He released his most famous film in 1927: *Berlin, Die Sinfonie der Grosstadt* (*Berlin: Symphony of City*) and made a similar film in 1928 and 1929, *Melodie der Welt* (*World Melody*), Germany's first full-length sound film. Another milestone in his career was a film he made in Italy in 1932, *Acciaio* (*Steel*). Ruttmann's later career became controversial as he assisted Leni Riefenstahl on *Triumph des Willens* (*Triumph of the Will*), the notorious Nazi propaganda film (his scene was later removed), and *Olympia* (Bock, 2009, 405; Pidhajny Milestone Press Kit, 2001). He became a staunch Hitler supporter and used his talents in UFA's advertising department, making films that praised the Nazi party and glorified the Third Reich. He died on July 15, 1941, after a failed operation in Germany, although some sources claim he died on the Russian front while filming (Milestone Press Kit, 2001).

Berthold Bartosch (1893–1968) had already collaborated with Reiniger on her first silhouette film *Das Ornament des verliebten Herzens* in 1919. His animation skills continued to get him work, including advertising projects from Julius Pinschewer. In 1922, he made a complete film entitled *The Battle of Skagerrak* in eight days (Russett & Starr, 1976, 83). The following year, Reiniger and Koch contacted him to work on their ambitious and lengthy silhouette film and he accepted. Bartosch used his expertise to create astounding visual effects, many of which he invented through his own experimentation.

There is a debate over whether Bartosch or Ruttmann animated the genie's magical appearance from the lamp. Bartosch is shown in a production still manipulating the sand used for the special effect, while Reiniger was adamant it was Ruttmann (Jouvanceau, 2004, 230).

While Reiniger animated her silhouette films in Berlin, Lore Bierling animated her own and made title cards in Munich. All of her films fall into the lost film category, but fine examples of her cutout skills remain. Due to the similarity of their work, Pierre Jouvanceau in his book *The Silhouette Film* explains that many people believed Bierling contributed to *Prinzen Achmed*'s animation. When he asked Primrose Productions (Reiniger's later production company) about Bierling, they "categorically denied any involvement" (2004, 39).

Having assembled her crew, Reiniger set forth on animating the silhouettes for *Die Abenteuer des Prinzen Achmed* over the course of the next three years, from 1923 to1926. The animation studio situated above Hagen's garage was outfitted with the second tricktisch she ever worked with. Designed by her husband, it was built to specifications, adding wooden stands to place glass plates, that made it easier to animate different effects. Their goal was to make the animation process as modern as possible, so they took the advice of Guenther Rittau, a cinematographer of note who had worked for Fritz Lang, and installed a special motor to sequence the stop-motion. Reiniger had used a bicycle pump at the institute and preferred it, because "it had to be set to work by a lever, a movement which distracted me from my attention to the figures on the glass plate … whilst the reclining movement of pulling the string of the good bicycle pump allowed my eyes to be fixed perpetually" (Reiniger, 1970b, 3).

The ceiling in the studio was also extremely low, so the animators were hunched over and working at floor level. While animating her silhouettes, Reiniger sat on a seat taken from a car, which she preferred over the swivel chairs she used later in her career (Reiniger, 1970b, 3). Reiniger, Koch and their team animated while Hagen's private school still held classes on the property. Some of the students visited the studio and watched the animators at work, including Louis Hagen, Jr., who sat by Reiniger's side. Hagen, Jr., remarked in Katja Raganelli's documentary *Lotte Reiniger: Homage to the Inventor of the Silhouette Film* that the animators worked for hours in the studio, sometimes to midnight or one in the morning. He added,

We all had lunch together: the pupils, teachers, the assistants, such as Bartosch and Ruttmann.... And when the bell rang for lunch, we heard all kinds of moans and grunts as if they had been in some kind of torture chamber. The reason was the studio wasn't very high and all the animation on the table had to be done at floor level. So Lotte, Carl, and the assistants had to work on their knees. So you can imagine if you spent hours crawling on your knees, it's bound to be painful when you get up [1999].

The animation process was heavily detailed and repetitious. Reiniger handled the delicate animation of the silhouette puppets, placing them just so on the tricktisch to achieve the illusion of human movement and expression. In 1938, Walt Disney said of the animation process: "Our most important aim is to develop definite personalities in our cartoon characters. We don't want them to be just shadows, for merely as moving figures they would provoke no emotional response from the public" (qt. in Crafton, 2013, 1). Reiniger breathed life into each of her puppets and often she was inspired by those around her: "I initially made lots of drawings of the dramatic scenes that occur in the film. And while I was doing this, the shape of the hero gradually developed. He very much resembled the banker who financed the film, by the way. He was a very handsome young man. I liked him a lot" (qt. in Marschall *et al.*, 2012). Hagen has forever been immortalized as the handsome Prince Achmed, but the predevelopment phase was as staggering as the animation process itself due to the world-building Reiniger had to invent out of her own imagination; she didn't have any previous feature-length works to turn to for inspiration.

Bartosch took the lead when it came to the special effects. White wrote a glowing account of his process in his essay:

The results he obtains are staggering when compared to the means of which he disposes. For an effect of stars he will take a piece of cardboard, pin-prick it and photograph it moving slowly before the camera with a strong light behind it. He will then take the same piece of cardboard upside down, move it in a different direction and at a different speed, and superimpose the second shot upon the first. The result is a sky of stars moving slowly and (apparently) in different directions and at different speeds, nothing could be simpler or more effective [1931, 24].

In one sequence that Bartosch animated, Aladdin crossed the sea during a torrential storm. His boat was tossed and heaved in waves that are still visually striking. Bartosch spent months animating the waves using "superimposed pieces of semi-transparent tissue paper. Then he moves with such consummate skill as to convey the impression of the sea's natural sway and surge. Moonlit water he depicts by means of silver paper; in this case the waves overlap more broadly, and the scene has to be lit from in front (above)" (White, 1931, 25). To achieve the cloud, mist and other foggy animation, "they were painted on a glass shelf situated under the trick table, between the silhouette play and the lighting" (White, 1931, 25). The magic fight between the African Sorcerer and the Fire Witch use these effects to the sheer wonderment of the audience.

Bartosch was so obsessed with making the special effects look real and beautiful that he endlessly experimented with animation methods, such as making the waves fit his idea of perfection. Reiniger, Bartosch and the other artists spent weeks and months experimenting with alternate methods using sand, soap and paint on the various glass plate levels on the tricktisch. Finally Koch, who acted as a producer along with Hagen, forced them to stop and move onto the next scene (Reiniger, 1970b, 3; Russett & Starr, 1976, 83). While Reiniger could have played forever posing and filming her silhouettes, she would eventually have to complete the picture. She was grateful that her husband was able to rein in the playful experimentation. Michael Schurig of the Deutsches Filminstitut studied *Prinzen Achmed* frame by frame and noticed she left a piece of herself on film: "If you watch the film at the editing table, and look frame by frame at the static images, you can see the effort and how precise the work was. It's an immense piece of work.... If you watch closely you can occasionally see Lotte Reiniger's hand when she pulled it back too slow. It makes everything more vivid and I think it's a charming detail" (qt. in Marschall *et al.*, 2012).

Another resourceful German animator indirectly involved with *Prinzen Achmed* was Oskar Fischinger, who was at the beginning of his abstract film career. He had experimented with wax for an abstract film, using different colors, oils and other ingredients for a visually stimulating display. His experiments took place in the family bathtub and he aggravated his elder sister, whose job it was to clean. She gave him the idea to make a wax-slicing machine after a "happy accident," when she moved one of Fischinger's wax trays into the sunlight (Moritz, 2004, 7). Fischinger wrote to Ruttmann, curious if he would be interested in using the wax-slicing machine in his films. Ruttmann, who was just about to begin working on *Prinzen Achmed*, figured it would be a useful device for special effects in the film (Moritz, 2004, 8).

Ruttmann paid Fischinger to license the wax-slicing machine in November 1922 and a commercial model was delivered to Ruttmann in 1923 (Moritz, 2004, 8). It "cut slivers off swirled coloured waxes while a camera shutter, synchronized with the movement of the blade, filmed the changing features traced by the multicoloured whorls and striations of wax" (Leslie, 2002, 48–49). Oskar was sure he had developed a fantastic new animation tool and it would having amazing results, but…

> Ruttmann used it immediately to create the Sorcerer's magic conjuring of the flying horse in the opening sequence of *Prinz Achmed* [sic]. He had intended to use it much more widely in the film, but he reported to Oskar that it did not run as smoothly as expected—the slices would only be sharp and clean if the wax block remained very cold, and the hot film lights tended to heat it up before the shooting was done. Oskar insisted that if the proper mixture of wax and kaolin clay were used in the preparation of the block, melting or warping should not be a problem. Ruttmann insisted that the slices simply were not accurate enough for character animation, gave up using the machine, and asked Oskar to come take it away [Moritz, 2004, 9].

Fischinger wasn't deterred by the machine's failure. After a string of jobs, he emigrated to the U.S. in 1936 to work for Paramount and to escape the hold Joseph Goebbels had on the German film industry. When his Paramount job fell through, MGM hired him and he animated the abstract short *An Optical Poem*. Fred Quimby was tasked with creating an internal animation department and he didn't think abstract films were profitable, so he let Fischinger go. Quimby would go on to produce *Tom and Jerry* cartoons at MGM (Moritz, 2004, 78–79).

For a brief period, Fischinger worked for Walt Disney to avoid deportation, but it wasn't a good partnership. Fischinger was hired as a "motion picture cartoon effects animator," with high hopes that since Disney Studios was the best animation studio in the world, he would get the chance to experiment and challenge himself (Moritz, 2004, 83–84). He animated the Blue Fairy's magic wand in *Pinocchio* and influenced aspects of *Dumbo*, but Fischinger was sour over *Fantasia* (Moritz, 2004, 84).

Fischinger and Walt Disney had had similar ideas about setting animated pictures to music. Fischinger felt that more credit was due to him than Walt Disney was willing to give. When Fischinger worked at Paramount, Leopold Stokowski, the conductor in

Fantasia, was filmed in a similar manner in *Big Broadcast of 1937* as he later would be in the animated music feature. Moritz wonders who came up with filming Stokowski in shadow: was it the conductor, director Mitchell Leisen, or Fischinger? When Stokowski and Fischinger were at Paramount, they had discussed "collaborating on films for which Stokowski would supply the music and Oskar the animation. In one letter Oskar suggests the film begin with images of Stokowski's hands, which would guide the viewer's eyes off into visual space..." (Moritz, 2004, 75–76). It would have contributed to Fischinger's ire if he hadn't received credit for his idea; it might have been outright stolen from him, or Stokowski could have forgotten the conversation.[3] Fischinger was given only one segment in *Fantasia*, Bach's *Toccata* and *Fugue in D Minor*, under another animator and his ideas were constantly reworked (Moritz, 2004, 84). Fischinger's terminated his contract early and "in the terms of his severance contract, he specified that Disney could not use his name in relationship with *Fantasia*. He was confident that he would be more famous than Disney in the long run, and did not want Disney to be able to use his name to sell their 'geschmacklos' [tasteless] product" (Moritz, 2004, 85). He would have a restless career in experimental films with extreme highs and lows. During the last 20 years of his life, he never made another film or returned to Germany.

Reiniger had hoped to work with Fischinger at some point but never had the opportunity. In a 1970 interview, she said:

> I never saw Fischinger's silhouette animations, but I saw several types of his abstractions, and I was very impressed. Walther Ruttmann had some of the films, and he admired Fischinger so much, he told me Fischinger was a real genius of animation. Of course, I thought, well, why not get him to work with me like Bartosch and Ruttmann? But each time I tried to arrange a meeting with Fischinger, Ruttmann managed to cause some snag, so it never came about. Finally Ruttmann admitted that he had done it on purpose, because he was afraid that if I once worked with Fischinger, I would never want to work with Ruttmann again! [qt. in Moritz, 2004, 161].

Prinzen Achmed's three-year animation process was grueling for Reiniger and her team. For modern animated films, production requires a huge amount of teamwork. Individual departments work on different pieces of the film, which are constantly reviewed and edited, so that when all the pieces are put together, the final product is seamless. Reiniger and Koch had to weave together the works of the varying assistants, which was based on their own conceptions, and more than likely didn't coincide with Reiniger's vision at all times. While experimenting was fun for Reiniger, Bartosch and the others, there were instances when they also wanted to push forward with a scene but were held back because they had to "rehearse" their silhouettes to achieve the desired result. Even more stressful for Reiniger: she was not able to instantly watch the film during production. Early animation required that the scenes be shot and printed, and then they could be reviewed; animators crossed their fingers that the sequences met their expectations, otherwise they had to go back and redo it. Reiniger wrote, "The anxiety of this process was sometimes almost unbearable. Whilst working, you only see your figures on your composition in one position. What will it look like when it moves, or what the two compositions, which might look all right in themselves, will look like when they are printed, were riddles whose solution could only be awaited with hope" (Reiniger, 1970b, 3).

Whether those three years were over too quickly or crawled by slowly, Reiniger doesn't tell. But at the end of production she and her team had animated 250,000 frames of which they used 96,000 for a 65-minute film (Ratner, 2006, 47). Reiniger explained in the introduction she wrote to accompany the film that it took 24 frames to animate a single second (Pidhajny Milestone Press Kit, 2001). *Die Abenteuer des Prinzen Achmed* was a black and white 35mm silent film, accentuated by hand-tinted colored backgrounds, intertitles that described the action and carried dialogue, and new animation techniques. Famous fairy tale illustrator Edmund Dulac contributed his timeless skill to creating the intertitles for *Prinzen Achmed* (I can't find any sources that explain how Reiniger and Koch knew him) (Coté, 1954, 17). Silent films were accompanied by a recording or live music to establish a mood, but rather than have a generic soundtrack for her film, Reiniger hired a composer to write an original score that evoked the correct feelings in the audience. Throughout the film's production, Reiniger and Koch had Wolfgang Zeller compose the music to fit each scene, including sound effects, a march and a glockenspiel. Synchronization between the music and film was important, so film scenes were pasted onto the film score so the conductor knew to play the correct notes at the proper moment[4] (Reiniger, 1970b, 3). Silent film scores are a perplexing item to study in the modern era as most were not written down, Zeller and Reiniger had the forethought to transcribe the music as it was a necessity for synchronization. John Bishop in his review "German Film Scores from the Silent Era" critiqued a 2008 orchestral rendering of Zeller's music for *Prinzen Achmed* edited by Jens Schubbe. He wrote that these scores

> i.e. through-composed and consisting entirely of original material cohesively linked through motive recurrence, [were] a particular European phenomenon. From the vantage point of the sound-film era, these scores also come closer to what the general listener might assume the very term "film score" to signify—a potentially misleading assumption that warrants much qualification. Even some of the greatest and grandest of American silent scores ... drew heavily upon borrowed, as well as original material. Finally, as bears endless repeating to students of film music, nearly *all* silent-film music was intrinsically variable, performance-based phenomenon dependent upon the musical resources present at the theater in which the film was screened [2013, 185].

While Zeller wrote an original score, based on the practices of the day, he probably borrowed music from other composers, if he was not merely inspired by them. Also, even if the musical scores did exist, theaters were confused by the notion of the film's material and likely "butchered" Zeller's score or even substituted their own pieces. After working on *Prinzen Achmed,* Zeller composed the score for Ruttmann's *Melodie der Welt.* He had a prominent career composing music for German cinema that lasted until 1959.

Pierre Jouvanceau puzzled over why Reiniger had Zeller remain on the production team during *Prinzen Achmed*'s entire filming. Zeller was contracted to write an original soundtrack, but as Jouvanceau noted, "this commercial decision alone would not have justified the presence, throughout the whole production period and even before the first frame was shot, of the composer Wolfgang Zeller, nor have accounted for the specific nature of the task he was given" (2004, 202). Jouvanceau downplays the foresight that Reiniger had about the importance of musical synchronization with visual scenes. Reiniger knew from the start that, in order to invoke the proper emotions, enhance the special effects and have the audience identify with the silhouette characters, sound held as much power as the images on screen.

> The differing techniques of producing an animated, as opposed to a live-action film call for correspondingly different working relationships between directors and composers not to mention the many others whose special skills contribute to the art of animation. This is true because of the relatively complex microcosmic planning required for animated films, for which the sight and sound elements of each frame must be accounted before filming.... For one thing, the animation director

conceives his [or her] film knowing that he must control its contents and timing in increments of one twenty-fourth of a second, the time it takes each frame to pass through the projector [Newsom, 1980, 280].

Die Abenteuer des Prinzen Achmed was a brand new cinematic endeavor and just as American audiences were skeptical about Walt Disney's "Folly" and Argentineans scratched their heads at Cristiani's moving drawings, more than sight had to be mentally engaged in viewing the film. The inclusion of sound invited audiences to audibly engage with the characters during the adventures, in a way making them more lifelike.

Jouvanceau did note that Reiniger's desire for synchronization was a concept that sound pioneers, such as Rudolf Pfenninger and Nikolai Voinov, had experimented with in relation to matching sound with animated images, and he even went as far as saying she invented it (2004, 203). Animated synchronization is called "mickeymousing" in the animation industry, because Walt Disney made abundant use of the process for his early musical series *Silly Symphonies* (1929–1939). "It was no mere chance that animation invented, very early on, mickeymousing. It needed to create, artificially, the sound environment it originally lacked," which would then carry over into live action films as directors realized sound added more stimulation with talkies (Jouvanceau, 2004, 203).

Unlike later sound cartoons, Reiniger's silhouette films used synchronous music not as a sound effect, but as the context to understand the film's story (Jouvanceau, 2004, 205). Reiniger was in tune with her characters via cutting and designing them, but also through the musical selections she selected to bring them to life. She never relied on dialogue to convey her meaning (although the beloved bird catcher does sing in *Papageno* as do the lovers in *Zehn Minuten Mozart*). This was more of a personal preference, and it might otherwise have disrupted the artfulness of her films. For Reiniger, actions spoke much louder than words, and music carried the plot along. In many of her later works, Reiniger would rely on a narrator accompanied by music to tell the story, but music always remained her preferred brand of narration. Reiniger set the standard for later silhouette animators to follow in her paper-cutting footsteps, but total reliance on music as the only method to tell a story in silhouettes is a severe limitation and locks silhouette animation into only one trick.

Other animators who have taken silhouette animation down different pathways rely on traditional dialogue or use sound in brand new ways to tell their stories. When it comes to Reiniger's films, Jouvanceau wrote a beautiful, succinct passage that conceded music's importance:

> This ideal correspondence between music and image is not only theoretical. The spatial contribution of this music is a reality for the animator, who like Reiniger in her major films, works with pre-existing music. Music in such films really rules the destiny of the image and the characters. Lotte Reiniger would drink in the atmosphere of the music she had chosen before doing anything else, and work out from it the basic organisation of rhythms and movements, the sequence of shots but also the framing, the placing of the set and position of the puppets in the field.... [T]he whole film is carried by the music: its trace is perceptible even in the images themselves. Reiniger, who said in 1936: "Film is motion ... just pure and simple motion on the screen," must have felt that this aural concept, which mixes music into the genesis of the images, was the only one that could work for the silhouette film [2004, 206].

With a complete film, Reiniger and Koch were ready to share it with the world, but no one wanted to play it. For three years, they were cloistered in an attic studio above a garage in Potsdam. The strict production schedule kept them busy, without time to leave the studio to network. When they finished the film in 1926, they didn't have press contacts and no one was aware of it or if they were, they were not interested in an animated film. Reiniger remembered that after spending three years making the film, she and Koch, were so poor that "Carl and I had to write out by hand more than 8000 invitations to the premiere" (Coté, 1954, 17). They *were* able to arrange a showing on a Sunday morning, May 2, 1926, and with the help of their friend Bertolt Brecht the famous German playwright (1898–1956), the press was in attendance. Along with the press and Brecht, G.W. Pabst, László Moholy-Nagy, Karl With, Fritz Lang and Thea von Harbou were in the audience (Beckerman, 1974, 40). Reiniger's wrote in her article "The Adventures of Prince Achmed or What May Happen to Somebody Trying to Make a Full Length Cartoon in 1926":

> So we arranged on our own a first performance at the Volksbuehne, a theatre in the north of Berlin, where Wolfgang Zeller was in charge of the orchestra. His musicians had consented to play for us on a Sunday morning for his sake. We invited the press and all the people we could think of on postcards.... It had to be on a Sunday morning, and as it was spring and good weather had broken out, we did not think that many people would sacrifice a beautiful morning to see a mysterious, never-heard-of silhouette film in an out-of-the way theatre. But they all came and the theatre was overcrowded.
>
> There were rows going on among the audience about their seats, which were not numbered, and some people took the numbers of their cloakroom tickets for seat numbers and claimed them angrily. I also saw people who were of great importance to us, like Fritz Lang and Thea von Harbou, sitting on quite unfavorable seats right in front of the screen. Then Dr. Karl With, a renowned expert on the arts, started his opening speech, and the audience calmed down. But became restless again as he talked on and on, much to my amazement, as we had agreed that his address should only be short. Anyhow, finally he stopped and the film started, and the audience reacted very favorably to it.
>
> Only when I went behind the curtain in the first interval (by this time films were projected in reels) I heard what had happened. Just before the start, the projector lens had broken. It was Sunday morning, where on earth could we get another one? ... In his despair, my husband took a taxi and drove to the big Ufa house. He well knew that it was closed on Sundays, so.... He stood there and looked at the brilliant equipment displayed in the windows, when a gentleman approached [with a] key, and proceeded to open the door. Koch dashed towards him and told him ... of our desperate situation ... and the gentleman was not only willing to help, but could help. So Koch arrived back at the theater triumphantly with another lens, and Karl With could stop his unwillingly prolonged speech.
>
> ... In the middle of the performance ... a policeman arrived behind stage and ordered us to stop the performance for the theatre was overcrowded. Koch ... took flight, climbing a ladder into the upper stage, where the wings were hung, like in a Marx Brothers film. He came down only when the end of the next reel was acknowledged by the audience with a burst of applause. Koch grabbed me by the arm, and introduced me to the baffled policeman as the budding artist on the brink of an obvious success, who would be completely ruined.... The audience clapped on, and I went out to take my bow with a heartrending look at the stern defender of the law and order, who said threateningly, "You will hear from me..." and went away.
>
> ... In the last reel of that film there is a big battle between black and white spirits, but I saw suddenly something on the screen, something which was neither of those spirits, but obviously smoke. As I knew full well that we had not shot any smoke in that sequence, my heart stood still. Something must be burning on stage. I ran there very frightened, for in that period film was still very inflammable, and if the audience would get the faintest inkling what the smoke meant, panic would be the result. (How right the policeman had been.) But the reason was harmless enough: the stagehands, who wanted to see the film, had placed some wet sacks on the central heating and forgotten to take them away, and they had started smouldering just in front of the projector. The audience, however, had taken the clouds as an artistically intended effect! [pp. 3–4].

The audience loved *Prinzen Achmed*. After this unofficial first showing, an official premiere was held on July 1, 1926, at Louis Jouvet Théâtre des Champs-Élysées in Paris and it ran continuously for six or nine months (various sources consulted for this book say one or the other). The Société Française des Films Artistiques (the French Society of Artistic Films) held a press conference breakfast for Reiniger and Koch, where they became acquainted with Jean Renoir, who would become their lifelong friend and artistic partner. Reiniger was self-conscious at the event due to her limited French. Happ recalled her impressions of Renoir:

> I sat at the end of a long table surrounded by the president of the film society and the president of the press. My husband sat at the other end, happily speaking with a young man, and I envied him. I dared not to speak a word, since I only spoke a little French. One president gave a speech, the other answered, and it was about me. I thought, my God, I must run. It was horrible. I kept looking at my husband, who still spoke with the young man. With tears in my voice, "I said I couldn't speak French, but I am very happy and asked if they would please excuse me." And then the young man [Jean Renoir] said, "Qu'elle est charming!" That got me to my legs and perked me up…. From that day on we were great friends [2004, 26].

Weimar cinema finally took notice of *Die Abenteuer des Prinzen Achmed* and under UFA's rental program it had a grander German premiere at the Gloria Palace on September 3, 1926. Happ described the premiere as a huge festivity; the UFA newsreel first played on the screen, followed by a musical piece from Franz Schubert's "Rosamunde," then the dancer-film star-cabaret performer Valeska Gert danced a number. Finally *Die Abenteuer des Prinzen Achmed* ran, with Zeller's music played by a live orchestra conducted by Max Roth (2003, 27). According to Guy Coté, *Prinzen Achmed*'s premiere was successful in Berlin but it was "spurned by the German commercial distributors." When the German distributors shipped the film to theaters, "it was advertised as a 'detective' film. Disappointed exhibitors took to running the first reel and forgetting about the rest of the picture. In retaliation Carl Koch would jump upon the stage to protest against this mutilation of their masterpiece. Sometimes, they had to carry him off to jail, gesticulating" (Coté, 1954, 17–18). The latter claim about Koch jumping on the stage to protest the film's incomplete showings rings true with his personality, but it is unlikely he went to every theater in Germany to make his objections.

Across the English Channel, *Prinzen Achmed*'s uniqueness and popularity spread: "In 1926 the London Film Society administered write-in ballots to its members to determine which films they would most like to screen in the upcoming seasons. *Prince Achmed* ranked first in popularity…" (K.V. Taylor, 2011, 1–2). The London Film Society imported *Prinzen Achmed,* among other German films, inserted English intertitles and showed it before a British audience for the first time on May 8, 1927, at the New Gallery Cinema (Fogg, 2007, 5). The animated silhouette film would also journey to Japan, a future animation powerhouse, where it premiered in June 1929 at the Tokyo Musashino Theater, with possible screenings in Osaka and Kyoto (Yokota & Hu, 2013, 113).

Getting the film shown in the U.S. was an obstacle that even Achmed and the Fire Witch would have had trouble conquering. According to Donald Crafton, "Although *Prince Achmed* was well-known in Europe, its American release was delayed, apparently because the production Comenius-Film sold exclusive rights to the University Film Foundation of Harvard, which did not actively promote it" (1993, 366). A 1931 issue of the *Harvard Crimson* reveals more details how *Prinzen Achmed* was imported: "[It] was discovered in Paris about two years ago by J.A. Haeseler, a director of the University Film Foundation, when filming pictures in Europe. He was immediately attracted by the novel picture, but was forced to follow the film from city to city, and even back to New York before he could obtain the American rights to the film" (1931).

The University Film Foundation was a non-profit organization along the lines of the Institut für Kulturforschung. While it was associated with Harvard, it stood alone as its own organization until Harvard took over its services in 1934 (*The Harvard Crimson*, 1934). It is probably due to its standing as an individual organization that the University Film Foundation never promoted the film.

According to the *Annual Report (Fogg Art Museum)*, "A somewhat new departure for the Museum was the showing of *The Adventures of Prince Achmed*, a silhouette film fantasy, the only film of its sort in the world. Two showings were given on February 14 [1931] and because of the demand for tickets two additional performances were given on February 21" (1931, 9). It was shown under the "sponsorship of the Cambridge School of the Drama and the Department of Fine Arts of the University on Saturday afternoon and evening in the Large Lecture Hall of the Fogg Art Museum" (Harvard Crimson, 1931).

Harvard professor Robert Feild respected animation as an art form and he would curate an in-depth study of Walt Disney Animation within the studio and published a book on his observations, 1942's *The Art of Walt Disney* (Hahn & Miller-Zarneke, 2015, 298). During his research on animation, he never once mentioned Lotte Reiniger or *Die Abenteuer des Prinzen Achmed* despite the Harvard connection. I was hoping this would have established some connection between Reiniger and Walt Disney, but when I contacted the Harvard Art Museums Archives and the Harvard Film Archives, we were unable to find any relationship.

After the Fogg Museum showings, *Prinzen Achmed* had two screenings on February 26, 1931, for a charity show at the Town Hall, a performance space in New York City (Hall, 1931). One wonders how it ended up playing there, considering how the University Film Foundation of Harvard wasn't proactive with showings and that the Town Hall is a performance space, not a movie theater. *New York Times* reviewer Mordaunt Hall noted, "A number of youngsters were in the first audience and the cutouts that appeared as players on the screen soon enlisted their interest and sympathy. It is a wonderfully artistic production, in which there are countless ingenious ideas.... It may not be exactly new to perceive silhouette figures on the screen, but it is quite another matter as they are offered here."

The "official" showing was on January 16, 1942, one month after the Japanese bombed Pearl Harbor and when the U.S. finally joined the war. It is curious that a U.S. theater would show a German film one month after declaring war on Germany. Yet on the other hand, "German cinema was far and away the most popular alternative to the domestic product" and in 1932 there were around 200 theaters that specialized in "'German tongue talkers' with twenty of the venues operating in New York City alone" (Doherty, 2013, 176–77). Between 65 and 70 percent of the German cinema fan base were German-speaking Jews, but they boycotted once Hitler became chancellor (Doherty, 2015, 177–78).

Prinzen Achmed premiered at the Fifth Avenue Playhouse, one of the premier art houses in Greenwich Village with 273 seats (Heller, 2016). The Playhouse showed it during

Opposite: *Die Abenteuer des Prinzen Achmed*'s official premiere occurred in January 1942, one month after Pearl Harbor, at the Fifth Avenue Playhouse in New York City during the Surrealist and Fantastic Film Festival (courtesy Steven Heller).

4. The Adventures of Prince Achmed

its Surrealist and Fantastic Film Festival alongside Leni Riefenstahl's *The Blue Light*, even more cause for raised eyebrows than Reiniger's silhouette animated film based on *1001 Arabian Nights*. Despite the surreal nature of both films, I wonder whether to qualify the selections as audacious or dedication to art. In the program accompanying the festival was this note from the managing directors of the Playhouse:

> In presenting this Surrealistic and Fantastic Film Festival, we don't expect to revolutionize the motion picture industry. Nor do we expect that Cocteau and Man Ray will have the same appeal as Gable and Boyer. Indeed many moviegoers will probably be frightened by the title of this series. It is not intended to conjure nightmares. We offer it merely to whet the jaded film appetite.
>
> For too long, audiences have been surfeited by millions of reels of film that produce a soporific effect upon their mental, emotional and physical processes. We don't want to cause suspicions, BUT! Hollywood films are complete in themselves. They are enjoyable to look at and often forgotten as soon as one leaves the theatre…
>
> The surrealistic, abstract or fantastic film is designed purposely to disturb and shock one's balance. Surrealism attempts, we are told, "to discover and explore the more real than the real world behind the real." In surrealist film it is never the plot that receives attention but rather the wealth of innuendo which accompanies each action and which forms an emotional pattern far richer than the usual straight story…
>
> We would not be the least perturbed if our audience feels inclined to engage in verbal and even pitched battles. Some purpose will then have been accomplished. For these pictures will either release your inhibitions, phobias and frustrations, or you will emerge with an entirely new set of complexes [Fifth Avenue Playhouse, 1942].

Advertising was limited for the Surrealist and Fantastic Film Festival. An ad was published in *The New York Post* on Thursday, January 15, and Friday the 16th in the movie section alongside ads for Disney's *Fantasia*, *Remember the Day*, *Ball of Fire*, *Louisiana Purchase*, *Nothing but the Truth*, *Two-Faced Woman*, *I Wake Up Screaming*, *The Corsican Brothers* and *Hellzapoppin*. *The Post* even printed a short blurb about *Prinzen Achmed* in Richard Manson's "Going Out Tonight?":

> *Adventures of Prince Achmed,* a film entire [sic] in silhouette, conceived and executed by Reiniger, has its first public showing at the 5th Avenue Playhouse, 66 Fifth Ave., at 12th St., at 7:30 and 9:40. This is the second program in the theatre's Surrealist and Fantastic Film Festival, and an added feature is the revival of *The Blue Light*, pre–Hitler fantasy. 55 cents after 6 [1942, 14].

The festival's program was more excited about *Prinzen Achmed* than *The Post*'s movie columnist:

> For fantastic charm and truly remarkable artistry it is doubtful whether anything has yet been produced to compare with this picture. The work of a German artist, now in exile, Lotte Reiniger, who spent three years perfecting the delicate silhouettes, is said to have photographed 250,000 of them all, it stands as a monument not only of industry but of art in miniature. The tiny figures move with grace and ease or with grotesque stiffness according to the demands of the story. Palaces rise and sail through the air—winged monsters appear from nowhere and vanish—genii materialize out of the air and flying horses are a mere commonplace.
>
> Contrasting these eye-filling delights are the ludicrous goose-stepping extras, the grotesque caliph and emperor, and the horrific sorcerer, ogress, spirits, dragons and nondescript monsters of the magic world. This film is both imaginative and entertaining. Better than flesh and blood players, the puppets catch and set forth the fantasies of the Arabian Nights. The African sorcerer grins maliciously, rolls his eyes with evil satisfaction. The magic horse roars impatiently, flies blindly up into the region of the stars until the helpless Achmed on his back finds the lever at the creature's tail. Those scenes and others make *The Adventures of Prince Achmed* an enchanting spectacle of instant and haunting charm [Fifth Avenue Playhouse, 1942].

Audiences were pleased with the film, although its viewing might have been soured by its German origin. Manson's blurb notes that Riefenstahl's film is a "pre–Hitler fantasy" to clarify its distinction from her then current filmography. Reiniger's offering was less offensive and given her lack of Hitler connections, that aspect didn't need a caution label.

Despite the film's popularity (in most countries) with audiences and critics, it was overshadowed when the first talkies revolutionized film and World War II didn't help matters.

The original negative of *Die Abenteuer des Prinzen Achmed* was destroyed in the Battle of Berlin bombings in 1945. Postwar, it was considered a lost film until the British Film Institute discovered they had a copy in their archives.

Lotte Reiniger wrote the five-act story for *Die Abenteuer des Prinzen Achmed*, combining details from several stories in the popular *1001 Arabian Nights* saga: "The Tale of the Second Dervish" aka "The Tale of the Second Qalandar," "Aladdin and the Amazing Lamp," "The Tale of the Magic Horse" aka "The Ebony Horse" and "Prince Achmed and the Fairy Peri Banu." The villain in the film is now universally called the African Sorcerer, but a poster for the September 1926 screening at the Gloria Palast labeled him as "Der amerikanische Zauberer" or "The American Sorcerer"; that might have been a misprint (Jouvanceau, 2004, 68). She wrote in her article "Die Geschichte meines Prinzen Achmed" how she "employed" the prince and his family with her characteristic self-deprecating humor:

> For centuries Prince Achmed on his magic horse had lived a comfortable life as a well-loved fairy tale figure of the Arabian nights [sic] and was well contented with that. But one day he was thrown out of this peaceful existence by a film company which wanted to employ him and many other characters of the same stories for an animated film. For this purpose he had to be recreated like many other unfortunate fellows from tales of other literary regions [qt. in Wizansky, 2004, 103].

It begins with a powerful and ugly African Sorcerer conjuring a mechanical horse that can soar through the air. He flies on the horse to the beautiful city of Baghdad, bedecked with spiraling minarets, where the caliph is hosting a celebration in honor of his own birthday. The evil Sorcerer lands in front of the caliph, who wishes to purchase the horse. The Sorcerer won't sell the flying steed for gold, so the caliph offers him any of his treasures instead. The one treasure that appeals to the Sorcerer is the caliph's lovely daughter Dinarsade, but Prince Achmed refuses to allow his sister to be the wife of such a man. Upset by Achmed's actions, the Sorcerer persuades the prince to get on the flying horse and it takes off, straight into the sky.

Astonished and angry that his beloved son has disappeared, the caliph places the Sorcerer under guard. Achmed is trapped ascending among the clouds, when a stroke of luck helps him figure out how to work the horse. He lands on the islands of Wak-Wak and walks into a servants' quarters filled with pretty serving maids. The maids are smitten with Achmed and wish for him to stay among them forever, but when they quarrel over his attentions, the prince flees away on the horse.

Achmed steers the horse towards a neighboring island with an immense lake and descends, unaware that the ruler of the Islands of Wak-Wak, Peri Banu, uses it to take her toilette. Achmed hides among the plants and watches as three exquisite birds land, shed their feathers and transform into women. As they begin to bathe, Achmed falls in love with Peri Banu and steals her feather dress. When the three maidens finish bathing, Achmed reveals himself and two of the maidens fly away, but Peri Banu is left frightened.

He asks her to return to Baghdad with him. She demands he return her feathers, runs away and faints from fear.

As delicately as he can, Achmed carries Peri Banu to the horse and whisks her away to China. There she awakens and, despite reassurances from Achmed that he'll serve her for all of his days, she still wants her feather dress and to return to Wak-Wak, because the demons will come searching for her. Achmed says if she'll marry him, Allah will protect them both.

Back in the dungeon, the Sorcerer scries for his magic horse. He turns into a bat to escape the prison.

Achmed continues to plead with Peri Banu and tells her to forget Wak-Wak. Through desperate tears, she begs for her feather dress. Not wanting to hurt her any longer, Achmed returns it. The prince is torn that Peri Banu rejects him and she is overcome by his pain and handsome features. She agrees to travel with him and Achmed is ecstatic. The Sorcerer finds them and steals the feather dress by turning into a kangaroo. The Sorcerer throws the feathers across a ravine. Achmed pursues him, but the prince gets trapped by the steep sides.

The Sorcerer shape-shifts again, this time into a Chinese servant, and lures Peri Banu away with a robe, claiming that it's a gift from Achmed. Peri Banu is kidnapped and the Sorcerer flies away with her on the horse.

A huge viper attacks Achmed, but the prince is battle-savvy and quickly vanquishes the reptile. He uses the snake's body to climb out of the ravine. The Sorcerer takes Peri Banu to the Chinese emperor, who loves to listen to his hunchbacked dwarf play chimes, and sells her to him. The Sorcerer takes the bag of gold from the emperor and transforms them into winged afreets (demons) to go after Achmed. Devastated over the loss of his love, Achmed mourns but is interrupted by the attacking afreets.

The emperor attempts to woo Peri Banu, but she spurns his advances. Out of anger, the emperor gives her to the hunchbacked dwarf and screams, "Kill her or make her your wife!"

The afreets carry Achmed to a mountain and torture him. The Sorcerer orders his creatures to leave Achmed there to die, so he can claim Dinarsade.

On the mountain dwells another powerful magic maker: the Witch of the Flaming Mountain. The Witch smells Achmed and orders her minions to bring him to her. She's furious that Achmed has invaded her home and the prince lashes out and yells that he was brought there against his will. The pair fight, but the Witch relents when she learns that the African Sorcerer, her greatest enemy, is the root of all the trouble. Deciding to help Achmed, the Witch magically creates armor, a helmet, sword and a bow and quiver of arrows for him.

The Chinese celebrate as Peri Banu is wed to the dwarf. After the ceremony, Peri Banu and her new husband are taken to the bridal chamber. Achmed hides in the chamber, startling Peri Banu as she enters. She fights off Achmed until she realizes it's him, and then they kiss and embrace. The Wak-Wak demons, searching for their ruler, discover her in China. Reclaiming their ruler, the demons fly off and Achmed fights them. He manages to subdue one of the demons and forces it to carry him to Wak-Wak. Achmed arrives too late: The gates of Wak-Wak have closed and will only open to the one who possesses Aladdin's magic lamp.

Achmed is pondering how he will track down Aladdin and the magic lamp, when he spies a man being attacked by a monster. Achmed slays it with one arrow. The grateful

Brave Prince Achmed ready for battle (courtesy Paul Gelder, ©Primrose Productions).

man falls at Achmed's feet and calls himself Aladdin. Alas, Aladdin no longer possesses the lamp. He tells Achmed he was once a poor tailor in the caliph's great city, when one day a stranger (the Sorcerer in disguise) led him to the palace. They both viewed Dinarsade from a distance and the stranger told Aladdin that if he did him a small service, the princess would be his. They went to a cave, where Aladdin climbed down to fetch the lamp. At the cave's entrance, the stranger ordered Aladdin to hand over the lamp. Aladdin suspected the stranger was trying to deceive him, so he refused unless the stranger let him out. The stranger refused to let Aladdin out and the poor tailor fell deep into the cave, alone with the lamp.

Aladdin lit the lamp and a genie appeared in a cloud of smoke. The genie called Aladdin his master and said that the genies of the lamp would grant any wish he desired.

Aladdin wished himself home. With joy in his heart, Aladdin knew how he would win Dinarsade's heart: he used his wishes to create jewels to bestow upon her and built a palace overnight. The next morning the caliph visited Aladdin and was so taken with him that he allowed Dinarsade to marry him.

Overcome with excitement, Achmed embraces Aladdin and informs him that he is Achmed, the caliph's son and Dinarsade's brother. Aladdin continues his story and tells how one day all of his wealth, including his palace with Dinarsade, disappeared. The caliph was angered by the loss of his daughter. Aladdin ran away to the sea and secured a small boat to sail away on. A sudden storm tossed him about and washed him up on a foreign shore. When Aladdin woke up, he was attacked by a monster, and Achmed saved him.

Achmed is outraged and asks Aladdin who committed such atrocities. It was the evil Sorcerer. The Sorcerer is still obsessed with making Dinarsade his bride, so he stole Aladdin's palace, wealth and wife. The Witch comes across Aladdin and Achmed and realizes that the Wak-Wak demons are going to kill Peri-Banu unless Achmed can stop them. They can't open the Wak-Wak gates without the lamp and the only way they can retrieve it is to kill the Sorcerer. Determined to save his beloved, Achmed begs the witch to fight the Sorcerer and resolutely she agrees.

She summons the Sorcerer with her magic and they begin a fight of cunning shape-shifting. The Sorcerer morphs into a lion, only to be attacked by the Witch as a snake, but he quickly changes into a scorpion. Not to be taken, the witch shifts into a fighting cockerel, when the Sorcerer comes back with a vulture. Both turn into fish when the air battle proves futile, then resume their human forms when neither can defeat each other. Altering their tactics, the Witch and Sorcerer shoot flames at the other. Their battle heats up, growing more intense as the seconds tick by, when at last the Witch overpowers the Sorcerer!

The Witch reclaims the lamp, to the joy of Aladdin and Achmed. The Wak-Wak demons rise up against their unfaithful ruler. They are about to throw her over a cliff, when Achmed demands Peri Banu's release. He calls for Aladdin to release the genies. In a beautiful force of white lights, the spirits of the lamp fight the black demons of Wak-Wak. Achmed shields his love, when suddenly the Witch takes the lamp and joins her magic to its might. She releases hundreds of good spirits, forcing the demons to retreat, yet they still aren't quelled. A many-headed hydra attacks Achmed, Aladdin and Peri Banu and the prince defeats it with the Witch's aid.

Aladdin's palace floats through the air, returning to its master. Peri Banu, Achmed and Aladdin bid the Witch farewell with profuse thanks and she wishes them happiness in the land of mortals. As Achmed and his companions head to the palace, the Witch closes the mountain to prevent the Wak-Wak demons from escaping again. The palace flies off, when Aladdin realizes that his beloved Dinarsade must be somewhere within its passages. He finds her hidden and they passionately embrace. Achmed and Dinarsade are overjoyed to be reunited as well. They drift over their home kingdom with their father eagerly watching the palace. The caliph is overcome with happiness seeing the return of his two children and their partners. Their joy is quietened when the sound for morning prayers resounds through the minarets and they bow their heads to pray.

One of the biggest questions I asked myself while researching *Die Abenteuer des Prinzen Achmed* was why Lotte Reiniger selected *1001 Arabian Nights* as her source material. When she was a child, Germany was awash in fairytales and vibrant mythology that

4. The Adventures of Prince Achmed 71

Aladdin summons the spirits of the lamp to fight the demons of Wak-Wak (courtesy Paul Gelder).

still inspires many fantasy stories, so common sense tells us that she would turn to the familiar fairytales for her first grand epic. While western fairytales are regular source material for animated films and puppet shows, they've achieved an overused trope status with Disney's films, their "kid friendly" status being the root cause. Western fairytales have achieved a sense of literary normalcy that may seem overdone now, and was firmly established in Reiniger's day as well.

Europe had been enchanted with ideas of the Far East, India, Africa and Arabia, collectively known as Orientalism, for centuries. Most westerners had failed to journey to these exotic locales, but they were enamored with the idea of the "heathen" cultures and developed romantic notions about them, enhanced by art, films and literature—especially *1001 Arabian Nights*. Orientalism had been strong in Germany since the eighteenth century, "but the late nineteenth and early twentieth centuries witnesses especially lively publishing around the *Nights*" leading to a surge of public interest. Donald Haase and Ulrich Marzolph described the major *1001 Arabian Nights* translations were published in Germany:

- Translated by Johann Heinrich Voss, based off Antoine Galland's French translation 1781–1785
- Translated by Maximilian Habicht 1832–1838 (although the Arabic manuscripts he used proved to be forgeries)
- Translated by Gustav Weil from various Arabic sources 1838–1841

- Translated by Max Henning, published by Reclaim 1895–1899
- Translated by Felix Paul Greve, based off Sir Richard Burton's English translation 1907–1909
- Translated by Enno Littmann from the Arabic 1921–1928 (Haase 2004, p. 261; Marzolph email author, 20 Jan. 2016).

Haase also shares that there was "a steady stream of selections and adaptations for a juvenile audience" with lavish illustrations to stir the reader's imagination just from glancing at the cover (2004, 261).

Reiniger adored reading, watching and listening to fairytales in her youth and, like any voracious child with a hobby, she probably read several of the *1001 Arabian Nights* juvenile versions. She may have even adapted a tale or two for the shadow plays she performed for friends and family. She was probably just as familiar with these Arabian fairytales as she was with the Brothers Grimm.

During *Prinzen Achmed*'s production, Reiniger needed to refer to source material and according to Marzolph she could have been aware and used any of these translations to write the script (Marzolph email to author, January 20, 2016). Deducing what version she used can be determined by copyright dates and limited availability to obtain books in the early twentieth century. Reiniger most likely used the Littmann, Henning or Greve translation. Littmann's translation wasn't complete until 1928, two years after she completed *Prinzen Achmed*. Henning's version was over 20 years old by the time production began on *Prinzen Achmed* and it was probably not in wide circulation by 1923. The primary *1001 Arabian Nights* story Reiniger used for her film was "Prince Achmed and the Fairy Peri Banu." Littmann didn't publish this particular tale until 1925 in his third volume as "Der Geschichte von dem Prinzen Ahmed und der Fee Peri Banu," well into the film's production, so it couldn't have been used. "The Tale of the Second Qalandar" is in the first volume from 1921; "Aladdin" was published in 1922 in the second volume; "The Ebony Horse" was in the third volume. Reiniger may have read Littmann's first and second volumes, but based on how well she interwove the four tales together, without the two tales in the third volume she couldn't have relied on this translation for *Prinzen Achmed*. With Henning and Littmann eliminated, that leaves Greve's translation as the most recent and complete German version prior to production. Also, it would have been easier to obtain than Henning's version.

Stephen Cavalier wrote in *The World History of Animation* that Reiniger adapted *Prinzen Achmed* from Andrew Lang's *The Blue Fairy Book*, published in 1889 (2011, 68). *The Blue Fairy Book* included three stories from *1001 Arabian Nights*: "The Forty Thieves," "Aladdin and the Wonderful Lamp" and "The Story of Prince Ahmed and the Fairy Paribanu." Cavalier said that *The Blue Fairy Book* "translated Middle Eastern and Asian fairy tales and folklore into English for the first time" (2011, 68). Cavalier's claim has huge discrepancies. While Lang's *Fairy Books* were popular in Great Britain and the U.S., especially with children, his popularity was limited to an English-speaking audience. When it came to fairy tales, Germany preferred its own Brothers Grimm.

Another item to consider is that Lang was not the first person to translate Middle Eastern stories into English. French scholar Antoine Galland translated the *1001 Arabian Nights* from Arabic documents and published it in 12 volumes between 1704 and 1715 as *Mille et une Nuits* (Marzolph & van Leeuwen, 2004, 558). *Mille et une Nuits* took Europe by storm, resulting in translations "into all major European languages… [T]his craze for the *Arabian Nights* resulted in the discovery or intentional production of a number of other manuscripts of the *Arabian Nights*. Moreover, the mania Galland initiated also contributed to the rising concept of Orientalism, which in its turn influenced numerous European authors of the eighteenth and nineteenth centuries" (Marzolph & van Leeuwen, 2004, 559–60). Some scholars speculate that Galland took liberties with *Mille et une Nuits* and added stories he wrote himself. These are called the orphan stories, as they don't have an original Arabic version (Marzolph & van Leeuwen, 2004, 559). Reiniger used two orphan stories for *Prinzen Achmed,* "Aladdin and the Amazing Lamp" and "Prince Achmed and the Fairy Peri Banu."

Lang translated many stories into English for the first time, but *1001 Arabian Nights* was not among them. In his *Blue Fairy Book* preface, Lang credited the original translators, and when it comes to *1001 Arabian Nights*: "'The Fairy Paribanou' is abridged from the old English translation of Galland" (Andrew Lang's Fairy Books). *The Blue Fairy Book* was "intended for children, who will like, it is hoped, the old stories that have pleased so many generations" (Andrew Lang's Fairy Books). My research didn't turn up a German version of it, under the supposition that Reiniger might have had a copy as a child. Even if Reiniger possessed a copy, I can say without a doubt that she didn't use Andrew Lang's *The Blue Fairy Book* to adapt *Prinzen Achmed*.

Reiniger's interpretation of *1001 Arabian Nights* instead came from an English writer. Galland may have translated the first *1001 Arabian Nights* that launched the entire Orientalism craze, but Sir Richard Burton's English ten-volume translation published in 1885 (with six supplemental volumes between 1886 and 1888) is the best-known version in the English language. Burton's *The Book of the Thousand Nights and a Night* has resonated in part to Burton's own fame as a Victorian traveler and, the other, to his overt concentration on the saga's sexual activities. "It was published as a private edition under the label of the Kama Shastra Society to circumvent the strict rules of the Obscene Publications Act of 1857 and persecution by the Society for the Suppression of Vice. This was no unnecessary measure, since Burton used the translation to demonstrate his vast knowledge of the erotic customs of Orientals on sexual issues and to criticize Victorian public morality" (Marzolph & van Leeuwen, 2004, 506). Isabel Burton, his wife, released a cleaner version to appeal to more genteel tastes in 1886 and 1887 (Marzolph & van Leeuwen, 2004, 559).

The popularity of *The Book of the Thousand Nights and a Night* usurped Galland's dominance as the ideal *1001 Arabian Nights* translation and, like Galland's, it was translated into the major European languages. Felix Paul Greve relied on Burton's text for his 1907–1909 German translation. For his *1001 Arabian Nights*, Enno Littmann returned to the original Arabic documents and "produced an objective, technically almost perfect translation, aiming to meet the requirements of both modern linguistics and philology" in the German language (Marzolph & van Leeuwen, 2004, 624). He did include the orphan stories, however, to fulfill audience's expectations and he used Burton's English version for their translation (Littmann, 1925; Marzolph email to author, January 20, 2016).

From this information, I can deduce that Reiniger read Greve's *1001 Arabian Nights* because it is Burton's translation rendered in German. Or she might have read Burton in the original English (I don't know when she learned to speak English). It makes more sense for Reiniger to have read Greve's German version, because when doing research of any kind it is easier to read material in one's native language. Reiniger did show proficiency in English in her later life, due to living in England for many years, but she wrote *Prinzen Achmed*'s script as a young woman when she lived in Germany. Reiniger appeared to be self-conscious when it came to her language skills at this period (I'm referring to the situation between her and Renoir at the movie's premiere). Whether she read Greve in German or Burton in English, Reiniger adapted *Die Abenteuer des Prinzen Achmed* from Burton's translation. This can be inferred by Burton's popularity and the number of *1001 Arabian Nights* translations that turned to him as the authoritative text over his predecessor Galland.

Christiane Schönfeld infers that Reiniger turned to a popular version: *Arabische Nächte: Erzählungen aus Tausend und eine Nacht* by Ernst Ludwig Schellenberg, illustrated by Edmund Dulac and published by Kiepenheuer in 1914 (2006, 178). She points to the third story in the book, "Die Geschichte von dem Zauberpferde" ("The Story of the Magic Horse"), as proof for Reiniger's inspiration, but her summary reads very much like other versions of *The Ebony Horse*. However, if this was the version Reiniger read, it would explain the connection between her and Dulac: She loved his illustrations for the Kiepenheuer edition and contacted him to paint intertitles for *Prinzen Achmed*.

As Orientalism peaked in the publishing world, the German movie industry turned to the *1001 Arabian Nights* saga for inspiration. Ernst Lubitsch directed *Sumurun* (*One Arabian Night*) in 1920 and Fritz Lang used a frame story narrative for his 1921 *Der müde Tod* (*Destiny*), Reiniger easily could have seen both these movies and was drawn to the possibility of using the *1001 Arabian Nights* for her film (Haase, 2004, 262). In his essay "The *Arabian Nights*, Visual Culture, and Early German Cinema," Donald Haase discusses how the saga is rich with visual experiences that drew readers into the stories and stimulated all the senses. These visual experiences in turn attracted the attention of Weimar moviemakers, who wanted to capture the rich world of the Orient on screen (2004, 261–68). Herman G. Weinberg said, "The challenge of evoking the Arabian Nights on the screen was irresistible" (qt. in Haase, 2004, 268). While Weimar films were products of a culture steeped in new art forms, German film studios didn't make art for art's sake, but for profit. Taking an example from modern-day Hollywood, many popular books were eventually adapted into a movie with the hopes of creating a profitable franchise. Wizansky also notes that Reiniger selected this saga, because the stories' familiarity grounded the German viewer when presented with the odd idea of an animated feature-length silhouette film (2004, 104). *1001 Arabian Nights* was a popular read and it offered an endless supply of possible stories set in a visual-based fantasy world, perfect fodder for a new medium.

Also remember that Weimar cinema exploded after World War I and, much like how the U.S. movie industry did during the Depression, people were looking for escapism. "In her classic study of early German cinema, Lotte Eisner had observed that the many German costume films appearing between 1919 and 1924 expressed the 'escapism of a poverty-stricken nation which, moreover, had always been fond of the glitter of parades'" (qt. in Haase, 2004, 268). Haase also makes a point about how the saga's serial nature was directly related to the "flow of images" on screen, "[erasing] the distinction between storyteller and filmmaker. The narrative set of the *Arabian Nights* ... becomes identical to filmmaking turning the filmmaker into a storyteller" (Haase, 2004, 269). The storyteller role is one that Reiniger eagerly accepted. It goes without question that,

> just as male editors in their own collections during the transition from oral to print culture, so did male filmmakers appropriate the literary tales and narrative techniques of Shahrazad and cast themselves as the serial storyteller during the developing years of visual culture. We might well prove not only the implications of this phenomenon but also the reception of the *Arabian Nights* by women filmmakers, in particular Lotte Reiniger's remarkable silhouette film of 1926, *Die Abenteuer des Prinzen Achmed* [Haase, 2004, 272].

From a storytelling perspective, Reiniger chose to adapt *1001 Arabian Nights* because it was as exotic as the Brothers Grimm was familiar. For Europeans and all of western society, Arabia (now the Middle East) came across as an intriguing, alien world. It is very similar to how people viewed the New World before western imperialism: ancient, alluring, mysterious and even magical. "The choice of story certainly fell to Reiniger. Her passion for fairy tales, in conjunction with the vogue for orientalism, which was at the time on the rise in Germany, made an adaptation of the *Thousand and One Nights* seem a good idea. The plot is rich in adventure, sudden reversals, amazing feats and interesting characters. As in all fairy tales, archetypes abound, as do potential fantasy scenes" (Jouvanceau, 2004, 40).

Reiniger's Orient is an idealized version that draws on the traditional European archetypes, but also plays into stereotypes of the area.

> In this film, the Orient exists for the West because a Western woman creates Oriental images in order to enchant a Western audience, but Reiniger's representation of the Orient is only marginally constructed in relation to the West. The Orient here is the "Other" in the sense that it is unreal and magical—it remains a fairy tale, just like its literary source. Lotte Reiniger looked for magic and for the boundaries of cinematic representation in order to transgress them [Schönfeld, 2006, 182].

A more modern example of people being attracted to the "exotic" and "foreign" would be the huge anime explosion in the U.S. from the late 1990s to mid–2000s. Fans were drawn to Japanese animation's diverse storytelling, often with mature themes that weren't reflected in the majority of western cartoons at that time, and unique visual stylizations brand new to most animation fans. It created a huge popular surge centered on Japanese culture among American otaku. ("Otaku" is a Japanese word with a negative connotation for "anime fan," but among western fandoms it has taken on a positive meaning.)

The fantastical plot elements in *1001 Arabian Nights* also had the potential to be a spectacular visual feast using the special effects Reiniger, Bartosch and Ruttmann developed. A European fairytale might call for magic, but the standard quota of fairies, witches and mythical creatures were run-of-the-mill compared to the powerful jinn, disappearing castles, shape-shifting sorcerer and the demons of Wak-Wak. These were fantasy elements surrounded by a new setting and unfamiliar culture to the Europeans (although a German woman took creative license). The exotic setting and creatures combined with the trick film special effects made a pseudo–Arabian world even more magical for Reiniger to turn into a feature film.

Returning again to the question on why Reiniger selected fairytales as her main subject matter, another possibility is that she selected *1001 Arabian Nights* based on the pure nostalgia factor. Nostalgia is a powerful tool, especially for generations raised on an endless sea of television, movies, books and other media, and adults ceaselessly chase after it in hopes of reclaiming a period perceived to be more innocent. During the Weimar years, Germans longed for the time before the Great War and the economic devastation, when their country was safe and prosperous. Films allowed German audiences a greater escape than books and even the theater, because they were visually and later audibly transported to another world made real by suspended disbelief. "Reiniger secularises her story not only by omitting repeated thanks to Allah, but by depicting fate as wo/man-made (or possibly demon-driven) but not as part of Allah's plan as the literary source might suggest. The 'Orient' here provides a magical springboard of opportunities for a new artform to prove its potential" (Schönfeld, 2006, 181).

The *1001 Arabian Nights* was one of the most distant and surreal lands that they could escape to and Reiniger wanted this to be the world she brought to life.

K. Vivian Taylor reminds us that *1001 Arabian Nights* is a text rich with sexual activities. "[Reiniger's] adaptation of tales from the traditionally risqué *Arabian Nights* for *Prince Achmed* was an attempt to attract adult audiences" (K.V. Taylor, 2011, 91). If Reiniger did read the Burton edition only available through mail order, she was treated to quite the imaginative spectacle and it further enhanced her decision to select it as her source material to appeal to mature minds interested in the more taboo aspects of the *1001 Arabian Nights*.

The *1001 Arabian Nights* has many fantastical elements both familiar and strange to western imaginations. It is the combination of foreign exoticism and the stalwart fairytales that make the *1001 Arabian Nights* saga appealing source material. *Prinzen Achmed*'s biggest pull, however, is its position in the fairytale genre: reliable fodder for animated film stories. As the first feature-length animated fairytale film, *Prinzen Achmed* is the ancestor of all animated fairytales, even Disney's *Snow White*.

The Walt Disney Company undeniably dominates the animated fairytale genre. An example from my own past demonstrates this case: from the ages of one to seven I believed that Disney fairytales were the only acceptable fairytale versions and considered all other animated adaptations of the original stories as generic rip-offs.[5] My official stance on Disney's fairytales as the only "real thing" fueled frenzied arguments on the playground, until a fairytale unit in the second grade set me straight.[6] Richard Schickel observed the Disney formula in *The Disney Version* and described it in an aggressive manner reminiscent of my playground rants:

> Indeed, there was something arrogant about the way the studio took over these works [*Alice in Wonderland* and *Peter Pan*]. Grist for a mighty mill, they were in the ineffable Hollywood term, "properties" to do with as the proprietor of the machine would. You could throw jarring popular songs into the brew, you could gag them up, you could sentimentalize them. You had, in short, no obligation to the originals or to the cultural tradition they represented. In fact, when it came to billing, J.M. Barrie's *Peter Pan* somehow became Walt Disney's *Peter Pan*, and Lewis Carroll's *Alice* became Walt Disney's *Alice*. It could be argued that this was a true reflection of what happened to the works in the process of getting to the screen, but the egotism that insists on making another man's work your own through wanton tampering and by advertising claim is not an attractive form of egotism, however it is rationalized. And this kind of annexation was to be constant in the later life of Disney. The only defense that one can enter for him is that of invincible ignorance: He really didn't see what he was doing, didn't know how some people could be offended by it, and certainly could not see that what was basically at fault was his insistence that there was only one true style for the animated film—his style [1968, 296–297].

Schickel's views coincide with my Disney dissociative theory about the Mouse House rewriting history to suit its own purpose. Beyond my experience with Disney fairytale domination, I have already discussed Disney's influence on the genre in a prior chapter, but didn't include my observations when Lotte Reiniger and her silhouettes are tossed into the fray.

When one turns back the clock on the fairytale film before December 1937, the genre did follow the formulaic "once upon a time and happily ever after" story to generate profit. It was easy to replicate with different characters and settings without taking big investment risks, and audiences enjoyed seeing the old tale made new on film. In Zipes' opinion, "the classical fairy-tale narrative stamped film narrative and the canonical Hollywood narrative long before Hollywood even existed. I would even argue that it laid the groundwork for classical European films, especially the melodrama" (2011, 20).

In the 1920s, filmmakers were freer to explore more fantastic plots with special effects that slowly dwindled into more conservative realism as World War II drew closer.

When it came to Walt Disney making *Snow White* as his first film: "Although he had turned to fairy tales when he first began making cartoons at Laugh-O-Gram, there was nothing automatic about Disney's choice of a fairy tale as the subject of his first feature. Given the popularity of Mickey Mouse, he could easily have put his star into a feature-length comedy..." (Barrier, 2007, 101). Walt Disney loved fairytales and one large facet of his personality was his childlike wonder. Although this is consistently reinforced by the Disney Company with the "Uncle Walt" image, it is credible to state that he wanted to make a fairytale film to simply please this part of himself.

> Walt was inspired to use *Snow White*, because one of the first motion pictures he saw was a live action version of *Snow White* starring Marguerite Clark. [He said,] "I thought it was a perfect story." If nothing else, he knew from that film that the Grimms' story could be expanded without strain to feature length. Many other fairy tales, like the few he had already made into *Silly Symphonies,* could not. Fairy tales are as a rule rather stark. Disney's challenge in adapting one of them for an animated film was to enrich the characterizations without destroying the story's structure [Barrier, 2007, 102].

After *Snow White* premiered in December 1937, Disney challenged fairytale films to bring more magic to the screen. He raised the bar, but it was by reinventing the old with new technology:

> With the shift into Technicolor and high-fidelity RCA sound that the enlarged budgets made possible, Disney started a full-fledged series of musical fairy-tale adaptations. It proved a pivotal turning point. The re-casting of fairy-tale classics as playlets with song and dance was itself nothing new. In Europe, Lotte Reiniger and Ladislas Starevich had been doing it for years, and Tony Sarg's cutout silhouettes from Latin America had been popular in the United States throughout the 1920s. Looked at from one perspective, Disney himself was simply adapting the formulas of American marionette theater, which in turn had been influenced by turn-of-the-century fairyland operettas and stage musicals [Merritt, 2005, 4].

For a fairytale film to be successful after *Snow White*, it had to leave behind the whimsical trappings of the silent film era and include a greater amount of depth in the characters, setting, costumes, story and especially special effects as sound added a new dimension and color brought the world to life over grainy black and white. Fairytales needed to take an audience's breath away and that extra dash of movie magic meant the difference between true escapism or a dismal flop. Returning to Schickel's opinion, while Disney did relabel these works as his own, they did rework them and introduce them to a new audience, which is done with all fairytale adaptations.

MGM's *Wizard of Oz* (1939), *Münchhausen* (*The Adventures of Baron Munchausen,* 1934)—the Nazi fantasy meant to rival the story of Dorothy and her ruby slippers—and *La Belle et la bête* (*Beauty and the Beast,* 1946) are considered by many to be the most magical of all live-action fairytale films. They are all examples of post–*Snow White* films that rose to the challenge to make a convincing fantasy with movie magic. They proved to be so popular that all three remain staples in the fantasy genre and demonstrate how to correctly transfer a fairytale to the screen. Each also exemplifies how to create a fairytale film *sans* Disney influence.

Snow White did have a lingering effect on the fairytale genre in that studios and filmmakers wanted to replicate its success as well as the awe-inspiring moments the film gave audiences, except they didn't want to replicate the animation. It wasn't until the 1950s, when the Walt Disney Company diversified its entertainment offerings, that a seed for the Disney fairytale formula was planted. Disney offered wholesome family entertainment and established this trend in the postwar culture. It slowly sprouted through the decades before taking full bloom in the late 1980s and spreading its roots during the Disney Renaissance. The Disney fairytale combined with family entertainment, along with Disney's public relations and marketing departments, made the Disney version the *only* version. And it proved successful. "In its review of [*Snow White* in the 1930s], *Pour Vous* lamented 'the number of today's parents who voluntarily leave their children in ignorance of fairy tales ... the poor children ... who don't have the joy of learning to read from the marvelous stories of Perrault, Anderson [sic], the Brothers Grimm.' The producer of *Snow White* then took his place among these giants of children's literature: 'Thanks to Walt Disney for renewing the tradition of storytelling, for reinvigorating and perpetuating the fairy stories that have enchanted the imaginations of all people for centuries'" (qt. in Smoodin, 2012, 89).

When Hollywood and other entertainment industries realize the earning potential of a genre, actor, medium, etc., it's dissected to the core elements and repeatedly cloned until it's no longer popular or profitable. With his usual candidness, Zipes wrote a critical view of this approach in *Happily Ever After*:

> In [modern times] the creation of fairy tales in all their forms; their effective use by individual artists, corporations, and institutions; and their reception by different audiences take place within the culture industry. Simply put, all art, whether high or low, is subject to commodification.... In order to maximize profit, the culture industry has to instill standard expectations in audiences so that they think they are getting what they want, and that by getting what they supposedly want, they can become like the stars with whom they identify. When accused of "dumbing down" their programs and products, corporate representatives in the culture industry are fond of announcing that they are conceding to the wishes of the public and are only as guilty as their audiences. Of course, they never mention that they seek to control these audiences through their own polls and conditioning processes. The culture industry is indeed "totalitarian"—perhaps one should use the word *global* today, given the globalization of corporate capitalism—in its intention to totally take over markets and dominate demands in wishes [1997, 6–7].

While Zipes' latter thought about complete world domination is based on facts, it paints the entertainment corporations as the evil villains and the audiences as mindless peasants. Global economics isn't the key here, rather the fairytale commodification is. For years, only fairytale films that followed the Disney formula were released. If, however, you feed audiences the same meal over and over, it will get stale, as seen with Disney's slump in the 2000s and allowed upstart Pixar to reign supreme over the animation industry. The company only recovered when Michael Eisner was booted from his CEO office, replaced by Bob Iger, who then subsequently purchased Pixar, made John Lasseter chief creative officer, and invested in new properties (Marvel, *Star Wars* and the Muppets) and restructured the animation department. Lasseter, Iger and Ed Catmull knew they had to revamp Disney's fairytale formula, but other filmmakers were aware of this long before Disney.

It cannot be said that Lotte Reiniger was not formulaic in her work, she simply followed her own formula rather than giving in to popular demands. Zipes noted in *The Enchanted Screen*, "Reiniger did not greatly change the narrative plots of the classical fairy tales that she cut out in unique forms" (2011, 83). The biggest criticism of her work (other than using the same animation process for over 60 years) was how her stories mirrored their origins way too much. "The worst thing is that, during the course of her life, Reniger [sic] made at least fifty films, and it's eighty times the same thing" (qt. in Jouvanceau, 2004, 207) The critic who wrote this was tossing Reiniger's films into the standard Disney fairytale formula and doesn't consider that "this [fairytale movie] idea, though not usually expressed so brutally or forthrightly, also pervades many general [films]," especially movies made in the current Hollywood factory (Jouvanceau, 2004, 207).

What the critic also failed to recognize was that *Die Abenteuer des Prinzen Achmed* and her other films were animated during an era when most movies followed a predictable pattern to appeal to audiences and generate a profit. Films that challenged the status quo were made, but they were met with resistance from critics and audiences for upsetting the pattern or questioning social conventions, religion and government. An example from Reiniger's life is her experience with the Nazis and their rigid propaganda ideals. Her silhouette films and subject matter were too degenerate or avant-garde for Hitler's regime and her own personal beliefs led her and Koch to flee Germany. Movies in the earlier twentieth century, however, were products of a fledgling medium and their stories had to be simple to compliment the rudimentary process. As filmmaking technology advanced, screenwriters were able to develop stories better.

Reiniger did adapt fairytales for most of her career and while fairytales are simplistic at first glance, they are drenched with hidden meanings. *Prinzen Achmed* can be considered a purer adaptation of the actual *1001 Arabian Nights* folktales, because she made the film 11 years before Disney standardized the genre and she made it away from a for-profit studio. No one can doubt that Reiniger loved fairytales, but creating a beautiful art film was just as important to her, if not more so, depending on the project. Zipes continued, "She was more interested in embellishing stories that agreed with her ideological world view. For the most part, her films focused on the struggles of the underdog and closely followed the outlines of the original tales. However, in her very first major fairy-tale project she proved herself to be a most imaginative and impressive storyteller" (2011, 83).

As the first animated fairytale film, Reiniger's influence on the modern animated and live action film is more indirect than Disney's process. "Despite the intricate nature of her specialized technique of filming, the importance of the story must not be underestimated in Ms. Reiniger's work. The magic of the fairytale has always been her greatest fascination, yet her own interpretations contain a unique quality" (Isaacs, 1971). The quality being that story carried as much weight as the animation, achieving a perfect balance. Within her story process, she reworked the fairytales to suit her desires. Her goal was to animate the fairytales she wanted and make them as beautiful as possible to reflect her ideal world.

Film critic Béla Balázs wrote, "It's the brilliantly cut silhouettes which make the beautifully filigreed silhouette films of Lotte Reiniger so outstanding. For invention doesn't begin with the story, but with the visual arrival of these beings. Their appearance is a fairytale. The story doesn't determine the fairytale quality, but the shapes do" (qt. in Raganelli, 1999). As in the shapes of her silhouettes.

Due to the formulaic narrative in Reiniger's technique, her silhouettes are the uniqueness that give her films their magical, ethereal quality. She achieved a delicate elegance often lacking in computer animation and even traditional cel animation due to the actual hands-on manufacturing required to make the puppets. She animated her films with only her husband or a small team and that gave her total control. She even added a bit of herself in the films, when she'd accidentally photograph her hand by mistake. Borrowing from the *1001 Arabian Nights*, a simple yet accurate metaphor is to compare her to Scheherazade, the teller of all 1001 tales. Marina Warner and K. Vivian Taylor each had their own take on the Scheherazade metaphor. Taylor wrote from the perspective that Reiniger is self-inserting herself in *Prinzen Achmed* as an invisible character:

By omitting Scheherazade, Reiniger replaces her. Reiniger inserts herself into the narrative by excluding Scheherazade; she implies her own presence. Self-figuration was a prominent tendency among Weimar filmmakers who portrayed themselves, often overtly, as showmen and wizards within their films to comment upon the ambiguous position of Weimar filmmakers as both artists and entertainers eager to use a new technology yet wary of the film industry [K.V. Taylor, 2011, 51].

Warner takes a similar approach, but rather than making Reiniger the wizard behind the curtain, she is identified as the iconic female storyteller:

> The famous frame story is set aside, and instead Reiniger places herself, invisibly, in Shahrazad's role: she is the mistress of the feast, and she snips and stitches her tales together, creating a lively cycle of romances from several other stories beside "The Ebony Horse." Abandoning the disconnected, episodic sequence of the original book, she trims and tidies the originals to bind elements from them into a series of adventures which close with happy endings [Warner, 2011, 393–394].

Reiniger is Scheherazade in *Die Abenteuer des Prinzen Achmed* and she inhabits that role in each of her films that can be considered another night she tells a story to the sultan or the audience. The important factor to take away from Reiniger's role as Scheherazade is that she made all of the fairytales her own by recreating them in a manner that was new, paid homage to the original, and fulfills their original purpose as being entertaining. This is how Reiniger influences the modern fairytale film: she set a course to make creative animated films that fulfilled her unique vision instead of ceaselessly repeating the same storyline and format that has became commonplace with the Disney fairytale formula.

Disney's original film *Snow White and the Seven Dwarfs* inspired others to create fairytale films, hoping to replicate the same magic. The problem is that the Disney fairytale formula is tired. Zipes comments in *The Enchanted Screen*,

> In some ways, filmmakers are similar to fairy-tale protagonists in that they want to keep the narrative tradition of wondrous storytelling flowing. They are the champion tellers and projectors of fairy tales. Some do this by relying on the canonic mode of telling and showing fairy tales as Disney came to do. Others, fully aware of the normative schemata of the canonical and/or classical fairy tales, have sought to contest the norms and introduce alternative ways of employing and visualizing fairy tales through film [2011, 22].

Zipes quoted Eric Smoodin in his earlier work *Happily Ever After* that explains how the Disney fairytale formula is part of an entertainment juggernaut and doesn't always allow the filmmakers to pursue their vision:

> Animation was not produced within a system of fixed institutions and social practices, which, as conventional wisdom might have it, always and unproblematically reduced cartoons to children's entertainment, or which uniformly enforced censorship restrictions. Instead, the Hollywood cartoon from the classical era developed from, expressed, and was frequently controlled by a number of shifting and often contradictory discourses, about, for instance, sexuality, race, gender, class, leisure and creativity [Smoodin qt. in Zipes, 1997, 90].

Smoodin refers to short cartoons from the Golden Age, but Zipes is accurate to connect it with the animated feature film. It's a problem still faced today as Andrew Stanton, director of *Wall-E, A Bug's Life, Finding Nemo* and *Finding Dory*, pointed out in a TED talk entitled *The Clues to a Great Story*. Stanton shared his experience as a storyteller, stressing the importance of making an emotional link with audiences. The cringeworthy part is when he relates writing *Toy Story*:

> In our earliest days at Pixar, before we truly understood the invisible workings of a story, we were simply a group of guys just going on our gut, going on our instincts. And it's interesting to see how

that led us places that were actually pretty good. You've got to remember in this time of year, 1993, what was considered a successful animated picture was *The Little Mermaid, Beauty and the Beast, Aladdin, Lion King*. So when we pitched *Toy Story* to Tom Hanks for the first time, he walked in and said, "You don't want me to sing, do you?" And I thought that epitomized perfectly what everybody thought animation had to be at that time. But what we really wanted to prove was that you could tell stories completely different in animation.

So we didn't have any influence then, so we had a little secret list of rules that we kept to ourselves. And they were: no songs, no "I want" moment, no happy village, no love story, no villain. And the irony is that, in the first year, our story was not working at all and Disney was panicking. So they privately got advice from a famous lyricist, who I won't name, and he faxed them some suggestions. And we got hold of that fax and the fax said: there should be songs, there should be an "I want" song, there should be a happy village song, there should be a love story, and there should be a villain. And thank goodness we were just too young, rebellious, and contrarian at the time. That just gave us more determination to prove that you could prove a better story. And a year after that we did conquer it and it just went to prove that storytelling has guidelines, not hard fast rules [Stanton, 2012].

Fairytale films are changing, because the filmmakers have pulled away from the Disney formula and they want to reinterpret the fairytales in new ways that push the stories over the edge into the same new, unexplored territory that Silverlock and Golias notice in their journey across the Commonwealth of Letters.[7] Reiniger reimagined her fairytales as a bridge between the old European fairytales and modern cinema. Disney reimagined his fairytales as means to display animation film's potential and fulfill his longing to create magic in the world.

Reiniger's films present an alternative to the Disney formula and allow animators and filmmakers to see the potential within the fairytale and animation beyond established, preconceived notions that need to be laid to rest. In *Fairy-Tale Films Beyond Disney: International Perspectives,* Zipes explains the role fairytales play in modern culture

> In my opinion, the fairy tale has become the dominant cultural form of storytelling in our daily lives, thanks in large part to film and other mass-mediated technologies. Consequently, as an accessible and memetic popular genre, the fairy-tale film, along with other adaptations such as literature, drama, opera, cartoon and so on, purposely brings people together to share relevant stories that speak to common problems. The more bewildering, if not distorted and perverted, our lives become, the more people seek refuge and meaning in fairy tales and other figments of the human imagination like religion. Yet, unlike religion, fairy tales have a secular wondrous appeal geared to help us order our lives and endorse our hope for harmony and peace [2016].

Fairytales' current cultural role harkens back to how they fulfilled humanity's need to be entertained to stave off the darkness. Instead of fighting off the unknown darkness, fairytales are used to instill a sense of wonder about life. That, in turn, fuels the imagination. Zipes continues this thought again with *Happily Ever After*:

> Going beyond Disney is therefore the realization that fairy tales do not begin and end with Disney and that one can make one's own life resemble a fairy tale that transcends antiquated notions of patriarchy and racism. Going beyond Disney means realizing that there are no prescriptions for fairy tales or for happiness. To paraphrase a famous quotation from the German romantic writer Novalis—"Menschwerdern ist eine Kunst"—learning how to become a compassionate human being involves learning to live life as an artist—and I might add, learning to transform our fairy-tale dreams into narratives of our own making [1997, 110].

Reiniger personifies the very ideal of an artist whose art transforms fairytale dreams into her own narratives. She said multiple times that she lived a fairytale life and her films allowed her to inhabit a world of her own making. Her influences extend to other artists who make their own fairytale narratives, shaping the modern films to be different from Disney and create something never seen before.

Die Abenteuer des Prinzen Achmed has a complex plot compared to *Snow White and the Seven Dwarfs,* which began the commoditization of fairytale films. A "rivalry" exists between Walt Disney's Technicolor, musical, hand-drawn celluloid animated film and Lotte Reiniger's silent epic, special effects-laden, hand-cut paper silhouette, stop-motion animated film. Both films were the first of their kind in the entire world and have had an effect on the animation industry that still ripples to this day, although the Disney film is much better documented than Reiniger's masterpiece. According to K. Vivian Taylor, "More frequently her major accomplishments are attributed to the Disney Company, among others. The conspicuous lack of in-depth scholarship about the sixty-year-long filmmaking career of the inventor of the silhouette film genre, multiplane camera and the animated feature film genre seems groundless" (2011, 3).

When it comes to naming the first animated film, for years Walt Disney Studios claimed that *Snow White and the Seven Dwarfs* held the honor and it was backed up by many valid resources. From a marketing standpoint, the Walt Disney Company probably didn't argue the point, because it further cemented their founder's already legendary status in animation history and advanced the company's status as an industry leader ("It began with the mouse"). No one argued the point, because any remnants of several of the other contenders to the title were considered lost films and references to them were scarce. A lost film is a term that applies to films that existed at one point in time, but there are now no known copies. Nearly all of cinematographer George Melies' catalogue once had lost film status, which contributed to the decline of his career. (The subsequent discovery of his films in collections reignited interest in his work late in his life and established his importance in film history.) Fortunately, the BFI kept a copy of D*ie Abenteuer des Prinzen Achmed*!

Another reason why *Snow White* was mistakenly called the first animated film: animation films were not well-documented until the latter half of the twentieth century. Steve Schneider said it best: "The problem was, no one ever really paid much mind. In all the encyclopedias of film history, in all the vivisections of popular culture, non–Disney animation was either ignored, scorned, or given the shortest of shrift" (1990, 17–18). Many animation studios, including Warner Brothers, the Walt Disney Company, Rankin Bass, Fleischer and others, trashed their paperwork and cels (although some animators scavenged pieces and took them home), until a light bulb went on over someone's head that it might be worth saving these materials. Animation historian Jerry Beck acknowledges that when he and Leonard Maitlin began writing *Of Mice and Magic,* information about animation from the 1920s, '30s and '40s was scarce and incomplete (1987, vii). Bruno Edera wrote in *Full Length Animated Feature Films,* "In the sphere of full-length animated films, references are harder to come by. Very few works are devoted to this particular subject, especially to the period between the early days of the cinema and the end of the Second World War in 1945. In compiling a precise catalogue, one comes up against considerable obstacles, practically in countries where no historian has ever considered the animation cinema within its own terms of reference" (1977, 25). When Beck, Maitlin, Edera and other future animation historians began chronicling animation's history, they were blessed that many animation pioneers were still alive and available for interviews. The international animation industry hadn't been documented consistently either.

While the educated and invested animation enthusiasts were aware that *Snow White and the Seven Dwarfs* wasn't the first animated film, popular convention was against them. John Canemaker said, "*Snow White* could be called the first feature-length animated cartoon. That would be legit. There are other films that go back to the silent era that were lengthy as well. Max Fleischer did a film on the theory of relativity. There is some controversy about a film that was made in Argentina that was also rather lengthy. But for many [animation scholars], *Prince Achmed* is [considered] the first animated feature" (qt. in Liebenson, 2001). Cecile Starr counters with another observation about the power of Disney, "[*Prinzen Achmed*] only revises animation history to those people who are willing to revise. Columbus discovered America, and it doesn't matter that there were people who came before. That's the way the story goes and that's the popular version, and it's going to be very hard to shake it. Disney will always be first to those who are going to believe the Disney version, no matter what evidence is presented to the contrary" (qt. in Liebenson, 2001). The facts are black and white, though: *Snow White and the Seven Dwarfs* is not the first animated film. It does, however, have several other firsts for an animated film:

- First feature-length animated film made in the U.S.
- First feature-length animated film in Technicolor
- First feature-length animated musical
- First feature-length animated film that used the cel animation process
- First feature-length animated film to be made by a studio

While *Snow White* might have a notable lists of "firsts," there are at least six other films, including *Prinzen Achmed*, that could qualify for the title "first animated film ever made." (While many of the earliest examples of animation are stop-motion films, especially by pioneers such as Willis H. O'Brien, Vladislav Starevich and Ray Harryhausen, for consideration in this book they have been left out due to their length or due to their combination with live action; these films included stop-motion animated sequences interspersed with live action segments. Some noted examples are *King Kong, The Ghost of Slumber Mountain, The Lost World, Miest Kinomatograficheskovo Operatora* [*The Cameraman's Revenge*] and *Aviacionnaya Nedelya Nasekomykh* [*Insect's Aviation Week*]. *The Dream Doll* includes only a few live action segments, but it is predominantly stop-motion animated.)

Title	Country of Origin	Director	Production Company	Release Date	Animation Type	Length
El Apóstel	Argentina	Quirino Cristiani	Actualidades Valle	November 9, 1917	Stop-motion with hand drawn paper cutouts	70 min
The Dream Doll	USA	Howard Moss	Essanay Film Manufacturing	December 10, 1917	Stop-motion with dolls, includes live action	—
Sin dejar rastros	Argentina	Quirino Cristiani	—	Shown for one day in 1918	Stop-motion with hand drawn paper cutouts	—
The Einstein Theory of Relativity	USA	Max and Dave Fleischer	Fleischer Studios	February 11, 1923	Hand drawn, includes live action and still photographs	Two versions: 20 min/ 50 min.
Evolution or *Darwin's Theory of Evolution*	USA	Max and Dave Fleischer	Red Seal Pictures	July 12, 1925	Hand drawn, includes live action	41 min.

Title	Country of Origin	Director	Production Company	Release Date	Animation Type	Length
Die Abenteuer des Prinzen Achmed	Germany	Lotte Reiniger	Comenius Films	May 2, 1926	Stop-motion with silhouette figures	62 or 65 min.

Italian-born Argentine animator Quirino Cristiani made both *El Apóstel* and *Sin dejar rastros* in subsequent years. Always interested in drawing, Cristiani became enthralled with animation after viewing Émile Cohl's 1908 stop-motion film *Les Allumettes animées* (*Animated Matches*). He was obsessed with figuring out how Cohl made the matches move and finally discovered that it was through patience and repetitious photos (Bendazzi, 2008, 43).

Cristiani became known for his caricatures and was hired by Federico Valle to make an experimental political film for his *Actualidades Valle*. Cristiani taught himself basic animation principles, having studied Cohl's methods. His first film was a short called *La intervención a la provincia de Buenos Aires* (*Intervention in the Province of Buenos Aires*). Cristiani wanted to make a longer animated film, noting the same possibilities of the medium that Reiniger and Disney had decades later. He directed *El Apóstel* (*The Apostle*) with the help of Diógenes "El Mono" Taborda, who designed the characters, and Andrés Ducaud, who made models for a fire sequence. It was based on a book by Alfredo de Laferrere, a political satire with mythological imagery about President Hipólito Irigoyen. The film had limited distribution, and audiences loved it, but not a single copy exists today (Bendazzi, 1999, 50; Pidhajny, 2001).

His animation process was an "original technique for animating cutout figures, which he patented in 1917 under number 15.498," which used a combination of stop-motion and cel animation (Bendazzi, 1999, 50). Quirino's method relied on puppets he dubbed "munitos" and each puppet required individual drawings of body parts, connected with string so they could perform any movement. Cristiani drew characters and scenery in a white outline on black paper, then redrew the characters, slightly shifting their positions and facial features resulting in hundreds of copies of the characters. Cristiani animated the characters by using the same technique as Reiniger, except he switched out the paper cutouts instead of altering articulated puppets. When the scenes were filmed and developed, the white-on-black reversed in the negative exposure to have black lines on white backgrounds. By using silhouette puppets, Reiniger sped up the animation process by not having to switch out the characters; she only had to adjust the movement while it was still on the animation table.

Spurred by his success, Cristiani made *Sin dejar rastros* (*Without a Trace*) about the Germans trying to force Argentina to enter World War I as an Axis Power by torpedoing an Argentine ship and blaming the English and French. Argentina discovered the ruse and were angered that Germany would dismiss their neutrality. "[T]he film was shown for only one day, confiscated for political reasons, it disappeared in the basement of some government office" (Bendazzi, 1999, 50). Cristiani continued to animate, separating himself from Valle to form his own studio. He made the first sound animated film, *Peludópolis*, in 1931. *Peludópolis* was about a pirate captain, El Peludo, who commandeers a ship and expulses the old captain. El Peludo and the pirates sailed the ocean until they landed on an island and had adventures. General Provisional arrives on the island intending to bring order. It was another of Cristiani's political satires (Bendazzi, 2006, 101). The film premiered on September 16 or 18, 1931. Unfortunately for Cristiani, it wasn't a success.

The Guinness Book of World Records states that Cristiani created the first animated film with *El Apóstel*, but the biggest problem it faces is the lack of an actual copy of the film and documented evidence outside of Argentina. Bendazzi sums up the situation: "No copy of this film exists today and we must rely on a few written sources and Cristiani's memory. Whether or not *El Apóstel* was actually a feature film is still uncertain" (1994, 50).

We're given the impression that all information regarding *El Apóstel* was destroyed. Zucchelli shows in his documentary *Quirino Cristiani: The Mystery of the First Animated Movies*, however, that there is printed evidence to support Cristiani's claim to title "first animated film" by literally visiting the archives that house the information. The Cristiani family maintains their own personal archives, including a few remaining munitos. While speculation still remains, the printed evidence is enough to support the claim sans the reels. *El Apóstel* clocks in at 70 minutes using 50,000 frames played at 14 frames per second (Pidhajny, 2001).

Other than the lack of a physical print, there is doubt about *El Apóstel* being a feature film which would disqualify it from the running. The length standard for feature films as defined by the American Film Institute, British Film Institute and Academy of Motion Picture Art and Sciences is 40 minutes or longer. While *El Apóstel* runs 70 minutes, it is speculated that it could have been padded with content from other films (Pidhajny, 2001). *Prinzen Achmed* used a larger amount of frames and from the beginning it was intended to be a feature-length film, but it's known that Reiniger created the entire movie from scratch and didn't lengthen it with pre-made content. While Cristiani's memories provide the most reliable account, he claimed he made a feature-length film and never discussed the padded content. Bendazzi and Zucchelli don't mention it either. His second film *Sin dejar rastros* is another contender, but it had an even shorter lifespan than its predecessor and it fell victim to the same fate: only written hard evidence remains to support its claim.

There is enough written proof for Cristiani to have a concrete platform for the distinction "first animated movie," but it does remain built on sand given the lack of a physical reel.

William Moritz brings to attention stop-motion animator Ladislas Starevitch and his daughter Irene, who both animated *Le Roman de Renard* (*Reynard the Fox*), a stop-motion film using puppets. Film planning evidently took place in the 1920s, but it wasn't until that *Prinzen Achmed* was complete would the Starevitch father and daughter start production. Moritz sums up the entire reason why it doesn't even fall into consideration, "[I]t was largely shot in Paris around 1930, has been completely ignored in discussions of 'the first feature-length animation film' because it finally received its finishing funds from German sources [UFA provided the remaining money] (since Goethe had written a classic version of the Reynard legend) and had its world premiere in Berlin in April 1937, still eight months before Disney's *Snow White*..." (1997, 230).

The other three candidates, *The Dream Doll*, *The Darwin Theory of Evolution* and *The Einstein Theory of Relativity*, can be discounted because they aren't entirely animated. *The Dream Doll* is a hybrid of live action and stop-motion animation, the ancestor of films by Ray Harryhausen, Tim Burton, Peter Lord, David Sproxton and Henry Selick. The Fleischer brothers' educational films *The Einstein Theory of Relativity* and *The Darwin Theory of Evolution* are much shorter than Reiniger and Cristiani's films. *The Einstein Theory of Relativity* consisted of "live action, still photographs, charts, and some simple animation." Albert Einstein enjoyed the film, but that is not enough to keep it in the running (Solomon, 1994, 32). It can be assumed that *The Darwin Theory of Evolution* was made with a similar structure as *The Einstein Theory of Relativity* due its teaching purpose, but "but it is alleged that it contains footage from [Willis H.] O'Brien's *The Ghost of Slumber Mountain*" from 1918 (Langer qt. in Pidhajny, 2001). If *The Darwin Theory of Evolution* used pre-made content and was made like *The Darwin Theory of Evolution*, then it is also disqualified.

Reiniger's *Die Abenteuer des Prinzen Achmed* vies for the title "first animated film made" because from the start it was intended to be a feature, it is not a lost film, and there is ample evidence supporting its production, including the actual silhouette puppets Reiniger used to make the film at the Tübingen Stadtmuseum. Reiniger with *Die Abenteuer des Prinzen Achmed* has her own line of firsts:

- First feature-length animated silhouette film
- First feature-length animated film created by a woman
- First feature-length animated film made in Europe
- First feature-length animated film with a fictional narrative

Die Abenteuer des Prinzen Achmed has the honor of being the oldest surviving feature-length animated film, which is a title neither Disney nor Cristiani can take away, unless the latter's works spontaneously rematerialize. There will be supporters for both *Die Abenteuer des Prinzen Achmed* and *El Apóstel* as the first animated film ever made. Walter Schobert of the Deutsches Filminstitut am Main summarizes why many people believe Reiniger should have the title:

> She is the pioneer. Not only of the silhouette films, but of animation films per se. There are one or two indications that probably someone in Argentina made an animation film in 1910, but it hasn't been proved. Since there's no sign of any film, I can say with impunity she made the first full feature animated film in the history of the cinema, *The Adventures of Prince Achmed*. I would even accentuate that her significance isn't just to be found in the genre she chose. She's a great and important filmmaker quite apart from this. *Prince Achmed* is not only vitally important, because of its technique, but through its content and message, which is still persuasive and meaningful. I think it should be shown to people for the healing power it projects. For these reasons, it belongs to the greatest films of the twentieth century cinema [qt. in Raganelli, 1999].

As the world's leading animation studio, the Walt Disney Company likes to set itself apart from others in that it has a unique approach when it comes to making animated films. This ideal dates back to the early days with Walt Disney and how he promoted his studio as a place where magical things happen. In actuality, Disney Animation Studios is an entertainment company like many others and while it does have its own unique qualities, there are still multiple similarities with other studios when it comes to the animation process, especially when animation was in its infancy. J.B. Kaufman in *The Fairest One of All* argues that Disney made *Snow White* different from prior animated films and cartoons and he wanted to make a movie that would set itself apart: "[W]hile all these films technically could be described as a) feature length and b) wholly or partly animated, none of them was anything like the picture Walt now had in mind. His vision involved more than the simple technical challenge of increasing the *length* of the film; an entirely different kind of story would be required" (2012, 32).

Reiniger was aware years before Disney that simply making a longer animated film would be a challenge, but an even bigger hurdle was writing a story that was more engrossing than the standard comedic short. She held fast to Pixar's mantra "Story Is King"[8] and wrote a complex, compelling script with intricacies that Disney's *Snow White* lacks. Dr. Morkovin interviewed Art Babbitt to gain insight about Babbitt's "Gag Manual Project" and the transcript was saved in the Disney Archives:

> The measurement of the success of a gag depends on the degree to which the spectator has identified himself with the character on the screen, the degree in which he was able to forget himself in the action and adventures of the story character, both in mind and body.... There are two ways of doing this: one, thru the mental channel—sympathy with the character and antipathy or antagonism towards the menace. That is story building. The other method is thru empathy.... The principle of empathy is involved in cartoons as well as in other expressions. You must get into the body of your spectator. In order to do that you must make your character so living, his action so convincing, that identification is possible ... [Hahn & Miller-Zarneke, 2015, 42–43].

Reiniger embodied these two principles not just through laying down heavy storylines and creating heroic/evil romantic characters, but also through the very movement of her silhouette puppets as she replicated the human image to make them lifelike and identifiable. These were the exact lessons Disney implemented in *Snow White*. For later films, she didn't rely on scripts (Jouvanceau & Roda, 1980). Solomon stated, "*Snow White* established the basic pattern for almost every subsequent American animated feature, and its influence can be seen in films made decades later" (1994, 62). Not only is the Disney formula replicated in the U.S., but it has become prevalent in Europe, Australia and parts of Asia.

In *The Enchanted Screen*, Zipes examined how the Disney fairytale film thrusts an idealized version of life onto the audience, deluding them to believe that only an elitist group can have power and happiness (2011, 23). The Disney formula teamed with the company's impeccable talent of product endorsement and advertising deftly shaves and carves the imagination with children being the primary targets. As the children grow up and reproduce, they are ingrained with the Disney belief system; in turn they teach it to their offspring. The cyclical Disney lifestyle, if not kept in check, leaves a person with a disillusioned, inactive view of reality.

> ... Disney set limits on the possibilities of utopia that laid out a prescribed way of ordering the world and curbing the imagination. In fact, he sought to establish ownership of utopia [through his theme parks] ... [but they] were nothing but a continuation of degenerated notions of utopia in the fairy-tale films ... they lead the viewer on a quest the *THAT? legitimates a reality of violence and injustice by making it appear, through fixed stereotypes and values fostering violence and exploitations, that contradictions can be reconciled through a collective fantasy, namely the sets of images that constitute a Disney fairy-tale film [Zipes, 2011, 25].

By repeating the Disney formula, animated movies have developed a standardized pattern that has influenced the medium being prescribed as a "children's genre" and has also made the animated film "lazy." Repackaging the same story over and over again reinforces the Disney belief system, but it also limits the animators' and writers' creativity. No matter how many times you change the formula's costumes, the same themes, archetypes, plot and characters are revealed when the mask is taken off. Replicating the formula stunts the fairytale genre's growth, which is contrary how the stories organically grew through the oral tradition hundreds of years before the Brothers Grimm had the notion to transcribe them.

The 1001 Arabian Nights, which inspired *Prinzen Achmed*, uses the "story within a story" motif or framed narrative, where the storyteller Scheherazade narrates one story a night for 1001 nights to prevent her sultan husband from beheading her. Scheherazade frames her stories so that one stems from another, sometimes even building intricate story webs within each other that would collapse without being shaped and changed. Reiniger continues with Scheherazade's tradition by altering tales from *1001 Arabian Nights* and transforming them into her own *Arabian Nights* epic.

The familiar Disney fairytales were adapted from stories that went through dozens of versions for centuries. Scholars have examined why the fairytales evolved the way they did. *Cinderella* is the most retold fairytale, with versions ranging from ancient Egypt to China, the common factor being a poor peasant gaining fortune and marriage with magic or luck. The prevalence of the Disney formula, however, stops the evolution and forces the said Disney version of classic fairytales to be taken as canon. It could be argued that the Disney Company expanded on their versions of the fairytales with the infamous sequels and original content made for franchise lines. The sequels were poorly received (dubbed "cheap-quels" in some circles for their low production budgets and story quality) and content derived from franchises, i.e., Disney Princesses, are thin veils for product placements; it's all an effort by the Mouse House to turn a quick profit. The sequels and franchise content exacerbate fairytale stagnation, because they don't add anything significant to the stories. Unlike the animated films, the spawned derivative works aren't made with the same high craftsmanship or story standards. They might continue the Disney fairytale after the credits roll, fulfilling a child's desire to experience more of their favorite character's adventures, but it's also indulging consumerism. The fairytales haven't evolved; instead they have devolved from promoting curiosity and intellect into marketable products made in Asia, sold at retail stores, and are putting a brand name on the imagination. Humanity's consciousness feeds off imagination and fairytales are very much the embodiment of the human consciousness, which is supposed to grow and adapt as humanity ages.

Fairytales and other stories are supposed to ignite the imagination, but when the Disney formula became even lazier with the cheap-quels, something had to be done. Robert Iger, John Lasseter and other higher-ups realized it. They so despised the cheap-quels that when Disney and Pixar merged in 2006, two of the conditions to the merger was to make Lasseter the chief creative officer of Walt Disney Animation, Pixar and DisneyToon Studios and end the mass-produced sequels, reinvesting the resources into more lucrative projects. When Lasseter took charge of Walt Disney Animation and DisneyToon Studios, he revamped the place and expressed his opinion on the sequels:

> His first aim, he says, was to make Disney Animation "a film-makers' studio" once again. How did he go about it? "I got rid of idiot executives. Disney had got away from quality," he claims. "Their currency seemed to be doing things to make a buck rather than quality." He doesn't stop there. Some of Disney's straight-to-DVD titles "sucked," he insists. "And I'm against making really bad sequels to movies that Walt Disney made at the height of his talent—which we were doing" [Gritten, 2009].

Despite the changes from the Pixar-Disney merger and alterations to the Disney formula,[9] its bones still remains the same. No one can deny the quality of Disney's animated movies that contributes to their longevity. As Catmull wrote in his book *Creativity Inc.*, "Disney Animation's embrace of the new would take on steam, ironically, when it finally figured out how to reframe and rethink: the fairy tale..." (2014, 271). The animation is always of the highest grade for its time (if not high quality for posterity) and if the stories have the same bones, they are altered enough to keep audiences flocking to the theaters and the parks.

While Disney is one of the main factors contributing to stunted fairytale growth, it hasn't stopped the fairytale movie from being an alluring genre to filmmakers. Zipes jokes:

[W]e must never forget that, just as drug addicts can save themselves through detoxification programs, the fairy-tale film—and the fairy-tale film in general—can save itself through de–Disneyfication programs, and perhaps we can also rescue ourselves and restore our vision so we can play with the fairy-tale and social reality on our own terms [2011, 26].

De-Disneyfication is happening in the fairytale genre as well with animated movies. Some of the leading causes are female animation fans who are calling for proactive, non-princess heroines, writers who reimagine the old tales free of Disney tropes, and entertainment studios searching for more original content. (While this always happens in Hollywood, the hunger for new ideas is stronger as audiences consume content at a higher rate with easier access via the Internet.) It is also pertinent to mention that the Internet paired with social media has allowed creators to express their own versions of fairytales and gaining notoriety.

Despite the arguments against the Disney formula, when it was first conceived it was original. Walt Disney wanted to create an animated film that would leave a huge impact, and it did. However, like many creators, he didn't know how large it would become. For a moment, think about Sir Arthur Conan Doyle's Sherlock Holmes stories. If you read them today, the stories are laid out like most modern crime and detective shows. Why? Because Doyle set the standards for detective fiction, which writers have been copying ever since. The same is true with most animated films with a fairytale theme.

Reiniger wrote her script in an effort comparable to Disney (or vice versa since she made her film first) in that she wanted to make something brand new. Beyond what Reiniger and Disney took for their inspiration, they both relied on fairytale adaptations, and their alternate animation styles pioneered storytelling methods within a new medium that altered the way audiences viewed the animation medium. Reiniger and Disney accepted the challenge of a different story required for an animated film, turning to one of the oldest story modes: the fairytale. They conceived new versions of older stories, following in the tradition of modifying a fairytale to suit the times, and received high praise for their efforts.

After viewing *Snow White*, a fan in France wrote to the French film magazine *Pour Vous*: "Not only does the film make its mark in the history of animation, but also, quite simply, in the history of cinema. This is a masterpiece that one must see many times … so as not to miss a single detail" (qt. in Smoodin, 2012, 7). The fan was referring to *Snow White*, but her phrases should also be applied to *Prinzen Achmed* as both films were prime accomplishments in the history of animation. While Disney won eight Academy Awards for *Snow White* (one normal-sized statue with seven complimentary miniature ones), Reiniger fell into the shadows and had her film blown to smithereens in World War II.

5

Sound Cartoons and Miscredited Ideas

> I have had a stubborn, blind confidence in the cartoon medium, a determination to show the skeptics that the animated cartoon was deserving of a better place; that it was more than a mere "filler" on a program; that it was more than novelty; that it could be one of the greatest mediums of fantasy and entertainment yet developed. That faith, confidence and determination and unselfish attitude has brought the cartoon to the place that it now occupies in the entertainment world.—Walt Disney (quoted in Barrier, 2007, 4)

Lotte Reiniger: Eine Dokumentation collects many of the *Prinzen Achmed* reviews. The critics praised her animation work, the story and characters, but amongst the general aplomb was confusion because they didn't know how to react to it. "*Die Geschichte des Prinzen Achmed* was considered unusual by reviewers, not because it presented a screen vision that had never yet been seen, but because it refigured the parameters within which cut paper silhouettes had been viewed in 1920s films. It crossed over from the sphere of the Institut für Kulturforschung's research-oriented into that of feature-length cinema [and a brand new use of the animation medium]" (Wizansky, 2004, 85). They were removed from their live-action comfort zones, placed in a silhouette world and asked to suspend their disbelief that animation could be longer and not strictly comedic.

The reactions to *Prinzen Achmed* are comparable to how U.S. audiences responded in 2000 to Studio Ghibli's *Princess Mononoke* (1997), directed by Hayao Miyazaki. They couldn't separate animation from the children's genre notion and many parents took their children to the theater expecting a family-friendly film; after all, the title had "princess" in it. *Princess Mononoke* is a mature film with scenes featuring graphic depictions of blood, violence and death related to an environmentalist theme. The parents, needless to say, left the theater, because they weren't able to wrap their heads around the concept of an animated film portraying realistic violence or the idea of an animated film with a thought-provoking message about life. Neil Gaiman adapted *Princess Mononoke*'s script for the American dub, produced by Disney's Miramax. He said about the film's differences, "The biggest thing this film is going to have to overcome is the idea of the limitations of animation. You can compare it to [British director] David Lean or [Japanese director Akira] Kurosawa with much more ease than you can to Disney. It's not a film aimed at children. It has a complicated world view, complex people with complex problems and things to be overcome" (qt. in Ealy, 1999). Hayao Miyazaki thought differently about his film:

> Miyazaki says he doesn't think *Princess Mononoke* will frustrate older children, should parents let them see it. "They will understand it intuitively." Miyazaki says he made the film, in part, because "the greatest burden to children ... is that they take out their aggressions on themselves and on others and that they don't have a good understanding of how to manage and control this terrible aggression.
> "Children can't articulate this by themselves, and that's the biggest problem that confronts them," he says. "*Princess Mononoke* is an attempt to help them articulate. Just making films that say, 'You should grow up and be happy and hopeful,' well, children aren't going to fall for that. If we don't want to continue to feed children a bundle of lies, then we have to make such films" [qt. in Ealy, 1999]

Prinzen Achmed didn't have as heavy a message as *Princess Mononoke*, but it did have the burden of being compared to kitsch:

> Reviewing the premiere of *Die Geschichte des Prinzen Achmed* at UFA's Gloria Palast Theater, the critic began by describing his initial skepticism about the artistic possibilities of visual forms from the realm of mass produced kitsch: "[O]ne thinks of bad picture postcards, and of saccharine book illustrations." Other reviews characterized silhouettes as poor relations of miniature painting and tied hand-cut silhouettes and silhouette puppetry to spheres conventionally associated with non-critical visual art practices, including pre-war German parlor culture, and Asian and Middle Eastern shadow play [Wizansky, 2004, 86].

Critic Freddy Chevalley commented on the film's length, the same problem Walt Disney faced with *Snow White* 11 years later, "Films of purely visual interest, in which life manifests itself only under appearances far removed from reality, provoke a nervous tension which becomes the more pronounced the longer the projection" (Russett & Starr, 1976, 75). A similar observation was published in *Vorwärts*: "Everything is an artificial world, but with the story it is the only way the film could have been realized. For the audience, it is very tiring and difficult to follow such a film, which always provides new and unfamiliar stimuli..." (1969/1926, 53).

Despite some critics not comprehending Reiniger's pioneering ambitions, many were amazed that she and her team were able to tell a story with shadows and mesmerizing special effects. A renowned German publicist wrote,

> At a time when German film is struggling, Lotte Reiniger presents her great shadow feature of several acts. At times, when it has become doubtful that her traditional ways alone will accomplish something, Lotte Reiniger is breaking new ground. An attempt? An exploration and an experiment? More than that: the consistent execution of revolutionary ideas.... This film is visual poetry, a miracle to be experienced, as exciting as it is artful [qt. in Schönfeld, 2006, 176].

L. Steffens wrote for the *Die Weltbühne* newspaper a minimalist review that expresses the adventurous depth Reiniger wanted her audience to experience:

> People skeptically enter the Zuckerguss Palast on Kurfürstendamm. Silhouettes [make] them think of bad postcards, on mellifluous book illustrations. The film starts. They're not used to seeing silhouettes in movies. So they're initially tired [of seeing them]. But gradually they become increasingly excited, delighted and enraptured. They love, suffer, fight with the hero; fairytales that used to go in one ear and out the other live again. Yes, as they used to read and experience in childhood's long lost land. Yes, that was it, so it must have been, and if I never knew, magicians can turn into bats and escape through barred windows—now I know it; so and not otherwise ... [1969/1926, 55].

The New York Times published the Herman G. Scheffauer article "New Shadow Film Enriches the Screen: Arabian Nights' Story Lives" in 1926, one of the rare U.S. publicity items during the film's first circulation. Scheffauer eschewed the usual film review in favor of an educational piece that provided a first-hand account from Reiniger about her animation process before it transitions into a poetic compliment that fits within the film's romantic quality. He wrote:

> There have been shadow and silhouette films before, but *The Story of Prince Achmed* is praised as the most ambitious and successful effort of the sort that has yet been undertaken.... The complication of movements simultaneous and differentiated, proved almost appalling, and demanded from Miss Reiniger an almost celestial patience. Some conception of the wearying detail of the process may be gained from the fact that some fifty-two separated exposures were necessary to make a section of film.... The grace, beauty and magic of this amalgamated tale of Prince Achmed ... is something that releases in us a distinct esthetic sensation and makes us feel that new territory in the realm of the future's possibilities. A new form of expression has been achieved.... The movements of the figures are, of course, as close to human as possible; but the mere manner of manipulation brings about a certain slowness and dignity of movement, a conventionalization of step or gesture, which leads additional charm to these products of scissors and movie-camera.... As moderns we may admire the dexterity and subtlety by means of which these fairy-like effects are achieved, but it is as children that we can enter into the spirit that produced this piece of art, and it is only as children that we can realize the real power and significance of an old world recreated in such a form that is once more new. It is, in fact, only the resuscitation of a young immortal world in a world that is perhaps growing old [1926, SM6].

General audiences were enthralled and in Paris the film was held over for months. They were even more astounded that it took so long to make *Die Abenteuer des Prinzen Achmed*, but Reiniger, Bartosch and Ruttmann's constant experimentation to invent new techniques and the tedious animation process were brand new and it took time to perfect the film's effects and style. Reiniger and Koch's friend Bertolt Brecht "had expressed a similar idea, noting approvingly that *Die Geschichte des Prinzen Achmed* was the product of collaborative effort by artistic individuals, who were not earning wages from the national film industry. Brecht felt that this alone endowed it with cultural significance irrespective of its questionable ability to survive the economic pressures of the film production and distribution system and the tastes of the typical film spectator" (Wizansky, 2004, 90). Jean Renoir's lifelong friendship with Koch and Reiniger blossomed from the French premiere; the director became obsessed with the film. Randolph T. Weaver documented Renoir's enthusiasm for *Prinzen Achmed* and it reads like a modern-day description of an excited fan:

> I came to know of [Prince Achmed] through Jean Renoir ... and his wife [Catherine Hessling], who had just gone into the movies and were enthusiastic about the art and everything connected with it. As beginners their enthusiasm was naturally as lively as it was sincere, and I was rather inclined to discount their exuberance when they told me one day about their discovery of the Prince. They could talk of nothing else. They had violent discussions about him, his qualities and defects, his portrayal, his makeup, the scenes he had played in, the success of his interpretation [1931, 505].

Accounts vary about the financial success of *Prinzen Achmed*, Louis Hagen, Jr., said, "From a financial standpoint it was a disaster. It only began to pay its way fifty years later" (qt. in Raganelli, 1999).

Reiniger and Koch did make a nice profit off the film and Hagen financed a trip to Egypt from December 1926 to February 1927. Reiniger was impressed by the Egyptian art: "Looking at the works of the ancient Egyptian artists, revealed in them is the purest and most pronounced profile art that was ever created.... [T]his perception incessantly worked on me" (Happ, 2004, 28). She was similarly touched by art when she and Koch traveled to Greece in 1936, noting how the ancient artists mastered the art of the silhouette:

> What did the master artists of the past have to give the outline more expression? We see Egyptian reliefs and the Greek vases, they are the acknowledged masters of the art profile. Behold, they have found the solution! They show [the face and] the feet in the profile, but they also show the two shoulders, and thus both arms, thereby broadening the expressive ability. We want to imitate them [Happ, 2004, 29].

Rejuvenated and inspired by the ancient artists, Reiniger and Koch returned to Germany. After their trip, she probably began work on silhouette special effects for producer-director Friedrich Zelnik's 1927–28 film *Heut' tanzt Mariette* (*Marietta's Dancing Day*) (Moritz, 1996a, 22). Zelnik specialized in period operetta movies and promoted his ballet dancer wife's acting career by casting her as the leading lady in films opposite popular male stars. In *Heut' tanzt Mariette*, Harry Halm was her love interest (Bock, 2009, 548). She also worked on a short film, *Grotesken im Schnee*[1] (*Cartoons in the Snow*), in Berlin 1928 with her avant-garde filmmaker friend Alex Strasser. A montage of winter activities, it features stop-motion, silhouette and live action footage (Mebold, 2008, 19).

Reiniger's second full-length animated project was a six-film series based on the British children's author Hugh Lofting's *Dr. Dolittle* books. GM BH Berlin produced the films and Reiniger worked on the first three from September 1927 to September 1928. The films had their world premiere in December 15, 1928, at the Alhambra in Berlin. The entire film series was titled *Dr. Dolittle und seine Tiere* (*Dr. Dolittle and His Animals*) and the individual film chapters were "Die Reise nach Afrika" ("The Journey to Africa"), "Die Affenbrücke" ("The Monkey Bridge" or "In Cannibal Land") and "Die Affenkrankheit" ("The Monkey Illness" or "In the Lion's Den"). It was originally released as three different films, but Louis Hagen helped Reiniger combine the three into one 25-minute film.

Dr. Dolittle und seine Tiere is about the famous veterinarian who can walk and talk with animals. It opens with a preface that explains the animation process in hopes to further compliment the "illusion of life":

> The characters in this little comedy have no real existence. They have been designed and cut out of a sheet of black paper and are made to move on backgrounds lit from below and photographed from above. This brief explanation is not offered as an apology for their lack of life but to make you marvel that they have so much.

In Reiniger's version of Lofting's story, intertitles explain the action and the translator was kind enough to make the titles rhyme in English. The first chapter starts with Dr. Dolittle living in a house with his animal companions: a duck, a parrot, a crocodile, a dog, an ape and a pig. One day a swallow informs the doctor about an epidemic befalling all the apes in Africa. Dr. Dolittle packs his medical bag and he sails to Africa. In a storm, the ship is smashed against rocks. Dr. Dolittle and his animal friends survive and reach the shore. The second chapter picks up with Dr. Dolittle and his companions travelling to the apes' home. Cannibals capture all but the parrot. The parrot plays a tennis match against the chief's son and helps the prisoners escape, which is followed by a chase that ends at a gorge. The apes appear and form a bridge for Dr. Dolittle and the animals to cross and flee the cannibals. Chapter three places Dr. Dolittle and his friends in the apes' homeland, where all types of simians await medical treatment. The task seems impossible for the doctor to accomplish alone, but other animals want to assist the apes as well. The lion, king of the jungle, doesn't want his subjects to help Dr. Dolittle and he chases them away. Things change quickly when the lion's son gets a thorn stuck in his paw and requires Dr. Dolittle's attention. Dr. Dolittle removes the thorn and the lion allows the other animals to help with treating the sick apes.[2]

Bartosch worked his special effects magic on the *Dr. Dolittle* films by animating the snowstorm and the sea voyages. He parted ways with Reiniger and Koch in 1930 (White, 1931, 24): Moving to Paris, he married and began working on *L'Idée* (*The Idea*), his most famous work. *L'Idée* was an experimental and technological animation film that clocked in at 30 minutes and used 45,000 frames. It was based on Franz Massereel's allegorical book (consisting of 83 wood block prints—one of the earliest graphic novels) about an idea's life: it's birth, propagation and eventual suppression. Bartosch took two years to animate *L'Idée* and he released it in 1932 (Russett & Starr, 1976, 84).

Reiniger shared her thoughts on Bartosch and *L'Idée* at a 1936 London lecture concerning cartoons of the '20s and '30s. She stated that *L'Idée* was the best film demonstrating the use of special effects in animation as well as telling a story about a serious topic (Happ, 2004, 31). She also noted that Bartosch had outgrown her animation group: "[H]e was too much of an independent personality to be content … in the shadow of my productions. We were indeed very sad to lose him, but we were very relieved and happy that he finally started something of his own (Happ, 2004, 31)." One can imagine that after being acquainted with the biggest names in German animation (Viking Eggeling, Hans Richter and Oskar Fischinger), Bartosch was restless and ready to animate his own stories (Russett & Starr, 1976, 84).

Paul Dessau arranged the music for the films, using original compositions he wrote as well as pieces from Igor Stravinsky and Paul Hindemith (Happ, 2004, 29). Audiences were keen to see Reiniger's next film and critics had accepted the new cinematic art. Upon viewing *Dr. Dolittle*, writer Hans Sahl shared his impressions:

> An artistic event. Lotte Reiniger animated the *Dr. Dolittle* story … in the custom manner of the subtle silhouette fairytale delicacy. She has perfected the technique of paper cutting. The animals' movements fabulously flow, hover, flutter, dissolve and disappear into each image. It is a childlike colorful, drawing filled world of symbols…. It is a shadow art that bewitches with the simple and lively picture book allegories [qt. Happ, 2004, 29].

The magazine *Close Up* reviewed her films as well:

> [Reiniger's Dr. Dolittle films] have been shown in Berlin with very great success. The decorative effect and the mood of these three films is a delightful harmony, full of constant surprises, not the least of which is the contrast in feeling and execution to *Prince Achmed*, her former experiment, with which most people are familiar…. If we miss the astral mysticism of the Unknown Lands in *Achmed*, we are recompensed by the richer, more kindly shapes of the Dolittle *ménage*. The fantasy has mirth and gaiety. It is less frail, less intricately spun than the fantasy of *Achmed*. There is nothing dour or frightening…. The Dolittle films will please everybody. Their charm is quite effervescent [1929, 97].

Dr. Dolittle even impressed the famous critic Rudolf Arnheim:

> It is not easy to bring fairy tales to life because the magical power, with which children imagine stories, is far too easily weakened by every picture. The magical technique of film alone hardly touches the sovereign buoyancy of young fantasy; in the lovely story tale films of Starewitsch (1), the most artfully construed animals have something terribly robotic about them—uncanny, somnambulant machines. Lotte Reiniger uses the ideal technique: the silhouette film. The silhouette is not as close to reality as a plastic thing, yet is perceived so fantastically; thus it enshrines from the audience, especially the children, the horror that ensues when fairy tale things become, up to a certain point of clarity, a tangible reality. The mobile silhouettes maintain, with charm, just the right boundary between

art product and life; one believes enough to be spellbound, and one does not quite believe enough to get goosebumps by experiencing the supernatural [1969/1928, 5].

Despite praise, the film was unsuccessful and Reiniger attributed her first relative failure to the advent of sound cinema (Jouvanceau, 2004, 44). GM BH Berlin didn't provide Reiniger with funds to finish the remaining three films; the company felt it wasn't economically feasible and halted production, probably due to the new talkies. Reiniger was upset by this news, because she had already made the silhouette puppets and film designs. This also left *Dr. Dolittle und seine Tiere* ending on a cliffhanger, alluding to more adventures that were never animated.

Dr. Dolittle wasn't Reiniger's only adventure with Hugh Lofting's work. She illustrated *Der böse Gutsherr und die guten Tiere*, a German translation of his *The Story of Mrs. Tubbs* (1923).

During production of the *Dr. Dolittle* films, Koch and Reiniger's friend Bertold Brecht visited them. At the time, he was creating his famous *Threepenny Opera* with Kurt Weill. Koch, Reiniger, Bartosch and Brecht were good friends, so after the first two *Dolittle* films were finished in April 1928, they decided to vacation together and went to southern France, Marseille and Bandol in June 1928 (Happ, 2004, 31). During the trip, they reacquainted themselves with Jean Renoir and watched him work on his short film *La Petite Marchande d'allumettes* (*The Little Matchstick Girl*). While Koch and Reiniger worked on the third *Dr. Dolittle* film, *The Threepenny Opera* opened on August 31, 1928, in the Theater am Schiffbauerdamm and they celebrated with Brecht early in the morning when the first positive reviews appeared in the papers (Happ, 2004, 31). Reiniger cut scherenschnitte pieces depicting scenes from the opera for Brecht and they were displayed in the Theater am Schiffbauerdamm and later illustrated a newspaper article (Happ, 2004, 32).

Between *Prinzen Achmed* and *Dr. Dolittle*, Reiniger made another film, *Der scheintote Chinese* (*The Seemingly Dead Chinaman*). Originally it was intended to be a *Prinzen Achmed* segment, but it was cut from the already long film (White, 1931, 15). Reiniger also wanted to include a pair of men kissing, so children would view homosexuality as a natural occurrence rather than a shameful act (Osmond, 2011, 10). Christel Strobel wrote that it was a minor work between two of Reiniger's bigger projects; the character development and subtle humor were affected (Strobel). The nine-minute *Der scheintote Chinese* is about the emperor's favorite, spoiled Ping Pong. One day he ventures outside the court and causes a huge scene. An older couple invite him to share a meal with them to stop him from creating more of a ruckus, but he accidentally swallows a fishbone and dies. The older couple pass the body off to a doctor and his assistant, who in turn dump Ping Pong on a drunk and a miser. The miser and the drunk are taken to the gallows. Feelings of guilt overwhelm the doctor and the old couple. Each person orders the hangman to kill him or her. Suddenly Ping Pong coughs up the bone and lives.

The Weimar years were rife with creative artists, including those in Reiniger and Koch's circle, who tried their hand at different media. Brecht experimented with projects outside his operatic discipline and he created *Badener Lehrstück vom Einverständnis* (*The Baden-Baden Lesson on Consent*), which world-premiered on July 28, 1929. It was a musical multimedia piece with a film Carl Koch directed, *The Dance of Death*, a dance number with Valeska Gert. Brecht also wanted Reiniger to make a silhouette film for him and he specifically wrote a piece for her, *The Kaffessackschmeisser*. The sequence was cut because of heightened political tensions (Happ, 2004, 33).

Reiniger was also drawn to explore different film experimentation avenues. While she remained dedicated to silhouette animation, she had an idea for a live action film. Koch, Reiniger and Bartosch visited Renoir, she explained her film idea to him and the group came to the conclusion that it was the perfect time to turn it into a film (Happ, 2004, 33). Alex Strasser[3] is credited with inventing the concept with Reiniger and he also joined the writing team. It would be called *Die Jagd nach dem Glück* (*The Pursuit of Happiness* or *Chasing Luck* or *Running After Luck*) and it would feature an international cast: Russian Alexander Murski, French Catherine Hessling and Jean Renoir, German Berthold Bartosch and the American Amy Wells. Rochus Gliese co-directed the film with Koch and Reiniger; she and Koch also wrote the script with Gliese. Alex Strasser joined the group and famous cinematographer Fritz Arno Wagner (he worked on *M, Nosferatu* and *Das Testament des Dr. Mabuse*) manned the camera. Theo Mackeben wrote an original musical accompaniment for it (White, 1931, 28). The film was a metaphor for destiny, life and the history of film. Reiniger described *Die Jagd nach dem Glück*'s theme: "This is a story that tells of the film's ancestral state. From the static image to the transition of moving pictures.... It is in its simplicity a symbol of all life" (Happ, 2004, 33). She gave a less metaphorical description in another interview: "A young couple hitches up with a show booth owner who is exhibiting wax works of Napoleon, Charlie Chaplin, and the Goddess Fortuna. After a while they plan a new sensation, a shadow theater, replacing the stiff old, wax figure cabinet. In the end they succeed" (qt. in Raganelli, 1999).

The silent film is "a love story set in the milieu of a carnival shadow-puppet theater" and consists of live action scenes shot in Ciotat, France, and two silhouette films Reiniger made at her Potsdam studio (Moritz, 1996b, 42; Happ, 2004, 34). Everything was set for *Die Jagd nach dem Glück* to be a success, but it was a bomb. It premiered in Berlin on May 27, 1930, and closed soon after. Reiniger, Renoir and Koch hadn't speculated that a silent film would fare so badly, despite the failure with *Dr. Dolittle*.[4] Silent movies were no longer popular with the advent of sound. Audiences raved about "talkies" and were eager to hear actors speak in sync with the pictures on the screen. *Die Jagd nach dem Glück* "was converted into a sound film using the voices of professional actors, but the lip-synch was far from perfect, and though critics praised Reiniger's script, direction, and animation, the film couldn't compete with the sharp, elaborate UFA musical [*The Love Waltz*] or the impressive ... war film, *The Last Company* [or *Thirteen Men and a Girl*], which opened in the weeks preceding Reiniger's feature" (Moritz, 1996b, 42). The two silhouette sequences would be removed from the film. They were later shown at the London Film Society, but the remainder of the film is now lost (Happ, 2004, 34).

Reiniger's silhouette segments demonstrate the lengths of creativity and how she stepped outside her wheelhouse to animate a compelling story without a fairytale theme. The 19-minute segment features a personified Lady Luck costumed as a ballerina with a bouquet of flowers. As she dances across the globe, she bestows her flower petals on a selected few. She happens to grace a young man with her petals, but she quickly leaves him and he decides to chase Lady Luck around the world, despite already having a loving paramour. As the young man chases Lady Luck, she bestows her gifts on other people, swiftly eluding her pursuer whenever he draws too close. The young man returns home to his steadfast love and she accepts him without hesitation. Lady Luck entices him once more, but he leaves her behind and Luck decides to bless him with one of her flowers. The last intertitle contains one large word, SLUT, pointing out Lady Luck's fickleness and

5. Sound Cartoons and Miscredited Ideas 97

Reiniger's sense of humor. The young man's pursuit is narrated with quaint poem that doesn't include a line about the happy ending.

> Happiness around the globe does blissfully dance stopping whenever she fancies a glance.
> A young man is very lonesome. Yet he longs for a harmonious twosome.
> But the moment is a fleeting one, and happiness is so quickly gone.
> Happiness, however, shows its graces to he who awaits with patient pace.
> Of Happiness we are often oblivious even when it's right behind us.
> No path too steep, no leap too far, happiness he chases unyieldingly in his car.
> He begins to think Fortune must reside, in faraway lands he has not yet espied.
> In quiet corners now and then happiness loves to bring joy to men.
> Happiness can do as it doth please, the hardest chore is a breeze.
> Happiness oft follows the rich man, who has something to offer his fan.
> Now and again Happiness has a foible, for brute strength and toil.
> Off he goes to battle, Hoping Happiness will help him prove his mettle.
> Exhausted he quits the game, for too much and in vain.
> Pursue happiness with fervour galore, return empty-handed and sore.

Motion pictures would forever be changed with the addition of sound. Rather than relying on intertitles, exaggerated acting techniques and recorded or live music to convey the story, audiences were introduced to the wonderful cacophony of vocal talents and whatever foley artists could dish out of their sound closets. Warner Brothers' *The Jazz Singer* revolutionized live action films, but animation still relied on the old-fashion silent film sound tricks. Walt Disney's *Steamboat Willie*, which premiered on November 18, 1928, would do for animation what *The Jazz Singer* did for live action features. *Steamboat Willie* is not the first sound cartoon; the Fleischer brothers had been using music in their sing-along *Song Car Tunes* since 1924 with the Phonofilm system and they initiated the first vocal synchronization in the cartoon *My Old Kentucky Home* in 1926 (Solomon, 1994, 40; Lee & Madej, 2012, 36). The first cartoon character to speak on screen was a dog who told viewers to, "Follow the ball, and join in, everybody." Paul Terry announced his synchronized sound cartoon on August 18, 1928, although it premiered on September 1, named *Dinner Time*, Terry's cartoon was part of his *Aesop's Fables* series and used the RCA Photophone to match a vocal track with the animation and play orchestral music in the background (Crafton, 1993, 211). It included the cartoon character to speak on screen, it was a dog who told viewers to, "Follow the ball, and join in, everybody." Disney was granted a special sneak preview of *Dinner Time* and his reaction was less than positive:

> In a letter to Roy Disney and Ub Iwerks, he exclaimed "MY GOSH—TERRIBLE—A lot of racket and nothing else. I was honestly disappointed. I really expected to see something half-way decent. BUT HONESTLY—it was nothing but one of the rottenest fables I believe that I ever saw, and I should because I have seen almost all of them. It merely had an orchestra playing and adding some noises. The talking part does not mean a thing. It doesn't even match. We sure have nothing to worry about from these quarters" [qt. in Crafton, 1993, 211–212].

Disney was never one to mask his true opinion and he used his competition's failures to bolster his own success. While *Steamboat Willie* isn't the first sound cartoon, it is the first to show the amazing possibilities for sound cartoons. What makes Disney really notable with sound cartoons was his drive to "master sound technology for its own sake" and he was able to do so as an independent filmmaker (Crafton, 1993, 212). Other studios, such as Van Buren, Mintz and once more the Fleischer Brothers, would release their own sound cartoons, as they too had been experimenting with sound, but Disney would remain the undisputed animation leader in American animation (Crafton, 1993, 212). Eric Walter White wrote, "The important discovery made by Walt Disney in his cartoon films concerns the unexpected relations that exist between visual and aural phenomena" (1931, 28–29). After *Steamboat Willie*, it seemed that Walt Disney had a plethora of opportunities waiting for him, but animator Wilfred Jackson remembered Disney said to him in 1928, "Some day I'm going to make a cartoon as good as a Fable" (qt. in Barrier, 2007, 67). Michael Barrier wrote that this "was not much of an ambition. Paul Terry's *Fables* were furiously busy cartoons, but that was about all" (Barrier, 2007, 67). It demonstrates that Disney didn't have limitless confidence and admired his fellow animators' works, but it also fueled his relentless pursuit to be the best cartoon producer and employ new and better techniques than his colleagues. As for silent films and cartoons, Solomon eloquently wrote, "When Mickey Mouse whistled 'Steamboat Bill' in the opening scene, he unwittingly sounded the death knell of the silent era in American animation" (1993, 41).

It is more apt to say that Mickey Mouse whistled a tune that resounded around the world and became the first note on synchronized soundtracks for animation. By making *Die Jagd nach dem Glück,* Reiniger learned a lesson about the sound's future importance for the animation medium. In hindsight, it is better that she suffered a disappointment on an experimental film, rather than one of her more popular silhouette animations. Had Reiniger made an animated silhouette film and the sound was an afterthought in the production (thusly very poor quality and not matching the standards of her animation skill), her career might have ended. Reiniger, however, was a huge music fan, especially of Mozart's operas, an obsession that dated back to her student days at Max Reinhardt Drama School.

She was aware that she would have to adapt her films to remain appealing to audiences. A factor working against her was that her silhouettes lacked the rubber hose and elastic body movements and electric expressions of other animated films. While puppets can convey emotion with a slight angle of the head, body movements or mouth gesture, silhouettes can lack the emotional depth due to static blackness and lack of discernible facial features. (Up until Jim Henson revisualized puppetry design in the 1960s with Don Sahlin and Kermit Love, puppets were traditionally made using methods that dated back hundreds of years. The puppets lacked the ability to move their faces, unless it was a ventriloquist's dummy. Audiences had more to focus on if the puppet wore a costume, had a face, and was painted.) It takes a master hand to guarantee that lifeless and emotionless black silhouette puppets convey the illusion of emotion and life, which Reiniger had mastered by 1930. Reiniger realized that music and sound could only augment her silhouette films. She had been aware of the importance of sound when she worked with Wolfgang Zeller to create a musical score for *Die Abenteuer des Prinzen Achmed.*

Reiniger adjusted her animation process to make music a more integral part. "Before I had to work out the action in a movie and then search for the right music. Today I first look for the music and then [animate] the appropriate action" (qt. in Happ, 2004, 36). In the fall of that year, she animated *Zehn Minuten Mozart* (*Ten Minutes of Mozart*) and partnered with Zeller to provide a compilation of "Eine kleine Nachtmusik" and an operatic duet from *Così fan tutte*. It was planned to be the first in a series of *commedia dell'arte*-inspired films (White mentions the romantic pair in the film are Harlequin and Columbine); *Harlekin, Carmen* and *Papageno* complete the series. Her first sound film premiered on December 14, 1930, at the Film Society of London (White, 1931, 14–15, 21).

Reiniger crafted a sweet love story to the maestro's music: a young man sees a beau-

Lovers dance in *Zehn Minuten Mozart* (©Primrose Productions).

tiful girl attending a ball, but his bedraggled appearance bars his entry. The young man borrows a mask and cloak from a stranger and infiltrates the ball, discovering that the object of his affections has wandered out to the gardens. The pair sing a duet, the young man reveals himself and they venture back inside to dance.

Zehn Minuten Mozart was Reiniger's first attempt at merging silhouette animation with music. At this point, she had achieved more fluid grace with her figures: the puppets have lost their stilted movements noticeable in *Prinzen Achmed* and they move naturally across the screen. The music adds an evocative atmosphere, but it's off-putting when the young man and woman begin to sing the duet. While Reiniger's enchantment isn't broken, these two small, black silhouettes have grandiose voices booming from their small frames. Their bodies move appropriately to the lyrics' content, but their mouths don't move and the voices don't necessary reflect that bodies they "belong" too. The illusion carries on when the lovers return to the ball. While it's not perfect, *Zehn Minuten Mozart* does set a high standard. Reiniger commented, "I was proud to hear from those who make it their business to help German workers appreciate good music that these men have shown a marked preference for my film *Ten Minutes with Mozart*. Usually such people are bored by concerts and classical music; but they agreed that this film had made them understand and enjoy Mozart's music for the first time" (Reiniger, 1936b, 157).

Jouvanceau believes that silhouette films and sound repel each other, but Reiniger was never opposed to sound in her films (2004, 188). He points to the John Halas–Roger Manvells book *The Technique of Film Animation*, where Reiniger and Koch contributed a step-by-step list of their production process. From step one in her process, transcribed in Chapter 3, music is noted an integral part of her silhouette filmmaking. Reiniger takes into consideration how music affects her characters and setting, "We explore imaginary scenes or situations conjured up by the general atmosphere of the characters and setting, as well as, of course, the music." On what will please the audience: "We select those phases of the music that suit best the story treatment we are devising and contain the airs likely to be most familiar to our audience." How the music shapes the script: "Next, with the music in mind, we prepare a written script of our story" (1976, 279–80). Reiniger said in a 1979 interview, "With the talkies, [filmmaking] assumed a ballet-like character, and I liked that a lot, as I was interested in dance, and danced well in my youth. When I was at drama school, I had studied ballet and so on. So we made the opera-based material. I liked opera very much and I liked to make fun of it" (qt. in Marschall et al., 2012).

Once sound became a standard feature in films, Reiniger relied on it to supply the general atmosphere, if not the plot, of her films. I believe she preferred to rely on music, because of her love for opera and ballet, and it saved it from having to deal with the complexity of writing dialogue.

From May to July 1930, Koch and Reiniger visited Renoir in Fontainebleau. At this time, Renoir introduced Reiniger to the next theme for her silhouette films: *commedia dell'arte*, the classic Italian theater known for its masked stock characters and improvisation (Happ, 2004, 37). Randolph T. Weaver met Reiniger when he visited Renoir, and observed a makeshift tricktisch. Reiniger must have mentioned her permanent studio in Berlin and he wrote, "In Berlin she now has an elaborate equipment, set up in what she says is probably the smallest studio in the world. It is hardly larger than a clothes closet, but unfortunately it is the best she can afford" (1931, 507).

Inspired by *commedia dell'arte*, Reiniger animated *Harlekin* (*Harlequin*) in early 1931. When Reiniger lived in London in 1936, she explained her thoughts when making *Harlekin*: "I tried to show my love for music of the seventeenth and eighteenth century and the *commedia dell'arte*, which I had always been attracted to as the basis of the whole theater life, and the immortal characters have inspired film artists since then" (qt. in Happ, 2004, 39).

Throughout this time, Koch and Reiniger had maintained their friendship with the English teacher from Louis Hagen's private school, Eric Walter White. In 1931, White published *Walking Shadows*, an essay about Reiniger's silhouette films, through Leonard and Virginia Woolf Press. It was one of the few works in English about her. White wrote a few years later that *Harlekin* "with its rich and highly concentrated plot demanded a period musical accompaniment of the utmost discretion, one of that should preserve the atmosphere and underline the action, but never assert its own intrinsic aesthetic independence" (1936, 8). The music would, in fact, be a figural part, but not overwhelm it or even be the main reliance for story communication.

Harlekin's story follows romantic hero Harlequin as he attempts a series of illicit affairs. He watches the beautiful Columbine bathing and after an unsuccessful wooing attempt he falls in love with her. Columbine works as a maid in La Signora's household. La Signora is being courted by the pompous Pantalone; La Signora spurns Pantalone's suit, but Harlequin helps the rejected lover by delivering a note to her. La Signora believes the note is from the king and prepares to visit him, but she is attacked by bandits. Meanwhile, Harlequin has won Columbine's heart and they sneak off for a *tête-à-tête*. One of La Signora's servants escaped the bandits and runs to them for help. Harlequin bargains for La Signora's release and wins her affections at the same time. Columbine is dismayed, but Harlequin rejects La Signora and they reunite at the regal's lady home. La Signora faints when she sees Columbine and Harlequin. Pantalone witnesses the event and accuses

Harlequin of treachery. La Signora falls in love with Pantalone, while Harlequin is taken to court and sentenced to death. Columbine defends him to no avail and he is shot in the chest. All of Harlequin's romantic interests mourn his death, but none more than Columbine and she yells at the judge for his harsh sentence. The devil comes to claim Harlequin's soul, but an angel comes down from Heaven and brings him back to life, much to Columbine's delight.

Following *Harlekin,* Reiniger set her sights on another opera, Bizet's *Carmen.* She animated *Carmen* from April to May 1933. Little did she know that *Carmen* would become the first of many conflicts she and Koch would have with the growing Nazi party.

Despite the negative rumblings from the Nazi upstarts, sound innovation allowed Reiniger to marry her love for music with her dark silhouettes. Her silhouette films were filled with the illusion of life that animation is supposed to mimic, but despite the beautiful frills and minute details, the addition of sound to films rendered her work as only simplistic black figures captured on film. Reiniger needed the glory of sound to add a new layer to her work, and also demonstrate to audiences that within her characters, depths of complex emotion were hidden. Reiniger embraced sound and her love for music came into play as it led her to experiment with different composers and operas.

Reiniger was raised at the turn of the century in Berlin, one of Europe's cultural epicenters. During the Golden Twenties, the Weimar Republic attracted artists from around the globe interested in infusing their paintings, films and music with Berlin's modern sensibilities. While Weimar culture is noted for its revolutionary cinematic achievements, musicians experimented with new techniques (headed by Paul Dessau, Kurt Weill, Arnold Schoenberg, Hanns Eisler and Alban Berg) that laid the groundwork for modern musical compositions. The new wave musicians maintained strong ties to classic German composers and it was reflected in their work. Reiniger was exposed to renowned classical composers as well as musicians who thrived during the Weimar Republic and later gained the same status as their forbearers. She wasn't opposed to the popular music of times, but her personal tastes favored the classical composers over their modern brethren.

While new sounds floated on radio waves, silent movies were shot lacking a syncopated soundtrack, but they were hardly a quiet affair. Most theaters had a house band or orchestra or a pianist, but the "audience of a silent film would very possibly hear a different accompaniment to the same film in a different cinema, or even from one screening to the next; in each case it would hear a continuous musical accompaniment which bore a loose relationship with the narrative" (Davison, 2004, 19). For larger productions, studios did attempt to have special scores with musical cues sent around to theaters along with the movie reels, "signaling a first attempt by studios to take control of the music which accompanied the exhibition of their films" (Marks qt. in Davison 2004, 19). Unless a theater owner took particular interest in playing the same original music each time a film played, sound wasn't deemed important.

That perspective changed in the mid–1920s when studios became aware of a marketing opportunity to cash in on the special scores. "When savvy producers discovered that sheet music was a nifty marketing tool for their pictures—and sometimes produced a hit—they urged composers to incorporate tunes specifically written either for the score or as pure promotion for the picture" (Burlingame, 2001, 1). These often yielded hit songs and it is a trend that still continues with modern soundtracks (Pallant, 2011, 22).

Filmmakers were unaware of how sound could texturize their work, but Reiniger played with sound for her films and knew that music added an extra dimension to them. Her theatrical background and being a musical fan demonstrated the power music could have and when teamed with a film it gave audiences a more powerful experience. For *Prinzen Achmed*, she worked with Wolfgang Zeller to score original music in a forebear to the modern soundtrack. One could say that Reiniger had unknowingly been waiting for the marriage of film and sound, so she could direct an animated musical or an animated opera.

One of the biggest differences between Walt Disney and Reiniger lays in their approach to sound and most of it is due to cultural perspectives. Reiniger's German cultural identity leaned more towards opera and classical music, while Disney's work, fueled by the young American culture, reflected more jazz, Dixie, blues and even rock'n'roll genres combined with classical music and musical numbers that set the standard for the modern movie musical. Disney was a fan of classical musicals, he just spun the pieces to his own tune and added animated stories, best exemplified by *Fantasia* (1940) and *Silly Symphonies* (1929–1939).

Walt Disney and his studio have had the monopoly on animated musicals from the moment Mickey Mouse's boat puttered across the screen with synchronized sound and set the pace for the genre when Snow White trilled her first musical note. Unlike Disney, Reiniger had the penchant to create original adaptations of pre-existing musical pieces, but the two animation pioneers were both triggered to write stories inspired by music. Disney employed in-house composers who wrote original numbers to accompany his films in a manner that mirrored live-action studios. Frank Churchill and Larry Morrell composed the songs for *Snow White and the Seven Dwarfs* (now iconic tracks on any Disney playlist) and Paul J. Smith and Leigh Harline wrote the incidental score.

While *Snow White and the Seven Dwarfs* was the first animated musical, movie musicals sang and danced across the screen since the advent of *The Jazz Singer*. Studios still released special movie musical scores, but "nobody thought to recommodify the songs, as performed in the film, in the form of a phonographic record" (Pallant, 2011, 22). Disney, ever the entrepreneur to make money to fund his next project (the studio had a habit of operating in the red), released the first soundtrack using actual soundtracks from *Snow White* (Pallant, 2011, 22–23). "The main reason that Disney had the confidence to release the *Snow White* original soundtrack was because it was from a family film, and children's fare was considered marketable" (Pallant, 2011, 23). It would further cement Disney's corner on the animated movie musical, but it would help imprint on audience's minds the notion that animation was a children's medium.

Reiniger worked closely with composers and musicians to create the perfect soundtrack for her films. She and Koch remained independent from the larger studios, so they never had an in-house composer at any of the studios they worked for or owned. Many of the composers who teamed with them were selected from friends and artistic communities they socialized within. Reiniger oversaw all the music that accompanied her films, adding a personal signature as well as an appreciation for the music. With *Zehn Minuten Mozart* she wrote her first original silhouette film since *Prinzen Achmed*.

While Reiniger paid special attention to the music that accompanied her silhouette films as a music and opera connoisseur, but after *Prinzen Achmed,* her films never again included an original soundtrack. She was more inclined to make her films around the music and prewritten stories that already accompanied them. Her creative imagination displayed itself as she reimagined the stories to fit her own desires as a writer, but it was also as if she was in charge of her own stage production of the shows.

5. Sound Cartoons and Miscredited Ideas

After the advent of sound and experimentation with *Prinzen Achmed* and *Zehn Minuten Mozart*, Reiniger stressed the importance music played in her animation process. In the early part of her career, the music became one of her starting points: she considered it wise "to have the sound track made first, measure it carefully and only commence the film after this has been done" (1936a, 15 & 18). Reiniger's "ideal musical state" was to complete the animation, then compose the music, but in her early career it wasn't economically feasible (1936a, 15). She later had this luxury, but in 1936 she predicted what later became an industry standard in regards to music: compose it after the animation is complete.

Music was a form of expression for both Disney and Reiniger. They were aware of how music conveyed moods, engaged the audience, and even acted as a storytelling tool. Both animators relied on "mickeymousing," but they had different goals with the process and using it to make their own versions of the "illusion of life." Disney used sound to imitate the "sound of life" augmented by music to create exciting cartoon adventures for his characters, while Reiniger wanted to capture a finer quality of life based on refined movement and traditional stories. Reiniger's use of music has a sophisticated air and preserves the idea of fine art, while Disney moved forward with testing the boundaries and creating a brand new art form. In other words, Reiniger was more traditional in her use of music, while Disney challenged musical convention.

Reiniger clung to her love for classical composers and opera, animating stories to augment the legendary music using the fascinating animation method. Reiniger said in one of her famous interviews,

> I have always been regarded with suspicion by the film trade, because I have never disguised my preference for eighteenth-century music. I have acted on the assumption that in the cinema this music would sound unusual and remote, churchlike to some, almost revolutionary to others, whereas actually it is as clear as water and underlines with perfect discretion the very formal style of silhouette movement and action [Reiniger, 1936b, 159].

She proved that the traditional art forms could be adapted to screen and entertain audiences, predating Warner Brothers' *The Rabbit of Seville* (1950) and *What's Opera, Doc?* (1957) with less cartoonish humor. Chuck Jones directed both of those cartoons. In an 1982 interview John Lewell told him, "In fact, animation is a logical development of Western Art, adding the element of movement to the artist's vocabulary." Jones responded, "That's true. But animation—and films in general—probably have more to do with music than other forms of graphic art. This is because animation is a series of visual impacts. Music is a series of auditory impacts. You hear notes in relation to other notes, and the same is true of film. It has a time factor. If you didn't retain the visual image, the accents wouldn't work" (Lewell, 1982, 133).

Jones and Reiniger followed the same string of musical notes as they both related the importance of music to animation. Jones loved the musical side, but he was more interested in making himself laugh, while Reiniger loved the stories and music. "[T]he real sensation for me has always been—and will always be—the discovery of various possibilities of screen rhythm which, to my experience, is the most essential part of film art. For here rules are to be found that have nothing to do with other arts and essentially belong to the screen, and the screen alone" (Reiniger, 1936a, 15). Jones loved pushing the animation boundaries, but his explorations were less poetic and more frank about entertaining than Reiniger.

With screen rhythm, Reiniger was referring to the literal movement of her silhouette puppets on her tricktisch's flat surface. This form is unique to the screen alone, because silhouette stop-motion animation makes shadows come alive without apparent human influence. Silhouettes and other puppets used in stop-motion are inanimate objects, but unlike hand-drawn cels or computer generated images, they exist in our relative environment as tangible objects. "The creator of trick-film movement can be compared with the choreographer of the ballet—only he has not the space of the stage, but the more flat conditions of the screen to consider" (Reiniger, 1936a, 15). A stop-motion animator must remain conscious of music on a different level than a traditional or computer animator, because while they control the environment, the puppets do not always obey and the environment is a huge concern. Reiniger drew a storyboard to document her puppets' every single action, match the music and avoid mistakes, while fresh problems arose as she filmed. The initial planning was "one of the most pleasant parts of the whole film" (Reiniger, 1936a, 18).

When Reiniger had studied to be an actress at Max Reinhardt's drama school, she took dance lessons. Although that potential career path never blossomed for her, Reiniger felt that the new sound films exhibited a different type of movement. Silent films became more realistic, but while Reiniger was able to escape the realism demand, she still had to change her silhouettes' movements to reflect it. She said that actors "may try to do justice to the change by singing and dancing; but ... they have lost the strong personal touch. A different kind of movement must be found to-day, and there the example of the ballet extending the human body to music is an excellent mentor and guide" (1936b, 159). She paid particular attention to how her puppets moved across the tricktisch's glass pane: noting how they fit within the frame, how different puppets were needed for different movements and dances, audiences' eye movements across the screen, and how to exploit linear directions for the best advantage (Reiniger, 1936b, 160–63). All these considerations were kept in mind when she animated to the music. Moving an animated character one tiny bit at a time might seem to be an easy, time-consuming process, but Reiniger took many factors into consideration such as music, movement, scenery, timing and more to make a cohesive film.

Technology pioneered or augmented for her silhouette films, especially the multiplane camera and tricktisch or animation desk, impacted animation history. Much like how *Snow White and the Seven Dwarfs* is often mistaken for the first animated film, Walt Disney is often credited as the inventor of the multiplane camera and animation desks, both invaluable tools in the animation industry until more advanced technology took over their functions.

The tricktisch's functions and importance to Reiniger's animation process were discussed in Chapter 3, especially how it streamlined the stop-motion animation technique. As for the multiplane camera, it projected false depth on two-dimensional drawings to give them a sense of existing in three-dimensions. In *Hollywood Cartoons*, Michael Barrier provides a simple but effective explanation of how a multiplane camera works:

> For multiplane scenes, the animation, background paintings, and overlay paintings might be on as many as six different levels, with the backgrounds and overlays painted on sheets of mounted glass a foot or more apart. As the camera trucked forward, different levels would come in and out of focus, as if they had been photographed by a live-action camera [Barrier, 1999, 249].

The above quotation refers to the first Disney cartoon to be filmed with the multiplane camera, *The Old Mill*, released by RKO in November 1937 one month before *Snow White*. What is ironic about the release and making of *The Old Mill* and *Snow White* is that from 1923 to 1926, Reiniger used a multiplane camera when she animated *Prinzen Achmed* (and possibly with her first film *Das Ornament des verliebten Herzens* [K.V. Taylor, 2011, 100]), but Disney historical records and marketing material sprinkle pixie dust on the camera and animation desk as if they were brand new inventions and had not been used by other animators for years.

The multiplane camera was an essential component of Reiniger's tricktisch, which was specifically designed to mount the camera and film the glass plates at varying distances. Reiniger drafted the blueprints for the tricktisch used to animate *Prinzen Achmed* and she continued to use the desk and similar designs until her death. (She mentioned having to leave behind her tricktisch when she fled Germany during World War II.)

Disney taking credit for the multiplane camera and the tricktisch is not a plagiarism case. At the same time Reiniger animated her film, Disney was occupied with running his Laugh-O-Gram Studios, subsequently losing the studio to bankruptcy, then establishing the Disney Brothers' Studio (later renamed the Walt Disney Company) and producing the *Alice* comedies. There isn't any recorded incident of Disney or his immediate team traveling to Germany, much less "spying" on Reiniger in her garage studio. The multiplane camera and animation desk is a case of simultaneous invention, where people invented similar devices within the same time frame. The early animation community was a small forum and animators were generally familiar with trends in their field through literature, film and shared correspondence or collaboration. Animators didn't exist in a vacuum and were given to experimentation to solve problems; after all, this was a brand new entertainment medium and most of the earliest animators are described as avant-garde or abstract so it is only natural to assume they came across the same solution. Ideas about how to improve the animation process, generate special effects, and how it could be used were free-flowing and absorbed by vested individuals. Similar knowledge allocation happened in other fields and people acted on it by creating an invention, process or theory. There are multiple cases of simultaneous invention, including the radio, modern flush toilet, calculus, theory of evolution, telephone and theory of relativity. It was only attributed to a person when they visited the patent office (or earned acclaim by the scientific community).

As for the development of the multiplane camera,[5] several technicians worked on the project but the first manager of the Disney Studio William "Bill" Garity (responsible for the sound in *Steamboat Willie*) is credited with developing Disney's multiplane camera. "'Bill Garity is an unsung hero of Disney history,' Dave Smith, Disney's chief archivist emeritus, once said. 'With his pioneering efforts in sound and camera techniques, he helped set Disney Studios apart from others, while his planning and supervisory expertise resulted in the building of a highly efficient studio in Burbank'" (qt. in D23). Garity was a technical mastermind and while he was the manager, he also became the de facto leader of the special effects department where he led 18 engineers to design and develop the Walt Disney cartoon (D23). His technical genius would also cause him to lead the team that developed Disney's version of the multiplane camera (D23; Thomas and Johnston, 1981, 264).

Walt wanted to make his first feature film as realistic as possible, so while he already had a patent for a mounted camera on a table he called the "Art of Animation," he needed a camera with more freedom to move (Smith, 1987, 40). Art director Ken Anderson remembered Walt discussing this issue as early as 1935 and he experimented with dimen-

April 23, 1940. W. E. GARITY 2,198,006
CONTROL DEVICE FOR ANIMATION
Filed Nov. 16, 1938 10 Sheets-Sheet 1

FIG. 1.

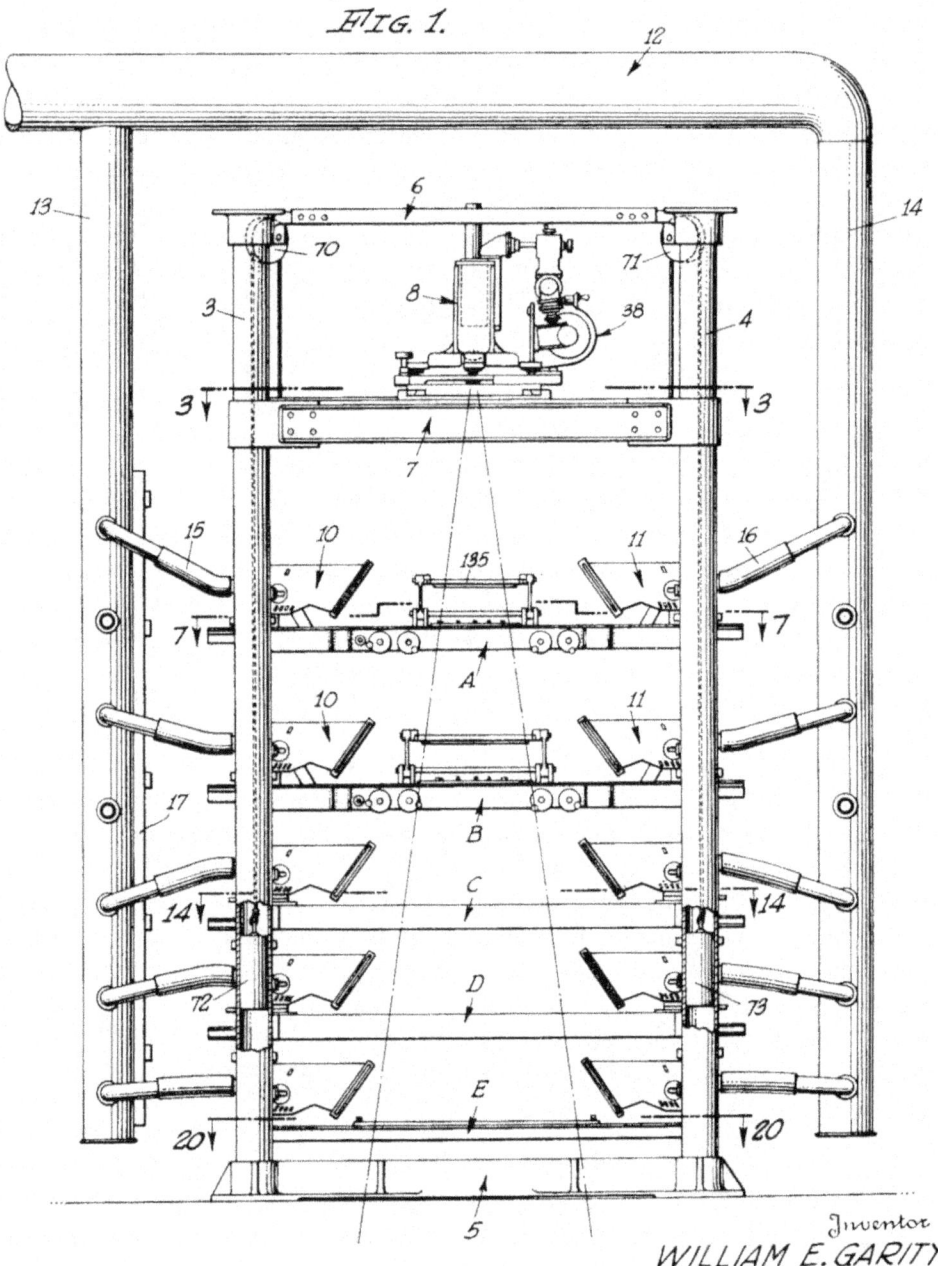

Inventor
WILLIAM E. GARITY
By
Attorney

sionality and perspective in the cartoon short *Three Orphan Kittens*. Anderson didn't really like his work on the short, but the boss was pleased. This resulted in Anderson joining a team with Garity, effects animator Cy Young and expert light technician Hal Helvenston (Smith, 1987, 40–41). A series of initial experiments using a horizontal setup led to a vertical multiplane crane and it was decided to test its ability in *The Old Mill* that had been on the drawing board for months (Smith, 1987, 42). Animation on *The Old Mill* began in mid–1937 and it was released on November 5, more than one month before *Snow White*'s premiere. Disney would win an Oscar for this short as well as another in the Scientific or Technical class "for the design and application of the Multi-Plane Camera" (Smith, 1987. p. 49). Disney's multiplane camera cost over $70,000 and a team of five or six technicians was needed to operate and figure out how to shoot the cartoon, so it was used for feature films only (Smith, 1987, 40 & 49).

Garity filed a patent for Disney's multiplane camera on November 16, 1938, under the name "Control Device for Animation." His massive machine is a huge technical upgrade compared to Reiniger's glass panes mounted at various distances on her tricktisch. Garity's camera resembles an elaborate science fiction invention, while Reiniger's looks like it came from a pre-industrial age. On April 23, 1940, Garity received U.S. patent number 2,198,006.

There is another example of simultaneous invention involving the multiplane camera. After a dispute with Walt Disney, Ub Iwerks left his old partner and the Disney Studios in 1930. Pat Powers had offered Iwerks a contract to form his own animation with Powers as the backer. Iwerks Studio opened the same year and released his first short starring Flip the Frog, *Fiddlesticks with Flip the Frog*. At his studio, Iwerks fabricated his own version of the multiplane camera in 1934 out of old Chevy car parts he purchased for $350 (Schönfeld, 2006, 183; Iwerks and Kenworthy, 2001, 148). Unlike Reiniger's tricktisch with the multiplane camera, Iwerks' camera had a horizontal layout. It was mounted on a standard rig and glass panes were mounted like billboards at varied distances from the camera lens, from which the camera would shoot the scene through the glass panels. The horizontal multiplane camera was used in *Fantasia, The Headless Horseman* (for P.A. Powers), *The Gallant Little Tailor, Pinocchio* and the unreleased stop-motion film *The Toy Parade* (Iwerks and Kenworthy, 2001, 146; Thomas and Johnston, 1981, 264). Iwerks returned to the Disney Studios on September 9, 1940, as a "technician, engineer, and inventor" (Iwerks and Kenworthy, 2001, 148).

While the vertical multiplane camera was used to film *Snow White and the Seven Dwarfs*, the Disney technicians discovered working on *Pinocchio* that if a horizontal camera was used, the orientation could capture backgrounds double the size and it permitted shooting *Pinocchio* "on the same principle as motion-picture photography in a live-action studio" (*New York Times* qt. in Barrier, 1999, 262). Iwerks had been the one to first use the horizontal multiplane camera at his own studio, but Disney had explored a horizontal setup when first developing their own multiplane camera with early tests; after *Snow White*, they made a more elaborate horizontal model. When Iwerks worked for Disney once again he "especially enjoyed the parts of his job that involved planning the movements of Disney's multiplane camera, which had previously been under the direction of Bill Garity" (Iwerks and Kenworthy, 2001, 148).[6]

Opposite: U.S. Patent 2198006, Bill Garity's patent for the multiplane camera, registered on April 23, 1940 (courtesy the U.S. Patent Office).

Prior to development on the multiplane camera, Walt Disney had applied for a patent for his own version of a tricktisch or what he called "The Art of Animation" on September 1, 1936. It was granted May 21, 1940, with U.S. patent number 220,1689. The patent office requires diagrams, description and other supportive evidence for an application. With his application, Disney included a diagram that bears a strong resemblance to Reiniger's animation table. Disney, however, was the first to register the idea and one can argue that he didn't submit an exact duplicate to the patent office.

The patent's description begins, "This invention is particularly directed to improvements in the art of producing what are generally known as animated cartoons; this term being applicable to all instances in which drawn or painted representations of objects, characters, scenes and the like are recorded upon continuous mm so that projection thereof creates the appearance of animation or movement in such drawn or painted characters and scenes" (U.S. Patent No. 2,20,1689, 1940). Schönfeld broke down the coincidental development of the multiplane camera on both sides of the Atlantic without mentioning Garity:

> The drawings supplied with the patent application shows a "Tricktisch," an animation table, with the cameras. The figures attached to the patent application illustrate the "form of apparatus in which the method of the invention may be carried out." The stated aim was on the one hand, to provide the production with "greater fidelity and ease" and on the other, to create animation that suggests three-dimensional space.... The main difference between Lotte Reiniger's invention of 1924 and this animation table of 1936 is the fact that in the case of the latter the lower pane is not flat but rather like a box that made the illusion of three dimensionality much easier to achieve. Reiniger used glass panes one above the other on which foregrounds and backgrounds, silhouette figures and atmospheric storms were placed in order to achieve visual depth. Therefore, her idea of mounting the camera horizontally above a table of two glass panes was replaced by Disney with a table that replaced the lower one with a curved, stagelike background. Or as the patent application states: "the method of this invention comprises forming a three dimensional model of the desired background" and "projecting the image of the foreground character upon such three dimensional background" [2006, 183].

Walt Disney, Iwerks and Garity augmented concepts that were essentially the same as Reiniger's technological endeavors. Pallant used an apt biologic metaphor to describe Disney's take on the camera and animation desk: "[The Walt Disney Studio's] multiplane apparatus was, in reality, purely the latest evolution of depth in animation" (Pallant, 2011, 28). Speculation has arisen about whether or not Reiniger would have or should have sued Disney for "stealing" her idea. As stated before, the idea for the camera and animation desk arose from common knowledge the circulated in the animation field. Neither Reiniger, Iwerks, Garity nor Disney might have even been aware of the other's invention, especially due to the international barriers, studios keeping their secrets, lack of modern means of information access, and lack of materials about animation processes. As animation progressed, publications on animation increased and information dissemination advanced, Reiniger, Disney and Iwerks were more than likely to be aware of the other and the multiplane camera invention.[7]

Reiniger had more than ample evidence to prove that she invented the multiplane camera and animation desk as she used them to film *Prinzen Achmed*. If she had decided to sue the Walt Disney Company, she would have encountered more than one problem. After World War II, Reiniger was at the height of her popularity in Europe and while she was earning a decent income, it would not have been substantial to pursue an international case against the Walt Disney Company. There was also the problem of her nationality. The world frowned on Germany for many years following the war and Reiniger would have more than likely been harangued for "attacking" Uncle Walt and Mickey Mouse, two of the most beloved international icons. While she would have had her supporters, her ploy would have been frowned on by the media and legions of Disney fans. Reiniger would also have been suing the Walt Disney Company, a beast to be reckoned with.

Reiniger was not interested in pursuing legal action, because it wasn't in her congenial personality and she preferred to openly share her knowledge. "But rather than engaging in a patent suit or attempting to claim the 'Art of Animation' for herself, Lotte Reiniger published her *Shadow Theatres and Shadow Films* in 1970, in which she gives detailed descriptions, illustrations and photographs of her 'trick table' with step-by-step instructions as to how to build one at home. Quite clearly, animation for her never became a commodity, but rather an art that would never lose its magic" (Schönfeld, 2006, 184).

Throughout his entire animation career, Disney was obsessed with any new technology that improved the illusion of life. The multiplane camera was the first in a long line of inventions he used to make his films, but it is the first he is credited with and this has mistakenly solidified his claim on its creation.

K. Vivian Taylor and Chris Pallant both build on Zipes' writings about Disney's fairytale movie dominance by exploring what Bruce Edera dubbed the "Disney myth" and what in popular culture has become verbs: Disneyfied or Disneyized—Walt Disney's and his company's attempt to paint over history and assert Uncle Walt's magical innovation and status as the first man of animation (Edera, 1977, 31). Douglas Brode explained more about the infamous Disney verbs: "The term 'Disneyfication' long ago entered into our idiomatic American English as a stigma. Whenever anything is said to have been Disneyised or Disneyified, a harsh criticism is implied" (2004, x).

Taylor's use of the term "Disney myth" and her arguments in her thesis "National Identity, Gender, and Genre: The Multiple Marginalization of Lotte Reiniger and *The Adventures of Prince Achmed*" provide a thorough examination about how and why the Walt Disney Company have Disneyfied animation history. But it is too loose of a term to explain the actions.

The term myth refers to stories that are used to explain a natural or social occurrence and usually involves supernatural elements; a legend, on the other hand, is based on unauthenticated historical fact interwoven with dramatic storytelling elements to convey a story about a person or event. Despite the pixie dust Tinkerbell tossed on Walt Disney during *Walt Disney Presents* and the movie magic that made it seem as if he had superhuman abilities, Disney was an ordinary man with extraordinary talent and drive that became the stuff of legend when he passed.

In Internet nomenclature, "Disney myth" is commonly used to reference urban legends, interesting facts and untold stories that mention the parks, movies, people and other items associated the Walt Disney Company that often have a negative connotation. Conducting a basic Internet search will return results that fit this description, mostly driven by websites that subsist on entertaining people's appetite for dark facts about the "happiest place on Earth" and the "world's most beloved entertainer." Myths do not revise history as they only are used to explain, but legends do glance over facts in order to tell an exciting story. Referring to Disney and his studio's habit of rewriting history as a legend, doesn't convey the same meaning either.

Without doubt, Walt Disney is a legend. Facts about him have been misconstrued, but he is one of the leading animation pioneers and Disney films have kept the medium at the forefront of people's minds, although it is tied to children's entertainment. All other animation studios that began around the same time as Disney are now either defunct or absorbed by other companies. The Walt Disney Company also has trademarked the term "Disney Legends" as an award given to individuals who have made an indelible contribution to the company.

The best way to describe Disney's rewriting habit puts Walter Benjamin's quote "History is written by the victors" into play. Disney "won" the animation industry by portraying himself as the sole pioneer of the medium and his company has since built this impression up, transforming him into a magical storytelling being and making people believe he did everything by himself, leaving out all of the man's unbecoming traits. Disney was involved in every aspect of his studio, but he didn't do everything and relied on his team. In fact,

> he didn't write, direct, animate or even produce the vast majority of movies bearing his name. Disney himself was fascinated with this, often relating a favorite story: "I was stunned one day when a little boy asked, 'Do you draw Mickey Mouse?' I had to admit I did not…. 'Then you think up all the jokes and ideas?' 'No,' I said, 'I don't do that.' Finally, he looked at me and said, 'Mr. Disney, just what do you do?'" Ultimately, Disney's only answer was, "Sometimes I think of myself as a little bee. I go from one area of the studio to another, and gather pollen and sort of stimulate everybody" [qt. in Brode, 2004, xvii].

Since Disney "won," other animation pioneers have been swept into history's crevices, but none more so than Lotte Reiniger. "Disney revisionist actions" is a proper, all-inclusive description that sums up the Mouse House's revision of animation history.

Along with the Disney revisionist actions, however, comes a danger of ruining the beloved "Uncle Walt" belief amongst the millions of Disney fans. For many people (and there is a large, diverse crowd of Disney lovers), being a Disney fan is more than a hobby it is a lifestyle passed from parent to child and upheld with vacations to Disney theme parks, purchasing merchandise, watching the Disney films and even eating licensed Disney food. The Disney lifestyle is one of the many interesting facets of fandom subculture (the "geek-nerd culture"). What marks the Disney lifestyle as a spectacle is similar to how *Star Wars* fans run away with their excitement with the release of every new film. Some fans have a strong devotion to the Walt Disney Company and any expression of "badmouthing" it is seen as blasphemous. Taylor wrote, "[T]o debunk the Disney myth is to introduce logic into and therefore spoil the magic of an American tale. To debunk the Disney myth is to question the American dream. To debunk the Disney myth is to be unpatriotic, perhaps even a Communist [sic], a cynic, a skeptic, an intellectual" (2011, 96).[8]

It is an extremist view to label a person who challenges Disney revisionist actions as un–American, much less a communist, but as animation is viewed as a pure American product, citing Reiniger as an earlier animation pioneer with achievements usually attributed to Disney would rankle some fans. "The Disney myth emerged in post–WWII [sic] American culture as a pleasant alternative to the 'unnatural' and 'unpleasant' German, feminine, and avant-garde origins of animated film, as originating in Reiniger's *Prince Achmed*" (K.V. Taylor, 2011, 97). After World War II, the Walt Disney Company was more embedded than ever as a symbol of American pride. When the 1950s rolled around with the Red Scare[9] and Cold War, Americans wouldn't have rested well with the knowledge that a German woman made an animated fairytale feature film 11 years before Disney.

The biggest opponent of the false Walt Disney image was none other than his eldest daughter Diane Disney Miller (1933–2013). She detested the urban legends and slander

5. Sound Cartoons and Miscredited Ideas 111

that sprang up around her father's name and legacy and she was the first person to acknowledge that Walt was an ordinary man with extraordinary gifts. Many times when she was asked what it was like to grow up with her famous father, she replied that he was just her dad and he was good to her and her sister Sharon.

> While devoting her earlier life to raising her seven children, over the past two decades, Diane undertook an active advocacy to document the life and accomplishments of her father, who has been the subject of poorly researched biographies and inaccurate rumors. She was also concerned that his name had become more of a corporate identity than a reference to the man himself [Walt Disney Family Museum, 2013].

Taylor, Pallant and I have tracked numerous documents that credit Disney as the inventor of the multiplane camera, including Robert Feild's *The Art of Walt Disney*, Leonard Maltin's *The Disney Films*, Christopher Finch's *The Art of Walt Disney* and many more. There are countless manuscripts that cite Disney as the creator of the first animated movie. Resources that mistakenly credit Disney as the creator of the first animated movie are easily found.[10] Disney's revisionist actions are most often perpetuated by the Walt Disney Company. "Much post–WWII [sic] animation and biographical scholarship that mistakenly attributes production of the first feature-length animated film, and invention of the multiplane camera, and perfection of the animation technique to Disney was funded/or authorized by the Disney Company" (K.V. Taylor, 2011, 101). Most of the above list, sans marked items, are published by Disney's own publication companies, written by Disney scholars or personnel, or the studio funded or authorized the works (K.V. Taylor, 2011, 101).

The animation technique and history manuscript *The Illusion of Life* is one of the most notable examples. It was written by Johnston and Thomas, two of the Nine Old Men; later editions published were by Disney Editions (earlier editions were published by Abbeville Press); and it is one of the company's most prominent books. The title is one of the many popular definitions of "what" animation is and it is *still* used by industry professionals. *The Illusion of Life* was written with a congenial rapport about the animation process, how studio life was during Disney's Golden Age, and a description of how Walt Disney worked with his crew. He sat at the top of a pyramid and collaborated with individuals asking two common questions, "Can you do it?" and "What can you do here?" Then he brought different talents together to form teams, "cameraman, carpenter, stylist, colorist, technician, artist—they formed teams as needed with no money for expenses, no time to research, only their own inventive minds, and Walt's enthusiasm to guide them" (Thomas & Johnston, 1981, 263–64). Disney had a bubbling spring of ideas and constantly asked his employees to create something based on nothing more than a thought. *The Illusion of Life* gives the impression the multiplane camera was born this way:

> Once they were asked to build an arrangement that could hold separate layers of artwork at varying distances from a still camera, so that the ensuing photograph would have the appearance of depth. It was built of wood and glue and tape—as Bill McFadden said, "You couldn't build anything without tape, y'know." But it worked and Walt liked the result and suddenly was talking about building another one, larger and more complicated, that might be used for shooting animation. This was more of a problem and called for engineering knowledge, but on the records it was built by Special Effects! And so the first multiplane camera was born [1981, 264].

The book gives the illusion that the apparatus was built strictly due to Disney's prodding (Thomas & Johnston, 1981, 262). However, the Walt Disney Company, with "the 1938 [sic] patent filed for this camera, coupled with its industrial notoriety, frequently obscures the developmental history of the device pre–Disney" (Pallant, 2011, 28). The patent is signed by William Garity, so in the end they awarded the credit to him. Disney revisionist actions are detrimental to animation's overall history, because it leaves the story incomplete and negates the important contributions of animators like Reiniger. It might be "to the victor goes the spoils," but it ends up being an oversaturated marketing campaign that started with one man's dream and ego and continued by his namesake company: "[T]his history overvalues the output of the Disney Company at the expense of other animators" (K.V. Taylor, 2011, 101).

The miscredit of the multiplane camera is an example of how history can be construed and influenced by powerful entities. The Walt Disney Studio overshadowed Reiniger's own contributions to the camera's development by nixing her completely out of their own history and they even took credit for the accomplishment of the first feature film to heighten their hold on the animation medium. These actions black out Reiniger's (and Cristiani's) importance in animation history and how she influenced future feature-length animated films, including Disney's own movies.

Technology aided and harmed Lotte Reiniger's career. When "talkies" overtook the industry, by adapting to sound she added a new, intriguing level to her silhouette films. Then multiplane camera gave them illusional depth to mirror real life. Other animators changed their styles and techniques as the technology progressed, but Reiniger remained dedicated to her silhouette films. While it made them enduring and they had their devotees, general audiences were more drawn to flashy productions and mainstream features, rather than independent animation.

While Walt Disney drew on European folklore and art for his films, instead of taking something old and reimagining it, Disney reinvented it. Disney took the raw animation process and flipped it to suit his needs. Unafraid to experiment, he created new techniques and styles within animation. Disney's story fits the traditional American dream formula (similar to how modern animated fairytale films fit the Disney formula). While that has drawn criticism from some angles, it is one of the aspects that shaped Disney's career.

The U.S. was a country less than 200 years old at the time Reiniger and Disney started their careers. Its citizens were (and are) able to pursue ideas relatively free of old social conventions and tradition. Animation was a prime medium for Disney to invest his talent in, because he was able to explore and shape it without social constructs to hold him back. The fact that animation was a new medium didn't hurt his cause either.

Reiniger, on the other hand, swam in traditional mindsets despite the more liberal mentalities of the Weimar Republic in the Golden Twenties. Reiniger was a determined woman and although she made animation for animation's sake, Germany's rich culture had a deep impact on her. While Reiniger was just as eager as Disney to experiment with animation technique, she didn't use the modern celluloid process. Instead she stuck with silhouettes, a traditional European art form. Her musical tasted veered towards the more classical forms: opera and composers such as Bach and Mozart. Her cultural identity remained rooted in her German heritage and was reflected through her animated films.

At the beginning of her career and especially prior to World War II, Reiniger's film perpetuated her German cultural heritage. Other German filmmakers did the same, the most notable being Fritz Lang's *Die Nibelungen*. Once Reiniger traveled more, became world-weary after the war, and then migrated to Britain, her films reflected her pan-experience. Oliver Wendell Holmes Jr.'s quote became very apt for her: "A mind that is stretched by a new experience can never go back to its old dimensions," although her films did maintain a sweet innocence due to their content and Reiniger's intent. It brings to mind that conversation she had with Walter Ruttmann about 1923 during *Prinzen Achmed*'s production.

One constant aesthetic in Reiniger's work was her love affair with beauty and femininity. Scherenschnitte had become a traditional women's craft and making silhouettes was a job title held by both sexes. Paper-cutting artists developed their own style and nuances—that is to say, not all silhouettes and paper cuttings are cut out to be equals. A Lotte Reiniger silhouette is much different from one by the famous American artist Kara Walker, who adopted the silhouette to depict black history in America. The same is true for a silhouette puppet rendered by puppeteer Richard Bradshaw or an animated shadow by Michel Ocelot. All of these artists work with in the same medium of opaque figures, but there are individual artist marks.

Reiniger's mark on silhouette animation and shadow puppetry is the refined feministic style she cut into each of her puppets and backgrounds. Art nouveau like curlicues and flowing lines accent beautiful, youthful figures that are idealized portrayals of men and women. Even characters that are grotesque in nature have a defined quality that marks them as beautiful in their construction. Feminine nature is traditionally noted to be delicate, elegant, flowing and, of course, beautiful. Reiniger released the hidden beauty with her construction materials. Rather than it being an artistic choice to distinguish herself from other animators, she made beautiful things for the sheer pleasure of it. Paul Wells in *Understanding Animation* wrote that Reiniger is a pure feminine animator and was a sharp contrast to her male compatriots whose masculine styles dominated the industry until the 1970s (1998, 200). "[Her works] exhibit a feminist tendency in that the language of such work is couched most specifically in the lyrical movement of the figures, and he emotional intensity of *gesture*—a profound departure from the (male) agendas of the evolving cartoon" (Wells, 1998, 201).

While Reiniger took pleasure in making beauty, she did intend to have her style accent the stories to accentuated the world she created: "This lightness of touch, this subtlety of expression, this desire to delineate emotional states in [her] films" (Wells, 1998, 201).

6

Fanboy Hitler and the Short Life of Hansi and Schnuff

German history has been irrevocably stained by the actions of the Nazi party, from their rise in 1920 to their fall in 1945. With each passing year from 1920, the party grew in power, culminating when the amateur artist turned politician, Adolf Hitler, was appointed chancellor of Germany on January 30, 1933. Discussions about how the Nazi party gained power will forever be a psychological study of the human mentality and the cause and effect of human actions or inactions. It is fact that Nazi Germany combined with World War II was one of the darkest periods in modern history, still with rippling consequences. What remains intriguing about Hitler's plans for a thousand-year reich are how far the Nazi party inserted itself into the most mundane of daily activities to the glamorous world on the silver screen. Hitler's plans for the German entertainment industry are mirrored in modern dictatorships. North Korea, the Middle East and several African nations spring to mind.

Hitler was obsessed with the fine arts. Before World War I, he painted, sold watercolors of Vienna's scenery and applied to Vienna's Academy of Fine Arts. Twice he was rejected. He tried to study architecture, but he lacked the proper academic credentials. It can be speculated that within Hitler, a hatred festered due to his exclusion from the world of higher arts. The Weimar years are historically significant as a time when German artists were able to experiment in classic art, music, architecture and other disciplines, including the new and exciting moving pictures. Weimar cinema is still considered a pinnacle in world cinema. Seeing the success of others and his exclusion from this world, Hitler became determined to dominate and plunder art from across the European continent.[1]

While he rubbed his enemies' noses into his victories by stealing prized artworks, he wanted the Third Reich to become a film powerhouse to rival Hollywood. Reich Chancellor Hitler instituted changes to "repair" Germany's culture. All creative works from paintings to movies had to adhere to the strict Nazi guidelines of appropriateness and glorify Nazi idealism. If they didn't, they were labeled as degenerate and censored or banned.

Reiniger was usually uninterested in politics, preferring to spend her time in the happier themes found in fairytales. One of people's favorite quotes from her is, "I believe more in the truth of fairytales than I do newspapers." Her husband wasn't apolitical and was very outspoken about his political opinions. While Reiniger's sound films tested her skills as an animator, they also tested the Nazi cultural code just as Koch attracted unwanted attention. When Hitler's followers marched on the Kurfürstendamm in Berlin, Koch and Brecht stood on the roadside and called them philistines (Happ, 2004, 41). For Brecht, things didn't improve in Germany, when months later the Nazi party began its moves to purify German culture (i.e., destroying literary works that reflected an un–German spirit). On May 10, 1933, the German Student Union burned over 25,000 books, including Erich Kästner, Franz Kafka, Otto Dix, Helen Keller and Bertolt Brecht. Brecht had fled Germany with his family right after the February 27, 1933, Reichstag Fire.

Reiniger was fearful that something would happen to her husband. She said that Koch "was very careless with his utterances ... and was afraid of nothing" (Happ, 2004, 42). She had to put her fears aside to animate a ten-minute silhouette entr'acte for the operetta *Sissi* by Fritz Kreisler, about Austrian Kaiser Franz Josef and his courtship with Bavarian princess Elisabeth. The *Sissi* animation is quite delicate, but not as exciting as many of Reiniger's other works. It describes a carriage's journey with intertitles. They stop at a tollgate, then pick up another passenger while cherubs bless their voyage. Famous director G.W. Pabst asked for her services for a short animation sequence depicting medieval knights errant for his 1933 *Don Quichotte* (*Don Quixote*). Reiniger couldn't hide away in her silhouettes as tensions grew, and she feared for Koch's safety, but she had read that Renoir was in Paris working on another film and he left in April 1933 to work for Renoir on his film *Madame Bovary* (he helped write the script and co-direct). Reiniger visited him in August of that year and made paper cutting books for use in the film, but from the time Koch left in April to her visit months later, she was left alone in Berlin (Happ, 2004, 42).

To overcome her loneliness, she started work on transforming Bizet's *Carmen* into a humorous silhouette parody and also modeled the puppets on her friends' profiles. Renoir became the innkeeper Lillas Pastia, Catherine Hessling was the heroine Carmen, and her husband was an audience member watching the show through opera glasses (Happ, 2004, 44). Reiniger reimagined the seductive gypsy as more of a cunning trickster, a role traditionally fulfilled by a male. Carmen seduces Don José, captain of the dragoons, and lures him back to her camp, where he falls asleep. She proceeds to steal his clothes, sell them and buy herself a lovely Spanish mantilla and trousseau. In her new finery, Carmen wanders the street and is attracted to the toreador Escamillo. She tries to lure him, but he pushes her to the ground and leaves to attend his bullfight. Enraged, Carmen decides to defend her honor, while a confused Don José seeks his own revenge. At the Corrida del Toros, Escamillo fights the bull. Don José spies Carmen and slashes at her with a dagger. She jumps into the arena and is almost run over by the bull, when she tames him with her dancing skills. The bull bows to Carmen and dances with her. Escamillo is charmed, then he and Carmen ride the bull around the arena to celebrate their new love.

Reiniger had intended *Carmen*[2] to be the first in many operatic adaptations, but instead it drew the attention of Nazi censors (Happ, 2004, 44). None of the German theaters would show it. It would only be shown once in Germany, at the 1934 Berlin Film Festival, where Reiniger profusely thanked them for rescuing her film for the public to see. It again screened in Germany after the war ended in 1945 (Happ, 2004, 44). The film was well-received all around. The German Film Rating chamber wrote a positive review:

> With graceful shadow puppets the story of the beautiful, sultry Carmen, Don Jose, and the proud Escamillo is shown. The opera *Carmen* especially provides for a playful, high-spirited travesty.... The story of hot-blooded Carmen, beautiful Don Jose, and proud Escamillo is told with graceful silhou-

ettes. The opera *Carmen* offers good fundamentals that can be skillfully developed and artistically perfected for these kinds of playful, cocky travesties. The silhouette film *Carmen* should therefore have been recognized as artistic. The silhouette film *Carmen* should therefore be recognized be recognized as artistic ... [and] for an art award [Release Zeite 1 Number 29/30 qt. in Happ, 2004, 44].

The film "triggered stormy mirth and warm applause" at the 1934 Berlin Film Festival, but it was not enough to play the film again (Happ, 2004, 44). Reiniger was told if she had made a film featuring a German opera rather than a foreign one, it would have been shown without exception. A journalist had written an article about *Carmen* for the film festival and ended it with a quote that would later sum up Reiniger's departure from Germany: "German film, which is not exactly distinguished by an over-abundance of humorous, graceful, or even witty works, had a valuable asset in this artist [Reiniger], especially since it has already been proven more than once that her works are popular abroad" (qt. in Happ, 2004, 44).

After *Carmen*, Reiniger was presented with a new problem. Due to the new censorship laws, no one was interested in producing her films. Happ notes that Reiniger and Koch were proud of their independence outside of the main film studios and were able to make art films according to their own wishes, but it also placed Reiniger in a financial predicament. Reiniger was very angry at the film industry, because it recognized the hard work that went into making silhouette films, but film distributors were unwilling to take a risk on her films due to their classification as art and therefore they would not be popular with audiences (2004, 46). She and Eric Walter White did occupy themselves in the same year by working together on the book *Wander Birds*, the simple story of two vagabonds or wander birds (wandervögel) and their escapades one night in Geneva before they move on to the next place to repeat the pattern.

Reiniger did make two movies that were Nazi-approved. The first, 1934's *Das rollende Rad* (*The Rolling Wheel*), was about the history of locomotion. It would be used as a propaganda film, because it ended with Hitler at the Autobahn's groundbreaking ceremony. The story is told as a wheel spins through the different eras as a narrator explains about the wheel and vehicles before moving on to the silhouette animation. H.W. Whanslaw recounted,

> The film illustrates a complete history of transport from the earliest prehistoric times until the present day. This picture meant an enormous amount of research for it contains every kind of road vehicle imaginable and every detail is accurately drawn. Madame Reiniger spent many hours of careful and tedious work filming the action of a stage coach and horses crossing the scene only to find on projection that the wheels of the coach were running backwards which meant refilming the scene all over again [1950, 103–104].

Das gestohlene Herz (*The Stolen Heart*), also made in 1934 and the second to receive Nazi approval, was a cultural propaganda film with music by Carl Maria von Weber. Adapted from a story by Ernst Kleienburg, it was made with the intent to inspire people to make music (Happ, 2004, 48 & Strobel) While it was made under the guise of an educational film and escaped censorship, Reiniger cleverly masked her political views about the Nazi party in *Das gestohlene Herz*. It tells about an evil ogre that wants to control everything and everyone, including people's happiness. The musical instruments fight the ogre with their music, defeat him, and then return to their owners. Nazi propaganda minister Joseph Goebbels had a special showing of it without realizing her hidden message (Happ, 2004, 48, 51–52). Helga Happ, Alfred Happ's wife, said, "This is a film you can only understand in political terms. An evil spirit comes and takes away all their instruments, and all possibility of living and expressing themselves. But this evil spirit is vanquished" (qt. in Marschall *et al.*, 2012). Reiniger did manage to animate one fairytale in 1934, *Der Graf von Carabas* (*Puss in Boots*), but it would be her last silhouette fairytale in Germany for several years.

The year 1934 held special significance to Hamelin: It was the 650th anniversary of their favorite fairytale *The Pied Piper of Hamelin*. The Rulffs-Künstler-Puppenbühne wanted to reimagine the story as a hand puppet play, but were confounded about how to stage its more fantastic scenes. Reiniger was commissioned to make shadow plays of the "rats' nightly exodus, and later the exodus of about 130 children" from the town (Happ, 2004, 130).

As 1934 drew to an end, the popular entertainment rag *Film-Kurier* ran articles that discussed what Germany could expect in the New Year in relation to film. Amongst articles about Goebbels's plans were quotes from famous people in the arts. Some were Nazi supporters, others (like Reiniger and Fischinger) didn't wear swastikas willingly. Reiniger's quote reads:

> My plans for the New Year are simple: to make as many good silhouette films as possible. Last year, I had the pleasure to receive three film applications and the New Year already welcomed me with an order from Rota-Film A.G., which I intend to carry out with love and joy and when I travel to London, where *Das Rollende Rad* had a successful run, I will be hard at work. To the *Film-Kurier* and its readers, I wish a happy 1935! [1934]

Her New Year wishes proved bittersweet as 1935 would be a decisive year for Reiniger. It began with her animating the *Der kleine Schornsteinfeger* (*The Little Chimney Sweep*), a collaboration with her former teaching companion Eric Walter White. The pair was enchanted with the Orlando Gibbons composition "London Street Cries," a musical depiction of street sounds from seventeenth century England, accompanied by music by Handel, *The Beggar's Opera* and John Jenkin's dialogue (White, 1936, 10, 12). While Gibbons' music is a creative take on random din, "the scheme if carried out to its logical conclusion would have led to a silhouette documentary with little or no visual and tonal contrasts" (White, 1936, 8). While listening to the 74 different cries, they discerned that the chimney sweep's voice was the most prolific and it was decided to make him the hero (White, 1936, 10). With these details, White composed the music and wrote the short story "The Mohock and the Unicorn" for the film. Authenticity was key for Reiniger in this particular production, thus she based her silhouette puppets on characters in Marcellus Lauron's drawing series "The Cries of London" and paid strict attention to London's famous scenery, including Convent Garden Piazza, Westminster, Blackfriars and St. Paul's Cathedral (White, 1936, 10, 14–15).

White sets the story in London during Queen Anne's reign. Amongst the street cries, a little chimney sweep is at work. He falls down and startles the beautiful maiden Belinde. He charms Belinde with his song and she gives him her handkerchief embroidered with a unicorn as a present. Later that evening, Belinde and her parents attend the opera, when the evil Mohock tries to seduce her. Belinde fights him off and she returns home with her parents, but Mohock and his henchmen kidnap her. Mohock attempts to be gentler with Belinde, but she spurns his pretty words. Left alone, Belinde hears the chimney sweep and then sings his song to get his attention. The sweep finds her, then she throws down her handkerchief as a message for her parents. As the rogue tries to ravage Belinde, a besotted scullery maid alerts Mohock that Belinde's parents and the authorities are on their way. The rogue and his gang take off with Belinde to the docks, but the chimney sweep and the garrison fend him off. Belinde is saved and thanks the little chimney sweep for helping her.

Reiniger had very little time to animate *Der kleine Schornsteinfeger*, but she was lucky to find a distributor for the film. She had to start animating early in the New Year and complete it by February 16, 1935. "[T]here was no safety margin for possible errors at the time it was made. In spite of that, only one scene had to be retaken; and even then it was ultimately decided to use the original and not the revised version" (White, 1936, 12). The chimney sweep's voice rings out like the cries in William Blake's "The Chimney Sweeper" from *Songs of Experience*. *Der kleine Schornsteinfeger* was also published as a children's book in 1936.

Reiniger's two other animated films from 1935 showed her love for opera and music. *Papageno* featured a character from Mozart's opera *Die Zauberflöte* (*The Magic Flute*): Papageno is the jovial companion to the opera's hero, who has a love for food and wants nothing more than to find the love of his life. The short was presented for the first time in London on January 27, 1938, and Reiniger was as joyful and funny as the film's main character: "Today is Mozart's birthday and I'm happy to show the film for the first time in London. And I hope that Mozart would not roll over in his grave if he could see what is happening with his lovable character from *The Magic Flute*" (qt. in Happ, 2004, 39).

Papageno is indeed charming, Reiniger had perfected the art of synchronizing voices to her silhouettes' mouths. Papageno's singing about food with little birds transforming into his favorite dishes and the beautiful Papagena swaying her form like Josephine Baker demonstrate the subtle humor Reiniger was known for (Weigmann & Blattner, 2010, 7). Hitler found the film charming and was especially moved when Papageno and his beloved Papagena had many children and depicted clean eroticism (Happ, 2004, 48; qt. in Marschall *et al.*, 2012).

Galathea was based on the Greek myth *Pygmalion* and told the tale of the sculptor king who sculpts a beautiful woman, Galathea (or Galatea), and falls hopelessly in love with her. The gods are so moved by Pygmalion's love that they bring the statue to life. In Reiniger's version, Galathea shuns Pygmalion and his gifts. She would rather remain a free woman and dance naked in a local tavern. Pygmalion's maid is saddened by her master's plight (and is deeply in love with him). The townsmen lust after Galathea, while the women are in an uproar over her scandalous ways. The maid pleads with Aphrodite to end Galathea's raucous ways and her prayers (as well as the other womens') are answered when Galathea is transformed back into a statue. Pygmalion recognizes the maid's devotion and falls in love with her.

At the same London lecture, Reiniger shared details about making *Galathea*, the last silhouette film she animated in Germany: the music was written by a 14-year-old; Eric Walter White's brother provided the inspiration for the Pygmalion puppet when he visited (Happ, 2004, 46). *Galathea* and *Papageno* were unprofitable for Koch and Reiniger but they did remain art for art's sake, a huge no-no under the Nazi regime (Happ, 2004, 46).

The Nazi regime attacked Reiniger and Koch through criticism and passive aggressive comments on silhouette animation. Julius Pinschewer wanted to reuse Reiniger's *Barcarole* chocolate advertisement from the 1920s in German theaters, but it was opposed (Happ, 2004, 48). On October 16, 1935, the couple applied to the Film Kreditbank (the bank that oversaw money distribution for films in Nazi Germany) to make a film based on Hans Christian Andersen's fairytale *Däumelinchen* (*Thumbelina*) and were denied (Happ, 2004, 47). She was also interested in animating the German Arthurian story

One of Lotte Reiniger's favorite films was her 1935 *Papageno*. Here the bird catcher dances among his caged birds (courtesy the Tübingen Stadtmuseum).

Lohengrin, but Hitler forbade that as well (surprising as it was of German origin) (Bastiancich, 1991/1981, 13). The pro–Nazi actor Willy Krause wrote in *Deutsche Filmzeitung*:

> The silhouette film is not realistic, it is illusion and its form is romantic. Through speech, sounds, and music it preserves the artistically impeccable character of romantic irony. We no longer have a romantic space, but rather a realistic one. When the Reich Minister Dr. Goebbels announces the provisions for financial resources for the film during the next budget meeting for the Reich, that is how the funds will be raised [qt. in Happ, 2004, 48].

Krause sunk the knife in deeper when he mentioned the couple in a personal conversation: "We need healthy food for the German people. What they produce is caviar, which does not interest us" (Happ, 2004, 48).

Reiniger's films were never officially banned by the Nazi party, but all finances for

The townswomen are upset with Galathea, so they force Pygmalion to stop her (courtesy Mara Alper).

them had dried up by 1935. One would think that this would inspire Koch and Reiniger to emigrate, but they remained even though most of their friends had left the country. Reiniger held onto hope that the Nazis would cease their suffocating practices, but she realized things were not going to change in Germany when their composer friend Peter Gellhorn was targeted.

"Gellhorn arranged or composed the music for *Carmen…*, *Das Rollende Rad*, *Der Graf von Carabas*, *Der Kleine Schornsteinfeger*, and *Papageno*" (Happ, 2004, 49). Gellhorn loved working with Reiniger and Koch and said about them,

> Technically she wasn't a musician, but she was very musical. She had an instinct for music. Her husband Koch was a big help too. Once he said to me, "Gellhorn, this is really interesting good stuff. Lovely music, but for Lotte's films we need something more straightforward." He wasn't a musician either, but he gave me the right sense of style for Lotte's films. More than ever he knew himself. To me that was great fun. He was the director type, supervised everything from A to Z. He was her conscience? He said, "Lotte, it has to be done like this or like that." And they did work wonderfully together. It was a brilliant collaboration. The film industry would usually require far more than two people [qt. in Raganelli, 1999].

Gellhorn's father was Jewish, thus the Nazis labeled him as a half-Jew and he was only able to find work on Reiniger's silhouette film. She even included his name in the credits. In September 1935, the Reich Chamber of Film ordered Reiniger and Koch to stop working with Gellhorn and officially banned him from working on any other projects. Gellhorn took the opportunity to leave Germany and made it to Reiniger's friends in London after he was overlooked by a sleep-deprived immigration officer on his crossing from Dover (Happ, 2004, 49).

Reiniger and Koch took the hint as well and in late 1935 left Berlin for England. While the Nazi government and its regulations were the biggest reason for them to leave Germany, Eric Walter White had arranged for a Bristol museum to exhibit Reiniger's work (Happ, 2004, 52).

Running from December 6 to 28, 1935, the Bristol exhibit featured a technical examination of Reiniger's work from *Prinzen Achmed* and films she had made in the past few years, including shadow puppets, silhouettes, backgrounds and sketches (Happ, 2004, 52). Happ noted that the exhibition introduced Reiniger and Koch to British film notables, who were interested in animation (Thorold Dickinson, John Grierson and Basil Wright) as well as New Zealand experimental animator Len Lye and Russian animator Alexander Alexeieff (2004, 54). The exhibit proved so popular that it was suggested that Reiniger hold a show in London. She contacted James Lebrun from the Victoria and Albert Museum; he and the museum's director were enthralled with Reiniger's silhouette puppets and were even playing with them when they said they would exhibit her work through the Department of Engraving, Illustration, and Design. She became the first foreigner to exhibit at the Victoria and Albert Museum, and Reiniger was extremely proud she arranged for all of it on her own (Happ, 2004, 54). The museum now houses a small collection of her work.

The exhibit was held from February 3 to March 8, 1936. Another was held in Liverpool from March 13 to 19, 1936 (Happ, 2004, 54). The London Film Society showed Reiniger's films (*Papageno, Galathea,* and *Der kleine Schornsteinfeger*) to coincide with the exhibit and thus promoted her work (Happ, 2004, 54). She also gave lectures about animation. In the audience were new and familiar faces: Lye, Bartosch, Grierson, Fischinger, Alberto Cavalcanti and Walt Disney (Happ, 2004, 54).

While Walt Disney has become the poster boy for the American dream, from his youth he was inspired by European and German culture, if not from his own family history. Walt and his family lived on a Marceline, Kansas, farm for four years during his childhood and Walt would later idealize this period in his life. Robin Allan in *Walt Disney and Europe* explained:

> The cultural heritage of Europe, and in particular that of Germany, which the new Americans of the Midwest brought with them, cannot be over-emphasised. At the turn of the century more than 27 percent of Americans were of German stock.... The majority were from humble farming, artisan and later on proletarian backgrounds. Many were illiterate. They have relied on popular cultural forms for entertainment and education, including the live theatre, comic strips, picture books and, increasingly towards the end of the 19th century, the cinema [Allan, 1999, 16].

Disney only spent a short time in Marceline, but its impact had a profound effect on him. Through the small town country life, he was exposed to German culture. His maternal grandmother was also of German descent. Walt recalled her "reading him the tales of Grimm and Hans Andersen. 'It was the best time of the day for me ... and the stories and characters in them seemed quite as real as my schoolmates and our games. Of all the characters in the Fairy Tales, I loved *Snow White and the Seven Dwarfs* the best'" (Allan, 1999, 2 & 36). Allan speculates that Disney was enthralled with the fairytale because "his mind was uncluttered by formal education or direction, and he absorbed stories orally from his grandmother's readings or from the storytelling medium of popular film" (1999, 44). As we know, his love for fairytales would translate into his career and most of his early films are based on the German fairytale.

In 1935, Disney made a promotional trip to Europe during which he vacationed to combat the nervous breakdown symptoms he was exhibiting. His wife Lillian, Roy and Roy's wife Edna joined him and they visited England, France Austria, Germany, Switzerland and Italy. As much as Marceline impacted Disney's imagination, his 11-week European tour had an even greater influence. "Walt was already inclined to favor the European aesthetic..." and it rose even higher in his favor as he purchased 335 fairytale and folk story books ("90 ... from France, 81 from England, 149 from Germany and 15 from Italy"—note that the most came from Germany). Many featured classic examples of European illustration and all were conscripted to the Disney Studio Library (Allan, 1999, 31; Hahn & Miller-Zarneke, 2015, 341–42). These books inspired animators during the production of *Snow White* as well as later Disney feature films.

Lotte Reiniger animated *Prinzen Achmed* 11 years before Disney's *Snow White*. It is difficult to tie Reiniger and Disney together as the references are limited. Disney never set out to meet Reiniger. Solomon notes that Disney and his studio probably had heard of *Die Abenteuer des Prinzen Achmed*: "While it is unlikely that Disney or anyone on his staff had seen [Quirino] Cristiani's film, Reiniger's work had received considerable attention in Europe and the animators may have been aware of it" (1994, 62).

Like most creative individuals, Disney sought and collected talent to help him bring his visions to life. He or his team arranged to meet his contemporaries in the film business as well as artists, authors or anyone he was particularly interested in. He could have easily arranged a meeting with Reiniger on his trip to Germany. Reiniger could have delivered an unrecorded lecture in animation in 1935 Germany or England that Disney attended, but Reiniger doesn't write of ever meeting him. While Alfred Happ wrote that Walt Disney attended one of her lectures, I consulted the Walt Disney Company Archives to find a record of him meeting Reiniger, viewing *Prinzen Achmed* or any of her movies, and possibly using them to inspire some of the Disney animators. As of writing this book, a direct connection hasn't been found between the two pioneering animators.

Robin Allan wrote that during development for *Snow White*, the animation crew watched German expressionist films to establish the story and the atmosphere they wanted to create in the animated epic (1993, 44–45). Marc Davis, one of the Nine Old Men, said:

> Walt rented a studio up in North Hollywood and ... we would see a selection of films—anything from Charlie Chaplin to unusual subjects. Anything that might produce growth, that might be stimulating—the cutting of the scenes, the staging, and how a group of scenes was put together.... *The Cabinet of Dr. Caligari*, *Nosferatu* were things we saw. I remember *Metropolis*.... I would never want to see this film again because it had a very strong impact on me. I have built it up in my mind and I want to leave it that way [qt. in Allan, 1999, 45].

According to Allan, German expressionism

> is the background to the powerful scenes of Snow White's flight through the forest and the Queen's transformation scene.... Gothic elements echo F.W. Murnau's *Nosferatu* (1922) and Fritz Lang's *Metropolis* (1926) where Rotwang's house looks like an early model for the dwarfs' cottage. Jonathan Rosenbaum also cites Leni Riefenstahl's *The Blue Light* (1932) as an influence indicating its striking resemblance to [Disney's opening sequence for *Snow White*] [Allan, 1999, 45].

As discussed in prior chapters, the German expressionist filmmakers and other avant-garde artists were Reiniger and Koch's contemporaries and friends. One German filmmaker's project inspired another and their activities were written about in the papers and film magazines. Reiniger and Koch received attention for *Die Abenteuer des Prinzen Achmed* and were mentioned in association with this artistic crowd. Marc Davis recalled that Walt wanted himself and his animators to be exposed to new ideas and forms of filmmaking and relied heavily on Weimar cinema, so it goes without saying he would have heard about Reiniger's silhouette films. He might have showcased some of her reels at the North Hollywood studio, perhaps even getting a *Prinzen Achmed* copy out of Harvard's iron grip due to his powerful status. As Charles Solomon inferred in *Enchanted Drawings* and given how insular the animation community was at this period in time, some Walt Disney animators were probably aware of Reiniger and it is more than probable they viewed any available films, especially to study how a German woman handled an epic fairytale. None of them, however, felt it was worth recording.[3]

Given how extraordinary Walt Disney's influence was on animation on a global basis, two animation pioneers remember meeting him with great clarity and reverence: Osamu Tezuka and Quirino Cristiani. I can only assume that Reiniger would have written about meeting Disney with her own opinions about the man behind the mouse. Cristiani and Tezuka's meetings with Disney left an imprint on both memories as a noteworthy moment in their careers.

In 1941, Walt Disney and a crew of 16 Disney employees embarked on a South American goodwill tour for the U.S. government. The goal was to collect information and inspiration to create a series of films based on South American cultures (these would be *Saludos Amigos* [1942] and *The Three Caballeros* [1944]) with the underlying hope that Walt Disney would curb any animosity and prevent South America from allying with the Axis Powers. The tour group, nicknamed "Walt and el groupo," toured Chile, Brazil, Argentina and many other countries for ten weeks. (Yet another reason Disney traveled was to get away from his studio as his animators were on strike.) During the Argentina leg on the journey, he met Quirino Cristiani. Cristiani recounted the tale of meeting Disney many times. It was also recorded on film and Zucchelli included it in his documentary:

> [Disney] had been informed that in Buenos Aires there was an artist, the only one making animation. Because I had the film laboratory with a mini cinema[4] I showed him one act from *Peludópolis*. He said to [Frank] Thomas: "What a strange humour this man has, and how effective it is!" And he asked how long it took to finish *Peludópolis*. I said that the film had seven acts. He wanted to know how long and how many people. I said: "Seven to eight months." "And how many people?" I said: "One ... me. Not only the drawing but also the filming." "Impossible!" said Walt Disney. "When we make a movie we use 50 people. And this man made it on his own?" He said: "Invite him to come and join us as team supervisor for a movie about gauchos." I said it was a great honour, but I had my own studio to run and I declined the offer [qt. in Zucchelli, 2010].

Cristiani was then 45, a father, had his own studio, and he wasn't keen on traveling. He would have had to uproot himself and his family and move to California, learn a new language and learn how to work with a team of animators as well as acclimate to the Disney culture. It wasn't worth the risk to him; like Fischinger, Chuck Jones and Reiniger, Cristiani liked being his own boss and didn't want to report to a superior (Zucchelli, 2010). According to Zucchelli's documentary, Disney's offer was Cristiani's real opportunity to return to animation and he eased into retirement afterwards (2010). Cristiani did recommend that Disney contact cartoonist Florencio Molina Campos, who became an artistic consultant to the studio.

In postwar Japan, Douglas MacArthur and the U.S. forces instituted sweeping reforms on the country's government, economy and even entertainment. Everything related to traditional Japanese culture were banned and American media were imported for the first time in years, making a profound impact on a young Osamu Tezuka. As Tezuka evolved into a renowned manga and anime writer and artist, the influence from U.S. animation studios and comics was apparent. "Tezuka once wrote, '[Tetsuwan] Atom's father was in effect Mighty Mouse, whose father was Superman.' ... At other times, Tezuka did not hesitate to speculate on the similarities between Mighty Atom[5] and Mickey Mouse" (Schodt, 2007, 45). Tezuka visited New York for the 1964 World's Fair, which has gone down in Disney history for four pavilions that the Disney Company designed, including the beloved It's a Small World for Pepsi. Tezuka was at the World's Fair as a reporter for the *Sankei* newspaper and to represent himself. Walt was in attendance one day at the Small World pavilion and as Tezuka watched,

> Disney addressed an adoring audience of hundreds at the pavilion. Later, Tezuka drew cartoons of the event, showing Disney with a halo around his head, or being treated like royalty. After Disney finished talking, Tezuka ran into him in the audience. As nervous and tongue-tied as a young fan, he managed to introduce himself as the head of an animation studio in Japan. Disney apparently replied with a disinterested pleasantry, but when Tezuka mentioned that he was the creator of *Astro Boy*, it pricked Disney's interest; he had seen it in Los Angeles, he said, and thought it was a wonderful show, a fascinating example of a story with a science theme. "Kids are going to be focused more and more on space in the future," Disney supposedly said, "so that's the sort of thing I'd like to make myself someday." Sometimes, in conversation, Tezuka would later embellish this story a bit and have Disney say that he "wished *he* had made *Astro Boy*" [Schodt, 2007, 91–92].

Reiniger expressed her displeasure for other animated films receiving funding and was not an avid Disney fan, but she did respect others' work and in her personal accounts would have recorded meeting Walt. Reiniger's friends also would have recounted the tale, especially Jean Renoir, Alfred Happ and Christel Strobel. Based on my own research, I can conclude that Disney and Reiniger never met and he never attended Reiniger's lectures in 1936.

Reiniger and Koch intended to return to Berlin when the Nazi insurgency died down, but they found England's atmosphere to be friendlier and more welcoming, especially considering the stifling regulations they left behind. Their time in England would later influence their decision to settle there after the war and become British citizens. Buoyed by the positive reception she received in England, Reiniger decided to break from her work and seek inspiration in Athens, Greece. From late August to September 1936, Reiniger and Eric Walter White spent time in Greece, the home of Antonis "Mollas" Papoulias, a shadow puppeteer who specialized in Karagiozis (Happ, 2004. p. 55).

Reiniger attended many of Mollas' performances that took place at a street cafe with "a motley crowd that filled all the seats" (Happ, 2004. p. 55). Reiniger wanted to see Mollas, because the Nazis were adamant that silhouette puppetry was unsuitable for audiences. Reiniger, Koch, their friends and the audiences that attended her films were aware this was a false claim. When Reiniger was subjected to the negative Nazi environment, she was filled with self-doubt, psychologically affected, and needed to rekindle her inspiration. Reiniger wrote to her husband after seeing Mollas' performance: "I'm a puppeteer. That's one of the most gratifying results of this trip.... I'm glad I went" (Happ, 2004, 55).

Returning to England, Reiniger set out to create a new film in the fall of 1936 entitled *The King's Breakfast.* Koch and Thorold Dickinson had become well acquainted, even collaborating on a few film projects, and Dickinson hired Reiniger for his new company

Facts and Fantasies to animate A.A. Milne's poem about a king who wants butter for his bread, but he is told marmalade is the more popular choice. It was a sound film, using H. Fraser-Simon's music, with an orchestra conducted by Ernest Irving. Olive Groves and George Baker sang the poem (Happ, 2004, 56). Dickinson would hire Reiniger to make another film for him, *Dream Circus*. The concept behind *Dream Circus* fell into Reiniger's wheelhouse: using music from Stravinsky's ballet *Pulcinella* (based on a famous *commedia dell'arte* character), Reiniger crafted a story about a boy and girl who attend a circus at night and dance a ballet with elephants. She had the story brewing in her mind for some time and finished half the film, but Facts and Fantasies had financial difficulties and *Dream Circus* was never completed (Happ, 2004, 56).

Koch crossed the Channel and visited his close friend Renoir in Paris on January 1, 1937. Renoir was a respected film director at the height of his success in the 1930s. He associated with many famous names and introduced Koch to cameraman Henri Cartier Bresson, movie star Erich von Stroheim, and Count Luchino Visconti di Modrone of Lonate Pozzolo (Happ, 2004, 57). Count Luchino Visconti di Modrone was an Italian film, opera and theater director as well as a screenwriter. Renoir was planning what is regarded as one of his finest films, *La Grande Illusion* (*The Grand Illusion*), a World War I drama inspired by his own experiences as a French reconnaissance pilot. Renoir asked Koch to work on the film as a technical consultant, as he too had survived the Great War and experienced it from the German side. *La Grande Illusion* is about French soldiers imprisoned in a German POW camp and their many complicated escape attempts. Escaping, they make their way to neutral territory. Koch remained in France to work on *La Grande Illusion*. The separation was difficult for the couple and they relied on letters and the occasional visit to keep in touch. Koch spent the next two years working on Renoir's films; he also included Reiniger's silhouettes in *La Marseillaise*. Koch became an essential component for Renoir's *La Grande Illusion* and the famous director wrote, "I owe a great deal to the Germans. I owe them Karl Koch, without whom *La Grande Illusion* could not have been what it is" (1974, 94). Filming *La Grande Illusion* was a challenge for Renoir. He sought historical accuracy, including having actor Jean Gabin wear his old pilot uniform. In his memoir, Renoir recounts that Stroheim and Koch got into an argument about a hospital nurse costume. Koch said it was too elaborate and Stroheim defended taking creative licenses:

> ... Koch [replied that Stroheim] had not fought in the war and should therefore keep his mouth shut. Stroheim's answer was to call Koch a petty-bourgeois, an unjust accusation, for Koch was an aristocrat in spirit. Koch was so angered he threw a wine glass at Stroheim, who left the room and shut the door just as it shattered behind him. The entire time Stroheim had played a joke on Koch, angering him, eventually they settled their differences over wine [Renoir, 1974, 164–65].

During filming, Koch donned a uniform and worked as an extra during some of the prison scenes. It would be one of the few times he was captured on camera.

While Koch saturated himself in white wine, John Grierson[6] became more interested in Reiniger's work. He ran the General Post Office (GPO) and would later be a famous figure in British documentary films. The GPO had a film unit that was used to market the United Kingdom's postal services via documentary films. Any type of film could be made as long as it related to postal services. Many well-known figures in British film history worked for the GPO Film Unit, including animator Norman McLaren. While Reiniger initially was hired by Grierson, he departed for Canada and she worked closely with Alberto Cavalcanti (Happ, 2004, 58). At a 1974 Goethe Institute event honoring Reiniger, panelist Richard Kaplan (who sponsored Reiniger's work in the 1950s) said that "some of Reiniger's most remarkable work was done at this time—very short theatre commercials which he described as 'lovely, exquisite, delicate pieces of work'" (Starr, 1980, 18).

The first film she made for the GPO was for presentation at the Empire Exhibition at Glasgow, a music festival, in the summer of 1937: *The Tocher* featured Benjamin Britten's Rossini arrangements (Whanslaw, 1950, 103; Happ, 2004, 170). "The word 'Tocher' is Scottish and means 'a marriage portion'" (Whanslaw, 1950, 103). While meant to advertise the GPO savings book, the film is a grand drama starring the lovers Angus and Rhona. Angus wishes to marry Rhona, but her father objects. As sorrowful as any love-stricken prince, Angus laments near an enchanted pond that bequeaths the lover a magical gift that is sure to please Rhona's father. Rhona is being forced to marry another man, but when Angus appears and gives her father the gift, a GPO savings book, he stops the wedding and allows the lovers to be together.

At this point, Koch was working on another Renoir film, *La Marseillaise*, that showcased the French Revolution from the perspective of people directly involved. Renoir requested that Reiniger pay homage to the famous French shadow performer François Dominique Séraphin and his popular play *Le Pont cassé* (*The Broken Bridge*). Koch wrote Reiniger and explained that Renoir offered to pay her £30 for the "short but impressive scene" if she had the time (Happ, 2004, 59). Reiniger heartily accepted and she designed scenes and characters: the king of France and Madame la France, an anthropomorphized version of the country, with a broken bridge between them. The king points at the bridge and cries, "The bridge is broken between us." The sequence was shot in mid-November and it might have been short, but it was heavy with metaphor about the French Revolution and foreshadowed the storm brewing in Germany.

In 1938, after *La Marseillaise*, Koch worked on Renoir's *La Règle du jeu* (*The Rules of the Game*), a movie that was a flop at the time, but has gone on to being regarded as one of his best. A satirical comment on the aristocratic lifestyle, it featured adulterous behavior, lack of regard for human life, and other topics that riled French and German censors. Renoir edited the film multiple times because of the censors' regulations. It has been restored as much as possible, but a complete cut doesn't exist today. When it was released in 1939, it was banned after one month in France. When the Nazis invaded, they took great pride in destroying the copies. Very much like Reiniger's *Prinzen Achmed*, *La Règle du Jeu* was considered a lost film until several copies were found and edited together. The Nazis didn't like Renoir or his work.

Reiniger had returned to England and received another film job from the GPO. She animated *The HPO: Heavenly Post Office*, where angels delivered greetings via telegrams during happy occasions. Reiniger decided to experiment again by animating with color, and *HPO* was her first color silhouette film (Happ, 2004, 59). Reiniger once more pulled out all her storytelling skills and made a commercial where life's happiest moments are augmented by warm greetings received through the GPO (cherubs deliver the happy messages); it finished with the line, "It's heaven to receive a greetings telegram. Be an angel and send one." While Reiniger preferred to film in black and white, she would adapt most of her post–World War II films to include color backgrounds. According to Eric Walter White, "[W]hatever the technical difficulties of this new medium may be, the use of flat colour is going to add enormously to the expressiveness of the chiaroscuro of her silhouettes" (1939, 47).

The following year, Reiniger drew on her theatrical background and her love for opera when the Toynbee Hall Theatre Club hired her to make sets and costumes for two productions: Christoph Willibald Gluck's *Orpheus* (Gellhorn conducted the orchestra) in January and Molière's *The Imaginary Invalid* in June (Happ, 2004, 59).

The year 1939 wasn't quiet for Europe and Reiniger and Koch were wise to have left Germany when they did. Renoir recalled, "[T]he failure of *La Règle du jeu* so depressed me that I resolved either to give up the cinema or to leave France" (1974, 173). He didn't quit his film career, rather he accepted Benito Mussolini's invitation to make films in Italy. On August 4, 1939, Renoir, his new wife actress Dido Freire and Koch left for Rome (Happ, 2004, 60). Renoir's next project was a film based on the opera *Tosca* and Reiniger wanted to join her husband, but on September 1, 1939, Hitler invaded Poland. She left one day before England and Germany declared war. She had traveled from London to Paris to Nice, then booked passage on one of the last trains between Italy and France. Reiniger remembered, "As the train drove into a tunnel, I had a sudden overpowering thought, here I go into fascist Italy." She met her friends in Rome the night of September 2, 1939 (Happ, 2004, 60).

Not long after arriving in Italy, Scalera Film commissioned Reiniger to make a shadow film based on Gaetano Donizetti's comic opera *L'Elisir d'amore* (*The Elixir of Love*). Scalera Film was established in 1938 and Mussolini supported it, due to his obsession to centralize the Italian film industry. Continuing with her love for music and opera, Reiniger was ecstatic to be making a silhouette film based on the opera:

> The task ... to make a silhouette film from an Italian opera was very exciting for me. To me, *L'Elisir dAmore* is one of the loveliest operas of all time. Everything is presented with the most beautiful melodies.... However, it was not an easy task to transform Donizetti's graceful work, which commands the opera stage for three hours. When it plays as a short film [it] may take twenty minutes without losing ... too much of the opera's poetic charm. But I think I have succeeded. The story is told with a few changes, which occurs in the opera, and the main songs are mostly sung in their original length [qt. in Happ, 2004, 60–61].

Animated during the fall of 1939, *L'Elisir d'amore* premiered on May 11, 1940. It is now a lost film (Happ, 2004, 61).

It was not simple to make a movie during World War II and Renoir was dealt a blow not long after *Tosca*'s script was complete. He began filming on May 6, 1940, with Luchiano Visconti as his assistant director, but the Germans were infiltrating Rome and on May 19, 1940, there was an incident:

> The only Italian paper favoring France was that of the Vatican, the *Osservatore Romano*. The Nazis hired a gang of local thugs ... and posted them at all the newspaper kiosks selling the paper. Prospective purchasers were beaten up. Within 24 hours even neutral papers had become pro–German. I myself was one of the sufferers. I asked for the *Osservatore Romano* in a restaurant and was duly set upon. Things would have gone badly with me if I had not invoked the name of Mussolini, who was, after all, responsible for my being there [Renoir, 1974, 176–77].

Under advice from the French ambassador, Renoir immediately left the country for the U.S. with his wife. As a German citizen, Koch was not an enemy of the Italian government; his only problem was that Germany might force him to come back. One month later, on June 10, 1940, Koch became *Tosca*'s director with Reiniger as his assistant. Two days later they resumed filming (Happ, 2004, 64).

Alongside *Tosca*, the couple worked on an Italian version of an American western called *Una Signora dell'ovest* (*Girl of the Golden West*), but it didn't go very well for Reiniger. She and Koch had written the script, but she didn't know anything about the

American west, so she wrote down her husband's ideas (Happ, 2004, 64). Reiniger also disliked the lead actress Isa Pola, who happened to be the mistress of the head of Scalera Film, and he called her a "horrible cow" (Happ, 2004, 64). The film premiered on January 1, 1941, in Rome and Reiniger made plans for other silhouette films. She planned to make a film in 1942 called *Mustafa* with an Asian theme where she wrote the script and made the costumes, but it never came about (Jouvanceau, 2004 p. 48; Happ, 2004, 64). She did hand-publish *Das Plantenbuch* (*The Planet Book*) on February 14, 1942, featuring her watercolor landscapes, silhouettes on mythological themes, and linocut prints with the planetary symbols (Happ, 2004, 64).

The following year would prove to be very bad for Reiniger and Koch. She didn't make one silhouette film and the war drew closer to their haven with Count Luchino Visconti di Modrone. Allied troops invaded Sicily on July 10, 1943, and nine days an air raid later destroyed much of Rome. On July 25, Mussolini was arrested, followed by the Italian armistice on September 8. It was apparent that Rome wasn't safe any more, so Koch and Reiniger fled to Venice. "Both earned their livelihood with contributions to the entertainment part of Wehrmacht newspapers. Koch wrote articles on the Alpine Pass and Napoleon, Reiniger illustrated classical literature with pen drawings" (Happ, 2004, 64). They remained in Venice until Christmas 1943, when Reiniger got word that her mother was ill. There were stressful political tensions due to their German citizenship, so reluctantly they decided to return to Berlin. They celebrated Christmas on December 23, and the next morning left Venice at 5:00 a.m. and arrived in Berlin by train at 9:00 p.m., returning to the city they abandoned eight years prior.

Koch and Reiniger were more than nervous about returning to Berlin. They were disliked by the Reichstag for their political beliefs, they didn't have jobs—and Berlin was the epicenter of the war and a prime target for Allied forces. Their lives were in danger from the moment they returned to their native soil, but the couple fared better than expected. The second week of January, Reiniger visited her old friend and mentor Paul Wegener; in December 1944, for his seventieth birthday, she cut him a special silhouette displaying his most famous roles (Happ, 2004, 18). Reiniger found work with the National Institute for Film and Picture in Science and Education, while UFA commissioned Koch to write a screenplay that would never be produced. Reiniger didn't want to work in films when she returned to Germany, because all films had to be made with the Nazi seal of approval. She discovered that working for the National Institute for Film and Picture was better than she expected: "When I came back to Berlin during the war, I did not like having to go back to the film industry, because [all films were made by] the Reich Chamber of Film. And I did not want to belong to an organization. But the Institute was a harmless thing..." (Happ, 2004, 66). Reiniger began work on *Die goldene Gans* (*The Golden Goose*) in January 1944, her first and only film made officially for the Nazi party.

While Reiniger and Koch despised the Nazis, they had to rely on the party for survival. All the money they earned for making *Die goldene Gans* was put towards food and other necessities to live in the crumbling city with her ailing mother. During 1944, the Allies continuously bombed Berlin to break the German morale and wipe out the country's capital, but one of their main targets was to destroy transportation to cut off supplies. By this time, Hitler and the Nazis felt outward pressure as the Allies drew closer to Germany from all sides, which led to inward stresses as Hitler struggled to bolster his army with dwindling supplies and heavy losses. The army lacked a fresh stock of soldiers and were forced to draft older men and even place young boys at the front. Koch received a

The princess is amused by the golden goose (©Primrose Productions).

draft notice on February 1, 1945, but he was able to return home in the evenings and continue work on *Die goldene Gans* (Happ, 2004, 66). *Die goldene Gans* provided a respite from the raging battle and the couple were able to disappear into their world of fairytales, where bombs and Nazism didn't exist.

The evenings spent in a fairytale world were shattered when Koch's troop was ordered to defend eastern Berlin against the impending Russians in April, without a weapon and wearing an old firefighter's uniform (Happ, 2004, 66). On April 21, Koch managed to escape and he spent two weeks hiding from German and Russian soldiers. Reiniger didn't have any idea what happened to him. Koch's entire tale that reads like a script from one of his films:

> Every man capable of bearing arms was mobilized for that defense of the city against the Russians. Koch, who was nearly 50, was drafted into a regiment armed with bazookas—a strange weapon which he was no more capable of using than his comrades. They were dressed in National Guard uniform dating from 1870 and sent to defend a small birch wood on the outskirts of town. A captain of territorials was in command. He posted his men behind the trees with the encouragement: "Hang on till the last of you is killed. The Russians must not pass." Despite this stirring exhortation, those amateur soldiers, having consulted together, decided to make a bolt for it.
>
> Koch fetched up in a village which was almost immediately occupied by the Russians, who rounded up everyone of military appearance in the marketplace. Koch found an NCO who spoke German and did his best to persuade him that the uniform he was wearing, although out-of-date, was nonetheless military, and that he was entitled to the soldier's chief privilege—namely not to be shot. The discussion was cut short by the arrival of a car containing a woman in officer's uniform who seemed to be the Russian commander. Koch rushed towards her, his face glowing with astonishment. "We met in Paris, don't you remember?" The lady was no less astonished, never having set eyes on him before. She asked in perfect German: "Who introduced us?" After a bare moment's hesitation

Koch came out with the name which seemed to him most improbable in Russian ears. "Lestringuez,"[7] he said. The lady's expression relaxed. She gave an order and Koch was released. Well done, Lestringuez! [1974, 178–79].

Meanwhile, Reiniger and her mother spent their time taking cover from the Battle of Berlin in the basement or an underground shaft (Happ, 2004, 66). She continued to work on *Die Goldene Gans* despite the bombing and invasion of the Red Army. Reiniger said that her friends believed she had died. "It was thought we'd committed suicide. The reason being a poem by Brecht. So I put some of my silhouettes in bookshop windows as a sign to our friends that we were still alive" (qt. in Raganelli, 1999). One day she had an alarming confrontation with a Russian soldier armed with a machine gun, who asked what she was doing in her home. Reiniger replied that she was making a film and after some deliberation the soldier told her to "carry on" with her work. Reiniger wrote that from that point, "I worked on this film under Goebbels, but from that point on it was made under the Russians" (Happ, 2004, 66).

Journalist Werner Fielder wrote about Reiniger's dedication to animation despite her sobering surroundings in the *Neue Zeite* on June 23, 1946:

> In a severely destroyed Berlin street, in the very house that almost challengely [sic] towers five storeys high over a row of ruins, a woman continues to work unperturbed. Up there under the roof, fragile, ornamented creatures climb up the wall like fantasy wallpaper. Mrs. Lotte Reiniger is back at work in the poor, bombed Berlin working on her new film plans with the same wonderful, irrepressible determination [qt. in Marschall *et al.*, 2012].

The Allied forces overwhelmed the Nazi army and the Battle of Berlin ended on May 2, 1945. It was followed by the end of war in Europe on May 8 with Germany's unconditional surrender. World War II would come to an official end when the Japanese Empire surrendered and signed a peace treaty on September 2, 1945. The war ended for Reiniger when Koch came home on May 9, the day Germany capitulated to the Soviet Union.

Animation has an interesting history as being used as a propaganda tool and World War II was an especially scintillating period as it was the first war when animation played a compelling role. As the world animation powerhouse, the U.S. pumped out cartoons to support the war effort in a zeitgeist that has never been replayed at a major animation studio due to anti-war advocates and political correctness. Donald Duck, Tom and Jerry, Daffy Duck, Popeye, Bugs Bunny, Mickey Mouse, Goofy and other famous characters spurred the home front to rally behind their troops and buy war bonds. These animated characters were placed in direct conflict with Nazis, Italians, Japanese and, until they changed sides, Soviet enemies. This often resulted in comical antics at their adversaries' expense. Seeing them at war placed a strong black and white division between the "good guys versus the bad guys." Cartoons of this era are noted for the simplistic plots crowned by "violent" hysterical action and reaction that defy the laws of physics and, if they were duplicated today, would be automatically censored. It is within this simplicity, however, that these cartoons have achieved their recognition, but also it gave audiences a simple rendering of heroes vs. villains transferable to the real world. If Donald Duck fought the Nazis, then everyone needed to fight the Nazis!

Perhaps the most famous U.S. World War II cartoon is Disney's *Der Führer's Face*, where Donald Duck dreams he works in a Nazi factory and wakes up to realize it was a horrible nightmare. *Der Führer's Face* sports a German oom-pah band with players sporting racist caricatures of Hideki Tojo, Benito Mussolini, Heinrich Himmler and an effeminate Herman Göring playing the popular namesake song. It won the 1943 Oscar for Best

Animated Short Film, while the following year MGM's *Yankee Doodle Mouse* won; both were animated propaganda shorts. The only other cartoon to vie for most popular U.S. World War II cartoon is Disney's *Victory Through Airpower* (1943), a partially animated film that depicted America's prestige in aerial combat and bombings. It was used to inspire faith in the U.S. Air Force just as Reiniger's *Das rollende Rad* showed German innovation with vehicular transportation. Other famous World War II cartoons were *Blitz Wolf, Confusions of a Nutzy Spy, Falling Hare, Secret Agent, Russian Rhapsody, Herr Meets Hare, A Jolly Good Furlough, Scrap Happy Daffy, Ration Fer the Duration*, the Private Snafu cartoons and a seven-film series following Donald Duck through his U.S. Army conscription to his first mission. Disney teamed with the National Film Board of Canada to make several cartoons starring the Disney characters supporting the war effort.

The Axis Powers also animated cartoons to fuel their own propaganda machines, but they relied more on live action films. The Japanese released their own propaganda cartoons, although they hadn't yet mastered animation (a sharp contrast to their current state). In pre-war Japan "because their films were unlikely to be seen in America ... Japanese animators of the 1930s freely 'borrowed' drawings and characters from American sources" and used them as homages to their origins (Knight, 2014). Mickey Mouse, Betty Boop, Felix the Cat, Bosko and animation styles from their creators were represented in Japan's early cartoons.

Taro's Monster Hunt (1930), made by Iwao Ashida, borrowed from Herman and Ising with a Bosko rendered samurai and "animation plundered from the first two Looney Tunes, *Sinkin' in the Bathtub* and *Congo Jazz*. Ikio Oishi drew heavily on Paul Terry and Otto Messmer in his 1931 *Home Alone Mice* and in 1934 Noburo Ofuji made *The Routing of the Tengu* that borrowed Myron Waldman and Fleischer-style animation (Knight, 2014).

As tensions heightened between the U.S. and Japan, Japanese animators used American cartoon characters and styles as a propaganda tool. *Momotaro vs. Mickey Mouse* (1934) animated by Yoshitsugu Tanaka, used the "international symbol of goodwill" Mickey Mouse as an enemy combatant with an army of duplicates attacking peaceful characters from Japanese folklore. The Japanese characters call upon the famous fairytale hero Momotaro to defeat the western scourge.

Osamu Tezuka felt the only one worth mentioning was *Momotaro: Umi no Shinpei* (*Momotaro's Divine Warriors*), released towards the end of 1945. The first full-length animated film made in Japan clocked in at 79 minutes (Schodt, 2007, 58). The Japanese Imperial Navy produced the film and it served as a sequel to *Momotaro no Umiwashi* (*Momotaro's Sea Eagles*) made two years earlier. (At 39 minutes, it was too short to be a full-length feature film [Schodt, 2007, 58)]. The story involved a group of animals freeing an island from evil white oppressors. "Tezuka often wrote how this film moved him, not for its theme so much as for its technical excellence and for the circumstances under which it was created" (Schodt, 2007, 58).

Germany might have had the first full-length animated movie made in Europe and the first documented uses of the multiplane camera, but its animated films consisted primarily of abstract experimental shorts "which, when the filmmakers were lucky, were shown and financed as advertising films" (Giesen & Storm, 2012, 5). In the 1920s and '30s, Reiniger was the only German animator who used a straightforward means of storytelling comparable to the popular U.S. cartoons. Her concentration on fairytales contained recognizable story elements: beginning, middle, end, villains, heroes, climax, conflict and a happy resolution. Her more "familiar" stories had a wider appeal than abstract shorts that required a deeper dive into the imagination and didn't allow the audience to be carried away into escapism. Since Reiniger didn't animate abstract films and was a woman, she wasn't as highly regarded in some artistic circles.

In the early twentieth century, Germany had a live action movie industry rivaled only by Hollywood. Imported U.S. cartoons generated a significant profit and German studios investigated the possibility of animating their own cartoons. Glamour studio UFA made an attempt to establish an animation studio in Germany. UFA was aware that many popular cartoon characters originated in comic books, but the country didn't have a surfeit of cartoonists with the exception of Otto Waffenschmied. He was one of the few German cartoonists with a successful career drawing the children's magazine *Dideldum*, so UFA contracted him in October 1934 to create a character to compete with U.S. characters. Inspired by German fairytales, he invented the "sylvan elf" Tilo Voss. After disagreements over the story's content because it "didn't have enough gags" and fluctuating budgets, the project was canceled in September 1935 (Giesen & Storm, 2012, 9). Ultra Film Berlin and a Fabry-financed company contracted UFA to make cartoons, but all negotiations fell off when *Snow White* premiered.

Walt Disney's *Snow White* had a huge global impact which didn't go unnoticed by Hitler, Goebbels and other Nazi cronies. "Hitler and Goebbels were cartoon aficionados.... They tried to establish a cartoon industry to rival Disney and competed with American producers in a love-hate relationship, studying their films behind locked doors" (Giesen & Storm, 2012, 1). The Nazis were just as invested in making their own cartoons, but they wanted to prove they were not only the master race, but also the master animators of the world. The master animator in the world's consciousness was Walt Disney, so Hitler, Goebbels and the rest of the Nazi gang not only wanted to become Walt Disney, they wanted to conquer his claim to the title. The Nazis were ambitious in their animation projects, but the desire was greater than the yield and their actual popularity, much like UFA's failed attempts.

Moritz wrote in his article "Resistance and Subversion in Animated Films of the Nazi Era," "The question of animation in the Nazi era has largely been ignored or even falsified" (1997, 230). He lists several known German animators who had the real release dates of the films falsified to avoid the association with Nazi Germany: Oskar Fischinger, the Diehl brothers, Ladislas Starevitch, Paul Peroff. Even Reiniger's *Das gestohlene Herz* is "given as 1932 or 1933, as if to suggest that they had not been made in Nazi Germany[8]" (Moritz, 1997, 230). No one wanted to acknowledge how the Nazis took over the German film industry and transformed it into part of their propaganda machine and along with it viewed animation as vehicle to promote their ideals. While German animators wanted to whitewash any connection with the Third Reich, very little has also been documented about German animation because (again) it wasn't viewed as a topic of value and Germany really isn't known for its animation.

Rolf Giesen and J.P. Storm wrote the quintessential guide to understanding the Nazi plan for their animation empire: *Animation Under the Swastika: A History of Trickfilm in Nazi Germany.* They open their book with the following quote from *Der Zeichen und Trickfilm: Neue Ausdrucksmöglichkeiten für die künstlerische Kinematographie*, published in 1935:

> It is the unique German mental and emotional world as it is expressed in medieval puppet plays and death dances in the fairy tales of the brothers Grimm, by Musaeus and Hauff, in the spooky tales of

E.T.A. Hoffman, the fantasies of Munchhausen etc., that should perform as the source of ideas for German animation films.... The German artist should be able to set against American style something totally equal, even superior and originally German with a little support. Certainly the idiosyncrasy of works inspired by the true German spirit should be successful beyond our borders in practice and for sentimental value and would mean important promotion of our culture [2012, ii].

Giesen and Storm selected this quote to start the book as it explains the Nazis' attempts to kickstart their own animation industry. Walt Disney was considered the pinnacle of American animation and in order to compete with Disney Animation and other studios, the Nazis needed something more than Reiniger's silhouette films and abstract films by Bartosch and Fischinger. Ruttmann had turned his attention to documentary films with Leni Riefenstahl, but had he lived he might have pursued more animation.

When the Nazis took power, they had to build an animation industry from the bottom up and master techniques that the American studios had spent more than a decade mastering. It would be no mean feat to rival Walt Disney and other animation studios that had financial backing and established reputations. Georg Pál of *Puppetoons* fame began his animation career at UFA, where he made a stop-motion commercial using cigarettes and other commercials. He wrote in a 1936 letter about the lack of sophistication and finances in the German animation industry, leading into how stop-motion was Germany's specialty:

I produced a great number of animated cartoons and was able to improve my technique considerably. Although these films were very favorably commented upon by the press and leading critics, I personally was never really satisfied with the work I turned out, because I felt that with the enormous resources the American trick film production could put behind their films, I would never be able to successfully compete with such productions. Plans, therefore, ripened in my mind to produce cartoons in the third dimension [qt. in Giesen & Storm, 2012, 162].

During the Weimar Republic an import quota on foreign films had been set, limiting the number of films available to German audiences, and once the war started all foreign films were banned. Prior to 1939, U.S. distributors still released films in Germany and when the U.S. stock market crashed in 1929, they heavily relied on foreign film distribution to make up the deficits, (Giesen & Storm, 2012, 12). More than 100 animated shorts were released in Germany, starring popular characters Mickey Mouse, Oswald the Lucky Rabbit, Popeye, Betty Boop, Felix the Cat and more (Giesen & Storm, 2012, 12). Walt Disney molded himself and his company into a powerful entertainment icon with the ability to influence the masses. Mickey Mouse's global reach influenced not only children, but also world leaders:

Disney's most famous creation, Mickey Mouse, became the most popular international figure of the era. In Japan, he was more popular than anyone but the emperor. In Britain, King George V reportedly refused to attend movies unless Mickey Mouse was playing. And by the mid–1930s the Mouse was being shown in 38 nations, and a wax image was on display in Madam Tussaud's museum in London. The League of Nations presented Disney with a scroll[9] in 1937 [sic] proclaiming Mickey Mouse an "international symbol of good will." The secret of Mickey Mouse's success involved the appeal of fantasy, bold colors, and uncomplicated messages. Mickey carried an egalitarian message celebrating the triumph of the little guy [Eckles & Zeiler, 2003, 102].

This quote, published in *Globalization and the American Century,* pulled its information from "L'Affaire Mickey Mouse" by Herbert Russell and published in 1937, the year *Snow White* premiered. Russell also mentions that Mussolini loved the Mouse, Queen Mother Mary "sent for him regularly," and that he palled around with President Roosevelt

(142). One might think that while Hitler and Goebbels were animation fans, they would wage an all-out war on the Mouse, especially given his prominence as a stalwart American symbol. Anti-foreign propaganda had circulated through Germany since World War I's end and more did once the Nazis came into power. On July 28, 1931, in the *Film-Kurier*, the Mouse was described as a promoter of indecency and undermined young people's intelligence:

> Blonde, freethinking, urban German youth tied to the apron strings of Jewish finance. Young people, where is your sense of self? Mickey Mouse is the shabbiest, most miserable ideal ever invented. Mickey Mouse is a recipe for mental enfeeblement sent over with capital from the Young Plan. Healthy instinct should tell every decent girl and honest boy that those filthy, dirt-caked vermin, the greatest carriers of bacteria in the animal kingdom, cannot be made into an ideal animal type. Have we nothing better to do than decorate our garments with filthy animals because Jewish business in America wants profits? Down with Jewish brainwashing of the people! Kick out the vermin! Down with Mickey Mouse, and up with the swastika![10] [p. 35].

There is also a famous incident when the Reichstag banned the Disney cartoon *Barnyard Battle* (1929) in 1930, because it drew on sour World War I memories: "The wearing of German military helmets by an army of cats which opposed a militia of mice is offensive to national dignity. Permission to exhibit this production in Germany is refused"[11] (Bulik, 2014). The ban didn't last long, because Hitler loved Mickey Mouse and lobbied to license *Snow White* in Germany. Goebbels knew how much the Führer loved the Mouse, so for Christmas 1937 he arranged a special gift for him. Written on December 20, 1937, in Goebbels' diary: "As a Christmas present I gave the Führer 30 top movies of the past few years and 18 Mickey Mouse films. He is pleased to no end. Glad to have that treasure which hopefully will give him joy and relaxation (qt. in Giesen & Storm, 2012, 13).

Ironically, while the Nazi leaders loved Mickey Mouse, someone thought the Mouse could be used to mock the Nazis. In response to the editorial denouncing Mickey as vermin, a response was published on July 28, 1931, claiming Disney and Mickey Mouse "should be taken up as a symbol of reason, against 'swastika and persecution.' Instead of the swastika emblems, patrons of Disney films were advised to buy the little Mickey Mouse pins from the cinemas and wear them to make an anti–Nazi statement" (Leslie, 2001, 80). While Mickey Mouse might be considered a representation of the "all-American dream," Russell counters with, "[N]one of these nations [Allies and Axis Powers alike] has been able to agree upon an interpretation of either Mickey or his activities. They see in him a mere reflection of their own ideologies or those of their enemies, according to their national psychology" (1937, 143). Goebbels had said, "We are convinced that the film is one of the most modern and far-reaching means for influencing the masses. A government can therefore not possibly leave the film world to itself" (qt. in Doherty, 2015, 19). Hitler and Goebbels understood the power Disney held and they wanted to manufacture a Nazi Mickey Mouse who could sway audiences to their political ideals.

Continuing on the same thought that Goebbels and Hitler wanted their own exploitable cartoon character, Esther Leslie drew on Clement Greenberg's article "Avant Garde and Kitsch," defining kitsch as the "culture of the industrialized masses.... [It] compromised both American commercial culture and the totalitarian art of Nazi Germany and the Soviet Union" (2002, 132). Hitler's totalitarian art never caught on with the masses, specifically because it displayed a generic and unimaginative glimpse into the Vaterland's ideal, non-existent statehood, which German citizens were unable to identify with, considering their steady diet of Weimar avant garde, World War I atrocities and the economic troubles. "In Nazi Germany, [kitsch] was monumental art, once again illusionistic and illusory. In America its quintessence was surely Disney" (Leslie, 2002, 133). Mickey Mouse and the Walt Disney Company represented the power to sway and control masses in a manner both entertaining and resonating. Mickey Mouse could be criticized, but his overall appeal was more positive than negative, unlike Hitler's regime in the early 1930s and arguably among many Germans who joined the Nazi party for fear of death. Mickey Mouse or a Nazi version of the character could masquerade as a harmless symbol to inoculate the Third Reich's doctrine into impressionable minds.[12]

A popular Disney myth is that Walt Disney held anti–Semitic beliefs. Numerous Disney scholars have disproven this but the idea persists with even some possible Nazi ties that have been blown out of proportion thanks to the Internet. Despite the truth, it can be intimated that there are similarities between Mickey Mouse and Hitler's tyrannical control over people, which demonstrate why Hitler was lured into creating his own cartoon empire. Russell paints a picture of Mickey Mouse Clubs that littered the U.S. in 1937: "Most of the organizations take in only children, who carry a Mickey Mouse emblem and take a Mickey Mouse oath, which on its face is an innocuous pledge of goodwill and patriotism. But they have a song, and a grip [handshake], and a password" (1937, 143).

Russell's description rings of the Hitler Youth, a social club built around Nazi beliefs. It was geared towards children, had official memorabilia, an oath of patriotism, and a handbook that told kids not to harm animals. Despite the similarities, the Hitler Youth is an extreme example of fascist and dictatorial governments establishing control by building a strong grip on people from childhood. The Mickey Mouse Club wasn't any different from other fan clubs that dominated American culture in the twentieth century, it just had a wide reach and was a marketing gimmick. The Mickey Mouse Club was a more wholesome type of fan club in the sense that it was geared towards children, didn't encourage hatred or reporting friends, neighbors or parents for disliking the government, had a positive message, and the kids had imaginary adventures with Mickey Mouse and his friends. Other cartoons, movie stars, TV shows, singers and rock groups had fan clubs with fine examples of fandom at its worst. Rudolph Valentino, the Beatles and Elvis Presley stirred up more social unrest with pandemic episodes of teenage girls and women swooning, sex appeal, gyrating hips and "promoting derelict activities." Mickey Mouse never claimed to be "bigger than God"; he supported more traditional family views, democracy and American capitalism with merchandising. The worst he did was encourage screaming kids to buy Disney products.[13]

There isn't a record of Hitler nor Goebbels and Disney meeting, although they came close in 1935 when Roy and Walt Disney traveled to Berlin after Mickey Mouse was honored as "an international symbol of good will" (Giesen & Storm, 2012, 13). Hitler was eager to play *Snow White* in German theaters. It's odd that Hitler, who ranted about the superiority of the Aryan race and German culture, wasn't as excited about Reiniger's animated film. *Prinzen Achmed* was a pure German domestic product made with six people compared to over 500 people Disney required for his first film; it relied on German ingenuity; was made 11 years before; has amazing special effects; was "the first" animated film (Hitler probably wasn't aware of Cristiani), and was made by a woman. Hitler could have argued Reiniger's gender in a way that one German woman was more creative than a crew of American men and it came first! *Prinzen Achmed* theoretically was the perfect film to lead the Nazi animation industry based on these indications, except for four factors: 1) The story was based on *1001 Arabian Nights*, and there isn't anything German about that; 2) Reiniger and Koch's political ties or lack thereof; they didn't like the Nazis; 3) Reiniger was still indirectly associated with the degenerate avant-garde; and 4) Koch and Reiniger had left the country. If Reiniger and Koch had different political allegiances and remained in the country, it can be assumed the Nazis would have showcased her work.

Snow White, on the other hand, was based on a Brothers Grimm German fairytale. It was the only American film to receive huge coverage in the National Socialist Press (Giesen & Storm, 2012, 13). Hitler ordered a copy of *Snow White*, adored it and added it to his private collection; Storm interviewed Hitler's projectionist, who said the Führer enjoyed laughing at the dwarfs' antics (Giesen & Storm, 2012, 14, 216). Both the Reichsminister of Propaganda and the Walt Disney company wanted a *Snow White* German premiere, Disney more so for the profit and Goebbels to satisfy his and Hitler's fandom. But negotiations never worked out because the Nazis couldn't raise the money to license the film (Giesen & Storm, 2012, 15–22). As the start of World War II neared, the Ministry of Enlightenment and Propaganda were forced to act against Hollywood's Anti-Nazi League. "[T]he Ministry and German film experts regarded *Snow White* as a film of high artistic calibre and a movie for which an exemption clause should be possible" (Giesen & Storm, 2012, 22). Esther Leslie wrote, "[I]t could not be denied that Disney had tapped into something dear to the Teutonic 'soul'" (Leslie, 2002, 132).

Despite the exemption clause, the Nazis eventually got around to criticizing Disney's work as "too American for German taste. German fairy tales, official reviewers said, are strictly a 'German matter'" (Giesen & Storm, 2012, 24). Goebbels wanted the Third Reich to have its own *Schneeweisschen* and ordered nature documentarian Hubert Schonger to film a live action version of the fairytale, but it was an inferior substitute. Schonger was told to film the German *Snow White*

> with "documentary" fidelity to the original Grimm fairytale version.... This "genuine German" *Snow White* [1939] turned out to be an awful bore (and awkwardly made), but never one to admit a mistake, Goebbels commissioned seven other live action fairytales (three of them feature-length) from Schonger, along with three short combined live-action and animation films, and four drawn-colour fairytale cartoons—all, apparently, of decidedly second-rate quality both in imagination and execution [Moritz, 1997, 232].

Perhaps Goebbels thought Germany had a chance to triumph over Disney's imagination, when Riefenstahl's documentary on the 1936 Olympics, *Olympia,* won the Best Film (Coppa Mussolini) at the Venice International Film Festival in 1938 over *Snow White*. Harold Smith, European representative for the Motion Picture Producers and Distributors of America, "argued that a documentary, not being a legitimate film, should not have been in competition. How else to explain how an obscure German documentary film' had beaten out the fairy-tale magic of Walt Disney?" (Doherty, 2015, 301). (Disney, however, didn't seem to hold it against her, and when Riefenstahl journeyed to the U.S. to sell Hollywood on Nazism and *Olympia,* she was shunned by the elite except for Walt Disney.)

Nazis were still curious about Walt Disney's origins, and in a manner similar to how the Japanese were granted Ehrenarier or "Honorary Aryan" status, Walt Disney became "Germanized." A man who helped Reiniger begin her animation career and introduced her to Carl Koch rewrote Disney's past. "On inquiry by Dr. Günther Schwarz, Reichsfilmkammer, in a letter dated May 5, 1941, documentary filmmaker Dr. Hans Cürlis falsely assured that he had heard Walt Disney was born in Germany, baptized 'Walter Distler,' and had worked for some years in Germany" (Giesen & Storm, 2012, 24). Disney was of German descent along with English on his mother's side. His father came from an Irish-Canadian pedigree.[14]

The Nazis weren't going to get *Snow White*, so Goebbels decided it was time to build an all-German animation studio fueled by the creative energy of strong Aryan animators, and their films would outpace Disney's pieces. Other German animators jumped on board with their own desires to create animated shorts and films to rival Disney, so Reiniger wasn't alone any longer in her use of fairytales and concrete storytelling. She and Koch abandoned Germany in favor of England, so she couldn't be tapped to lead any animation projects.

Wolfgang Kaskeline stepped up to the plate, but he failed to prove his Aryan ancestry (Giesen & Storm, 2012, 43–49). Hans Held wanted to make cartoons, but he had difficulty completing projects, was drafted, and had financial problems (Giesen & Storm, 2012, 52–57).

Kurt Stordel had the greatest desire to start a German animation studio after seeing a Mickey Mouse cartoon in the early 1930s, but he stressed he didn't want to copy Walt Disney (Giesen & Storm, 2012, 58, 60). Stordel said many times he wanted to distinguish himself from Disney, and even went as far to be critical of Disney's animation style: "Referring to the grotesque style of Walt Disney was consciously avoided. Stordel's films shall be funny, romantic, and folksy" (qt. in Giesen & Storm, 2012, 59). He was inspired by the same German fairytales and he animated a "German fairytale cycle" with *Graf Habenichts* (*Puss in Boots*), *Hansel und Gretel*, *Dornröschen* (*Sleeping Beauty*), *Rotkäpchen und der Wolf* (*Little Red Riding Hood*) and *Die Bremer Stadtmusikanten* (*The Bremen Town Musicians*) (Giesen & Storm, 2012, 59; Bendazzi, 1999, 81). In his first color cartoon, *Purzel, Brumm und Quack* (1938), Purzel the dwarf saves his friends from an evil spider. It was followed by *Purzel, der Zwerg, und die Reise vom Berg* the same year (Giesen & Storm, 2012, 59–61; Bendazzi, 1999, 81).

Stordel offered his services to the Ministry of Enlightenment and Propaganda and wrote a letter to State Secretary Hans Hinkel on September 25, 1939, stating his credentials as an animator and with the line, "I have particularly commissioned myself to replace the production of American Disney films by own German films…. I want to offer my services and manpower furthermore to propaganda in pictures" (qt. in Giesen & Storm, 2012, 63). He was referred to UFA and in March 1940 took a job as an animator on *Quick macht Hochzeit* (*Quick Marries*) to dodge the draft. The project failed, so he took another art job in July 1940 to once again avoid conscription (Giesen & Storm, 2012, 63). He continued to animate, but mostly information and promotional films, never achieving an animation career to compare with Walt Disney (Giesen & Storm, 2012, 168–69).

While individual animators attempted to jumpstart their careers and the German animation industry, Tobis Filmkunst, established in 1940 and funded by the Deutsche Kulturfilm Zentrale, was the first studio that actually stood a chance (Giesen & Storm, 2012, 65). Tobis Filmkunst hired Louis Seel to lead the studio in its first animated film *Rübezahl* (Giesen & Storm, 2012, 70). Seel had studied animation in the U.S., alongside the medium's earliest pioneers Winsor McCay, Bud Fisher and Eadweard Muybridge (Giesen & Storm, 2012, 70–71). Seel and his team only worked on *Rübezahl* for a year before the Ministry of Enlightenment and Propaganda got the brilliant idea to have a studio directly controlled by the ministry. *Rübezahl* production was shut down and Seel was out of a job. He attempted to form his own studio, but Karl Neumann (Goebbels's assistant, head of Deutsche Kulturfilm Zentrale, and soon to head the Nazi animation studio) feared Seel's competition and denied him permission to lead any animation projects (Giesen & Storm, 2012, 72). Seel never had a prominent animation career, even after his attempts in Prague (Giesen & Storm, 2012, 73).

Hans Fischerkoesen was the only person "that really delivered films of timeless quality to rival Disney" (Giesen and Storm, 2012, 107). He animated two short films written by Horst von Möllendorff: *Die verwitterte Melodie* (*Weather Beaten Melody*) and *Der Schneemann* (*The Snowman*). Fischerkoesen made one more cartoon, *Das dumme Gänslein* (*The Dumb Goose*), but it met with criticism because Möllendorff hadn't written it like the other two. Fischerkoesen hated that Möllendorff received more media attention than he did, so the pair split (Giesen & Storm, 2012, 112–20). It also meant the dissolution of Fischerkoesen's studio, but not before Neumann attempted to absorb it into the Nazi-run animation studio. Goebbels enjoyed Fischerkoesen's cartoons: "[T]here is another production from cartoon film producer Fischer-Kösen which Neumann would love to take over by force and integrate into his own production. I refuse temporarily. As long as new film production is in its infancy, it is good if there is competition" (qt. in Giesen and Storm, 2012, 120). It's funny that Goebbels would write that competition is good, considering that it is one of the main aspects of capitalism.

Neumann sat in Goebbels' pocket, and the Propaganda Reichsminister placed him at the head of the Deutsche Zeichenfilm G.m.b.H. (DZF) that translates as the German Animation Film Company. It opened on August 7, 1941 (Giesen & Storm, 2012, 72). According to Giesen and Storm, Neumann knew next to nothing about animation and only got the job because he was Goebbels' lapdog. Their description of Neumann would make any modern animation studio hiring director wince: "[A]s usual with Nazi parvenus he was a complete layman. Neumann's career was based on accounting, meat and sausages. In Goebbels' eyes, however, this seemed to qualify him perfectly for his task as supervisor of German animation" (Giesen & Storm, 2012, 74). The DZF, as it would be called, hired Gerhard Fieber as head of animation and Dr. Kruse Werner as the technical head (Giesen & Storm, 2012, 74, 77). While Neumann had Goebbels on his side, he had to convince the other ministry members that DZF would be able to produce the desired Nazi propaganda cartoons. On December 18, 1941, he wrote a letter to State Secretary Leopold Gutterer explaining what DZF would accomplish under his leadership (Giesen & Storm, 2012, 77).

Giesen and Storm reprinted Neumann's letter in its entirety and Neumann deserves credit for doing his best to justify the Reichstag funding an animation studio. Gutterer and his Nazi colleagues expressed their doubts about the success of a German animation studio and Neumann summarized the objections, which are now humorous to read:

1. They claimed that the wages paid to the artists are way too high…
2. Following the methods of English propaganda they invent incredibly short dates of delivery and then sarcastically ask when the first feature-length cartoon will be finished.
3. They spread the slogan that because everything that was tried in Germany in this field failed, the new task would be condemned to fail as well as according to natural law.
4. The distribution head of a big state company explained that one could not reach what Disney had achieved, as he is a unique genius. When Disney would die it

would be over with animated films. Regarding the German plans the same film mogul remarked that nobody has asked him.

  5. In [a] defeatist manner mouth-to-mouth propaganda has been employed that it (namely the establishment of an animation film production with the goal of producing feature-length films) never would come true. The working methods would be too expensive and schedule for much too long preproduction. The whole issue was begun with too much grandeur [2012, 78–80].

These Nazi bigwigs believed that Goebbels and Neumann were well out of their league and any funding dedicated to animation would be a huge money pit. What is astonishing is that Walt Disney was called "a unique genius" despite being an American; it was quickly refuted that the animation medium would die once Disney kicked the bucket. The Reichstag didn't believe German animation stood a chance and there were enough prior attempts to support their hesitations. Neumann was bound and determined to prove the doubters wrong, especially as this was Goebbels' pet project.

  Neumann countered with a pure Nazi statement: hatred of capitalism and ignorance of animation history. He wrote, "[A]ll attempts of German film industry to create the German animation film were started with so inadequate means and such a capitalist focus that they necessarily had to fail. If the recently started work will succeed all those people who were not able to create the German animation film and considered him dead would be made absolute fools" (2012, 80). Neumann glanced over Reiniger's full-length animated feature film and he also slammed past attempts to establish a German film industry as the fault of capitalist ventures. This was also a thinly veiled insult to American studios, especially Disney, which were founded to generate income and only became successful when they did (merchandising, anyone?).

  Neumann forgot that all animation studios in this time period started small and grew based on their capitalistic success. The German animation industry failed, because there wasn't enough financial gain, except in advertisements, and most of the animators were interested in experimental degenerate films. Reiniger successfully completed her film only because a banker with disposable income financed it. None of them wanted to make cartoons on par with Disney. It wasn't until the Nazis gained power in the 1930s that people like Stordel, Held, Seel and Kaskeline attempted to make such cartoons. They were set up for failure, though, because the Reichstag controlled everything, especially creative projects like animated cartoons.

  Neumann divided his letter in sections detailing how DZF would make the Third Reich proud. It contains endless comparisons to Disney Animation Studios, citing how DZF would be superior, even though Neumann was copying Walt Disney's own plans for a studio. In section one he explained how animators would be trained by attending art classes: "Instead of a trickfilm proletariat of technical supporting forces that without any passion and stoledly [sic] draws its lines, a professional type of responsible and creative artist craftsman of German animation must develop" (2012, 81). Section two contains projections of the studio's success, including employee estimations and film releases. The funniest bit is, "Of course Deutsche Zeichenfilm G.m.b.H can skip many of Walt Disney's years of apprenticeship provided one will not force upon it a narrow-minded, in too short deadline and less goal-directed" (2012, 81). Animators' years of drawing experience, studying animation and improving talent couldn't compare to the Nazi might which could overcome all obstacles, even lack of experience.

Neumann put his accounting background to use with budget and salary projections—the only part of the letter that was actually fact-based.

DZF sniffed around for ideas before settling on Hermann Krause's story about a caged canary who longs for freedom, but discovers that the outside world isn't as safe as his walled home. After several name changes, the film was finally called *Armer Hanzi*[15] (*Poor Hansi*) and released in 1943. It ran 18 minutes and 23,400 frames (Giesen and Storm, 2012, 90–95).

DZF never hid the fact from its employees that it was blatantly copying the Disney Studio. "Once a week, members of DZF were asked to get together and study Walt Disney films, especially techniques like rotoscoping, in order to copy them in their own work" (Giesen and Storm, 2012, 85). Animators who could draw Disney characters were always hired, such as Gerhard Fieber (Giesen and Storm, 2012, 93). Even the multiplane camera, which had origins in Reiniger's studio, was purloined by DZF, except they believed they were ripping off Disney's inventive camera (Giesen and Storm, 2012, 93). DZF had a training program and classes to teach animators figure and movement drawing, comparable to how Disney required his animators to continue their own artistic education. Quite unlike the Walt Disney Animation Studios, however, DZF employees weren't allowed to quit. Once they signed a contract, they signed a service obligation (Giesen and Storm, 2012, 100). Seventy percent of the employees were women and many were animators due to men having to fight in the war. Neumann "devoted himself to female artists," but if any of them didn't comply with the rules, he turned them over to the authorities (Giesen and Storm, 2012, 100)

While DZF appeared to be off to a promising start, the war progressed and unrest penetrated the studio. One of the founding members of the resistance group Rote Kapelle was a DZF writer, Frau Libertas Schulz-Boysen; she was later sentenced to death on December 19, 1942, and died three days later (Giesen and Storm, 2012, 92). In November 1943, the DZF buildings were bombed. The DZF was then split into five units in Berlin, Vienna, and Dachau (Giesen and Storm, 2012, 102).

> Dachau was the new home of German animation, but from the other side of the street there came an offensive smell like the smell of old meat. They noticed barbed wire fence and livestock wagons drawn by men. A female French artist got to know more when she got in touch with some SS men who let her see what was going on inside.... When she returned, none of her colleagues wanted to believe what she had to report. Actually, the protected area was a concentration camp [Giesen and Storm, 2012, 104–05].

It's ironic how an animation studio meant to glorify Nazism and the Third Reich via a medium in a Disney-esque romantic manner ended up across the street from a concentration camp, one of the Nazis' worst crimes against humanity.

Robert B. Sherman, half of the famous Disney songwriting duo with his brother Richard Sherman, were among the fighting force in Germany. Sherman and a contingent of eight men were separated from their unit in April 1945 and stumbled upon "a large fenced area of some sort" (Sherman, 2013, 25). The men later saw German soldiers abandoning the camp. When they investigated further, "a group of five thin, gray, faded and forlorn scarecrow men edged their way toward us" (Sherman, 2013, 25). Sherman's Dachau[16] description was brief in his autobiography *Moose: Chapters From My Life*:

> We took a brief walking tour of the camp. The small group of men closely followed us, making indecipherable comments. But we didn't hear anything that they mumbled. Our attention was fixed on the horrors we were witnessing. The world has been exposed to them now.... In half an hour I saw

enough to fill my nightmares for the remainder of my life (and that was more than 60 years ago) [2013, 26].

Despite the genocide across the street at Dachau, work on DZF's second short film continued. *Schnuff, der Nieser* had a similar theme to *Armer Hansi*: A puppy accidentally sneezes himself outside his warm house and must rely on other dogs to help him return home. Five hundred men were recruited for *Schnuff, der Nieser*, but it was asking for too many men and too much money at a time the Germans were doing poorly in the war (Giesen and Storm, 2012, 104). The Deutsche Zeichenfilm G.m.b.H. was officially shut down by the Ministry of Propaganda and Enlightenment on August 4, 1944, when Germany was in a state of total war and all available people were needed to work in armament factories (Giesen and Storm, 2012, 107). "Only Fieber was allowed to continue on *Schnuff, der Nieser*. *Schnuff*, however, was not finished under the Nazis. It was transformed into a DEFA, an East German film studio, production after the war and retitled *Purzelbaum ins Leben*" (Giesen and Storm, 2012, 107). Production cels, negatives and other art material related to *Schnuff, der Nieser*[17] were damaged by war-induced fires when they were shipped back to Berlin (Giesen and Storm, 2012, 103).

"On November 17, 1944, the Court Auditors of Deutsches Reich complained, 'The efforts of the company are in evident contrast with money spent. In a period lasting from August 7, 1941 until July 25, 1943, i.e., roughly two years, the company has finished a single cartoon'" (Giesen and Storm, 2012, 107). Dr. Hans Karbe and Heinrich Roellenbleg, who also worked at the DZF, also proposed a Europäischer Zeichenfilm Ring (an animation film ring) in 1944, to rescue the German film industry. It would consolidate animation studios around Europe (counting on the Nazis winning the war) controlled by one organization with assurances that it would "not transform into a second Deutsche Zeichenfilm G.m.b.H." and "offers an expert way to enhance the efforts of smaller 2D and puppet film studios considerably in quality" (qt. in Giesen and Storm, 2012, 127, 131). It never happened, because Goebbels still was for a "healthy artistic competition" and the Nazis were more preoccupied with the Allied forces in 1944 than animation cartoons (Giesen and Storm, 2012, 127, 135).

The DZF had been tilting windmills believing they would be able to compete with Disney and other U.S. facilities. The Ministry of Propaganda and Enlightenment's expectation to finish a feature-length animated film with Disney quality with a team of animation amateurs was unattainable and ridiculous. Two years is more or less enough time for expert animators to produce and complete an animated feature, so long as funds don't run dry, but the Nazis were only set up to produce shorts and only had enough experience to rival Disney and other studios in their early days. Had Goebbels taken a different route, hiring an experienced animator rather than a meat accountant to be in charge along with other artists and even some film experts, DZF might have stood a chance, because the Reichstag was funding the studio and it was a pet project.

Neumann didn't fare well when DZF closed. He was sent to an internment camp and was found hanged in a bathroom in June 1945 (Giesen and Storm, 2012, 108). "Fieber became a pioneer of German television," continuing on with animation[18]; he even created Germany's first hand-drawn animated feature film, 1949's *Tobias Knopp, Abenteuer eines Junggesellen* (*Tobias Knopp, Adventures of a Bachelor*) (Giesen and Storm, 2012, 109). "But when it was released it had no chance to compete with Disney's *Snow White* and other animated features that finally were shown in Germany as ours was only black and white, the American films, however, produced in Technicolor. It was like a dwarf fighting a giant!" (qt. in Giesen and Storm, 2012, 109).

German animators have since developed a domestic animation industry for TV shows, advertisements and even the occasional film. Some of the more popular shows and films gain notoriety outside the country, but usually only in European countries and very rarely in the U.S. The German animation industry in the 21st century is reflective of other European countries. With advanced technology and better access to animation software, it is easier to animate, but locating the funding for an animated film is difficult. France remains a champion for animation with directors such as Bibo Bergeron, Sylvain Chomet and Michel Ocelot at the helm, while Cartoon Saloon in Ireland headed by Tomm Moore, Paul Young and Nora Twomey stages beautiful films drawing on ancient traditions combined with modern art renderings. A bigger animation industry in Europe is a possibility in the future and Germany has a stake in the race. It all depends on funding and talent.

A Nazi-run German film industry was destined to sink. Some parties wanted a German film industry to invest in art styles from German animators and stop chasing that blasted Walt Disney and his *Snow White,* because it wasn't in the Germans' best interest. The *Lichtbildbühne* lamented in 1937 that German animation couldn't catch a break in "Deutscher Trickfilm weltmarktfähig" ("German Animated Films for the World Market"). Beginning with "Doesn't the German animator have imagination?" the piece included several other questions about Germany's lack of recognition before clarifying that Germans are known for their artistry and skill (qt. in Giesen and Storm, 2012, 26). As proof, it lists German animation accomplishments, including Reiniger's *Prinzen Achmed*, and explains that German trickfilm makers were waiting in reserve and they had fairytales and more stories as ammunition: "Sure do we have enough of such men and women among our filmmakers. Let them work, all those who are obsessed by trickfilm. Then German animation in brief time will be weltmarktfähig [ready to enter the world market]. Then it will compete—supported by German color film technicians and German art of music—with Felix, Mickey Mouse and all other film animals from USA, the 'country of the already limited possibilities'" (qt. in Giesen and Storm, 2012, 27).

The opposition against Walt Disney and *Snow White* was quite apparent in the memo "The Color Puppet Trickfilm: What it is—what it could be—what it will cost?" by Herbert Phris and Jürgen Clausen for Tobis Filmkunst in December 1941. They felt that German animation was best suited for stop-motion puppet films in color. The memo included their plans to develop a puppet film studio drawing on Georg Pál's techniques and how it was a huge potential moneymaker, citing color and toy merchandising. Prhis and Clausen felt that Disney had achieved the highest standard for hand-drawn animation, so it was silly to attempt to rival Disney; Germany needed to concentrate on puppet trick films: "[T]he puppet or spatial trick is located in European cultural space and no other country can be its more natural home than Germany. The German … profoundly imaginative, he is dreamy and contemplative" (qt. in Giesen and Storm, 2012, 30). Clausen and Phris never saw their plans surface as the Ministry of Enlightenment and Propaganda vetoed it (Giesen and Storm, 2012, 28–33).

Not surprising, Clausen and Phris neglected to mention Lotte Reiniger and her silhouette puppet films in their memo. It was probably due to her trick films animated in two dimensions instead of the preferred three dimensions. As mentioned in Chapter 3, Reiniger was often overlooked as no one knew how to define her animation, because it crossed both puppetry and animation media. The Nazis were only interested in pursuing traditional hand-drawn animation due to the success of Walt Disney and other animation studios, while a whole sub-medium of 3D stop-motion puppets gained popularity in Germany and in other countries. Reiniger and Koch just did not fit into the German culture surrounding animation, even more so as animation and puppetry evolved to more technologically, yet similarly artistic-creative methods.

Reiniger might not have associated herself with any political group or specific art movement, but she fit the definition of avant-garde animator because of her techniques with silhouette animation. She was doing something new and creative, and without a defined purpose. Examining her from a modern perspective, her fairytale and operatic films seem relatively harmless, not enough to trigger the ire of the Nazi party. The problem was even if her silhouette films could be tied to German glorification, her intent wasn't aligned with the tenets of the Third Reich. In a fascist government, all aspects of life must be in tune with the authoritarian and nationalistic frequency; anything that runs contrary to its ideals corrupts the signal. For an animated example of how totalitarian governments interfere in artists' work, Czechoslovakian puppet animator Jiri Trnka's film *The Hand* captures the experience.

In his article "Some Critical Perspectives of Lotte Reiniger," William Moritz discussed political points Reiniger made in her films: "[S]he thought consciously of a socialist responsibility to infuse these films (which would be seen by young, impressionable minds) with constructive and thought-provoking ideas" (1996b, 49). I find these observations to be thoughts that Moritz projected onto Reiniger's films.

She did want to make intelligent films, as Moritz stated; she may have believed in some of Koch's political beliefs; and she did make an anti–Nazi film disguised as a parable. But none of my research indicated she believed in anything more than common decency and wanted to pursue her art. Moritz claimed that her shadow play in Renoir's *La Marseillaise* was a message about revolution: "Reiniger's shadow puppets do not appear as 'ombres chinoises' of the idle aristocracy, but rather as a political theater of the revolutionaries, presenting a satirical fable." While it is a satire within *La Marseillaise,* Reiniger did it because it was a paying job (1996b, 49). He also admits that these are his own thoughts, rather than Reiniger's intention, when he says, "I, personally, have always imagined that there was something of the advanced socialist tolerance for birth control and abortion rights (suppressed by the Nazis) in the satirical literalness of the mad proliferation of little Papagenos and Papagenas at the end of Reiniger's 1935 *Papageno*" (1996b, 49).[19]

Entertainment and art that fed off raw emotions; that rejected rational thought and logic; that encouraged the dissemination of traditionalist views, and that excused radical, abstract actions: These were key themes in Germany in the 1920s and 1930s. This was the radical "pop culture" of the era and it fed into a society that was still hobbling along after the Great War. The Nazis wanted to eradicate expressionism, Dada, surrealism and any art movement associated with the avant garde. "The year 1937 saw the formation of a purposiveness in Nazi art policy, with the official outlawing of German expressionism and the promotion of classical, heroic art, a process undertaken in conjunction with the highly publicized exhibition of 'Entartete Kunst' ('Degenerate Art')" (Leslie, 2002, 144–45). The infamous Entartete Kunst was first exhibited in Munich before it went on tour in Germany.[20] It featured works by Marc Chagall, Hans Richter, Max Ernst, Wassily Kandinsky and others. Art and entertainment that fell into the degenerate movements didn't encourage a stable society; rather, it rallied the opposite, and Nazi leaders blasted this entertainment as one of the downfalls of the once proud German race. Reiniger's work exacerbated the culture problem. Reiniger wanted to make films that spread the noble message of love and challenged her artistic skills. Her desires were simple, but the Nazi party wanted propaganda churned out in support of their "Deutschland uber alles" mindset. Gentle silhouettes that didn't showcase German art and culture didn't make the cut. They also didn't have the same artistic quality as hand-drawn animation and, as described throughout this chapter, Goebbels and Hitler chased after traditional animation like Harlequin or Pepe Le Pew after their newest love interest/victim.

When Oskar Fischinger completed his *Komposition in Blau* in 1935, no German theaters wanted to risk playing it. Fischinger's friend Dr. Leonhard Fürst was a clever writer and could finesse his way in and out of situations, and he took it upon himself to get *Komposition in Blau* into theaters.

> ... Fürst managed to plant a whole page spread in the official Nazi film paper *Der Film* on 20 June 1935. Using a clever line drawing of a unicorn with a horn made of film, he posits a should-be-endangered species, "Das Zellhorn" [The celluloid unicorn], the stodgy distributor unwilling to take a chance on unusual films.... [H]e laments [that the "experimenter" in German film will die out]. In a last brilliant touch, Fürst reproduced ... a photo from a Czech newspaper in which their delegates to the recent film festival in Berlin are shown with swastikas air-brushed out of the NS flags in the background; the caption reads ... [Are they *that* afraid?] [qt. in Moritz, 2004, 59].

Fürst taunted the Nazis by questioning their artistic tastes and positing that they weren't interested in showcasing genuine German creativity. His metaphor of Das Zellhorn is apt in how the Nazis felt about experimental films: the Nazi experimental film would be as imaginary as a unicorn. In 1935, poking the Nazi bear was still tolerated to a degree and calling Nazi censors afraid to see an experimental film did achieve the desired goal, but it truly did describe that the Nazis were afraid of any idea that ran counter to their dogma, even a harmless animated film. The Nazis would be exceedingly daft in their observance of degenerate ideas, one of the reasons Reiniger's *Das gestohlene Herz* went over their heads, and violent due to their ignorance, which resulted in the destruction of thousands of cultural artifacts. Reiniger was a Zellhorn for the Nazi party and perhaps Germany. Her silhouette animation was not highly regarded by society at large, especially when the Nazis were in charge, but what supporters she did have weren't enough to prevent her "extinction" and being glossed over in history.

After World War II, anti–German sentiment rooted itself in American, European and other cultural mindsets that generated a stigma still felt in the contemporary zeitgeist. K.V. Taylor wrote, "I posit that the historical tendency to ignore or misappropriate Reiniger's contributions to the development of film has been caused, at least in part, by widespread anti–German sentiment, gaps in German history, contemporaneous domestic critical neglect of German film, and the independent production and distribution of *Prince Achmed*" (2011, 5). I have established that Reiniger and Koch never aligned with popular artistic circles on purpose and in this way, they were the most avant-garde of all the avant-garde artists. But being an independent has limited reach no matter how famous their friends were. *Prinzen Achmed*'s limited screenings in the U.S. and the official premiere in 1942 in the throes of World War II with German hatred at its highest, combined with Disney's dominance with color and sound cartoons, ruined Reiniger's chance of establishing a fanbase.

Taylor is good to recognize that Germany's interwar history played a role in

Reiniger's diminished importance. The German national identity was shattered after the war. As a whole, the survivors wanted to distance themselves from the bloody stain on their history, but it was at the expense of losing knowledge. Although Reiniger and Koch spent most of their time away from Germany and never upheld or participated in Nazism, they were still German. As Disney is considered to be synonymous with animation, for years after the war the world held a similar belief that all Germans were Nazis just as the Japanese were feared to be genetically disposed to be loyal to the emperor. It is a tragic association and due to a hideous period, Germany suffered and lost many talented people who renounced their former heritage or were too traumatized to remain or even return to their birth country.

There are many accounts of how World War scarred human history. The anti–German sentiment was firmly planted in people's minds in a description similar to an odious cartoon villain dressed in a black cape and takes slinking steps to harm the hero and his girl. Germany never gained traction as an animation giant, even though there are established studios that animate and distribute TV shows, advertisements and even the occasional film. Animation history is among the many topics that knowledge is scarce on, especially during the interwar years. For this account on how it harmed Reiniger's importance in animation history (and the lives of millions), Robert Sherman said it best: "In half an hour I saw enough to fill my nightmares for the remainder of my life" (2013, 26). That is what fueled people's anti–German sentiment and propelled some film historians to overlook Germany's Lotte Reiniger.

7

Animated Women and Lost Love

World War II had ended and all of Germany was in ruins. The German people were broken and lost, unsure of what the future held. Unlike World War I, the Germans weren't forced to pay war reparations; instead the Allied forces occupied Germany and helped rebuild the shattered nation, including the film industry.

In a year after the war, known as the Filmpause, not a single film was produced in Germany. The film industry eventually did restart and, using the war-torn landscape as a backdrop, the trümmerfilm (rubble films) period began with Wolfgang Staudte's *Die Mörder sind unter uns* (*Murders Among Us*), funded by the Soviet forces. While many Germans felt hopeless about pressing forward with their lives in ruins in around them, Reiniger and Koch were already planning to reignite their careers and began cutting silhouettes from paper. They might not have been as fazed in World War II's aftermath as their countrymen due to having spent the majority of the war abroad. They had been spared the majority of the Nazis' destructive practices on Germany and most of their friends survived the conflict. But their experience in Berlin in 1944 and '45 shouldn't be downplayed as they had witnessed the heaviest assault on Germany as the war crept to a close. Koch was shanghaied into military service, fearful that the next moment could be his last; for weeks, Reiniger didn't know if he was alive or dead. There were hundreds of thousands of people lost in the Battle of Berlin. For Koch, Reiniger and her mother to have survived the assault alive was a miracle.

Koch picked up his life by becoming involved with the new radio station, Berliner Rundfunk, set up by the Soviet Military Administration in Berlin-Charlottenburg, Reiniger's home town. It was located in the British sector of the future West Berlin (Happ, 2004, 67; Galle, 2003, 53). He was the chief editor of a Rundfunk segment entitled "Künstlerisches Wort" ("Artistic Word") about cultural and historical subjects (80 manuscripts still exist), something he was quite familiar with, having studied those subjects during his university years. He kept this position until 1948 (Happ, 2004, 67).

Reiniger returned to an activity of her youth, the performance and creation of shadow plays. Back in 1943, she had met Elsbeth Schulz, who operated a professional shadow theater, and in 1945, Reiniger and Schulz's paths crossed again and they combined their talents to establish the Berliner Schattenspiele (Berlin Shadow Play) (Happ, 2004, 67). Reiniger made the shadow puppets, scenery and other decorations for the shadow theater. The pair performed many shows together, including *Der gestiefelte Kater* (*Puss in Boots*), *Dornröschen* (*Sleeping Beauty*) and *Brüderchen und Schwesterchen* (*Brother and Sister*) (Happ, 2004, 67–68). Reiniger eventually left the Berliner Schattenspiele, but Schulz continued it for years (Happ, 2004, 68).

Once their lives were settled in postwar Berlin, Reiniger once again took up animating *Die goldene Gans* in the ruins of her neighborhood. She eventually shelved the film and wouldn't complete it until 1963. She said, "I made this film in the style of Penelope. I didn't want to finish it, because one needs groceries and all these sorts of problems. It was finished without me. One only had to add on the ending" (qt. in Happ, 2004, 68). When Reiniger wasn't working on her film or at the Berliner Schattenspiele, her friends hired her. Rochus Gliese had her create the poster, program, scenery, and other material for a fairytale play, *Onkel Demetrius und die fünf Freunde* (*Uncle Demetrius and the Five Friends*) at the Schiffbauerdamm Theater. She worked on two more productions for this theater in 1947 (Happ, 2004, 68). She occasionally found the time to relax and enjoy life once more, such as when the Rambert Dance Company came to Berlin in 1946. To show her appreciation, she gave them silhouette cuttings as a present (Mégroz, 1949, 113).

Renoir continued his long friendship with Koch and Reiniger via lengthy correspondence. He had emigrated to the U.S., became a naturalized citizen, and had a semi-successful Hollywood career during the war. With the end of the war, he wanted to try something new, so he traveled to India and filmed his first color production, *The River*. Reiniger and Koch weren't able to rendezvous with Renoir in India, due to Koch's illness. Renoir did send Koch a copy of the script and asked him to provide a Dutch perspective. Koch was paid and the money was used for his treatment (Happ, 2004, 70).

While Reiniger and Koch were able to find work in Berlin, the conditions weren't the best and the couple sought a way to return to England. Reiniger made a short visit to London in February 1948, but quickly returned in March when her husband became sick from malnutrition (Happ, 2004, 70). He had an operation and a long recovery period in the hospital, but the outlook was grim due to Germany's food shortage. They relied on friends once more to help them out in a crisis; their *Prinzen Achmed* collaborator Alexander Kardan opened his London home to them. Koch and Reiniger stayed in England from September to November 1948 (Happ, 2004, 70). In November, Reiniger showcased her work at the British Model and Puppet Theater Guild, culminating in an evening shadow puppet show (Happ, 2004, 70).

Reiniger was forced to return to Berlin on November 24 and had to deal with more food and power shortages. Despite the poor conditions, she continued to work and had the opportunity to open a studio in Düsseldorf to recover her old films, which she used to provide an income for her mother (Happ, 2004, 70, 72). She was faced with a hard choice: remain in Germany (which the Düsseldorf studio financier wanted) or cross the channel and join her husband in England. She cut her final ties to Germany and on January 31, 1949,[1] emigrated to London.

Upon her arrival in England, Reiniger fell sick from exhaustion and worry about her future and her husband. She found refuge with Jo Hodgkinson and his family in Didsbury, Manchester, and was laid up for three weeks (Happ, 2004, 71). Hodgkinson produced two plays in 1939, when he worked with Peter Gellhorn and Reiniger (Gellhorn was the musical director and Reiniger made scenery and props), and in England he held a government position and worked with the Manchester Arts Council (Happ, 2004, 73). During that time, Koch progressed well in his recovery. Reiniger had the potential to work once more with the GPO Film Unit (now called the Crown Film Unit, and part of the Central Office of Information), and she spoke with famous puppeteers Jan Bussell and Ann Hogarth about future opportunities with them at the Hogarth Puppet Theatre (Happ, 2004, 71, 73).

Bussell and Hogarth are still highly regarded in puppetry circles and they wrote of Reiniger in similar fashion in their book *Fanfare for Puppets*: "Each of [her films] required many thousands of frames; every limb of every figure had to be moved infinitesimally in each frame. Her sense of timing was phenomenal and this, combined with her wit, her style and elegance and her great humanity, as well as her feeling for the dramatic, makes her unique and quite unforgettable" (1985, 43–44). The couple might have emigrated to England, but they couldn't stay in the country unless they had jobs. In their favor, they had references from Jo Hodgkinson and old friends John Grierson and Eric Walter White (Happ, 2004, 73).

Reiniger and Koch relied heavily on their friends to help them transition to life in England. In late 1948, Martin Hürlimann, owner of the publishing house Atlantis Verlag, secured an illustration job for Reiniger on a children's book by expressionist Karl Otten. Otten and Reiniger became friends during work on the book (Happ, 2004, 73). *Der ewige Esel: Eine Jugenderzählung* (*The Eternal Donkey: A Children's Story*), published in 1949, was about a donkey's life from birth and his many sad and happy adventures.

Reiniger and Koch needed more permanent jobs, but to obtain them, they needed work permits. They received the proper documentation and they worked with Grierson, head of the Crown Film Unit, creating many films. Reiniger resumed her silhouette animation work and was considered a "suitable instructor for English animators." Among the many films she made for the Crown Film Unit were advertisement films, including ones for the General Post Office (Happ, 2004, 76). In 1950, she made several films; her famous *Post Early for Christmas* (aka *Christmas Is Coming*) was a silhouette film about Father Christmas going on strike because people forgot to mail their holiday cards early. This was followed by the "reverse silhouette film" (white figures on black paper) *Not Without License*, about renewing wireless licenses; it depicted a cheap man who forgets to pay his bills. *Here and There* was about properly addressing letters using a pinball machine to explain a letter's route. There was also another cartoon, *Greeting Telegrams* (Happ, 2004, 76).

Together with her husband, she made *The Dancing Fleece* aka *Wool Ballet*, a promotional film for the English Department of Labor about the wool industry; it involved some live action mixed with puppetry (Happ, 2004, 76). In it, a young man dreams he is in a puppet show and is spurned by the female dancers. As revenge, he turns them into sheep, herds them into a factory and forces them to manufacture fabric. They later ask to have garments made from the beautiful fabric and he grants their wish. The Ministry of Agriculture also hired Reiniger and Koch to make *Grain Harvest*, about Scotland's grain harvest in 1950 (Happ, 2004, 76).

"In the studios, Grierson gave Carl Koch the opportunity to shoot documentary-animated films on geographical ... topics"; the first film he made was 1949's *Introducing the Commonwealth* (Happ, 2004, 76). All seemed well until September 1949, when the Interior Ministry informed the couple their stay couldn't be extended and they had to leave the country by the end of the month (Happ, 2004, 75). Koch had asked for permission to engage in freelance work for American television, but this request was denied (Happ, 2004, 75). Luck was on their side: one day after their visas expired on October 1, the Minister of the Interior extended their residence permit and attached a direct note that they couldn't take on freelance work (Happ, 2004, 75).

Despite the setback, Koch continued making his documentary films. Two were released in 1951: one about the Antarctic, another entitled *Soil Science* about England's geographic history since the Ice Age (Happ, 2004, 76). In the early '50s, Reiniger got the chance to make a longer silhouette film in which she experimented with moving black figures on a colored background, a new technique that she would use for the fairytale films she made later in the decade. *Mary's Birthday*, made for the London Ministry of Health, explained the dangers of germs (Happ, 2004, 76). It's quite a beautiful and alarming piece. It appears to be a gentle story about Mary as she prepares for her birthday by watering her flowers. The flower fairies thank Mary for the water, but an evil fly warns the flower fairies that humans are bad and he plans to attack them at the party. The concerned fairies visit Mary that night, showing her the fly's plan by spreading germs. Mary defeats the germs by covering containers, emptying dustbins and washing her hands. Reiniger made such accurate representations of germs that still dissuade the viewer from allowing germs to incubate in their households.

When she emigrated to England, Reiniger met with Jan Bussell and Ann Hogarth to discuss the potential for her to collaborate with them. Hogarth Puppets was Britain's flagship puppet troupe, highly regarded for its artistic contributions to puppetry in the 1950s and 1960s. In 1948, she teamed with them on *Die Geschichte vom wilden Jäger* (*The Story of the Wild Hunter*), from Heinrich Hoffmann's *Struwwelpeter* (Happ, 2004, 79). Reiniger enjoyed her time with the Hogarth Puppets: "I was glad I could work together with Jan Bussell and Ann Hogarth, who showed shadow plays as an interlude in their marionette show. I had the great fortune of cutting figures and scenes for them" (qt. in Happ, 2004, 79). Reiniger taught the puppeteers how to make and perform shadow plays, using Oscar Wilde's *The Happy Prince*. For the production, she drew on the lessons she learned from the Greek shadow theater Mollas and it received high praise. Jan Bussell and Ann Hogarth explained their experience working with Reiniger on their shows, capturing her humor and thick accent:

> In 1950 we persuaded Lotte Reiniger to design and cut for us all the scenery and figures for a version of Oscar Wilde's *The Happy Prince* using three screens, comprising some 15 scene changes as the action as well as the basic and dramatic black silhouettes for which she was rightly so famous. She was a wonderful and inspiring person to work with, but also a very nerve-racking one as she never produced drawings to be working on a production at all—just "thinking." When we had already accepted a television engagement for *The Happy Prince* and were desperately needing to start rehearsals she said to us one day, "Don't worry! It is all here! [pointing at her head] I vill just do so ... and so ... and it will be ver' good!" We went off to perform somewhere and on our return about 12 hours later she was sitting on the floor in a mass of cardboard snippings, and surrounded by all the exquisite scenes and figures we have loved performing with ever since. It was indeed "ver" good! [1985, 46].

This led to another collaboration in 1951 on *The King's Breakfast*, which Reiniger had made into a silhouette film in 1936. All three puppet shows were shown on television (Happ, 2004, 79).

Reiniger and Koch had many successes in the early days of their English sojourn, but while England fared better in the postwar years than Germany, an economic downturn shut down the Central Office of Information's film unit in 1952. Without work, Reiniger and Koch would be forced to return to Germany, which they didn't want to do. Providence provided for them once more: Puffin Books commissioned Reiniger to create silhouette cutouts for an inexpensive "young adult" paperback about King Arthur and his knights, based on Sir Thomas Malory's *Le Morte Darthur*. For *King Arthur and the Knights of the Round Table* by Roger Lancelyn Green, she made a total of 38 cutouts inspired by the opening sequence she had made for Georg Wilhelm Pabst's *Don Quixote* (Happ, 2004,

77). A small note about Reiniger's work graces the front: "The artist, Lotte Reiniger, has used an entirely new method of illustration. Her pictures are not pen-and-ink drawings or woodcuts: they were cut out of thin black paper with a pair of special scissors. These delicate scissor-cuts were then mounted on transparent paper, and from them a set of much smaller pictures were made for this book" (1976). The King Arthur paper cuttings resemble medieval stained windows sans translucent, colorful glass. It was published in 1953, and Penguin has continued to reissue it to this day.

In January 1952, Reiniger was invited to create silhouette pieces for a televised ballet of *The Sleeping Beauty*. Christian Simpson produced the ballet, along with many others, for the BBC, and he hired Reiniger to create films that would be interspersed between the dance segments along with scenes with "magical" special effects. "She prepared animated films of animals, birds, insects and growing plants to embellish appropriate moments in the ballet, and a silhouette cutout of Carabosse" (Davis, 1996, 23). There were some problems, but her animated silhouettes were overall a success: she animated Carabosse's arrival, the wicked fairy, in a carriage pulled by mice, but there was a regrettable lack of coordination between the animated bats and the live-action dancers.

> This was because of technical limitations, which required the film to be superimposed from a different camera, so that the dancers could not actually see where the bats were. As for the bats themselves, [dancer] Gordon Smith applauded them as a replacement for the mice and creepy-crawlies that usually nibbled round Carabosse's skirts [Davis, 1996, 32].

An angel Reiniger made for Ann Hogarth and Jan Bussells' *The Happy Prince* production. It measures 40 cm high and the outline is made from clear plastic. Colored gel is adhered to the plastic with tape (courtesy Richard Bradshaw).

Simpson made *The Sleeping Beauty* specially for TV and he wanted to take advantage of the

A stunning example of Reiniger's cutout illustrations for Puffin's *King Arthur and the Knights of the Round Table* depicting the lovers Tristram and Iseult. © *Puffin Books*.

medium by using tricks like Reiniger's animation, camera angles and reworking the story and choreography. Some critics jeered, but others praised it as an innovation for the future of televised ballet performances.

The BBC then commissioned Reiniger to make fairytales shadow plays, such as *Jorinde and Joringel*, *The Frog Prince*, *Good King Wenceslas*, *Cinderella* and more, under producer Viviana Milroy (Happ, 2004, 80). The year 1952 brought another renewal on Koch and Reinigers' residential permit; without the BBC work, they would have been deported back to Germany. When Reiniger's silhouettes were televised, they not only provided exposure for her, but it presented a solution for work and finances, which came in the form of someone she taught as a child.

Lotte Reiniger spent three years animating *Die Abenteuer des Prinzen Achmed* in Louis Hagen's garage attic with her husband and colleagues. The attic quarters were cramped, but there was still enough room for students from the school to visit and watch them animate. Reiniger would even occasionally allow them to help her on a sequence. Among the visitors were Hagen's children, including Louis Hagen, Jr., also known as

Büdi (little brother). The younger Hagen had fond memories of watching Reiniger when she made her film: "From childhood, my siblings, friends and I were fascinated by all the fairytale things that arose from [Reiniger's] hands. No one could produce as many exciting glories with scissors and paper alone: figures with joints that run, jump, play and fight, houses made of cardboard with doors and windows that open and close, trees that lose their leaves in autumn and grow new leaves in the spring. Boats that sail through the water and so on… (qt. in Happ, 2004, 80).

Louis Hagen and his family were Jewish. Like many of their brethren, they fled Germany when the Nazis threatened their lives. Hagen Jr. didn't fare as well as the rest of his family. Three of his siblings went to the U.S. and his youngest sister to England, but in 1934 Büdi was thrown into the Schloss Lichtenburg concentration camp at age 15. Four months later, a high-ranking Nazi judge, the father of one of his school friends, liberated him. Büdi joined his sister in England, learned English, became a glider pilot in the war (he was awarded the Military Medal) and later was a war reporter and photographer in Asia. He also wrote several popular books, including the bestselling *Arnhem Lift*[2] (McFadyean, 2000).

After *Die Abenteuer des Prinzen Achmed's* production ended, Reiniger and Koch fell out of contact with Hagen, and the war made communication difficult. When Reiniger made the shadow plays for the BBC in the 1950s, Louis Hagen Jr. happened to see them and remembered Reiniger animating her silhouettes in the attic garage. Hagen Jr.'s nostalgic fascination was piqued after watching the plays and he reached out to Reiniger and her producer Viviana Milroy. Hagen Jr. followed in the footsteps as his father when he saw something special in Reiniger's work. "When my father heard that I'd spent quite a lot of time with Lotte, he told me, 'Don't get financially involved with Carl or Lotte or produce their films. I financed a lot of their films and I never got a brass farthing back. But I enjoyed it and could afford it. I was a wealthy banker, but you're a poor refugee.' I said, 'Papa, you're so right' and I went and did the opposite," Hagen Jr. said in an interview (qt. in Raganelli, 1999). He decided to invest his money in her silhouettes and in 1952, after discussions with Milroy, they founded Primrose Productions, a production company dedicated to making silhouette films for TV (Happ, 2004, 80).

As soon as Primrose Productions opened for business, the American TV and film producer Richard Kaplan contacted Reiniger to create a series of fairytale films for U.S. audiences and asked them to move to the U.S. There was one problem: Reiniger and Koch had German passports and they didn't want to disrupt their stay in England, lest they lose their residential permit (Happ, 2004, 81). It seemed that Reiniger would lose the opportunity to share her films with a brand new audience, but Hagen Jr. decided to bring Kaplan on board as a third partner in Primrose Productions and the fairytales were made under the new studio's label (Happ, 2004, 81).

With the creation of Primrose Productions, Reiniger and Koch needed a new physical location to do their work. In New Barnet, Hertfordshire, a half-hour outside London, art dealer William Ohly established the Abbey Arts Centre, an artist colony and museum, where creative individuals lived, worked and exhibited their art (Happ, 2004, 82; Coté, 1954, 16). Artists were given their own homes and work spaces, where they had formed a communal lifestyle. Reiniger and Koch were welcomed at the Abbey Arts Centre, finding that being around fellow artists helped inspire their own work. Reiniger said about the Abbey Art Center residents, "They live in their separate households, but close enough to inspire one another. The museum provided me with a number of artworks from

The Primrose Production credit screen (©Primrose Productions).

different parts of the world, it's not only ideas, but a widening creative atmosphere" (qt. in Happ, 2004, 82). The center would become Reiniger and Koch's home until his death and she would remain there.

At the new location, Hagen Jr. gave Reiniger a wonderful gift, a brand new tricktisch which she used for the remainder of her career. Guy Coté described her new workshop: "[N]owhere are to be seen the modern paraphernalia of arc lights, dolly tracks and sound booms. A single stop frame camera, a couple of photofloods and a glass-topped table are all Miss Reiniger needs to create the black and white world of charm and fantasy…" (1954, 16). He continued that there were "piles of long flat boxes labeled 'palaces,' 'forests,' 'witches,' 'animals'" and her sets were "great squares of white translucent paper" (Coté, 1954, 17). While Reiniger was excited about making new silhouette films, she had to adhere to a strict schedule Kaplan outlined in her contract. Reiniger needed to complete 13 ten-minute silhouette films by the middle of 1953, which would then premiere in 1954 (Happ, 2004, 82). Coté explained that she was contracted to make "26 one-reel films for American Television [sic]" in his 1954 article *Flatland Fairy Tales*, but only 13 fairytale films were made (Coté, 1954, 17). Kaplan later said that Reiniger couldn't churn the silhouette films out fast enough and it ended the distribution deal (Reiniger with Starr and others, 1978). He said at a 1978 seminar about Reiniger's career that working with Reiniger and Carl:

> could be difficult, challenging. Lotte was a personality who wasn't just making pretty little figures, she took her work very seriously. She was very adamant about what she wanted and how she wanted it done. I think working within the discipline of turning out films for American television at a specific length and a specific time was not the kind of thing Lotte had been used to. Except for when she worked for the GPO [*Reiniger with Starr and others*].

The 1950s would become Reiniger's most productive in the sheer amount of silhouette films she animated. She was successful in animating so many films due to several factors. The largest were that she wasn't in the direct path of a war and the government wasn't opposed to her work or political beliefs. She also had fluid funds, reliable resources such as equipment and support, and a permanent studio. The 13-episode fairytale series was a huge challenge, her biggest since making *Prinzen Achmed*. She met the challenge with the same vigor as she had with Hagen Sr. and *Prinzen Achmed*, which then led to similar successful results. Kaplan did say in 1974, "Both Carl and Lotte were artists in the very true sense of the term ... products of that German bohemianism, that Golden Age of avant-garde work in so many of the arts" (qt. in Starr, 1980, 17).

Reiniger, with her ever vigilant assistant and husband, animated ten new fairytale films, *Snow White and Rose Red*, *The Grasshopper and the Ant*, *The Three Wishes*, *Caliph Stork*, *The Gallant Little Tailor*, *Sleeping Beauty*, *Cinderella*, *Thumbelina*, *The Frog Prince* and *Hansel and Gretel*.

Snow White and Rose Red was released in 1953 with the subsequent films released in 1954. Three other films were part of Reiniger's contract with Kaplan, but instead of making all the films from scratch, she reused material from prior films. She abridged *Puss in Boots* (*Der gestiefelte Kater*) from her 1934 film and *The Little Chimney Sweep* (*Der kleine Schornsteinfeger*) and shortened them to the required ten minutes (Happ, 2004, 83). She also recycled the flying horse segments from *Prinzen Achmed* to make *The Magic Horse*, released in 1953 (Happ, 2004, 82).

She made many of these films in color to appease the Americans, but she managed to persuade the producers to allow her to animate *Thumbelina* in black and white as it stimulated the imagination more in Reiniger's opinion (Raganelli, 1999). The film series also allowed Reiniger to remake some stories from the past as well as animate stories she never had the chance to tell due to the Nazis. Reiniger finally made her Thumbelina piece, which she had attempted to make in 1935, and she reimagined the old classics *Sleeping Beauty* and *Cinderella*. While she was proud of these new films, Reiniger always felt that her best fairytale films were made in the pre-war years. She called the Weimar years "the golden age of German Films," continuing: "[A]t that time we lived in Berlin, there was a wonderful working atmosphere and international artistry.... [T]he movies I made then have their own character and more personal style compared with the fairytale film series from ... the '50s" (qt. in Happ, 2004, 41).

Cinderella, *Puss in Boots*, *Sleeping Beauty* and *The Magic Horse* were made into picture books using film stills. Published by Hutchinson of London in the 1950s, the four-book series had the subtitle "A Lotte Reiniger Story-Play" and were designed for young readers. A preface in each of the books reads:

> To uncles, aunts, parents and teachers who will be choosing these books for children[:] Lotte Reiniger's fascinating silhouette pictures have already won world-wide renown in the cinema and on television. One of her films gained first prize at the Venice Film Festival. Now for the first time they make their bow in book form.
>
> They are unique in that they appeal to not only children of all ages, but also to adults. Their economy of design, folklore themes and high artistic execution are among the chief reasons for their outstanding attraction. In particular they enable the acute imaginative powers of young children to have full play. These age-old fairy tales are told here in their simplest form, illustrated by enchanting silhouette figures. Those children fortunate enough to experience these tales for the first time in this form will remember them all their lives [*Cinderella*, 195?, i].

According to Kaplan, the books were unsuccessful (Reiniger with Starr and others).

Top: Thumbelina balances on a delicate silhouette flower (©Primrose Productions). *Bottom:* Puss models his new footwear (©Primrose Productions).

Primrose Productions also took an objective view of her work and decided to share with audiences how she made her films via a documentary. In 1953, *You've Asked for It— The Art of Lotte Reiniger* or *The Birth of the Silhouette Film* was made. Hagen Jr. also led efforts to track down her pre-war films that she deemed lost, but copies remained in other countries. Reiniger was grateful for all the work Hagen Jr. did to find her films, help her make new ones, and handling the business matters: "I am terribly sloppy and lose films and they are behind me, doing what they can. He is a good salesman, he brought them all into the television programs. He is excellent in his field" (qt. in Happ, 2004, 85).

When artists are given the opportunity to remake their earlier works, some balk at the idea because they consider the first incarnation the ideal version. Others seize the chance, as it allows them to try new techniques, experiment with alternate scenarios and fix mistakes. Reiniger loved her old films, but she also loved revisualizing them. The *Cinderella* and *Sleeping Beauty* films from 1954 aren't so much remakes as they are different takes on the same story. Fairytales run rampant with alternate versions of the same story and experts have spent years studying them along with the cultural and historical significance. Asked how she felt about remaking *Cinderella*, Reiniger said,

> Generally, I make my stories spontaneously and I don't think about children. But if you do a series for television, there are certain prerequisites. You have to align your mentality to a child's.... When I made *Cinderella* in 1922 Germany, everything was different. In the German version, there are pigeons that help Cinderella.... She gets her ball gown in the cemetery where her mother is buried under a tree.... Cinderella's sisters cut off the feet to fit into the shoe. The blood flows. The version I made in England is a much more elegant [version] … [qt. in Happ, 2004, 83].

Reiniger said in an interview with Pierre Jouvanceau for *Banc-Titre* that when she made the Primrose Productions fairytale films, she had to consider children's viewing needs (Jouvanceau & Roda, 1980). For instance, she showed mercy to the lackadaisical grasshopper in *The Ant and the Grasshopper* and allowed him to live; she said on animating the film that, "The film ends with the ant's triumph and I didn't want that. I favor the grasshopper" (qt. in Strobel, 2008, 18).

When it came to *Hansel and Gretel*, changes were made to the story in response to the Holocaust. The genocide of eleven million people (six million Jews and five million people the Nazis deemed undesirable) in concentration camps was still fresh in Europe's collective memory. Holocaust victims' bodies were disposed of through an assembly line process that involved cremation in huge ovens. "Reiniger wanted the witch to burn in the oven according to the original ending. However, the producers felt that they could not show the scene in a silhouette film so soon after the Holocaust" (Happ, 2004, 84). The witch instead broke into tiny pieces when Hansel and Gretel snapped her wand in half.

Reiniger also had to keep in mind western society's growing efforts to respect different ethnicities, and she animated true representations of them on screen.[3] Reiniger was a product of her era and while she was forward-thinking and apolitical, she did animate offensive portrayals of specific ethnic groups. It was common practice in the U.S. and Europe to depict non–European ethnic as offensive caricatures, but she did change her animation when she reused animation for *The Magic Horse* and *Aladdin* from *Prinzen Achmed*. Marina Warner noticed the changes in the African Magician character: he "lost his hooked nose and became a more cuddly, comic figure from Western nursery lore" due to his anti-Semitic profile (2011, 401). As for her rendition of Aladdin in *Prinzen Achmed*, "[T]he same slender elongated limbs, high-domed cranium and tight curly hair continue to appear but mixed in alongside a new puppet, who is younger, shorter, sturdier,

Cinderella meets her prince (©Primrose Productions).

with a snub nose, and more loosely wavy hair" (Warner, 2011, 402). Political correctness was not a priority in the 1950s, but Reiniger's changes to the reused *Prinzen Achmed* footage demonstrates how she retained her unprejudiced principles, and they evolved as she grew older.

Reiniger's silhouette films are considered gentler than traditional cel or stop-motion films, because the black visual elements are more bound to subjective themes of imagination than other animation forms that try to make the illusion of life more of a reflection of life. In 1928, Rudolf Arnheim wrote a review for *Weltbühne* about Reiniger's films that explains how her films are less "violent" than more realistic ones:

> Lotte Reiniger utilizes the ideal technique, the silhouette film. The silhouette is not as close to reality as a three-dimensional thing, no matter how imaginatively it may be thought out. It thus spares the viewer, particularly the child viewer, the fear that sets in when the fairy tale passes a certain point of vividness and becomes tangible reality. The movable silhouette charmingly maintains the right balance between the product of art and life; we believe it enough to be enthralled, and we do not believe it enough to get the goose bumps we get when experiencing the supernatural [1997, 141].

Cowan found another review about Reiniger's film in relation to how she represents mature themes without overwhelming children and "the difference lies precisely in the opposition between silhouette and photography" (2013, 796):

> The technique of the silhouette resides precisely in stylization. This form is predicated on a conscious renunciation of the principle of naturalism, for the silhouette—and this also goes for the silhouette film—is and remains absolutely two-dimensional, whereas photography gives us the impression of three-dimensionality. This natural stylization, which has nothing arbitrary about it and thus leaves no

The witch lures Hansel and Gretel with sweets (©Primrose Productions).

impression of artistry, makes things appear in a light that naturalism cannot attain. For naturalism appears raw and abrasive, whereas the silhouette remains light and graceful [qt. in Cowan, 2013, 796].

When the 13 films played in the U.S., England and other countries, audiences were enchanted with the silhouette puppets' deft movements, wondrous special effects and lulling narration. The most praised of all the films, *The Gallant Little Tailor* won the Venetian Silver Dolphin Award, the first prize for TV short films, and it was nominated for an award at the 1955 Edinburgh Film Festival. Earnings from the films allowed Koch and Reiniger to stay in England, much to their delight (Happ, 2004, 84).

In between animating her fairy tale films, Reiniger found the time to animate swans for another of Christian Simpson's televised ballets. His *Swan Lake* aired on June 9, 1954, and he once more met with success, although some critics disliked the silhouette swans (Davis, 1996, 36–38). After her fairytale film adventures, Reiniger animated *Jack and the Beanstalk* in 1955, featuring black silhouettes on a colored background. The colors were so striking against the black silhouettes that they leapt off the screen. In 1956, she decided to reanimate *The Star of Bethlehem*, her rendition of the Magi's journey to visit the newborn savior. It used the same animation technique as *Jack and the Beanstalk*, but she had the fun of working with her old friend Peter Gellhorn on the music; the Glyndebourne Festival Chorus performed the songs (Happ, 2004, 84; Mebold, 2008, 15). Reiniger's take on the Nativity is more like watching an epic fantasy as the Magi battle demons and Harrod and his soldiers as they make their way to pay homage to the Christ child. In 1956,

The Gallant Little Tailor kills seven flies in one blow (©Primrose Productions).

William Ohly died and as a memorial to him, she painted a stained glass window of St. Francis of Assisi in the Abbey (Raganelli, 1999).

While Reiniger was rebuilding her filmography with new pieces, Hagen Jr. was concerned about her older works that were left behind in Germany. As with the original print of *Die Abenteuer des Prinzen Achmed*, the original negatives for her other films were destroyed in the Battle of Berlin. Hagen Jr. wanted to share the old film with new audiences and stock up Primrose Productions' offering, but one can assume he also wanted to find them for posterity's sake (Happ, 2004, 84). He had a personal connection with *Prinzen Achmed* through his father and his own experiences, but he had a genuine affection for fairytales. His search was successful and yielded copies of *Prinzen Achmed* and other films stored at the British Film Institute and other British archives, which had the majority of her films. New York's Museum of Modern Art had *Carmen* and *Der kleine Schornsteinfeger* (Happ, 2004, 84). During his interview with her, Guy Coté said he had seen a print of *Papageno* and Reiniger exclaimed, "That old warhorse! Do you mean to say that there is still a print of that floating around in Canada?" (1954, 18)

After the discovery of the old films, Primrose Productions released them as classic Reiniger features and they were primarily new for audiences as they had been "lost" for a generation. Of note is the 12-minute film *Aladdin* that cut and pasted scenes from *Prinzen Achmed*. While it's technically a "new" film, it was shown as a classic and was also played along with the 13 fairytale films. The quality of some films were poor due to being copies of copies (Happ, 2004, 85).

The year 1956 was the sixtieth anniversary of cinema and to celebrate the medium, the British Film Institute teamed with Cinémathèque Francaise to hold an exhibition that honored cinema pioneers and other notables from June to September of that year in Trafalgar Square (Happ, 2004, 85). Richard Burke, head of the exhibition, said, "The first artist who I invited to design a room was Lotte Reiniger, whose silhouettes movies

Jack marvels at the sky as he climbs the beanstalk (©Primrose Productions).

I admired for a long time. Carl Koch, Reiniger's husband, had more good ideas than any other exhibition and he was the most enthusiastic colleague" (qt. in Happ, 2004, 85). The exhibition dedicated individual rooms to important cinema personages and the couple helped design two presentation rooms. The exhibition was highly praised and on July 9, 1956, Reiniger shared her own work. Her appearance apparently surprised many audiences who thought she died during World War II. Happ shared one comment someone made about her presence: "Lotte Reiniger, who presented to the public as a great personality of international film, and was thrilled to be able to participate in the exhibition, because, as she said, everyone believed that she was already dead already for a long time. Now she has impressively proven before an international audience that she is still alive and working" (qt. in Happ, 2004, 87).

While the 1950s were the steadiest time for Reiniger and helped reignite her animation career, not everything was well at Primrose Productions. Reiniger was happy to allow Hagen Jr. to handle business matters for the studio, because he was experienced and a "good salesperson," but she and Koch were suspicious that he went over her head and didn't share all matters with her (Happ, 2004, 87). Happ didn't delve further into this situation and he left out his own speculation as to why Reiniger and Hagen Jr. had a disagreement. He does acknowledge that he didn't know if Reiniger's suspicion was based on actual fact or if she just had a "bad feeling" (2004, 87). Whatever the cause, the two resolved the issue and decided that Primrose Production would continue to lease and profit from films she made specifically for that studio, but she and Koch branched out on their own and with the help of a few other people they established Fantasia Productions Ltd.

Reiniger made several new films under the Fantasia label. She shifted away from tried-and-true fairytales and once more returned to operas for inspiration. In 1957, she released *La belle Hélène* or *Helen la Belle* (*The Beautiful Helen*), adapted from Jacques Offenbach's operetta about Paris and Helen of Troy's elopement. After Discord's apple is thrown amongst them, the goddesses of Mount Olympus ask the youth Paris to select the fairest. He chooses Venus, who awards him Helen of Troy as his prize. Reiniger allowed her humor to come through the colored puppets as Cupid imitates Charlie Chaplin.[4]

> Lotte Reiniger said in a conversation: "I am a very good illustrator, I am really only an illustrator. My things are always illustrations of something." She said this quote as she looked back on her entire body of artwork. Once in awhile she receives commissions in the proper sense. It was like that earlier. In the late fifties, she was twice requested to complete a series of various illustrations of one of her favorite themes, ballet. Martin Hürlimann published in 1955 an issue of his newspaper *Atlantis* with emphasis on the theme of dance. He let Lotte Reiniger produce a "small history of ballet in paper cuts" for that. All cultures have passed down different ways (relief, vase painting, frescos, statues) of depicting images of dancing people. "Master of the paper cut Lotte Koch-Reiniger ... undertook this, some of the most interesting of these documents, the original of which usually are not satisfactorily reproduced, and made them consistent with her dainty art" [Happ, 2004, 89].

The following year, she made *The Abduction from the Seraglio* (aka *The Knight in the Harem*) from Mozart's opera about the hero Belmonte rescuing his beloved Konstanze from Pasha Selim's harem. (Gellhorn was in charge of the music arrangement for this film.) As this story goes, however, a newlywed couple are on their way to their honeymoon in a hot air balloon. Caught in a storm, they are stranded on an island, when suddenly they're attacked by desert bandits! The husband fights them off, but his bride is kidnapped, sold into a sultan's harem and imprisoned in a cage. Tied up and left to die, the husband cuts his bonds and wanders through the desert, until he comes to a well and accidentally releases a lion trapped in it. The grateful lion allows him to drink from a jug, when the husband discovers his bride's veil. The lion offers to help the husband rescue his wife as a thank you. Meanwhile the sultan's favorite is displaced she's been replaced by the bride. She discovers the husband and lion attempting to sneak into the seraglio and decides to help them to regain her status. While the sultan bathes, the favorite steals the key to the bride's cage. The husband releases his beloved and the newlyweds disguise the lion with the veil, then lock him in the cage. Just as they are about to escape, they're recaptured. The favorite pleads for the couple's release with the sultan, when suddenly the hot air balloon soars overhead in the sky. The sultan and his people bow in fright at the strange sight. Taking advantage of their captors' ignorance, the newlyweds escape.

Reiniger's first silhouette films with colored backgrounds started as an experiment that later became standard practice for her animation technique. She decided to use colored puppets for *La belle Hélène* and *The Abduction from the Seraglio*. Silhouette animation is a form of stop-motion animation noted for its use of opaque figures on a background, but when Reiniger gave her puppets discernable, colored features she stepped entirely out of the shadows for the first time in her career. While she used the same animation techniques on the same tricktisch, these films produced entirely in color cannot be considered silhouettes. They still rely on the stop-motion animation process, but they cross into cutout animation. Reiniger dubbed them "coloured cutouts" (Jouvanceau, 2004, 223).

Reiniger wasn't too pleased with the colored films, acknowledging that true silhouettes were indeed cast in black and white, but she relented that color was "the prevailing taste" (Happ, 2004, 88). "For Lotte Reiniger, the pure black is nothing less than *sine qua non* for the credibility of her figures. She had in fact noticed that 'when the puppets are not black the viewer does not believe in them'" (qt. in Jouvanceau, 2004, 73). Reiniger wanted to continue working in pure black and white in the latter portion of her career, but audiences demanded color. To make a living, she had to acquiesce and include some form of color in her silhouette films. While she might have been displeased with the colors, it did add more narrative depth to her films: "precise time a scene takes place" and more details to the character's environment (Jouvanceau, 2004, 214).

Reiniger considered her experimentation with colored cutout animation a "disappointing result" that came about due to the demand for color films and the colored tinting she had done in *Prinzen Achmed* (Jouvanceau, 2004, 224). Jouvanceau related how these films were flat, too color-dominated, and described the puppets and color fighting for dominance: "[T]he only possible outcome was the annihilation of one or the other of the antagonists" and thusly killed the silhouette film (Jouvanceau, 2004, 223).

The struggle for supremacy is an over-dramatic categorization of a different form of animation. Reiniger's colored cutout films are some of the most beautiful in her filmography as they demonstrate her painting, color competency and drawing skills that are otherwise hidden by the opaque silhouettes and grayscale backgrounds. Reiniger might have disliked them and scholars say they aren't the true reflection of her work, but they don't feel they fall into an entirely different form of stop-motion animation. *La belle Hélène*, *The Frog Prince* (1961) and *The Abduction from the Seraglio* demonstrate the range of capabilities she possessed. They lack an amateur's errors when experimenting with a new technique. Silhouette animation was Reiniger's preference for her filmmaking, but had she decided to switch her animation medium and practiced more with the alternate process, she might have embarked on a new, possibly even more successful part of her career.

Reiniger and Koch were unable to make much profit from Fantasia Productions. The company folded and they once more moved on to other projects.

Another fine example of Reiniger's versatile artistry was an illustration project she did for Cassell and Company on Gladys Davidson's children's book *Ballet Stories for Young People*. The compendium provides short biographies of legendary ballet choreographers and tells the stories of famous ballets such as *Giselle*, *The Nutcracker*, *Ondine*, *Coppelia* and *Swan Lake*. Instead of relying on her scissors, Reiniger solely used ink and ink to depict notable scenes in these ballets. As seen with her colored paper films, Reiniger's level of detail in her pen-and-ink drawings display a feminine grace reminiscent of old European fairytale illustrations and she also mimics different art movements (from art nouveau to early cartoon art) to highlight her fluid skills. Hiding within her ballet drawings, however, one notices that Reiniger used the same body shapes, facial features and stances from her silhouette characters.

Opposite: Reiniger mastered more than silhouettes. She was also gifted in painting with watercolors and pen and ink drawings, demonstrated in this drawing of *Le Spectre de la Rose* from the book *Ballet Stories for Young People* (© Cassell and Company).

7. Animated Women and Lost Love

Reiniger always had a pair of scissors in her hands and she was always cutting paper into silhouettes of people, animals and other figures. She gave these silhouettes to friends and family to the point where anyone who worked with Reiniger walked away with a silhouette as a gift. Continuously cutting silhouettes allowed Reiniger to practice and experiment with her art. One of the twentieth century's most famous English silhouettists, Hubert Leslie clipped two miniature portraits that are housed in the famous Doll's House at Windsor. He once wrote,

> There is no "painting," no hesitation, about cut paper. Even the very solidarity and flatness of the paper surface is a property inimitable in ink or paper. One other point in favour of scissor-cutting over other media is its own stout limitations. In pen-and-ink or paint it is not necessary that the design should "hang together" in one single piece; but in cutting paper this is essential. The whole picture must link up with itself, so as to remain one single piece of paper. This means that considerable ingenuity must be exercised in the designing of it, so that no "loose ends" are left unattached ... [qt. in Mégroz, 1949, 110–11].

Apparently Leslie and Reiniger crossed paths and befriended each other; Reiniger gave him silhouette figures of Ondine, a emperor and a nightingale inspired by Andersen's story. Mounted in a glass frame, Reiniger signed the trio, "FOR HUBERT LESLIE With All Best Wishes—Yours, Lotte Reiniger."[5]

In September 1960, Reiniger worked for ITV Granada on a small piece about the London Zoo, showing the mythological chimera. The animation is less than a minute; not much else is known about it (Mebold, 2008, 32).

Top: **Reiniger always had a pair of scissors in her hands and gave silhouettes to friends and family. This dancing couple has a gift for Mara Alper (courtesy Mara Alper).** *Right:* **A lovely Reiniger ballerina and her partner performing an extraordinary lift (courtesy Paul Gelder).**

Reiniger's friend Pauline Grant, who was in charge of the Coventry Theatre's Christmas pantomime, asked her to lend the theater her paper-cutting talents by making an original film for the holiday show (Happ, 2004, 88). In the United Kingdom, a Christmas pantomime is a yearly tradition. Pantomimes include acts one would have seen in a vaudeville show, and audience participation is welcomed. Reiniger was versed in pantomime history and she shared her knowledge in a magazine article: "[T]he pantomime emerged from the eighteenth century harlequinade and from jugglers and puppet theater, the puppets and shadow performances [were part] of a kind of world theater in the winter time in the streets of London. This in turn had its origins in the mystery plays of the Middle Ages" (qt. in Happ, 2004, 88)

Her silhouette films were used as interludes between acts in the pantomime. A canvas screen was dropped, then the film was projected on the screen accompanied by a live orchestra (Happ, 2004, 89). Her first Christmas pantomime at the Coventry Theatre was in 1960 and she animated the silhouette film *The Pied Piper of Hamelin* (she animated rats that ran across the screen and ate sausage links and other food), echoing back to the first major film project she did for Paul Wegener. The following year she presented *The Frog Prince*. Grant said of the shadow interludes, "Last year her moving silhouettes that opened for *The Pied Piper from Hamelin* were enthusiastically applauded, her wondrous invention gave the swarm of rats a precious quality. This year will be even more adventurous, as she shows in color the brave travels of the Frog Prince in the wells of the deep" (qt. in Happ, 2004, 89).

In 1962, Reiniger's career slowed, but she continued to keep her hands busy with a small job illustrating the dust jacket for Oswell Blakeston's *The Queen's Mate*. It was a very simple dust jacket, hardly a fine example of her skills, with two cameo portraits of a young and older man in contrasting black and white.

On December 19, 1962, Reiniger and Koch "took the oath of allegiance before the Commissioner of the Interior Ministry" and became naturalized citizens of the United Kingdom (Happ, 2004, 91). For Christmas 1962, Reiniger switched to the Glasgow Theatre for the yearly pantomime and made *Wee Sandy*. "It was about a shadow, who received a magical accordion and when [the shadow] played it, people would go crazy. For example, once he played at Trafalgar Square and then Nelson began to dance atop his pillar. And then the shadow went to the moon and played there and Scottish flags went up all over and the moon creatures put on kilts" (qt. in Happ, 2004, 89).

Reiniger's old publisher friend Martin Hürlimann continued to use Reiniger's silhouettes in his magazine *Atlantis* and for Bertelsmann-Lesering she made ten scherenschnitte to illustrate the 1963 book *Mondscheingärten: Gedichte* (*Moonlight Garden: Poetry*) by famous German romantic poet Eduard Mörike (Happ, 2004, 102). She returned to Coventry Theatre in 1963 for the Christmas pantomime, showcasing her third take on *Cinderella*. This time it was in color and "horrible to animate because it had six horses." This was the last project she made with her husband ("Lotte Reiniger Recording," 1976).

Carl Koch was diagnosed with chronic kidney inflammation in the fall of 1963. Though he was able to help Reiniger animate *Cinderella*, his health became worse and on December 1, he died of kidney failure in Barnet Hospital. His funeral was held on December 6. He was cremated and some of his ashes were spread while Reiniger safeguarded the rest in an urn. Louis Hagen, Jr., described the pair's relationship:

> Lotte and Carl were a happily married couple. Lotte was the introvert and Carl was the extrovert. If something didn't suit him, he went berserk; he made an awful noise, shouted the house down. If Lotte wasn't satisfied she got calmer and calmer until she didn't say anything at all. But in their work

they were completely harmonious. Carl often used to say, "Now Lotte, you've been overworking. Let me finish it off." He did it, but he never had her patience. He always started things nicely, but things got quicker and quicker. And when Lotte woke up or looked at the film the next day, "It's ghastly what you've done. I have to do it all again" [qt. in Raganelli, 1999].

Reiniger never truly got over his death and for many years she stopped animating silhouette films, because Koch had been her partner, inspiration, producer, assistant and more (she had a contract to film Ovid's *Metamorphoses*, but that fell through ["Lotte Reiniger Recording," 1976]. Reiniger said many things about her husband's death over the years, including,

> [I]t is terrible that my husband is gone, because you cannot imagine a better [partner] in the world. He always knew immediately what it was, if something did not work with the technology. He understood so much about films. Karl was my best critic. When I showed him something and he liked it, I was happy. When I lost my husband, I could not make any more movies. We have always worked very well together. It was wonderful. When he said that something is good, it made me stop worrying [qt. in Happ, 2004, 91–92].

Reiniger was very melancholic for the remainder of her life. Although she might never have displayed her depression outwardly, it followed her like Churchill's own black dog.

Renoir too was heartbroken over Koch's death and he said, "He was truly a remarkable man. He had a profound knowledge of human life and he had a sense of the absurd conditions of human life" (qt. in Happ, 2004, 92). Reiniger sold her tricktisch to the Düsseldorf Film Museum and intended never to animate again, but she did find it in herself to bring shadows to life on film once more.

One of the main reasons I set out to write about Lotte Reiniger was to share her contribution to animation and puppetry history, and also shine a spotlight on her female identity. Any woman who broke traditional gender roles usually made the history books and she is often the subject of modern introspective. Laurel Thatcher Ulrich said, "Well-behaved women seldom make history," and these women are held aloft as shining role models for the modern female. As stated before, there wasn't a lot of scholarship devoted to animation or puppetry outside their respective circles (although puppetry one-ups animation on academic research) and much less was applied to females within those mediums. K. Vivian Taylor also noted that there is a "general underrepresentation of female filmmakers working in an experimental multi-media genre (silhouette animation)" (2011, 11). While female filmmakers were marginalized due to their gender, the animation aspect of Reiniger's career worsened her obscurity. While animation is a male-dominated industry in its origins, it has since evolved to welcome more female personnel. The same can be said for puppetry as a traditional art dating back centuries.

There were women who left their hearth and home to pursue their interests in animation or puppetry, but their stories have not been discussed to a great extent. My interest in Reiniger stemmed from our shared love of the same mediums, her gender, and the lack of research surrounding her career. One of the primary reasons was her gender, because women who did more than ink and color in the lines were rare. Reiniger was someone for me to identify with and point to how women have influenced animation since its inception.

With any woman who ventured into a male-dominated world, they are lauded as a feminist icon. But it brings the question "What is a feminist?" into the conversation. Feminism and its supporters have received a negative reputation as crazy man-haters who blame all of society's ills on the opposite sex. Rush Limbaugh dubbed this type of feminist "feminazis" (Wilson, 2011, 55). I consider this a bad comparison and poor choice of words especially since the Nazis were against the basic tenets of feminism. According to John K. Wilson, "The comparison of feminists fighting for equality to the most brutal and murderous regime in human history should shock everyone" (2011, 55). I prefer to label so-called feminazis with the term hyper-feminists due to their extreme behaviors and beliefs. Hyper-feminists are a sensationalist topic and there are not as many as the media leads us to believe. It is due to the prevalence of hyper-feminists that many women do not call themselves feminists, even if they do believe in the equal and fair treatment of all women, because they don't want to be associated with negative connotations.

The existence of hyper-feminists is a nuisance for the calmer feminists who continuously must say, "I'm a feminist, but I'm not..." The basic definition of feminism is the advocacy of women's rights for equal and fair treatment in society, culture, economy and politics. A more liberal definition of feminism is the belief that any woman has the right to pursue her goals in a manner she sees fit. The latter definition gives credence to women who want to fulfill the traditional feminine roles, such as homemaker, but they do so because it is their own choice. The ability to choose is a big part of feminism and relates to Reiniger in that she chose to be an animator and puppeteer, but she also chose to be a wife and tell romantic stories in her silhouette films.

Based on this definition of feminism, Reiniger was a feminist, but she probably wouldn't have labeled herself as one. One must remember that no matter how forward-thinking a person is, they are still products of their time and immediate culture. The current agent for Primrose Productions, Christel Strobel, wrote that Reiniger "was one of the few women within the circle of filmmakers, in this regard she was a 'modern woman,' but she didn't step forward as a 'feminist'" (Strobel email to author, October 27, 2015). Reiniger was a very determined person right from her youth and her self-confidence grew from being an only child with indulging, supportive parents. She was a very expressive, outgoing woman with a clever sense of humor. While Reiniger and her husband socialized within elitist artist circles of 1920s Berlin, she was still a woman in a country that held to traditionalist roles and Reiniger adhered to them in her way. She didn't step forward as a feminist, because she didn't feel the need to. Animation scholar and film historian Cecile Starr wrote, "Reiniger herself did not feel disadvantaged in being a woman. What she did feel was a kind of resentment that the kind of films she wanted to make were so seldom financed by people who were turning out—to her—highly forgettable animation" (qt. in Liebenson, 2001).

K. Vivian Taylor also shares with us how Weimar Germany was a progressive and equal society on paper, but the reality was a sharp contrast to the facts:

> Much like the rest of modern life, the role of Weimar women was radically changing, and many women optimistically endorsed the new Weimar Republic's promises of gender equality. After receiving the vote in 1919, women became concerned with issues such as the prohibition of abortion, failure of political parties to follow through on various promises, equal pay for equal work, workplace treatment and conditions, and unrealistically glamorous women in the media. Although the Weimar constitution initially granted women the right to vote and promised equality, they remained objectified, restricted and subordinate.... Nothing much had truly changed since the Wilhelmine Empire for the working class women of Weimar [2011, 56].

Reiniger became more concerned with politics when the Nazi regime's militant doctrines overran her life and took away many of her close friends' rights. She did not seek to associate herself with any of the main movements of her life; her sole pleasure was to animate stories with her husband.

While most creators telling fiction-based stories follow the same creed of only wanting to tell a good story, themes sneak in and audiences interpreted them as they wish. Many academic studies declare that an author meant this or that through the employment of various artistic terms: metaphor, simile, allegory, parody, satire, *deus ex machina*, dramatic irony, poetic irony, etc. Fandom communities explore creative works in an analogous fashion with fanfiction, fanart and cosplay when they add their own interpretation to a creator's work. Academic works, however, are less flamboyant. Academic studies and fan works do overlap, especially when the academics happen to be a fan of a film or literature; think of all the hundreds of studies dedicated to the "hidden meanings" in *Harry Potter, Lord of the Rings, Doctor Who, Star Wars* and *Star Trek* and these franchises are only the threshold due to their more secular reach.

Most creators create for the pure joy of being able to use their talents and share their works with an audience. While some have noble intentions to spread a positive message from the start, many just want to the freedom to create. It's usually once they achieve security that a more noble purpose is attached to their work by themselves or via another party. Jim Henson fell in love with television and wanted to work in the medium, so he found a gimmick that worked for him and became a respected entertainer. After he had established himself by doing gigs on talk shows, commercials and TV specials, he applied his puppetry, leadership and artistic skills to spread a message about improving the world. The best examples are *Fraggle Rock, Sesame Street* and *Song of the Cloud Forest.*

Stylistically Reiniger veered away from overt messages in her films, because it would have hindered her creative expression. She was making art for art's sake as film was the epitome medium for her scherenschnitte, puppetry and animation skills. She made her silhouette films because she loved to make them, and if there was any message that Reiniger wanted viewers to take from her silhouette films it would be that love is a powerful and wonderful emotion *à la* "love conquers all." This simplistic and innocent theme is one of the oldest. One cannot ignore, however, that Reiniger was one of the few filmmakers in the world in the early twentieth century. Working in a male-dominated field and society probably led her to have some feelings about women's equality. While she played with animated puppets, within the shadows' featureless faces, female-empowered messages can be interpreted and they are conveyed through the puppets' subtle actions.

When first analyzing Reiniger's animated films, it appears her body of work supports more of a traditionalist view of society with women keeping to domestic duties and relying on men for protection. She spotlighted many female characters who play submissive and passive roles, but consider that she was adapting fairytales and this character archetype is a historic staple. Without a doubt Reiniger was vested in remaining true to the source material, but she did take artistic license to tell the story she wanted, and the versions she wanted to tell were with female characters fulfilling this archetype. It was her choice, but from a modern feminist analytical approach some scenes are cause for head-scratching and do remain a product of their time. The following observations are only meant to serve as examples of how Reiniger's filmography can be interpreted in a hyper-feminist fashion.

In her most famous film *Die Abenteuer des Prinzen Achmed,* female characters Princess Dinarsade and the fairy ruler Peri Banu are subject to the whims of their male counterparts. When Prince Achmed gains control of the mechanical flying horse, he lands the metal beast and journeys into a harem where he is voraciously attacked by women. Traditionalist views hold that women are emotional creatures and unable to control themselves, thus they must be cloistered for their own safety or they would be overtaken with their emotions as demonstrated by this seraglio scene. The women throw themselves at Achmed and fight over him. The harem's surfeit of emotion holds fast to the misconception that women become emotionally uncontrollable. It invokes the idea that women need to be reined in by men in order to keep their emotions in check. Achmed isn't the man to assert control over the seraglio, not only because the women are beyond reason, but also due to him being in another cock's henhouse. Overwhelmed by the female frenzy, Achmed escapes by taking off again on the mechanical horse.

The next questionable scene occurs when he lands the horse next to a moonlit lake in a grove. Within minutes of his descent, Peri Banu and her attendants descend in the shape of birds and shed their feathers to bathe in the lake. Achmed hides in the greenery and watches mystified like Actaeon spying on Artemis. Peri Banu doesn't curse Achmed like the virgin goddess did with her Peeping Tom; instead Achmed follows in the footsteps of the men in swan maiden and animal bride fairytales by stealing Peri Banu's feathery robe. Unable to flee, Achmed proceeds to kidnap Peri Banu and persuades her to be his wife.

While this scene between Peri Banu and Achmed bears all the classic elements of romantic fairytales and even myths, it still is a frightening exchange. Peri Banu is stripped naked and forcefully taken by a stranger who declares his love and proposes marriage. She is stripped of all her dignity and free will, then she must agree to Achmed's demands or face unknown consequences. It perpetuates an archaic ideal that women are objects that can be taken and subjected to the whims of their abductors, like war trophies. What's even worse is that poor Peri Banu is perpetually kidnapped and even sold throughout the movie. She never has the chance to actively save herself and must rely on Achmed to save her, a classic damsel-in-distress situation.

Achmed's sister Dinarsade, faces a similar fate. The evil magician tries to buy her from the caliph, but Achmed does stand up for his sister and objects to the union. It could arguably be more of a matter of pride, because the magician is old and ugly and lacks a pedigree. (Aladdin might be a poor tailor, but he becomes rich via magic.) She has the luck of Aladdin courting her and getting the chance to know him, before she chooses to marry him. The magician eventually kidnaps her and subjects her to his will; all speculation happens off-screen.

The women in *Prinzen Achmed* don't fare well in terms of female empowerment. The same applies to the women who star in Reiniger's silhouette fairytale adaptations: *Cinderella* (both versions), *Sleeping Beauty* (both versions), *Thumbelina* and *The Frog Prince*. The women in her fairytale films closely follow their story roots and the same old anti-feminist argument about fairytale applies: the heroines passively act out their parts, waiting for the plot to happen to them rather than asserting their own actions.

The trend continues with *The Grasshopper and the Ant*. Traditionally the title characters are played by personified male insects. Reiniger portrays the ant in the shadow of a stern German hausfrau, incapable of any pity or charity. The ant can be interpreted as representing a bitter old spinster, unhappy with her lot because she never found a husband, was never fulfilled by children.

In Reiniger's version of *Galathea*, the marble statue comes to life and instantly prefers a wild lifestyle. Pygmalion tries to persuade Galathea to join him in domestic bliss, including covering her shame with clothing and jewelry. Galathea only wants to dance naked at local taverns and have strange men praise her. Pygmalion's steadfast maid comforts

The repulsed princess feeds the Frog Prince from her own plate (©Primrose Productions).

him during the statue's crazy antics, despite her affections being rebuffed. Galathea's actions are only curbed by divine intervention when the men's wives and the maid plead with Aphrodite to transform the sinful statue back to marble. This silhouette film serves as an example of a sinful woman and a moral woman. Galathea serves as a metaphorical Eve, who once brought to life gives herself away to temptation. She rejects a domestic lifestyle in favor of sinful acts: spurning a man's wisdom, erotic dancing, shunning clothing, and luring husbands away from their wives. It takes an act of a god to strike her down and save people from her wickedness. The maid, on the other hand, is a symbol of domestic happiness. Remaining loyal to Pygmalion, she waits for him to forswear Galathea and come to his senses that she is the better mate. The maid is moral, domestic purity and through her, Pygmalion will find the happiness he sought with Galathea, because she is free of corruption that ruins a household.

Reiniger's other depiction of a classic myth is *Helen la Belle*, recounting the events that began the Trojan War. Goddesses Hera, Athena and Aphrodite argue over to whom Discord's Apple is for as it is enscribed with "For the fairest," so they ask Paris to make the decision. Women have been accused of vanity, dating as far back as Homer's time, and the three deities can't control their egos, so they bicker amongst themselves. An objective, masculine third party is selected to end the disagreement, but the goddesses must tempt Paris with their feminine charms and powers to sway his opinion. Paris declares Aphrodite the winner, when she bribed him with the most beautiful woman in the world, Helen of

Achmed whispering sweet words to Peri Banu (courtesy Paul Gelder, ©Primrose Productions).

Troy. The goddesses are overwhelmed by their egos for a meaningless title, while Helen is passed around like a prize. *Helen la Belle* disregards a woman's true worth as nothing more than shallow appearances; a woman is only as valuable as her outer beauty.

Its companion film *A Knight in the Harem* echoes Achmed's encounters in a harem. Newlyweds fly off on their honeymoon in a hot air balloon, but it's downed in a storm. Desert bandits kidnap the wife and sell her to a sultan with a harem. The husband must fill the traditional role of saving a damsel in distress before her virginity is compromised by the sultan. The sultan makes the bride his new favorite, but the former favorite is angry about being passed over. Out of jealously, she helps the husband save his wife. The bride is a traditional example of how a virgin bride is sweet, simple and meek. She can't function in the world without the protection of her husband. The favorite concubine is a fallen woman who has given herself over to corruption and uses her cunning to trick the sultan, so she can reclaim her place. The bride and the favorite serve as examples of the ideal and sinful woman, a duality theme often found in literature, theater and film.

In the opera *Carmen*, the leading lady is notorious for toying with men's hearts using her feminine wiles. She plants herself in the middle of a dangerous love triangle with Don José and the toreador Escamillo. In Reiniger's version, Carmen still toys with men's emotions, but she adds petty thievery to her charges. After a night together, she steals Don José's valuables and sells them for a beautiful dress and jewels, so she can flirt with Escamillo. Carmen doesn't care for any of the men she toys with as she is only interested in finding ways to amuse herself. She positions herself in an old feminine trope of a self-absorbed woman who relies on her beauty and charms to get by in life. Reiniger allows Carmen to reinforce the outdated trope.

Reiniger's *Harlekin* stars the comedic trickster Harlequin, whose romantic escapades get him in trouble. Harlequin is content with being a womanizer until the sweet and attractive Columbine makes him change his wanton ways. Their love is short-lived as Harlequin is punished for his crimes with the death penalty. Columbine's love calls him back to life and the pair are happily reunited. It was a common belief that a wanton man could be changed if he met the right woman to lead him into a life of domestic bliss. This plot idea, used in plays and books for hundreds of years, is still employed in Hollywood and Bollywood films. Columbine is thrust into the sweet virginal role and the plot happens to her rather than her interacting with it. Before his transformation, Harlequin almost rapes a maid, comes on to a wealthy woman, and spies on Columbine as she bathes. He's a scoundrel and the story tells women that they can change a man, which often ends up being a more dangerous situation for the woman.

There are other ways to underline the anti-feminist themes in Reiniger's work, but the examples above are the main ones. I made the examples brief, because too much focus on an anti-feminist argument goes against Reiniger's true intent and overshadows the fact that these were stories she wrote herself. She grew up in the early twentieth century, when these were accepted themes within the cultural paradigm, and she sought out romantic stories because this was her favorite genre. The anti-feminist argument must be addressed, however, due to modern ideology shifts and the common (yet sad) practice of forgetting how the past actually was.

As Strobel wrote, Reiniger was an independent woman who did what she was driven to do. These were the stories she wanted to tell, because they fulfilled her romantic notions and she had the opportunity to make them. A hyper-feminist would overlook these facts and paint Reiniger's films as prime examples of anti-feminism. I outlined the examples above and skewed them towards a extremist hyper-feminist perspective to demonstrate how they can be used to support anti-feminist principles. I used extremist examples because they are loud and easy to spot, contrary to subtle actions that can be used to support a feminist argument in Reiniger's work. While Reiniger is neither feminist nor anti-feminist, her films do portray animated female characters who lend themselves to assertive actions and qualities. "Some art historians fail to see artists' work in the context of the times they lived in and recognized the artists are not divorced from politics" (Sito, 2006, 23). The quote refers not to an artist's individual political ties, but rather how his or her work is viewed from an observer's political standpoint. In this case, we ignore Reiniger's early-twentieth-century perspective on feminism in favor of the more hyper-feministic approach. It's easy to glance over these portrayals and concentrate on the anti-feminist stance, but when found they prove to align more with modern heroine standards than expected.

Examining Reiniger's silhouette films from an objective feminist view raises less speculation when they are taken in context of the time period as well as the creator's intent. The kidnapping, harems and the more bawdy scenes are what they are, but they shouldn't overshadow an entire film; rather they should be viewed as advancing the story. When the heroines in Reiniger's films are met with a threatening situation, instead of bowing their heads and crying (although that does happen to some of the women), they fight back. The women resist the villains by running away, using their cunning, or even fighting tooth and nail. If Reiniger had made her films in recent times, she might have had a silhouette heroine scratch out her assailant's eyes or bludgeon them with a weapon.

Turning back to the biggest offender *Prinzen Achmed*, the hero Prince Achmed commits scandalous acts by spying on a naked Peri Banu and kidnapping her. This isn't the best way to start a courtship, much less win a woman's affections. Achmed's attempts at romance would now land him in prison, but in the source material *1001 Arabian Nights* it happened quite often as well as in myths and fairytales; women were as much the offenders as the men. After kidnapping Peri Banu, Achmed does realize his mistake and returns her feather robe. The movie has a dramatic pause after Achmed returns the robe, where both characters think about their current situation. Both are frightened and far from their homes. Peri Banu has the least control in the moment and decides to accept Achmed's affections and see where that leads. As Achmed and Peri Banu spend more time together, she does come to see him as her liberator, because it is indicated that Peri Banu was more of a prisoner than a ruler of Wak-Wak and Achmed freed her (this is never specifically addressed). Peri Banu takes a negative situation and seizes the opportunity to escape the demons of Wak-Wak, except before she has the chance to exercise her newfound freedom she is kidnapped again, sold to an emperor, and is forced into marriage with a humpback.

Despite having all of her power seized from her, Peri Banu does attempt to fight off her captors. Reiniger doesn't have any of her female characters go quietly into the night when they are kidnapped or placed in harm's way. Her heroines always attempt to fend off their attackers in any way they can, until they can attain freedom or stall until their lover can save them. Fending off the villains is a staple in Reiniger's silhouette films and it gives early twentieth century heroines more assertive actions than they had in other films of the time. Reiniger gives her heroines spunk and the willpower to fight. They might not always win and are forced to acquiesce to their captors, as Peri Banu and Dinarsade must, but they only do so with reluctance. Even though Reiniger's characters are mere shadows of real women, she delivers the message to fight for yourself.

Galathea and *Carmen* are two of Reiniger's more prominent films when it comes to feminist principles. Interestingly, they can be played for both the anti-feminist and the feminist camp. This aspect plays into Reiniger's sense of humor and wit. She loved to tell jokes and poke fun at herself and others; she injected a pinch of jest into her stories because it delighted her. *Galathea* and *Carmen* have a dual nature due to Reiniger's humor, making them more feminist than the anti as they make fun of stereotypical female characters as much as they fulfill them.

Galathea is a more satirical take on the classic myth than a lesson in morality. Pygmalion can't find his ideal women, despite his maid's pinings, so he has to make one. He thinks that a woman he made with his own hands will shape herself to his whims, but he didn't count on Aphrodite in the guise of Lotte Reiniger to give Galathea her own will and desires. An independent thinker, Galathea wants to indulge in the wild parts of life. She rebukes Pygmalion's misguided affections and fights for her freedom in a silhouette *tour de force*. Galathea succeeds and for a time basks in bacchanalian pleasures, especially dancing in the nude, but her "wicked" ways displease the more modest citizens and she dances back onto her pedestal. A saddened Pygmalion learned a valuable lesson that women, even false ones, have their own mind and won't fall into submission. Pygmalion's maid is also an example of feminism, because she doesn't compromise her own desires to attract his attention. While she might be waiting quietly, she's an example of a loyal and steadfast woman. She's dignified in her silence.

Carmen is the more street-smart version of Galathea. She is a thief and vain, but she is the antithesis of female heroines in the 1930s. Carmen is self-assured, assertive, strong, and knows what she wants. To get what she wants, she relies on her wits and beauty to charm Don José to her camp. When he falls asleep, she steals his valuables and sells them so that she can attract the famous toreador Escamillo's attentions. He spurns her attempts, because she's just another pretty face in the crowd to him. Carmen is determined to prove her mettle to Escamillo, so she dives into the bullring, challenges the bull, and triumphs over the beast and Escamillo with her dancing skills. An assertive heroine, Carmen had a goal and pursued it. Despite obstacles (Escamillo's ignoring her; Don José trying to catch her), she bests them by relying on her own strengths and getting her desire, even through devious means. It would be easy to toss Carmen into a con-artist's role, which would be a typical reaction to her thievery, seduction and vanity. Turning the tables, if a man committed the same acts that Carmen did, he would be viewed in a more romantic light, such as the humorous trickster or lovable vagabond. Reiniger made *Carmen* in hopes of creating a series of animated silhouette operas with her as stage manager, choreographer, costumer and director. She rewrote the classical opera to suit her own desires and she cast Carmen in a role usually reserved for a man.

Reiniger's *Carmen* is a self-assured heroine. Her actions fall more under a cunning personality. Carmen is very intelligent and knows how to use her natural beauty and dancing skills to flirt her way in and out of danger, but Reiniger's filmography includes other heroines who rely on their wits to escape precarious situations. Returning to *The Knight in the Harem*, the sultan's favorite initially appears to follow in Carmen's dance steps, but her character is more magnanimous. When the bride is sold to the sultan, he immediately makes her his new favorite concubine. The displaced concubine is unhappy and eager to regain her old title, and she risks her safety to sneak the husband into the harem and uses her knowledge of the sultan's schedule and palace activities to reunite the couple. The favorite makes smart, decisive moves and even adds a pinch of humor to the situation when they switch the bride with a lion dressed in a bridal veil. It can't be denied that the favorite has much to gain by freeing the bride, but she also has just as much to lose. She empathizes with the newlyweds and wants to help them escape the sultan. The favorite has many qualities of a feminist heroine: smart, empathic, quick-thinking, strong and determined. In a fashion, she can also be considered selfless as we don't know the conditions of life in the harem. It could be a "survival of the fittest" lifestyle with brutal and spiteful battles between the women as they vie for the sultan's affections. The favorite may hate this lifestyle, even though she has triumphed, and wants to spare the foreign bride from such suffering. However she is viewed, the favorite is the hero in *The Knight in the Harem*, because the newlyweds rely on her knowledge and actions to gain their freedom.

Der kleine Schornsteinfeger (*The Little Chimney Sweep*) is another story where a kidnapped woman must think quickly to escape. The heroine Belinde befriends a young chimney sweep after she enjoys his song and gives him a few gold coins and her handkerchief embroidered with a unicorn. Little does Belinde know that she is the target of a rake's kidnapping ploy and becomes a victim. Belinde never rests for a moment during her kidnapping; she screams and fights. When Mohock tries to seduce her again, she physically attacks him. Belinde isn't a cowed woman. Keeping her wits about her, she

Belinde meets her little chimney sweep. ©*Primrose Productions*.

hears the chimney sweep's familiar song. Sensing it as her only hope, Belinde whistles the same tune back to the boy. He hears it and promises to alert Belinde's parents of her whereabouts. After a dramatic chase, Belinde is safe and it was due to her quick thinking and reactions that she was able to start a chain reaction for her rescue. Belinde is a fine example of a woman who takes direct action to resolve her problems.

One of Reiniger's last films, *Aucassin and Nicolette*, is an adaptation of a chantefable that exudes feminism. Nicolette is set up to be a tragic heroine: her romance with Aucassin is forbidden, they're separated more than once, and she faces a forced marriage. Nicolette succeeds in not only winning her man

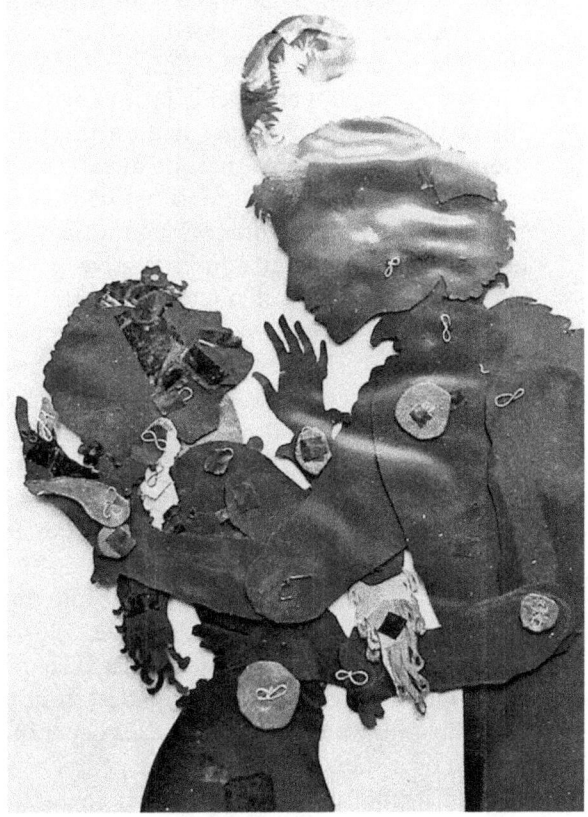

Backside view of the Nicolette and Aucassin silhouette puppets showing the various materials used in constructing the puppets (courtesy Mara Alper).

but also discovers the secrets of her past. Assassin's father forbids him from seeing Nicolette, so her adopted parents are forced to lock her in a tower. Nicolette refuses to play the Rapunzel card, so she escapes and searches for her beloved, only to discover that he was also imprisoned. She comforts Aucassin but, unable to free him, she hides in a forest and waits for him to find her. While this scenario doesn't seem too feminist, or polite for that matter, Nicolette wants to be sure that Aucassin truly loves her. It's a fidelity test, a popular way to determine true love in medieval literature, but rather than send Aucassin on a quest or save her, Nicolette simply waits. It's quite a noble way for her to conduct the test, because she's not putting herself or Aucassin in danger and she's also hiding to protect herself from imprisonment. It also might seem passive, but Nicolette's move is actually quite strategic.

Aucassin discovers Nicolette and they plan to leave the country. On their sea voyage, a storm shipwrecks them in different places. Nicolette is returned to her home country, only to remember that she's a princess. While she reclaims her title, she's once more imprisoned and this time faces an arranged marriage. Nicolette learns that Aucassin washed up on the shores of his homeland and inherited his father's title. She doesn't want her father to stop her, so Nicolette dresses like a minstrel boy. She makes her way to Aucassin's court and once more tests Aucassin to see if he truly loves her. She sings of her exploits and Aucassin recognizes that his lady love is the ministrel, they're then married. Not once during the entire story did Nicolette fulfill the trope of a weak, panicked maiden. She maneuvered her way through perils to evade capture, guarantee her lover's devotion, and avoid an unwanted marriage. She gave up comfort several times, her own choice, to live the life she wanted for herself.

Feminism is an open-ended argument that will be on the soap box for years to come, but when it comes to Lotte Reiniger, she can be held up as an admirable figure for the animation and puppetry fields for her scope of work who just happened to be female. One of the benefits Reiniger had partnering with her husband and working in small studio environments was that she didn't have to deal with the same treatment that other women in the animation industry faced. As stated before, animation was a man's game and no matter how talented women were, their presence was unwelcome in the studios (unless they did clerical, administrative or menial tasks in the animation process).

Female animated characters were also drawn to fulfill male fantasies (Betty Boop, Red Hot Riding Hood) or simply play a supporting role to the male counterpart (Minnie Mouse, Daisy Duck). Irene Kotlarz sums up how animated females were handled: "Human women, when they appeared, were usually a hybrid of signifiers of femininity comprising body parts like lips, hair, eyelashes, bosom, and so on, and were sometimes derived in part from actual women film stars. From Betty Boop to Jessica Rabbit, the standard character was, and still is, that of a showgirl designed to be looked at. Animated with squash and stretch, the female body in action was offered as the object of pleasure or amusement; there's many a gag based on the bouncing-tit routine" (1993, 102–03). Thankfully there is a flowing stream of female animators into the western animation industry. The showgirl routine has been toned down since the 1990s, and there is a large demand for more realistic and varied roles for female animated characters in movies and TV shows. The eastern animation industry, especially Japanese anime, continues to follow the trend of stylized, uber-gorgeous women with variances depending on the genre (bouncing boob jokes continue to be a staple in some anime genres). With Japanese anime, however, differences in feminist culture play a big factor. In the twenty-first century, one of the biggest achievements for animated girls is that they are no longer consigned to one job occupation (princess) and are given roles once reserved for animated males. Part of this is due to magical girl anime, where superhero girls are the main characters instead of a token team member.

"While I am not suggesting a male conspiracy—especially as many of the representations of women in cartoons suggest male anxiety as much as anything else—I am pointing out the process of signification with which animators engage. In animation there is no pointing the camera at a chosen subject and allowing 'reality' to speak for itself; everything you see has been put there by the animator" (Kotlarz, 1993, 103). Animation is not a happenstance product and everything on screen has been placed there on purpose based on an animator's direct action. Improvisation only occurs during the animation process and voice recording sessions. While female animated characters' treatment in the industry's early days has been brought up and is still vital, it is old school. "Women animators today are well aware of the cartoon tradition—its techniques, generic conventions and stereotypes; most use it, send it up or react against it on one way or another" (Kotlarz, 1993, 102). The key purpose for women in the modern animation industry is to remember where they have been, how far they have come, and go further with their work to take old traditions, remake them or invent something new.

Reiniger laid the groundwork for women in the animation industry as the director on *Prinzen Achmed* with Carl Koch, Walter Ruttmann Berthold Bartosch, Alexander Kardan, and Walter Turck, meaning she had full creative control and influence on the animation and story—so they followed her lead. A woman being in charge of story and lead animator was unheard of until the animation boom in the 1970s and onward. Even in the '70s, a woman holding any of these positions was uncommon.

Reiniger had the benefit of being able to express her individual artistic talents and transfer them to the silver screen, another trait which was exceedingly rare until the latter part of the twentieth century. If a woman in the U.S. had ambition to be an animator, it was like hitting a brick wall. Women who applied for an animation job were rejected or were sent to the Ink and Paint Department. Prime examples of the Disney Studio dealings with women are two infamous rejection letters. One was sent to Frances Brewer on May 9, 1939, and the latter was addressed to Mary V. Ford on June 7, 1938. The second paragraph on both letters must have shattered the dreams of many budding artists: "Women do not do any of the creative work in connection with preparing the cartoons for the screen, as that work is performed entirely by young men. For this reason, girls are not considered for the training school" (qt. in Sito, 2006, 25; Burg).

In his book *Drawing the Line*, Tom Sito describes women's trials and tribulations working at the Walt Disney Animation Studios. Prior to the women's liberation movements, "the largest single category of workers, by far, in an animation studio was ink-and-paint artists. They were, in the main, women who were held back by barriers to moving into the ranks of animator, layout, or direction" (Sito, 2006, 336). A favorite story told from the time was that a woman with a fantastic portfolio was only asked if she knew how to make coffee. Children's book illustrator Selby Kelly was ridiculed and told to hightail it to Ink and Paint (Sito, 2006, 24). Rae Medby McSpadden, who worked during Disney's Golden Age in the Ink and Paint Department, often heard that Walt Disney never hired any females to work in higher positions in the animation chain, because "each time they were beginning to get good they've quit to get married or something. So now he's thumbs down on girl animators" (qt. in Zohn, 2010). It was common practice for women to quit working once they were married, which made it justifiable in those times to limit women's advancement. Another argument that it was not worth investing in women animators was that they didn't have the same knack for storytelling and were more suited to capturing "action, personality, and caricature" (Zohn, 2010). This belief rang throughout Hollywood, not just the animation studios, and when women received screen credits of any kind, they often went only by their first and middle initials and last name.

Using marriage and "men are better at it" are a flimsy defense for the real reason. Painter Ruthie Thompson didn't mince words when she said, "It was a man's world all over the place.... [T]he stars were the beauties who sang and wiggled their fannies around—that's all girls were useful for" (qt. in Zohn, 2010). A "man's world" was another cause for segregation of the sexes. Women's workplaces at studios were dubbed "henhouses" (Sito, 2006, 26). Fraternization amongst male and female employees was forbidden, but that didn't stop male animators from flirting with the coeds. Reading descriptions of how ink-and-paint women were treated is not only distasteful, but would today cause an industry-wide sexual harassment suit. Catcalls, groping and unwanted attention were the norm. "A girl who complained about a butt pinch was called a killjoy or an old maid" (Sito, 2006, 27). It can still be common for a woman who calls out unwanted attention to be dismissed in a similar manner. Ironically, men and women were separated, because women would distract men from their work; but it seems men were more distracting to the women with their behavior.

Women at studios also had to adhere to regulations as did the men, although they were stricter for the former. Disney, for instance, enforced a female dress code where they could only wear dresses or skirts and weren't allowed to wear a lot of jewelry (Sito, 2006, 26). Sito also describes the "Disney shuffle," a gait that required the women to walk with small, soft steps and not pick their feet up too high, like how a Japanese woman shuffles in a kimono. The women were situated on the second floor and wore high heels, a poor combination when the animators wanted quiet (Sito, 2006, 26).

Despite the system stacked against them, some women gained animator status through their talent. "Those women who did attain the higher-paying positions did so through competence and persistence" (Beckerman, 2003, 42). During the production of *Snow White,* two women had the honor of being listed in the credits, Hazel Sewell and Dorothy Ann Blank (Smoodin, 2012, 31). Retta Scott, Mary Blair, Retta Davidson, Sylvia Moberly-Holland, Bea Selck, Janice Kenworthy, Elizabeth Case-Zwicker, Bianca Majolie, Sylvia Frye and Grace Stanzell worked at Disney. Lillian Friedman became the first female animator in the U.S. in 1933 at the Fleischer Studios when she was promoted from her inker position (Sito, 2006, 81). LaVerne Harding worked at Walter Lantz Studios from 1934 to 1960 and designed the Woody Woodpecker character design that was used from 1950 until 1999. Tissa David entered the animation scene early and in 1950 became the second woman to direct a feature film, *Bonjour Paris*, released in 1953. After working at Leon Schlesinger Productions and other studios, one ink-and-paint woman decided to go into business for herself: in 1954, Celine Miles formed her own company, Celine Miles Ink and Paint, that took over the time-consuming service. Celine Miles Ink and Paint worked on several Warner Brothers specials, Ralph Bakshi's *Fritz the Cat*, John Hubley projects and educational and medical films (Sigall, 2005, 184–86).

Behind the scenes was another woman responsible for promoting and distributing "the three most important animated-cartoon series of the silent era: Max Fleischer's 'Out of the Inkwell,' Pat Sullivan's 'Felix the Cat' and Walt Disney's 'Alice Comedies'" (Kaufman, 2004, 105–06). Margaret J. Winkler was a film distributor and had a profound influence on early American animation. Not only did she distribute now-legendary cartoons to theaters, but she also exerted some creative control over Disney's *Alice Comedies*, insisting that he add "as many gags as possible" (Kaufman, 2004, 108). She left the business after she married Charles Mintz, but "during a period of roughly three years, she brought to the screen the three foremost cartoon studios of her time. Despite some difficult business relationships, she not only promoted and distributed the films of those studios but exercised some influence over their content. In doing so, she earned an indelible place in American animation history" (Kaufman, 2004, 110).

Nelbert Chouinard, a passionate artist and teacher, became involved with a group of landscape painters in Pasadena, California, and also taught at a school that would become the California Institute of Technology, Otis Art Institute and Hollywood High School. She later opened the Chouinard School of Art in Los Angeles with an influential curriculum that caught Walt Disney's attention (Hahn & Miller-Zarneke, 2015, 21–22). "He was so motivated by her teaching that he would himself would drive his artists to her Friday-night class so they could learn to draw" (Hahn & Miller-Zarneke, 2015, 23). Her teaching methods set forth an innovative, rigorous teaching mantra and Disney would ally himself with Chouinard so his animators could augment their technique. Some of the Chouinard teachers were conscripted to work on *Snow White and the Seven Dwarfs* (Hahn & Miller-Zarneke, 2015, 26). Painter Millard Sheets recalled about Chouinard, "Oh, she was a terror. She was the sweetest, most wonderful person, if everybody behaved. But if they didn't, God, boy, look out. She was tough. Oh, I loved her with a passion" (qt. in Hahn & Miller-Zarneke, 2015, 25–26).

In the post–World War II years, the Chouinard School had financial difficulties and Walt Disney never forgot that she

> believed in him when no other Los Angeles art schools wanted anything to do with cartooning, and financially, because she had agreed to teach his animators when the Studio couldn't afford to pay for it.... When Nelbert suffered a stroke in 1957, she nearly lost control of the school. The Disney brothers stepped in to keep the Chouinard Art Institute running.... [They] pumped large sums of money into it to keep it solvent, and in 1961, they orchestrated a merger of the Chouinard Art Institute and the Los Angeles Conservatory of Music [Hahn & Miller-Zarneke, 2015, 438].

This merger formed a new school and Walt selected the board of trustees, including Chuck Jones, Millard Sheets and Alice and Marc Davis, to oversee the California Institute of Arts or CalArts, now one of the premier schools in the world to learn animation (Hahn & Miller-Zarneke, 2015, 438).

While the women despised their male co-workers' lewd and harassing behavior, many did love their jobs. "Though the work was tedious and unrelenting, it would be incorrect to suggest that there was little time for fun. On the contrary, many oldtimers remember those days as happy and fun-filled. The bringing together of so many youthful artists of both sexes made for a steady round of laughter and clowning" (Beckerman, 2003, 42). One of the few ink-and-paint ladies to write about her animation experiences was Martha Sigall in *Living Life Inside the Lines*. Her memoir documents how she "worked for just about every cartoon studio in existence then, with the exception of Disney. However, [she] did work on Disney cartoons when they faced a deadline and had to farm work out..." (2005, 11). Sigall revealed how studio life was filled with practical jokes, parties and romances. She found her career to be fulfilling and wrote of very few negative moments.

In the *Vanity Fair* article "Coloring the Kingdom," Patricia Zohn captured how Rae Medby McSpadden, Ruthie Thompson and their friends felt about working at Disney Animation Studios in the 1930s and 1940s. Zohn had her own preconceived notions about how the animation industry worked, but she "came to realize they were real-life models for the dedicated working girls who populated movie screens in the '30s and '40s. Neither downtrodden factory workers nor madcap flappers who jumped into fountains, they may have been caught in a sand trap of repetitive, highly precise work where eyes strained, waistlines shrank, and some even fainted, but they loved what they did and wanted to be the best" (2010).

The Disney ink-and-painting training program was rigorous with a "survival of the fittest" attitude very much like some of the animation trials male animators had to go through at studios to claim a job. Work schedules were stressful and during the production of *Snow White*, the ink-and-paint women clocked in so many hours that they "collapsed on the lawn, in the ladies' lounge, or even under their desks," in a fashion like the modern Japanese animation studio (Zohn, 2010). They were pushed to work faster and churn out cels to speed up production. One supervisor, Dot Smith, spouted, "Come on now, quick—like a bunny!" (Thompson, 2014) They took great pride in their work and the fact that they worked for Walt Disney. Warner Brothers inker Martha Sigall described Disney inkers: "[T]hey were kinda brainwashed ... they thought they were outstanding, that they were so lucky, that you have to be great to work at Disney, and they felt that" (qt. in Zohn, 2010). They added subtle contributions to the art, discovered errors, but mostly "their job was to make what the men did look good" (Zohn, 2010).

Prior to *Snow White*'s success, Disney Studios was more laidback. Animators and ink-and-paint ladies fraternized, and dating was even encouraged. Zohn includes a rival studio's press release about Disney romance: it was described as a "romantic paradise for young women employees ... for the amount of studio romances and marriages far exceeds that of any other studio" (2010). As the studio got bigger, the rules became stricter and segregation was enforced. The men called the animation building "the monastery" and the ink-and-paint department became "the nunnery" (Thompson, 2014)

Another popular urban legend about Walt Disney was that he was a misogynist, but Jim Korkis is quick to dispel this belief. Like Lotte Reiniger, he was progressive in many of his work practices. Korkis pointed to the biggest protector of Walt Disney's humanity, his own daughter Diane Disney Miller. She said her father "was very easy around women, and liked and respected them, with the exception of those who were pretentious or domineering, and I am aware of a few of those sorts that he complained about ... none family members!" (qt. in Korkis, 2014). Korkis explained that Walt Disney viewed ink and paint as a delicate craft, unsuitable for men. More women at Disney worked in non-ink-and-paint positions than at any other studio at the time and Disney himself was an advocate against sexual harassment.

> Walt insisted that the following memo be sent out to all men working as in-betweeners (IBT). It was dated January 17, 1939. Departmental conduct. "Attention has been called to the rather gross language that is being used by some members of the IBT Department in the presence of some of our female employees. It has always been Walt's hope that the Studio could be a place where girls can be employed without fear of embarrassment or humiliation. Your cooperation in this matter will be appreciated" [qt. in Korkis, 2014].

Korkis also points out that the infamous rejection letters were standard form letters, proved by the cited copies. Disney was a man who nurtured talent when he came across

Reiniger contemplating where to cut next (courtesy Paul Gelder).

it, including women artists, but his studio still kept to the male dominance status quo. Discriminatory rules and behavior were an industry standard just as much as the rejection letter. But enlightened minds have made the more horrid altercations things of the past. Buzzfeed news published "Inside the Persistent Boys Club of Animation" that included a quote about Mary Blair, one of the most lauded Disney artists and the go-to example for women's influence on Disney's animation: "Her niece [said that Mary Blair] was so unrivaled that she made the only piece of art by a Disney artist that Walt displayed in his home. She was an undeniably outstanding talent, which raises questions about the mediocrity of men who held similar positions" (Lange, 2015).

A disappointing fact was that even after the Women's Liberation movements in the 1960s and '70s, women were still limited in the animation industry and it wouldn't be until the late twentieth century cartoon boom that they began to assert themselves as more than support cogs and as vital to animation's future. I can't help but wonder how much talent was wasted due to misconceptions of the day. What would animation look like now if more women like Lotte Reiniger had been given the opportunity to pursue and practice their art in the so-called Golden Age?

We'll never know and speculation will only hold a person back. The key point to draw from the rejection letter is how far women in animation have come and will continue to go.

While I bemoan the lack of detailed resources on Reiniger's life in English, I was also astounded by the lack of information surrounding women in general in the animation industry. My research preference is skewed towards printed materials and academic databases, because their fact trails are easier to follow than a blind web search, but I was disappointed about the lack of old-school-style resource materials dedicated to women animators. A typical Internet search aided me more learning about women in the animation industry than the traditional outlets.

I was able to locate a few printed resources about women animators, but I was disappointed again that their copyright dates were prior to the Disney Renaissance and Nickelodeon's Golden Age. Not only was there limited information on women animators from the medium's early years, modern accounts are scattered as well.

The lack of documentation related to women in the animation industry has contributed to the lack of notoriety surrounding Reiniger's career. Despite the accomplishments of making a feature-length animated film 11 years prior to Disney and with a five-person staff, it didn't have a ripple effect on the animation community. Cutting silhouettes was considered a feminine art and an entire film using a feminine art created by a female artist failed to impress a male-dominated industry. Reiniger's co-animators on the film went on to receive recognition and scholars have devoted considerable efforts to documenting their work and lifestyles, again placing her in her normal role of footnote or two-sentence description. Reiniger's body of work is as or more impressive than many of her fellow animators. The quantity and quality is impressive for the husband-and-wife team, especially due to the roadblocks they encountered: World War II, financial setbacks, changes in the animation industry, German heritage, and (of course) Reiniger's gender. Her art also had the distinction to be categorized more as art than a "cartoon" (her films aren't cartoons), giving her a limited audience.

To many, Reiniger was only a small blip on the animation radar and she didn't register compared to the bigger studios with production teams, characters and animators who are now revered legends. Small blips aren't worth registering, because they are passed off as dust or even technical malfunction. Lotte Reiniger and her female animation brethren, however, have proven they're far from being annoying dust and that they too have stories worth being told.

8

The Fine Line Between Animation and Puppetry

> In the first silhouette films ... the figures moved alone in the middle of a white surface.... The movement of the silhouettes was choppier than today, because the frames in between were missing—but the humor stepped into its own rights. These traits stayed with the silhouette until today; it is the link between art and the cartoon. It is hardly thinkable that someone should come upon the idea to make a seriously-minded silhouette film, a sentimental drama, that sets the handkerchiefs of the ladies in the parquet and gallery into motion.—"The Silhouette Film" by M. Hiller

After her husband's death, Reiniger lost her motivation to animate. Carl Koch had been her animation, production and business partner since the beginning of her career and his love for her and devotion to her silhouettes was reflected in their collaborations. Without Koch, Reiniger felt that half of herself was missing, and continuing to animate would be a constant reminder that her beloved husband was no longer by her side to man the camera or help move the puppets. Reiniger didn't abandon her shadows, rather she channeled her grief through a medium she had played with in her youth: shadow puppetry.

Reiniger's childhood was a combination of fairytales, silent films, cutting scherenschnitte and puppetry. While her inspiration for making stop-motion animation is traced back to her love of film and Paul Wegener's urgings, it can also be tied to Germany's rich history of puppetry theater. Growing up in Berlin, one of Europe's cultural epicenters, and in a household that adored the arts, a young Lotte was probably in attendance at more than one show put on by a touring puppet troupe. She also might have played with a paper toy theater, miniature versions of live stage shows or films that could be cut and pasted like paper dolls, a common souvenir sold at theaters.

When she was young, Reiniger experimented with puppetry by making puppets with her scherenschnitte skills and entertained her friends and family with her performances. Many sources claim that she had witnessed Chinese shadow puppetry shows during her childhood. Alfio Bastiancich interviewed her in 1980 and asked her the pertinent question, "Were there any Chinese shadow theaters in Berlin?" Her reply was, "No, there were puppets in museums, which I actually didn't see until much later. It's not really true that I was influenced by Chinese shadow theatre" (1980/1992, 9). To prove she wasn't directly influenced by Chinese shadow puppetry, Reiniger went on, "There's a lot of differences between my way of animating characters and that of Chinese shadows: they move the characters in a kind of wavey [sic] ripple whilst I used a flat background and moved the characters through articulated joints. I also varied the lighting: theirs is frontal, mine was lit from above" (1980/1992, 9).

Germany and especially the capital city Berlin attracted artists from around the globe, including puppeteers. Hans R. Purschke in *The Puppet Theatre in Germany* wrote, "Germany, favoured by its geographical position, stood at the crossroads: a melting pot in which heterogeneous characteristics united with indigenous tradition to produce new forms and ideas" (1957, 7). Prior to stationary puppet theaters being built, puppeteers had to travel from place to place to make a living, often earning the name vagabond or gypsy along the way. Through their travels, they learned techniques from fellow practitioners and from the lands they visited. Given Germany's central position in Europe, shadow puppetry traveled along this chain of puppeteers and was adapted to suit German tastes, as was the art of paper-cutting when it traveled from the east. In this way, Reiniger could have indirectly been exposed to Chinese shadow puppetry, but whatever the case she did enjoy playing with her shadow puppets as a child just as much as an adult.

Reiniger began her career as a puppeteer, but when she transitioned to animation she considered herself a filmmaker. In the 1930s, changing politics, economy and audiences' tastes discarded the avant-garde and experimental period for realism. Despite continuing to make films, Reiniger was frustrated with new censorship laws and the Nazi political climate that made it harder to make her fanciful silhouettes. Faced with so many barriers, it was near impossible for her to work. Reiniger was in her thirties at this time and she had accomplished a great deal: Europe's first feature-length animated film, more than 20 films on her filmography, and respect as a great artist. Unable to practice her art and having done the same repetitious process since 1919, she was probably plagued by burnout along with self-doubt from the constant negative reinforcement.

In 1936, she traveled to Greece with Eric Walter White because they wanted to investigate the Greek shadow theater. She had (presumably) read an article in the 1930 *Atlantis* magazine issue about shadow puppetry's popularity in Greece and the famous puppeteer Antonis and she wanted to see them for herself (Happ, 2004, 116).

Shadow puppetry was, indeed popular in early twentieth century Greece, reaching its peak in 1930. Between 1928 and 1936, there were more than 120 professional shadow puppeteers performing in the country (Happ, 2004, 116). The most famous shadow puppet character was Karagiozis, and Mollas specialized in stories about the character that fulfills nearly every available archetype. Happ quotes a letter that Reiniger wrote to Koch on August 29, 1936, about her pure joy watching Mollas perform:

> I am infinitely happy here. I don't know how to explain everything.... I am happiest about the old puppeteer Mr. Mollas. He has had his theater for 30 years, his orchestra (all instruments) for 20 years. He has performed in about 300 shows, all ones he wrote himself, and he speaks and sings everything by heart. It's incredible watching him. The pieces are very popular. I am very delighted by the simplicity and naturalness and splendid naïveté. The great thing is: when one sees the vases in the Museum: [the puppets have] the same uninterrupted line. True folk art. He also makes all the characters himself. Magnificent figures. I could write volumes about that. The music is also interesting, and the layout of the pieces! [qt. in Happ, 2004, 118].

Earlier on the 29th, Reiniger had visited the Athens National Museum to see antiquity art, i.e., vases. Later that evening, when she caught Mollas' performance, she noticed the similarities between the Greek vases and the shadow puppets, referring to the "uninterrupted line" (Happ, 2004, 127). She also noted how Greek and Egyptian art resembled

Reiniger snipping a shadow puppet of a boy (courtesy Paul Gelder).

each other, which demonstrated the trade routes and influences the ancient kingdoms had on each other (Happ, 2004, 128).

Mollas' entire production impressed Reiniger and she was inspired to learn as much as she could from him. She intently studied his story process, puppet construction, the physical act of puppet manipulation, music and even the audience's reaction. She sketched his characters and she loved Karagiozis, especially Mollas' rendition, because he reminded her of Harlequin, her favorite *commedia dell'arte* character (Happ, 2004, 119).

Reiniger described her time in Athens in her book, where she documented in vivid detail her experience first viewing Mollas' shadow play[1]:

> It began in the hotel; when we asked where to find the Karaghiozis theatre, we were warned not to go there for it was supposed to be vulgar. But we found it in the end of the popular quarters and were shown into a kind of open-air café, seating about 200 people, filled with all sorts of people, sipping their coffee or *ouzo*, waiting for the beginning of the show on the large white screen erected at the far

side of the place, overhung by the dark blue sky and the shadows of trees. In front of the screen a small orchestra of five musicians was seated. Then the majestic figure of a stout man entered, clad in a white suit, a flat straw hat placed daringly on his black hair. He walked slowly alongside the crowd and vanished behind the screen. This was Mr. Mollas, by this time the most respected Karaghiozis player in Greece.

The orchestra played the overture and the screen lit up. The audience sighed with satisfaction. Two pieces of scenery were to be seen: on the left-hand side a miserable, dilapidated hut and on the right a palace in the Oriental style, both black with ornaments pierced through them. Then with enormous vivacity the figure of Kharaghiozis appeared and performed a lively dance. I was amazed by the richness of movement the figure had to offer and by the vividness of his colouring. I could not make out how this was achieved for I could not see any supporting rods, only some faint shadows above the figure following its movements. They were not distributing at all, on the contrary they seemed to emphasise the concentration on the action. But what pleased me more than anything was the spontaneous joyful reaction of the spectators. It came over at once, like the appearance of Punch to an audience of children, and so it remained the whole evening through.

Although I did not understand the language, I was perpetually entertained by the richness of gesture, the rustic simplicity of the figures and their colouring, and the ceaseless flow of their coming and going. Sometimes the character of the audience's laughter made one guess that the joke might have been somewhat rude and the gesture ambiguous, but the reaction was so natural that it became innocent. The most enjoyable element was the unity between performer and audience: they loved each other.

We were allowed to watch the performance from behind the screen and my admiration grew. Mr. Mollas practically did it all alone. He stood there, his figures in hand, pressing them against the screen with long rods over a line of tube lamps, speaking the lines for all of them with different voices. In addition to him were only his singer and one assistant, taking the figures away and handing him new ones, and a few children who occasionally were allowed to their pride to pass minor figures along when processions were indicated. Sometimes Mollas used this amplitude of his own body to press the rods of figures against his belly, when he had to handle more than two figures at a time. He had written the plays himself, too.

Innumerable figures made of parchment from animal skin were hung up all round, and ships and trees and aeroplanes all in a wonderful naïve peasant style. The rods were fixed to the figure with a leather loop, which enabled them to be turned round. Only one arm was articulated, not realistically, but so that a great variety of movement was possible. One never noticed that the figure was moving one arm only, for the things it did with the one arm were quite incredible. Seeing all this I became an addict of this playing with horizontal rods and have tried my hand with it ever since [1970a, 28–30].

When she left Athens, Mollas gifted her a set of her own colorful, cardboard shadow figures (Happ, 2004, 119).

Reiniger is noted most for her work cutting silhouettes and animating them on screen; however, her shadow plays left as great an impact on the puppetry world as her animation work. Reiniger experimented with shadow puppetry manipulation, because she wanted her shadow puppet figures to have as much expressionable ability as her film silhouette puppets. She emphasized that understanding how important movement was to expressing a puppet's emotions and she detested it when people believed the artistry was due to the puppets' mechanizations rather than the puppeteer. They were unaware how much of a person went into a performance (Happ, 2004, 103). She observed from her visit to Mollas and his shadow theater that shadow puppets are essentially constructed in the same fashion as silhouette puppets.

There was, however, one huge difference that made European shadow puppets more static and by employing a Mollas trick, Reiniger remedied the puppets' immobility. Eva Blattner and Karlheinz Weigmann described Reiniger's influence on Central Europe's shadow puppet theater, similar to how Jim Henson revisualized American puppetry:

Reiniger revolutionized shadow theatre in Central Europe with the adoption of the Southern European-Near Eastern performance technique.... In the summer of 1936 Lotte Reiniger was able to view the performances of the Greek shadow puppeteer Mollas. As was the custom in the Orient, he directed his figures with the aid of horizontally attached rods, which convey the silhouettes a considerably mobility. Figures controlled in this way were capable of executing leaps or withdrawing from the screen. Until Lotte Reiniger the shadow theatre tradition in Central Europe was characterized by fixed, vertical rods, so that her use of the new technique represented a significant enrichment for the genre [2010, 7–8].

Reiniger herself explained it in the documentary *Lotte Reiniger's Kunst*, "In traditional silhouette theater the figures are moved by rods. These figures are supported by vertical rods. These rods are used to move them across the screen. This is the preferred technique in oriental, Chinese and Turkish silhouette theater" (Isaacs & Hagen, 1964/1965). A problem with the horizontal rod is that characters' feet can get caught on the body with jumps or other aerial movements. For her silhouette characters to lay flat on the tricktisch, Reiniger made some of the body appendages from lead. So the shadow puppets' legs would resume their proper positions, she attached lead platelets to the feet (Happ, 2004, 126).

She had some opportunity to practice this technique, but World War II and concentration on producing films slowed her shadow play practice. She and Elsbeth Schulz created the Berlin Schattenspiele directly after the war, but it wasn't until the 1950s, when Reiniger worked with the Hogarth Puppet group, that she was able to further explore her puppetry techniques alongside professional puppeteers. The Hogarth puppeteers specialized in various puppetry forms and they hired Reiniger to help them develop shadow puppet shows. She used the horizontal rod technique with them for the first time (Happ, 2004, 125). Reiniger devoted most of her energy to her silhouette animation films until 1963, when Koch died and she no longer wished to animate. She concentrated on further developing her shadow puppetry skills by traveling with a small tabletop theater that she performed shows on for friends and groups of children. She also worked on larger theatrical productions and performed a series of Biblical stories for television (Happ, 2004, 132).

Reiniger's viable interest was her tabletop shadow theater and she spent a great deal of time designing its appearance—the front facing the audience. She noted that any art form from around the world could inspire the theater's ornamentation, but she designed hers after an old Venetian marionette theater she saw at the Victoria and Albert Museum (Happ, 2004, 132). Her small tabletop theater measured 45 centimeters wide by 25 centimeters high and a candle was used to light it (Happ, 2004, 132). This smaller theater proved insufficient for the horizontal rod method, so she expanded her theater to 55 centimeters wide and 37.5 centimeters high. The biggest theater she ever built was 135 centimeters wide and 75 centimeters high (Happ, 2004, 132).

Reiniger mentioned in her book that one time when she traveled, she needed a new theater to demonstrate the horizontal rod puppets and her small theater was insufficient for the task:

> I was far away from my home and my tools and looked round in despair for something I could quickly make a theater of. It was near Christmas time and I saw in a shop a display aimed at encouraging the customers to buy a certain stuffing for the Christmas turkey. This display incorporated a feature which had exactly the size and proportions I was aiming at. I succeeded in persuading the manager to let me have the thing and carried it home triumphantly, for it also possessed the most useful virtue for the theater of a strolling artist of folding up conveniently [1970a, 59–60].

While Reiniger's shadow plays were staged primarily in Germany and England, her collaboration with the Hogarth Puppets led to other shadow puppeteers learning her puppetry techniques. One of the most famous shadow puppeteers who carries on Reiniger's tradition, Australian Richard Bradshaw[2] is not only a shadow puppeteer but also a puppet show writer. He might be best recognized for his sense of humor and his Super Kangaroo skit. Bradshaw saw the Hogarth Puppets in 1952 when Jan Bussell, Ann Hogarth and their daughter Sally traveled to Australia to perform their marionettes. They didn't include their shadow puppet version of *The Happy Prince*, which Reiniger had made puppets for, in this performance. At this point in his career, Bradshaw focused on developing his skills in glove puppets and marionettes, but he would eventually encounter the art form that would become his trademark:

> In 1953 my school friend Arthur Cantrill did see the Hogarth Puppets' shadow show, as did an adult member of the Clovelly Puppet Theatre group in Sydney, Isobel Ferguson, and they decided to do a shadow puppet version of another Wilde story, *The Nightingale and the Rose*. I was invited to work with them, but it was mainly on technical aspects, although I did help with the manipulation.
>
> It wasn't until I began teaching some eight years later that I started making my own shadow puppets. I taught in a boarding school in Sydney and lived at the school, so I chose to make shadow puppets because they were easier to make in my bedroom! There was a feeling then that shadow puppets were for serious themes, and my first show was *Orpheus in the Underworld*. It wasn't wonderful! The lady who had directed Clovelly Puppet Theatre later asked me to make a shadow puppet for her to show in a talk on puppets she was to give to a girls' school in Sydney. I made an old man that tapped on a rock which turned out to be a "monster." There was a mighty laugh from the girls when I did the item and that was when I decide to use shadow puppets for humour [Bradshaw email to author, 18. Nov. 2015].

When *The Nightingale and the Rose* was worked on by the puppetry guild in Sydney, the borrowed Reiniger's films to view on film nights. Bradshaw remembered, "We were stunned by the quality of her work." He learned more about Reiniger's films through H.W. Whanslaw's *Shadow Play*, a book that included a short chapter on her career.

Bradshaw visited the Hogarth troupe and worked with them for a season in 1964, performing in London parks. While he worked with the Bussell and Hogarth, he finally saw *The Happy Prince*, except it was from behind as he sat backstage. Reiniger visited her old friends the same year and she met a young Bradshaw on August 1, 1964. Then he visited her at the Abbey Arts Centre on October 11, 1964. When he worked with Hogarth and Bussell, Bradshaw learned about Reiniger's developments with shadow puppetry. He said, "I made new puppets, that I controlled from behind with the horizontal rods," and, "I found that shadow puppets offered me a way to use widely varying characters, shapes and scale so I felt it offered me greater freedom than other forms" (qt. in Happ, 2004, 125–26; Bradshaw email to author, November 18, 2016). He also developed his own way of attaching the rods to the puppets, which was similar to a method Reiniger described in her book. Bradshaw has taught many workshops across the globe about shadow puppetry for decades, distributing his own techniques and love for the art to his students.

Bradshaw was initially stunned with amazement by Reiniger's work. As he grew to know her and her respected filmography, he became more awed:

> I think what struck me first on viewing Lotte's film was her wonderful sense of design. It's quite fascinating to look closely at things such as a series of bells, or a tiled floor to see how freely they are cut out where a lesser artist would try to measure things exactly. Yet she gets the effect without scrupulous accuracy. There is so much character in her figures … and something I appreciated much later is

the humour in much that she did. We are especially fond of her *Carmen* which is very witty. I have never tried working with stop-motion, and it seems such a tedious process. Yet Lotte somehow managed to get the movement right, even when there are many figures moving in the same scene [Bradshaw email to author, November 18, 2016].

Throughout this book, I've noted that Reiniger had a wonderful sense of humor and often made self-deprecating jokes. While Reiniger would have been the first to admit her faults, she also displayed self-confidence in her skills as a puppeteer and animator. Bradshaw noted, "Lotte knew she was good at what she did. Once she was telling Ann [Hogarth] Bussell about a very nice piece she had made. When Ann suggested that wasn't a very modest thing to say, Lotte replied that who could be a better judge of this kind of thing than Lotte herself! This doesn't mean that Lotte was vain ... it was just facing facts. In her field she was a genius" (Bradshaw email to author, November 18, 2016). Reiniger was modest to a point, but she would be the first to defend her skills.

Silhouettes and shadow puppetry are two vastly different yet intricately related art forms best differentiated by Currell's and Blackham's observations[3]:

A silhouette, unlike a shadow, exists in its own right and cannot be distorted; it is an image in solid black, silhouetted, not shadowed, against the light. Though not a shadow, this is a closely related phenomenon that produces similarly powerful images that can be more dramatic visually than the object itself. Olive Blackham ... noted this impact by highlighting the difference between the puppet placed flat on the table and the shadow it casts on the screen, suggesting that "the strength and impact of the solid shadow is quite different from that of the object" [2007, 12].

Both silhouettes and shadow puppetry have profound cultural and historical significance. They are as similar as they are different in relation to their significance, creation and usage. A common theme in Reiniger's silhouette films was love. She retold fairytales with a true love motif and a romantic author could say that the films were "made with love" because she filmed them with her husband Koch. The "made with love" metaphor can also be extended to Reiniger's passion for precise movement and detail in her puppets and fascination with animation as she loved these aspects of her work. What is interesting is that the origins of silhouettes and shadow puppetry revolve around the same theme of love.

While silhouettes have their origins in Paleolithic art with cave paintings, these were more reflections of daily life than intentions to capture the facade of a specific individual. The first recorded instance of an artist deliberating capturing an individual's silhouette likeness are found in Pliny the Elder's *Natural History*. In book 35, an account of paintings and colors, he describes how around 600 BC, Butades (sometimes referred to as Dibutades) and his daughter Core (also known as Kora or Callihoe) of Sicyon invented silhouette art:

Butades, a potter of Sicyon, was the first who invented, at Corinth, the art of modeling portraits in the earth which he used in his trade. It was through his daughter that he made the discovery; who, being deeply in love with a young man about to depart on a long journey, traced the profile of his face, as thrown upon the wall by the light of the lamp. Upon seeing this, her father filled in the outline, by compressing clay upon the surface, and so made a face in relief, which he then hardened by fire along with other articles of pottery [Pliny the Elder, 43:12].

By capturing her lover's shadow on the wall, Core also contributed to the invention of clay modeling as her father made her lover's exact likeness in clay. Emma Rutherford documents the historical precedence of Core's shadow-tracing in her book *Silhouette: The Art of Shadow*, where she refers to the maiden as Dibutrade. Rutherford notes that other artists and scholars referred to Core as the "Maid of Corinth" or "Corinthian Dame" (2009, 13). The sentimental origins of silhouette "appealed greatly to the eighteenth-century mind" and indirectly influenced the widespread adoption of silhouette portraiture of the same era (Rutherford, 2009, 13).

Silhouettes are a static art form unless they are animated in some way, à la the illusion of life, and shadow puppetry was in vogue long before silhouettes were deemed an art form. Shadow puppetry is the oldest form of puppetry in the world and China has the oldest myth of the practice's origins from 121 BC, although it is believed to be much older (Currell, 2007, 17). The ancient Chinese legend that explains shadow puppetry's origins mirror Core's grief for the loss of her lover:

> [Emperor Wu Ti/Di of the Han Dynasty was] overcome with grief when his favourite mistress died. All attempts to ease his sorrow failed until one of the court artists created a shadow figure likeness of her and, after much rehearsal to capture her gestures and voice accurately, presented his shadow show with the figure illuminated behind a silk screen. The emperor was comforted and the shadow show was born [Currell, 2007, 17; Blackham, 1960, 3].

Reiniger wrote in *Shadow Theater and Shadow Films* that there is a "more practical explanation of the origin of the Chinese shadow-theatre. This tells that as Chinese ladies were not allowed to visit live theater performances, the most successful plays were converted into shadow-shows, which would then be performed in the female quarters, much to the ladies' delight" (1970a, 16).

As the older account, a version of Pliny's *Natural History* could have traveled along the Silk Road and made its way into the hands of a Han Dynasty scholar, who translated the story and adapted it to suit the Chinese court or maybe even inspired the concubine's creation. Blackham also notes that Turkish shadow theater origin is similar to the Chinese myth, but it involves the trademark trickster Karagiozis (Karagöz) and his educated albeit airheaded sidekick Hacivat. Karagiozis and Hacivat were building a mosque, where they traded witty and humorous banter. The pair's chatter was so amusing that other workers stopped construction to listen to them. The sultan was enraged about the halted work, so he had Karagiozis and Hacivat executed. Unfortunately, the sultan had enjoyed the banter and he missed it, so the royal vizier used shadow puppetry to imitate Karagiozis and Hacivat's images and voices (Blackham, 1960, 46).

In her book, Reiniger tells of another story about the origins of Karagiozis and Hacivat: a sultan had two court jesters who were brothers and he loved their jokes. The sultan's advisors used the jesters to express their own political agenda. One day the sultan committed a folly that placed the country in danger, but no one was brave enough to confront the sultan. An advisor persuaded one of the jesters to comment on the situation in one of his jokes. The sultan became enraged at the jester's comment. Hoping to win the sultan's favor, the other jester drew a knife and stabbed his brother, but it had the opposite effect. The sultan missed the slain jester's wit and threatened to kill the other jester if the dead one wasn't restored. In his terror, the living jester recreated his brother with a shadow figure and a screen and imitated his voice. The sultan was pleased and forgave the jester. The jester's plays with his shadow puppet brother became the predecessor to the Karagiozis and Hacivat shadow plays (Reiniger, 1970a, 27).

While the Chinese shadow puppetry myth was created in the Han Dynasty (206 BC–AD 228), the first Chinese written accounts about the art were published in the Song Dynasty (AD 960–AD 1279) (Currell, 2007, 23). It is probable that the Turkish and Chinese origin myths are influenced by the same source, as the Turkish version originated during the Ottoman Empire (AD 1299–AD 1923) centuries later. Established trade routes encouraged more than the commerce of goods: stories, art and other entertainment forms were also exchanged. From his own research, Currell says that Chinese shadow puppetry "reached its height of artistry in the eleventh century and that this is the origin of the shadow play in the Middle East, introduced by Mongols in the thirteenth century. Indeed, some suggest that here lie the origins of shadow play throughout the east, if not the world" (Currell, 2007, 23). The Turkish shadow theater could also have its origins in Indonesia and Egypt, but Karagiozis and Hacivat were products of the Ottoman Empire (Currell, 2007, 24). As for the Greek Karagiozis, its origins are disputed. "Some suggest that it was carried from China by Greek merchants, others that it was invented by a Greek during Ottoman rule [1458–1821]; the legend of Karagiozis and Hacivat working in Bursa is also offered as another explanation. It is quite widely held that it actually came to Greece from Turkey in the nineteenth century" (Currell, 2007, 25). However the trickster character entered the Greek culture, it is this version that Reiniger was most familiar with and favored due to Antonis Mollas' performances.

It is unlikely that Core's story made its way into the Chinese scholarly accounts and likewise inspired the invention of shadow puppetry centuries later, but the two accounts for shadow art are striking in their similarities. Silhouettes and shadow puppetry are two sides of the same coin with origin stories that deal with the loss of a beloved individual (or individuals with Karagiozis and Hacivat, although they're only beloved in hindsight). It is another case of simultaneous invention, separated by centuries, as with Reiniger and Koch's multiplane camera and that of Walt Disney. It can be called simultaneous invention due to the lack of communication between China and Greece as well as the stark line between eastern and western civilization.

Silhouettes and shadow puppetry also both have ties to death and the afterlife. The term "shade," another term for silhouette, is also used to refer to ghosts or spirits of the departed. Rutherford said that in eighteenth century France, "the word silhouette was clearly synonymous with black shades" and silhouette was also translated from French into English using the word (2009, 27). The word "silhouette" came into popular use on the European continent from Johann Caspar Lavater's junk science book *Physiognomische Fragmente zur Beförderung der Menschenkenntnis und Menschenliebe* (*Essays on Physiognomy: Designed to Promote Knowledge and the Love of Mankind*), where "silhouette" was used to refer to a person's shadow profile (Rutherford, 2009, 27). Lavater's book was so influential that even Reiniger quoted him in her own work, although her contempt for his "science" is apparent: "[Lavater is] the great authority on the supposed science which purports to deduce the character individual from the features of the face or the form of the body" (1970a, 13). Having witnessed first hand the Nazis' persecution of her Jewish and "degenerate artist" friends, Reiniger's quotation can be considered a quiet opinion on "Aryan purity," its stupidity, and how with shadows nothing is determined about a person's genetics:

> [T]he shadow-picture of a man—of a human face—is the most feeble, the emptiest—but at the same time, if the light has been standing in the right distance, if the face has been falling on a pure surface and been parallel with that surface, the truest and most faithful picture which you can give of a man. For it is nothing positive, it is only negative, only the outline of half the face. The most faithful one, for it is the direct print of nature, such as one, not even the most skillful craftsman, would be able to make with a free hand from nature. What can be less the picture of a living man than a silhouette and yet how much is it able to say [qt. in Reiniger, 1970a, 13].

It is interesting how Reiniger defines the difference between silhouette and shadow: "The essential difference between a shadow and a silhouette is that the latter cannot be distorted. A silhouette can cast a shadow. When you see trees or figures against an evening sky, you would say, not that they are shadowed against the sky, but silhouetted against it. The silhouette exists it its own right" (1970a, 13). Shadows are inanimate objects that are constantly in motion and changing according to how the light changes, but silhouettes remain static once captured on paper, film or another medium. Silhouette puppets, in either puppet shows or animated films, bring life to inanimate objects, making them reflect real shadows or the illusion of life. "The shadow is born of a vivid movement, whereas the silhouette has to learn to walk first before it can play its film role convincingly" (Marschall et al., 2012).

Reiniger's ties to shadow theater, death and love also have another coincidental reference in Greek mythology as shades refer to a person's departed spirit; and Core (Kore or Cora) was another name for Persephone, Queen of the Underworld and Goddess of Spring. Core used a silhouette as a reminder of her lover, which can semantically be referred to as a shade. The fabled musician Orpheus journeyed into the Underworld to retrieve the shade of his beloved wife Eurydice. Hades, Persephone's husband and King of the Underworld, allowed Orpheus to reclaim his wife only if he never looked back at her on the return journey to the land of the living. Orpheus subsequently failed in his over-eagerness to greet his wife once he returned to sunlight and he looked back.

"Some cultures consider shadow puppets to exist at the intersection between the human and spiritual worlds. They inhabit the borderland between what physically exists and what does not. Viewers watch dramas enacted by characters, sets and props that have no concrete substance, that are nothing but the absence of light from area on a screen" (Blumenthal, 2005, 224). Asian countries were more apt to believe that shadow puppetry had ties to the dead and usually with religious overtones, but European countries stopped using religious puppetry during the Renaissance (Blumenthal, 2005, 224). The Indonesian island Java has the perspective of shadow puppetry and death and "the ritualistic nature of the performances also differentiates them from all other Shadow Shows [sic]" (Blackham, 1960, 18). The shows serve three consecutive purposes "simultaneously on different levels": entertainment, community activity and devotional act (Bell, 2002, 46). Javanese shadow plays are collectively known as wayang kulit. The most popular, the wayang purawa, tells stories from the Hindu *Ramayana* and *Mahabharata*. Large 24-inch puppets made from buffalo hide are treated until they are semi-transparent, then carved with traditional filigreed patterns that distinguish one character from another. The shape of the headdress, head angles, eyes and feet convey who the character is and what part it will play in the epic.

The Javanese shadow play's origins are believed to stem from ancestor worship. "The leather figures symbolized the spirits of the dead ancestors, and various rites were performed for these, before, during and after the performance, partly to propitiate these spirits and partly to make them look beneficially on the participants in the performance" (Blackham, 1960, 19). The wayang kulit is performed by a dalang, a puppeteer who takes on the role of priest as well as performer. "The dalang acts as a medium between the spirits and his audience. Clearly, whoever becomes a dalang must have an array of personal qualities far beyond that of entertainer and he is thus a highly respected artist" (Currell, 2007, 22). The wayang kulit puppets are similarly designed like silhouette figures Reiniger used in her films and shows.

After Koch's death, Reiniger turned to shadow plays to comfort herself in her grief. Her animated silhouette films were a product of a partnership between her and her husband; she was never a solo act. By concentrating on shadow plays, she was able to continue to express her love for her husband by concentrating her talents in another artistic shadow medium much as Core traced a silhouette likeness to remember her lover and the court artist comforted the Han emperor with a shadow image of his beloved concubine. Reiniger became a new Maid of Corinth and also a dalang. While she wasn't trying to communicate or resurrect the dead, she moved forward with her artistic endeavors, but she also channeled her prior films made with Koch. Reiniger visually communicated her love for her husband, thus she acts as a medium with her plays to recall the time they spent animating together.

In the latter part of her career, Reiniger crafted and performed shadow plays. Scenes from *The Lost Son* and *Santa's Mistake* can be viewed in the *Lotte Reiniger Gesamtausgabe* DVD collection. She animated a few more films at the urgings of the National Film Board of Canada and the Düsseldorf Stadtmuseum. What I find remarkable about Reiniger is that while she is highly esteemed by both puppetry and animation communities, no one has sought to bridge the gap between these two media for her. It is reminiscent of the shadow play she made for Renoir's film *La Marseillaise* about the bridge between Madame la France and the French king. The bridge between Reiniger's animation career and puppetry cry out to each other: "the bridge is broken between us."

Shadow theater didn't catch on in Europe until the eighteenth century, although there are records (especially in Germany) of performances that date back as early as 1683 and 1692 (von Boehn, 1932, 365). It entered Europe via Italy, then traveled to other countries. But as Max von Boehn wrote, "[T]he shadow-play could only get a footing in Germany [and the rest of the continent] after it had met approval in Paris" (1932, 366). In the eighteenth century, France was the pinnacle for haute culture in everything from clothing to entertainment. France still retains its glamorous place in western society, mostly in food and fashion, but the country is one of the last bastions for traditional animation and respects the art of the graphic novel. French society was enthralled with shadow plays that were dubbed "ombres chinoises" (Chinese shadows). "At this time there was a craze for 'chinoiserie,' popularised by the tales of travelers returning from China. Although the shadow theater, traversing as it did various lands, underwent many changes which left it bearing little resemblance to the Chinese archetype.... This designation is however inappropriate, for the Asian forms of shadow theater use translucent puppets of coloured, openwork design..." (Jouvanceau, 2004, 19). François Dominique Séraphin and Henri Rivière were two shadow puppeteers lauded for their visually stirring and masterful performances.

Séraphin debuted his ombres chinoises on September 8, 1784. He was "an artist, but he was a showman too; he had an excellent and varied repertoire of plays" (Whanslaw, 1950, 49–50). During the French Revolution, his shadow theater continued to entertain the masses mostly because "his showman's instinct told him to follow the line of least resistance, so his repertoire became inspired by current events" (Whanslaw, 1950, 50). His play *Le Pont cassé* appealed to the French people's patriotism. It was so popular that Renoir asked Reiniger to replicate it in his own film about the French Revolution. As for Séraphin's talent, he suffered the same "children's only" conundrum that still plagues puppeteers today. As M. Tronchet wrote in his 1815 guide book *Pictures of Paris*, "[I]t has long been looked upon as only fit for children" (qt. in Whanslaw, 1950, 48). M.

Tronchet is an example of a critic with a narrow viewpoint about puppetry art and his scope was indeed limited, for von Boehn quoted another critic, Thiéry from the *Pariser Führer*, in his *Dolls and Puppets* compendium: "The puppets represent human deportment very naturally. They dance on a tight rope [sic] and execute character dances with the greatest precision. Beasts of all kinds make their appearance here and move in their own special ways, and neither the strings nor the wires which hold and manipulate them can be seen" (qt. in von Boehn, 1932, 366). Séraphin's shadows were so *en vogue* that his shadow theater lasted until 1870, 70 years after the puppeteer's death.

When Séraphin's shadow finally dispersed, Henri Rivière cast his own shadow plays on a screen in the famous Le Chat Noir cabaret in 1886. The only remnants of Rivière's shadow plays are postcards with stills from his plays, but he was lauded for taking shadow plays to the next level in evolution with amazing technical achievements. He made 43 shows about classical mythology, the Bible and history. Max von Boehn praised Rivière with descriptions that bordered on poetry:

> Rivière's art provided a fantastic fairy-tale for the eye, deeply poetic in theme, of peculiar beauty in form, the whole a dream which vanished even as one strove to capture it. The artist made use of light and colour to steep his scenes in a mood made arresting through its strange magic. Before him there had been nothing similar to this ... [1932, 370].

Rivière used light and colored glasses to achieve great perspective and psychological effects, a "real audio-visual spectacle" (von Boehn, 1932, 370–71; Jouvanceau, 2004, 21). He introduced "perspective effects until then unknown in shadow theatre, to counteract the flatness of the representation. He used all the resources of his music hall lighting to create effects representing skies changing colour; he invented a system of tiered stage sets painted on glass, which could be moved at variable speeds, foreshadowing the multilayered animation Lotte Reiniger used for *Prince Achmed*, as well as Disney's multiplane system; he accompanied his images with sound effects, commentaries and mood music..." (Jouvanceau, 2004, 21). His tenure at Le Chat Noir lasted until the establishment closed in 1897. During that period, Le Chat Noir's shadow shows attained world fame, but shadow plays were becoming a thing of the past with other unique projection devices to replace them as the popular entertainment of choice. All of this would be pushed out of the way when moving images captured audiences' attention and would also be cheaper than the shadow play and other projection devices because "so many innovations were too expensive, took too long to set up and needed too many people to operate them" (Jouvanceau, 2004, 22). Cinematic pioneers like George Méliès took to the silver screen and camera and impressed audiences with their own forms of film puppetry, eventually giving birth to animation.

According to von Boehn, the shadow puppeteers who followed in Rivière's wake had limited success. Shadow plays and theaters would spring up, then fade away as audiences' attention drifted to other forms of entertainment. He said, "[T]hat such [shadow play] novelties should be copied in vulgarized forms in Berlin is comprehensible considering the ceaseless rush for sensation in that great city; such things commonly bear the mark of death on them at the very time of their birth" (1932, 380). While von Boehn's remark had an ominous tone, he did acknowledge that there were puppeteers attempting to revive the art and even noted that the shadow film held promise. On a funny note, von Boehn dedicated a chapter to the "Occidental Shadow Theatres" with most of the illustrations from Reiniger's own scherenschnitte portfolio and images from *Prinzen Achmed*. He said that when *Prinzen Achmed* premiered at the Volksbuhne, "[it] taught

Berlin that this was no mere amusement for aesthetics, but represented new possibilities for the film" (1932, 383). Other puppeteers saw the potential for animation and stop-motion films in the early twentieth century, while the silhouette film was regarded as a possible medium Reiniger was the only animator who achieved long-lasting success. Most of the puppeteers-turned-animators at this point were tired of opaque black shadows. They wanted characters and scenery with more details for visual stimulation and endowed the static images with the "illusion of life."

It is my opinion that Reiniger's work is the perfect marriage between animation and puppetry, because shadow puppetry is essentially the equivalent of animation performed in live action. Animated silhouette films also tie modern cinema to Asian shadow theaters, because unlike European theaters which are pure black puppets on a blank background, the shadow puppets were made in color. "[O]n the basis of nothing more than the presence of colour in both, people decided that the two modes of expression shared an indisputable family relationship, and that, thanks to its colour, the silhouette film was somehow reuniting with a tradition that the black and white films and, likewise, the European shadow theatre, had loftily ignored, and that it was now returning to the true source of this ancient art" (Jouvanceau, 2004, 217). The return to ancient Asian shadow puppetry has a romantic notion tied to it, but the coincidence is more than implied as cinematic features are an updated version of backlit flickering shadows on a screen.

Shadow figures are animated live on screen, and performed and animated according to the whims of a puppeteer or animator. Shadow puppetry was the only way for animation to be performed in real time, until several experimenting minds figured out how to use traditional animation in the same fashion. McCay's later vaudeville act with Gertie the Dinosaur, however, is not included, because McCay made Gertie "perform" to a script of pre-animated sequences, although the effect is still whimsical and magical even with today's technological advancements. It was actually a common trope for animators to cross the projected fourth wall in their films. Émile Cohl explored the idea in his *Fantasmagorie*; Walt Disney's Alice comedies featured a little girl jumping into an animated cartoon; in Warner Brothers' *The Cartoonist's Nightmare,* J. Stuart Blackton interacted with a drawn face in his *The Enchanted Drawing* (1900); and the Fleischer Brothers' *Out of the Inkwell* series demonstrated what happened when cartoon characters ran amok.

Throughout this book, I have referred to the "illusion of life" or, as Disney called it, a "caricature of life" that Reiniger sought the same accuracy in her films as Disney, albeit it more in the experimental quality. Donald Crafton wrote in his book *Shadow of a Mouse*:

> In Western puppet traditions, as in cartoons, the "illusion of life" is a powerful recurring trope. The mimetic accuracy of the characters' movements, the appropriateness of their voices, and their believability as actors are criteria for judging a successful "lifelike" show. Punch kills Judy, but she'll return for a curtain call. The mysterious creation of life, its tragic fragility, and the assurance of life after death are often figured as puppet stories, as in *Pinocchio*.... Such narratives re-perform the underlying human agency [2013, 63–64].

The problem has always been that animators were limited to the film screen and were never able to have characters react in real time, while shadow puppetry (and all puppetry for that matter) can instantly react to actions. Only with the development of more advanced computer animation techniques (dubbed digital puppetry) have animated characters been able to react to real-time actions. Walt Disney World ironically has the best examples of interactive digital puppetry with the attractions Monsters Inc. Laugh Floor and Turtle Talk with Crush.

While researching this book, I read several tomes on stop-motion films to learn more about early stop-motion animators, many of whom are considered Reiniger's compatriots. I was surprised that none of these books referenced Reiniger, who was indeed a pioneer stop-motion artist. It might be understandable that these books cannot cover all ground related to stop-motion, but Reiniger was at the beginning of stop-motion animation history and there weren't a lot of people doing it at the time. Some of Reiniger's greatest stop-motion compatriots were George Pál, Jiří Trnka, Ladislav Starevich, Aleksandr Lukich Ptushko, Willis O'Brien, Jan Svankmajer and brothers Ferdinand and Hermann Diehl.

Probably one of the most disappointing research avenues I encountered was *A Century of Stop Motion Animation* by Tony Dalton and none other than Ray Harryhausen. Harryhausen was one of the premier stop-motion animators and special effects artists in cinematic history. His book, a fantastic chronicle of stop-motion animation, cites the abovementioned animators, references Quirino Cristiani, and even notes puppeteer Tony Sarg's foray into silhouette animation.[4] Reiniger is omitted, despite the influences she's had on stop-motion animators today, including the renowned Henry Selick. I have found that Reiniger is constantly compared to Starevitch in older accounts (1920s through the '50s), and he apparently has more clout in stop-motion animation histories than Reiniger. Eric Walter White described her importance with a Starevitch comparison:

> Lotte Reiniger's work with such films as Starevitch's *Magic Clock* or [John] Grierson's marionette films, for Grierson and Starevitch (for the most part) work with artificially propelled puppets, whose antics are photographed straightforwardly and appear on the screen as they were seen by the eye; and even the *Secrets of Nature* are not trick films, although a trick camera is used to make them—they are no more than ordinary films of plant and animal life in fast or slow motion. With Lotte Reiniger's silhouette films it is different. In them, as in the animated cartoon films, every step has to be tricked; and her task is made more difficult by the fact she has to work almost entirely in two dimensions instead of three.... [B]ut when a silhouette artist like Lotte Reiniger has to work solely in black, white and tones of gray, it becomes a hundred times more difficult to make the figures plastic and to give the backgrounds depth. It will be seen later by what ways and means Lotte Reiniger overcomes these difficulties, how she manages to persuade her audience to accept the shadow for the substance ... [1931, 13–14].

Reiniger is not the only animator-puppeteer whose work is a perfect marriage between animation and puppetry, but they are usually not referred to as puppeteers. They are only called stop-motion animators or special effects artists. Pulling special effects artists into this category opens an even bigger can of worms. Bruce L. Holman declared, "It is difficult to draw a clear line regarding what *is* and what *is not* an animated puppet film"; after a basic description of stop-motion, he continues, "[W]ithin a study of puppet animation further delineation is necessary" (1975, 11). While Holman was referring to distinction between special effects, animated cartoons and puppet films, the distinction between art styles becomes more semantic than artistic in this regard. Jan Bussell and Ann Hogarth wrote,

> There is always controversy about which category stop-action puppets fit into. For example, we certainly consider Lotte Reiniger as a puppeteer, because not only did she occasionally give live shows herself, but has designed and cut several different productions for us to perform live. But of course her international fame rests on her pioneer work in the field of stop-action with her silhouette films. Yet the figures she uses for these are identical in construction to those she has made for us. In our case we attached them to rods and operated them against a vertical screen: in her case the figures and scenery were placed on a ground-glass tabletop with a light underneath and a camera above. She

would move each figure a minute fraction before taking each frame if the film-achieved by pulling a chain hanging from the camera.... Certainly this is puppetry [1985, 125].

Special effects artists' work is used to augment live action films, while stop-motion films are entirely animated such as what Reiniger did with her silhouettes. The lines becomes thinner as more films use CGI for special effects rather than special effects based in reality. It begs the question: will computer graphics- laden films cross into the animated film medium? Or is it better to wonder when all computer special effects films will be considered animated?

Puppetry (including shadow), special effects and animation of all types have come full circle since animation's birth with the advent of newer technology. Computer-generated images or 3D animation uses rendered images, controls and light in an artificial environment that an animator manipulates to generate a desired action very much like a puppeteer manipulates a puppet. A special effects artist's work is closely related, if not the same in some cases, to a computer animator. An animator using computer technology has essentially taken on the role of a puppeteer to create an animated film. "When the puppeteer stops working, the puppet loses its 'animation.' Profound human belief systems are mirrored and naturalized in these reassuring stories, as though we know them without having been told. These circular master narratives are parables of the shows' origins, emanating from puppet studios that remind us of animation shops" (Crafton, 2013, 64). It circles around to the early days of animation, when stop-motion was a more pervasive form of animation and special effects technique. It also echoes Gene Deitch's definition of cinematic animation. While intended to take into consideration future animation, he and others believe that live action animation is not genuine animation. Based on how new technology is making humans puppets, isn't it more apt to say that animation has gone full circle back to its puppetry origins?

Neil Pettigrew explains why stop-motion animation has more appeal than CGI at the moment: it's cheaper, doesn't allow real-time interaction between the animation and live action, and even questions the technology and makes the practicality argument (1997, 23). I've heard and read this same argument so many times. Radio people said TV would never amount to anything, some cartoonists still cling to the old newspaper system as the best way to sell comics, and don't forget about that horseless carriage and the Internet. Famous science fiction writer Douglas Adams wrote,

> I've come up with a set of rules that describe our reactions to technologies:
> 1. Anything that is in the world when you're born is normal and ordinary and is just a natural part of the way the world works.
> 2. Anything that's invented between when you're 15 and 35 is new and exciting and revolutionary and you can probably get a career in it.
> 3. Anything invented after you're 35 is against the natural order of things [2002, 95].

James Cameron said in regards to his fabulous *Avatar* feature being consider an animated film. "Odd, Cameron says that, because *Avatar*'s Pandora is now a new land at Disney World":

> I think the thing people need to keep very strongly in mind is that [*Avatar*] is not an animated film. These actors did not just stand at a lectern and do a voice-part, and then animators went off for the next two years and created the entire physicality of their performance.... Every nuance, every tiny bit of the performance that you see on the screen, was created by the actors. They had to run, they had to leap, they had to fight, they had to do all things that you see them doing in the film, and that's where the power of the performance comes from [qt. in Osmond, 2011, 5].

Brad Bird offers a rebuttal:

> I think the dirty little secret of most [motion capture] is that the really, really good stuff has been massaged by a lot by animators. And that's what people don't talk about, and I think that does a tremendous disservice to animators.... There's nothing wrong with animation. Animators are not technicians. They're artists, they think about performance.... The best [motion capture] I've seen has all been messed with by animation, in much the same way as the best rotoscope done in Disney's time was mucked with [qt. in Osmond, 2011, 5].

Henry Selick spans the bridge that exists between puppetry and animation as a stop-motion director. He said,

> There were early "Waldo" devices that allowed a puppeteer to manipulate an animated character live, but I didn't see that continuing to the extent I expected. And there's been years where mechanical and electronic interfaces and controls were used [by] puppeteers [to] manipulate metal and rubber and plastic creatures, like what Jim Henson's Creature Shop is/was known for. I think motion capture-performance capture has replaced both those things to a large degree. And however good the performance may be that is captured, there's still a lot of additional modeling and animation that has to be done. Certainly, in the CG animated world, they've come a long way from having to write math to make things move to the much more natural and intuitive experience of the Maya software and beyond [Selick email to author, March 29, 2016].

Perhaps the icing on the CGI cake is a 2002 interview with Walt Disney's nephew, Roy E. Disney:

> DISNEY: All the *Matrix* and *X-Men* kind of films that are out right now ... play on the very same thing: They look real, but of course they're not real at all, they're almost completely animated films, in one way of looking at it. You could go back to *Titanic*. You could almost consider *Titanic* an animated film because so much of it was unreal or not filmed in the real world at any rate.... [T]here's such a blurred line right now. I keep wondering why the Academy decided they needed a separate category for animated films just at a moment when there are a lot of people who couldn't tell you whether a film is animated or not.
> LEE: Is there a trade-off between traditional animation and CGI animation?
> DISNEY: Yes, there are definite tradeoffs; certainly one of the, at least traditionally, looks of *Toy Story* or a *Finding Nemo* is a kind of a plasticized look. That doesn't have to be what CG films look like, but it's, I think, the public conception of what a CG film looks like. Everything we've done since *Beauty and the Beast*, at Disney, had passed through the computer, so you could probably say that everything we've done for the last 12 or 14 years is, in a sense, computer graphics. All that means is that we have these wonderful tools at hand and we can make a movie look like anything we choose it to look like [Roy Disney qt. in Lee & Madej, 2012, 3].

Donald Crafton (indirectly) responded to Brad Bird's statement about animation and tied it to puppetry. He pointed out that while puppets can be dramatic, they were once considered superior to human actors:

> When [Brad] Bird tries to shift the agency in animated performance from the toon performers to the animators, he (presumably) is innocently reformulating a longstanding critical tradition that valorized puppets' agency over that of theatrical actors. Critics praised puppets for being devoid of sentiment, emotion, spontaneity and grace—in short, for lacking humanity. Being capable only of figuration, critics argued, counterintuitively made them superior to human actors, who invariably introduced their own personalities, experiences and unwanted interpretations into their roles. Embodied acting (of the kind lauded by Disney and the proponents of the Stanislavsky method) interfered with the purity of the author's intentions, the text, or the essential experience of the drama. As a result, puppet actors emerge as a radical alternative to human thespians. Because animated performers are (with rare exceptions) not blood actors, and since their agency is constrained like that of puppets, they might be even better standard-bearers for this critique of performance [Crafton, 2013, 64].

To put it another way: animators and puppeteers are superior performers. Animators are artists and know how to mimic life through their medium so that it appears real and resonates with people's emotions and hunger for exciting cinema. Animation and puppetry are more concentrated crafts devoid of human actors' hold-ups, because it is perfected by human hands to be the ideal version or illusion of life. The past critics praised these inanimate actors, because they achieved a true performance or embodiment of the characters and story. Puppets and animated characters were created for one purpose: to be whatever the artist intended and nothing more.

Animation is going full circle with newer technology that is recreating the first animated shows, puppetry, but instead of using inanimate objects, humans are becoming the puppets, thus upsetting the process and very definition of animation. However, when the humans are recorded and scanned into computers, they are manipulated in much the same way as animated characters. It is using different methods but a fundamental approach. At the Atlanta Center for Puppetry Arts exhibit I mentioned in the introduction, there was another quote, this one from Peter Hart: "In the fullest sense, puppeteers [and animators] are writers, designers, builders and performers. They are the force behind the objects, who animate the puppets and interpret their world for the audience" (Smith email to author, February 17, 2016).

Reiniger was a child when notable animation and special effects pioneers were busy practicing their art and their films played at cinemas. Reiniger had an extreme fondness for George Méliès. These pioneers combined with her inherent talent for scherenschnitte and Paul Wegener's 1918 speech ignited her career.

Stop-motion animation was discovered when filmmakers learned that when they stopped filming a sequence with the shutter closed, they could reposition people, making it appear as if they magically moved from one part of the screen to another when they continued to film. The mechanics for traditional hand-drawn animation were already known long before stop-motion entered the screen with inventions like flipbooks, zoetrope, praxinoscope and the phenakistoscope. The ability to capture and manipulate people in a manner similar to traditional animation could only be conceptualized with an actual motion picture camera. Once it was realized, "it was a logical step to introduce the practice of exposing the film one frame at a time to produce trick-films of inanimate objects moving" (Holman, 1975, 22).

A gap existed between animation and puppetry from the moment the first stop-motion puppets were animated shot by shot, but the gap has been widened as animation techniques improved. Puppetry and animation became even more separated with less stop-motion films being made and puppetry not being regarded as a popular entertainment form (with the exception of Jim Henson's creations) in the U.S.

Holman makes a poignant argument in his book *Puppet Animation in the Cinema* that stop-motion puppet films go against the semantic argument that animation, puppetry and special effects should remain in their distinctive realms:

> [A] puppet is a puppet. He is neither a live actor nor a cartoon film character, he is unique and in a medium of his own. To force a puppet animation beyond its point of efficiency by over-elaboration, or to waste carelessly the potentials which puppets possess, are violations.... This is not to say the last puppet film has been made nor must all others follow the forms which have already been established: there is ample latitude for experimentation and innovation within the field. The integrity of the medium, however, should be respected. Style and presentation, and much of the form itself, may change, but there should not be a conscious attempt to imitate other media, nor should puppet animation be forced into a configuration to which it does lend itself [1975, 76].

Holman[5] makes a valid point about respecting a medium's individual and unique creativity, but he fails to respect how the medium cross over into each and how newer technology would evaporate some distinctions. Many stop-motion animators would regard Holman's argument as a truth, but one needs to acknowledge that the origins of animation drew on puppetry and intermingle with modern techniques. It would be better to say that a medium's development should be left up to individual artists and their particular work. Reiniger was not a fan of the animation advances she witnessed in the latter half of the twentieth century, preferring her own paper-cut silhouettes, but she did admire the better equipment.

Animators and puppeteers like Lotte Reiniger overcome the barriers with the combination of both media drawing on different techniques from each other, but silhouette films still prove to be the truest representation of a perfect marriage. The silhouette film is not a recorded shadow play; rather it is an augmented version of the older art drawing on modern techniques to animate it. Cinematic special effects can be tossed into a silhouette film that would otherwise be impossible with a shadow play, especially live action presentations; but in contrast, the silhouette film still carries on with the world's oldest puppetry form by using techniques that haven't changed for centuries.

9

Fine Art and Resurgent Praise

> We awaken from the hallucination, stand up in the theater as if homeless, and walk out into the pompous splendor of the Kurfürstendamm. But we carry within ourselves warm feelings of gratitude towards the artist who created this work and donated it to us: we take Lotte Reiniger home with us.—L. Steffens, *Die Weltbühne*, September 28, 1926

Reiniger might have abandoned films for the time being, but she didn't leave the shadows. Throughout her career, she had been hired to create, write and perform shadow plays. After Koch's death, "I didn't want to make any more films and I dedicated myself to the shadow theater. I was never able to be a perfect shadow player, but I wanted to do it" (qt. in Happ, 2004, 92). Reiniger was always one to welcome new experiments, especially if they were exciting or could augment her own skills.

In 1962, she and Koch engaged in a shadow play experiment at Max Bührman's theater, known for his work in traditional Chinese shadow puppets (Happ, 2004, 92). He commissioned Reiniger to design characters and scenery for a take on the classic story *Undine*. His team took Reiniger's designs and made the physical puppets using Chinese puppetry construction methods, but things didn't go well. Something was lost between Reiniger's drawings and the puppets' actual renderings; *Undine* was scrapped after a few performances. Bührman even "banished them to the attic" and they weren't added to his collection (Happ, 2004, .93)

It had always been Reiniger's hobby to perform short shadow plays with a miniature Venetian theater she had constructed after seeing one on display in the Victoria and Albert Museum. She enjoyed these performances, because she could do them alone in front of the small audiences, including school groups, and was able to tell her beloved fairytales (Happ, 2004, 93). After Koch's death, Reiniger still performed these small shadow plays, but she wanted to do something bigger and grander. But that required a bigger theater and other performers who'd need to be trained (Happ, 2004, 93). The task didn't daunt Reiniger and she not only performed in many theaters over the next few years, but she also taught children and adults to be puppeteers. In August 1967, she worked at the Unicorn Theatre for Children and performed *The Story of the Seventeen Cows* and *Trip to the Moon*. These shows employed traditional black silhouettes and also colored puppets and backgrounds using transparent paper (Happ, 2004, 93). She once more collaborated with the Hogarth Puppets and made puppets for their production of the Indian fairytale *The Wise Jackal*.

While Reiniger had made England her permanent home by becoming a citizen, she continued to maintain ties to Germany, especially with friends and her husband's relatives in Nübrecht (Happ, 2004, 101). One of the many relationships she had in Berlin was with Else and Günther Wasmuth, a couple who owned a publishing house, Wasmuth Verlag; in 1926 they had published a tie-in book to *Prinzen Achmed* featuring 32 stills from the film (Happ, 2004, 101–02). When the Wasmuths' store was destroyed in the 1945 Battle of Berlin, they opened a new shop in Tübingen (Happ, 2004, 102). Reiniger's popularity in Germany kept growing as her fairytale films were replayed in theaters, television, museums and even added to the Munich Institut für Film und Bild in Wissenschaft und Unterricht (FWU) (Institute for Film and Picture in Science and Education) educational program. The FWU focused on making educational films and media and since Reiniger made her fairytale films in the 1950s, the FWU picked them up and played them in schools across Germany (Happ, 2004, 102). Children were exposed to her films in a school environment for decades and the FWU even asked Reiniger to finish her incomplete *Die goldene Gans*, which was added to the program in 1963 (Happ, 2004, 102).

As children watched Reiniger's fairytale films in their classrooms, Reiniger's contributions to German puppetry were finally being recognized. From June 6 to 9, 1968, she was a special guest at the Union Internationale de la Marionnette/International Puppetry Association (UNIMA) Festival, where she was given an award and made an honorary member (Happ, 2004, 102). Due to the attention from UNIMA, the top German puppet magazine *FigurenTheater*, published by the Deutschen Institut für Puppenspiel (German Institute for Puppetry), featured Reiniger in an article that described her importance to cinema history by introducing shadow puppetry to film (Happ, 2004, 102). When it came to puppetry, she disliked it when people viewed it from an academic perspective, forgetting to suspend their disbelief:

> One must be mindful to imagine the number of hours one wants to dedicate to the movement [in silhouette films] and to sympathize with a puppeteer who guides a marionette. For that reason I am always absolutely miserable, when I have to read in publications about shadow play that, in the opinion of the "direct" shadow player, the filming of this beautiful art implies a mechanization. If only they knew how much one shares of oneself through one's hands during one of these recordings [qt. in Happ, 2004, 103].

In 1969, the ATV network commissioned her to make 26 Biblical shadow plays for a children's show, *All Creatures Great and Small*, recorded in Birmingham, England. The shadow plays were recorded and made into individual films. Reiniger was dissatisfied with the work, finding that she didn't like the hectic pace of TV (having to cut new characters each week and perform them in a rush) (Happ, 2004, 94). "On television, you have no time to experiment around or do something really finished. Every week a recording date was set. Everything had to happen quickly. Thorough preparation was not possible. The result was correspondingly simple" (qt. in Happ, 2004, 94). What astounded Reiniger—surprising, considering the violence typical in fairytales—was that the Biblical shadow plays covered topics ranging from "fratricide to the resurrection of Jesus"[1] (Happ, 2004, 94).

Also in 1969, she was invited to the Deutschen Institut für Puppenspiel in Bochum to attend a puppetry academy from April 7 to 12, along with respected shadow puppeteers Rudolf Stössel and Otto Krämer (Happ, 2004, 103).

Praise continued for Reiniger in her golden years. To honor her work, the Deutsche Kinemathek held a film retrospective from September 18 to 20, 1969, and an exhibition that lasted until October 31 (Happ, 2004, 103). A tie-in book featured critiques of

Mary, Joseph, and a young shepherd watch over the newborn Jesus (©Primrose Productions).

Reiniger's films, a biography and a filmography. There was also a section for contemporary views on her films. Werner Dütsch, who had collected information about Reiniger for the Deutsche Kinemathek and would later become a documentary producer, pigeonholed Reiniger's work in the same manner that most uninformed people place animation, in the kiddie corner. Happ explained Dütsch's comments the best: "[He gave] Reiniger the pejorative label 'cute'" (Happ, 2004, 103).

The head of the Frankfurt municipal cinemas (and later the director of the Frankfurt am Main Deutsches Filminstitut), Walter Schobert loved Reiniger's films and he wanted to bring as much attention to them as possible (Happ, 2004, 105). He contacted her at the Abbey Arts Centre and arranged for her to visit theaters in Frankfurt and Munich around 1970, where she spoke about her life and making the films (Happ, 2004, 105).

Around this time, Reiniger decided to put her knowledge of silhouette animation and shadow theater on paper. While authors had written instructional manuals on animation and puppetry[2] as individual topics, Reiniger combined the two in one book. *Shadow Theatres and Shadow Films* teaches individuals not only how to animate their own silhouette or cutout animation but how to perform their own shadow plays. The book is the closest we have to an autobiography. Reiniger included filmmaking and puppetries stories from her long career and added her signature humor to the instructions to make the book a testament to her skills and personality. *Shadow Theatres and Shadow Films* was first published in English, printed in England, and released in 1970. Five years later it was retitled *Shadow Puppets, Shadow Theatres and Shadow Films*[3] for the U.S. audience and then translated into German in 1981 under the same title. Reiniger dedicated the book to Koch with the inscription, "To my late husband Carl Koch."

One of the few animation historians to write extensively about Reiniger was William "Bill" Moritz. He was the premier Oskar Fischinger scholar, but his research on the abstract animator often led him to write about Reiniger on the side and he even befriended her during her tenure at the Abbey Arts Centre. In his *Optical Poetry*, he recounted, "The summer of 1970 I had finished restoring a print of *Spiritual Constructions*, and I took it to London to show Lotte Reiniger, who had not seen it before, but liked it very much. She generously regaled me with anecdotes about Oskar (whom she knew only casually) as well as Bert Bartosch, Walther Ruttmann, Bert Brecht and Jean Renoir. And she cut some silhouette figures for me as well" (2004, 153).

Reiniger was passionate about Mozart's opera and music, having incorporated his work into her own whenever she had the chance. In 1970, she received a huge work order to design and cut silhouettes for a book showcasing Mozart's most popular operas *Figaro, Don Giovanni, Così fan tutte* and *Die Zauberflöte*. The silhouettes wouldn't be animated; rather they would be reprinted as static images in a book. This didn't displease Reiniger at all and one can imagine she was extremely excited that she had the opportunity to allow her talents to run free in the silhouettes' construction. The project was very important to Reiniger and she spent the winter months of 1970–1971 on the visual development process, gathering information about the history of the operas, listening to recordings, studying historical dress used in the operas, researching different versions of the characters and reading about the settings (Happ, 2004, 96). She drew pencil sketches of the silhouettes before deciding on the final images and in the summer of 1971, within one month she cut out 145 silhouettes (Happ, 2004, 96–97). She made sure to sketch out each silhouette on black paper to get them exactly right, because she hated questioning her cuts and having to glue two pieces together if she make a mistake (Happ, 2004, 97). It was important for Reiniger to achieve the perfect artist result and represent the silhouettes in the proper time and style of Mozart (Happ, 2004, 97). The end result was not only an illusion of life and astonishing feat, but the pinnacle of Reiniger's scherenschnitte skills. She had been cutting for over 60 years and her talent had grown from simplistic shadow cutouts to nearly living, breathing shadows.

By 1971, Reiniger's films had been incorporated into FWU's program for many years and the institute commissioned Primrose Productions to expand the 1953 documentary *You've Asked for It—The Art of Lotte Reiniger* aka *The Birth of the Silhouette Film* to include more about the technical aspects of her animation process. The documentary is "significant because on the one hand all of the silhouette techniques Lotte Reiniger developed are explained in detail for the first time and because on the other hand … the final results of this special type of animation are shown" (qt. in Happ, 2004, 106) It premiered in 1973.

One year earlier, 1972, Reiniger was recognized for her contribution to German cinema at the International Berlin Film Festival, more commonly known as the Berlinale. She was awarded a lifetime achievement award—the Deutsche Film Prize, Das Band von Gold—by the Minister of the Interior Hans-Dietrich Genscher for outstanding achievements in German film (Happ, 2004, 106).

Also in 1972, Schubert and Hans Strobel of the Munich Youth Film Television Work Center arranged for Reiniger to go on a lecture tour around Germany (Happ, 2004, 106).

Reiniger's fairytale films from the 1950s had circumnavigated the globe many times and become fan favorites.[4] The grand directory of *The Puppet Theatre in America* even devotes a sentence to Reiniger: "Lotte Reiniger's shadow films are allied to the early history of animation, and still delight American audiences," demonstrating how her films left a mark in the U.S., enough to warrant note in an American puppetry history tome (McPharlin, 1969, 573).

Walter Schobert said that everyone kept asking Reiniger to make another film:

> She always said, "After Carl died I didn't have the courage to make another film." You can say he was a good spirit. Naturally he was the technician in the background, the craftsman who worked out the figure animation. It wasn't easy at the time to motivate Lotte and say, "Come on get a grip on yourself and try again. The whole world is waiting for a new film." But she did it, but something completely different. She made *The Prodigal Son* for the German Bible Society. It wasn't a classical animation film like everything before. It was a filmed shadow theater [qt. in Raganelli, 1999].

After the major Mozart silhouette project, the Berlinale and her lecture tour, in the summer of 1974 Reiniger re-edited one of the Biblical shadow plays from *All Creatures Great and Small* as a standalone shadow play: *The Lost Son* (*The Prodigal Son*) was made using black puppets on colored acetate foil backgrounds. "I am pleased that I can now once again retell this important parable, a story that I have loved for a very long time" (qt. in Happ, 2004, 94).

By the 1970s, Reiniger's fame preceded her in more ways than one. She had achieved international fame in animation and puppetry circles and was a well-respected filmmaker in Germany. Her films continued to play in theaters and on television and the burgeoning video rental market helped spur popularity all over the world. She was invited to give lectures in the U.S., Canada, Turkey, Norway, France and other countries, to the delight of her fans. In 1974, Reiniger made her first journey to North America by invitation by Gordon Martin of the National Film Board of Canada. Reiniger also had friendships that drew her to Canada, along with the Goethe Institute, which sponsored her tour across North America (Roman, 1974). John Grierson, who had hired Reiniger to work at the GPO, worked in Canada during World War II and he brought Norman McLaren with him. McLaren was familiar with Reiniger; he encouraged her to come over along with Lena Lee and Alexander Alexejew, friends she knew before the war in London, and they later worked at the National Film Board of Canada (Happ, 2004, p. 98). (Reiniger, although, said she met Norman McLaren later in Canada and not when he was in England [Bastiancich, 1992/1981, p. 14].) In April 1974, she journeyed to Montreal and was immediately put on a very busy schedule, beginning with a five-day workshop and screenings of her films, continuing onto Toronto and the U.S. April 29 marked the official beginning of her North American tour, when it kicked off with a reception, followed by a personal appearance and screenings of her films in Quebec (NFB, 1974). "If you asked Lotte where she was off to next, she raised her hands in mock ignorance and despair and said, 'I'm just a package'" (Happ, 2004, 98).

The U.S. part of the whirlwind tour began in Boston on May 11 and took her to the West Coast and back again to the East Coast where she appeared at the Kennedy Center for the Performing Arts in Washington D.C. on May 21 (Ballard & Schubert, 1974, 39). She also gave lectures in New York and San Francisco (Roman, 1974, 9; 1976, 9). In San Francisco, she was overwhelmed and ecstatic about the large turnout. She was also amused by her first encounter with hippies. "I had a talk ... on a business day at 11 o'clock. There were a lot of people, all frightful hippies with tinsel and headbands.... [A]fterward when *Prince Achmed* was shown, the reaction was immensely strong. After the presentation, a noble hippie with a long robe and hair [came] to me, he looked like Sarastro: 'Tell me,' he said, 'how did you make that film in 1926?' I said, 'Probably because we were hippies ourselves. We dressed not so, but we felt so [like you]'" (qt. in Happ, 2004, 99).

By calling herself a hippie, Reiniger referred to the free-spirited mentality that epitomized the 1920s and early 1930s and took form in her via her avant-garde attitude to animating her own ideas without capitulating to the popular ideas of the time. The liberal avant-garde attitude morphed into the 1960s counterculture movement, which rippled into the 1970s as progressive social, art and political changes. The puppetry arts saw its greatest development in these years when Jim Henson decided to make puppets his main entertainment focus. He experimented with new construction techniques and performance methods that attracted Joan Ganz Cooney's attention. Cooney one of the founders of the Children's Television Network (now Sesame Workshop), thought Henson's puppet skits would work well on a new show. When she first met Henson, she commented,

> This was during the period of the Weathermen. There had been bombings and so on, and we knew there were some people who didn't like what we were doing. I was sitting up front with some CTW [Children's Television Workshop] people, and this man came in, dressed in what appeared to me to be hippie clothes with a hippie beard.... He walked into the back of the room and sat there, ramrod straight, rows and rows from the rest of us. I whispered to David Connell, "How do we know that man isn't going to kill us?" "It isn't very likely," Dave said. "That's Jim Henson" [qt. in Finch, 1993, 54].

Henson was indeed a hippie and the prevailing free-spirited ideas inspired his work, launching him into history as a TV and film icon.

When she was in California, Reiniger toured the Walt Disney Studios. When I consulted the Walt Disney Archives, they didn't have a record of her visit.

Whether she is categorized as a hippie or avant-garde animator, dozens of attendees flocked to her lectures. The Puppetry Guild of Greater New York member Shirley Roman attended Reiniger's lecture held in the Big Apple on May 20 at the Goethe Institute. At this lecture were panelists Richard Kaplan, Pat and Gordon Martin, National Film Board of Canada animator Grant Munro and silhouette-cutout artist Diana Bryan (Starr, 1980, 17–19). Roman wrote of the lecture: "Mrs. Reiniger introduced the evening with a brief, anecdote-filled talk on the early days of film in Berlin in the 1920's. Her charm and modesty were most endearing" (1974). The talk was followed by showings of Reiniger's *Papageno, The Grasshopper and the Ant* and *Die Abenteuer des Prinzen Achmed*, and it ended with a demonstration of her animation process (Roman, 1974). Cecile Starr, moderator of the Goethe Institute program, remembered that Reiniger stated, "My life is kind of an Andersen's fairytale" (1980, 17). Starr was a well-regarded film historian, critic and distributor, and even made her own documentaries. She dedicated a portion of her career to preserving the legacy of lesser known animators, including Reiniger, by distributing their films, often at her own expense (Keefer email to author, April 12, 2016).

Starr and Hagen Jr. corresponded with each other and discussed ways they could distribute Reiniger's films to a bigger audience than Germany. In 1994, Hagen Jr. commented on how people were critical about TV violence and believed that Reiniger's fairytale films could have a resurgence in the video market. In response, Starr wrote,

> The main problem here, it seems to me, is that as a nation we're addicted to violence on TV, in the movies and in real life. We pay lip service to art and culture and family values, but that's not where America puts its money. If I seem somewhat bitter about this, I guess I am. I hope to see a change for the better some day. You know I love Lotte's work—and I loved meeting her briefly here in New York and in England [June 28, 1994].

After the tour, Reiniger returned to Montreal. On the return flight, she discussed with the producers the details of a new silhouette film. She stated in a joking manner, "I told them that I have no technical understanding and not enough materials to engage with anyone. Then they asked me: 'If you had the chance, would you realise new film projects?' This was how they invited me to the National Film Board of Canada. I had always wanted to go there. That was the best place to make artful films. There I met great animators. They had so perfected an animation stand, that I did not dare to touch it. I made *Aucassin and Nicolette*" (qt. in Happ, 2004, 98).

Gordon Martin was convinced Reiniger had it within her to animate another film and he persuaded her to animate once more. "I did it with trembling hands thinking I couldn't do it any more" (qt. in Marschall *et al.*, 2012). In a letter, Gordon Martin wrote, "Now here is a woman who has pioneered in film animation and is still quite capable of making a film at age 73. We had dinner with her in London in December and she mentioned that she 'keeps in shape' by doing cutouts every day. Lack of sponsorship and her own modest means keep her from making another film" (NFB, 1974).

It was discussed that she would animate Joseph Maurice Ravel's opera *L'Enfant et les sortiléges* (*The Child and the Spells*), but she selected *Aucassin and Nicolette* instead (Jouvanceau, 2004, 52). She returned to Canada in August 1974 to animate *Aucassin and Nicolette*, based on a twelfth or thirteenth century chantefable about two lovers and their constant separation and reunification. She used classic black silhouettes on colored acetate backgrounds. When completed, it ran 16 minutes.

While Reiniger animated this new film, she became acquainted with Co Hoedeman, a Dutch-born Canadian animator who worked at the NFB for many years and became internationally known for his stop-motion prowess. In 1977, he won an Academy Award for his short film *Le Château de sable* (*The Sand Castle*), which served to inspire Henry Selick. Hoedeman had admired Reiniger's silhouettes and when she worked at the NFB's Montreal studio, he helped her set up the camera to film her puppets. Hoedeman developed a friendship with Reiniger: "In the cafeteria I would join her for lunch. She always had her tiny pair of scissors with her doing paper cutouts. She was incredibly adept doing cutouts and super-fast." Hoedeman became fascinated with the art of silhouette animation and decided to try his hand at it. "Only recently, after I left the NFB in 2004, did I make my first silhouette animation film called *55 Socks* in 2011, followed by *The Blue Marble* in 2014 and now *The Cardinal*. Soon I'll be finishing the film. I work basically out of my own basement studio at home with my digital camera and the articulated cutout puppets on a light box" (Hoedeman email to author, December 7, 2015). He follows in Reiniger's footsteps as she animated her films by herself and with a simple tricktisch rig, although she didn't have the technology available to Hoedeman.

Reiniger's animation for *Aucassin and Nicolette* is at its finest with defined silhouette characters and gorgeous colored backgrounds, but the story doesn't translate well to film. *Aucassin and Nicolette* is an epic medieval romance that is difficult to confine within 16 minutes; without the narration, the story would have flopped around like a fish. Had Reiniger animated more footage, it would have helped the film's performance. The Huggett Family, a group that performed vocal and instrumental ensemble music (specializing in folk, medieval, baroque and renaissance music), performed the music for *Aucassin and Nicolette*. It was shown in Ottawa at the 1976 International Animated Film Festival, where it won a special jury prize (Happ, 2004, 100).

When Reiniger animated the film, Patricia Martin, Gordon Martin's wife, and Jane

Suber assisted her (Jourvanceau, 2004, 52). During her time in Canada, she formed a strong friendship with Gordon and Pat Martin, who convinced her to stay a little longer in North America. Gordon headed a Montreal-based organization called Media & Education, which reviewed audio-visual methods and approaches, and through it he produced *Aucassin and Nicolette* (Roman, 1976, 9). When the film was finished, Gordon Martin used his powers of persuasion on Reiniger, encouraging her to attend a workshop where she would be the guest of honor, and also lead a group of participants in the rules of silhouette animation, puppet construction and how to make their own movie.

The seminar-workshop was a week-long affair held in August 1976. Most of the people it attracted were filmmakers, but ten puppeteers from Canada and the U.S. also went. Among the attendees: Janibeth Johnson, Emma Louise Warfield (former Puppeteers of America regional director), Ken McKay (former Puppeteers of America president), Mike Edelstein, Shirley Roman, Debbie Kleese (all three members of the Yueh Lung Shadow Theatre), David Malhoyt, Calvin Tamura, Betty Polus, Mara Alper, June Clearman, Michele Nixon and Marilyn Scott (Roman, 1976a, 10; 1976b, 19). Shirley Roman shared what occurred at during the week-long retreat:

Using his powers of persuasion Gordon Martin talked Lotte Reiniger into leading a four-day workshop in August 1976 demonstrating her silhouette animation and shadow puppetry techniques to participants (courtesy Gordon Martin and Lois Segal).

> Gordon Martin, director of Media & Education, arranged for the seminar-workshop to be held in a small, charming ski lodge, the Winsum Inn, in the Laurentian Mountains about 30 miles north of Montreal. We were the solo occupants and the staff went all-out to make the week perfect, catering to special diets where necessary, building screens and tables and whatever else was needed, running errands.... Martin, too, was a tower of strength, starting from the moment of our arrival at the Montreal Airport (and before, with registrations)...
>
> The seminar-workshops consisted of morning meetings with Miss Reiniger, afternoon and evening workshops (both film and puppet) and, of course, night-time showings of films—Miss Reiniger's but also Jean Renoir's antiwar classic, *Grand Illusion*, with which her husband had been closely associated. And, always, Miss Reiniger was there at meal times and between sessions and in the evenings, ready to explain, to discuss, to reminisce about film-making in Europe ... her "Adventures of Prince Achmet."
>
> Miss Reiniger illustrated and taught us how to make the silhouette figure which she so distinguishes her work, how to joint and move it—how to make an animated film. In fact, we did make a film; it consists of short scenes in which our own animated figures act or react against each other. Crude, unfinished, but definitely an example of knowledge gained and applied. An example, too, of

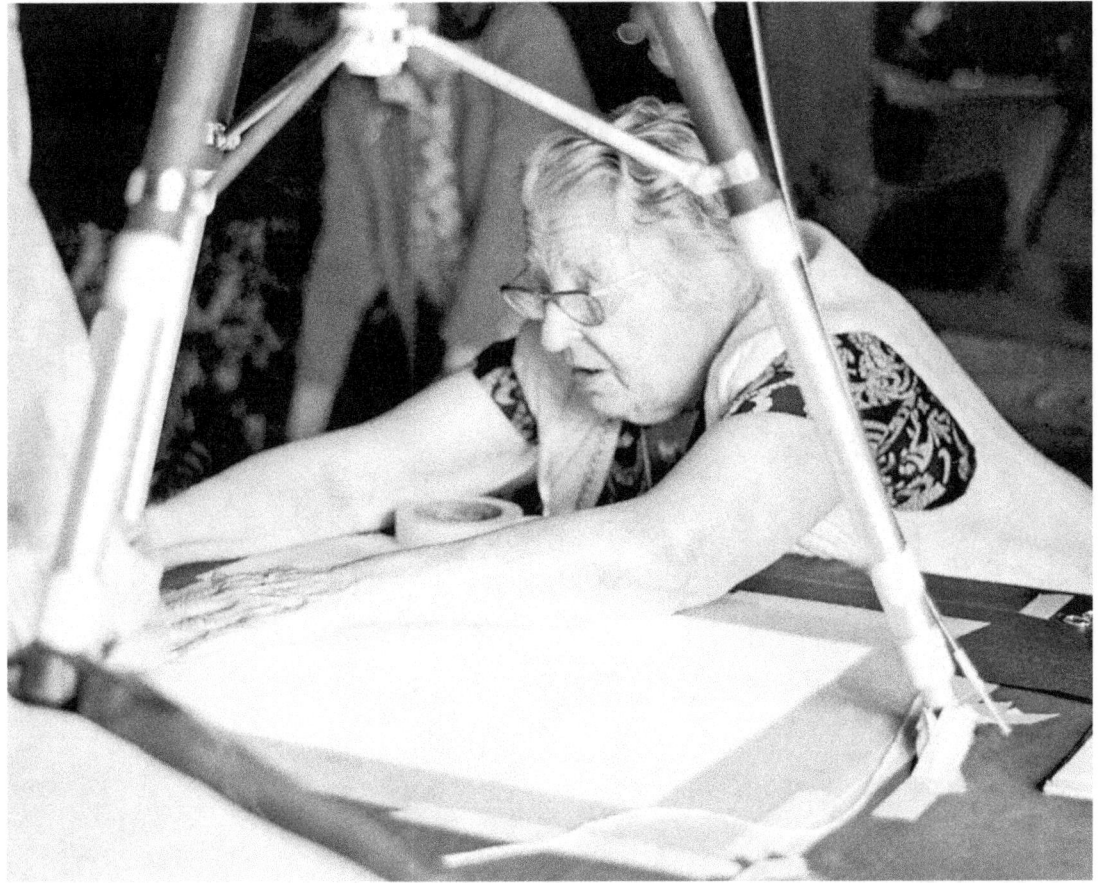

Reiniger demonstrating silhouette animation in 1976 (photo by Lois Segal).

some of the socializing that helped make Miss Reiniger's seminar-workshop so memorable: spilled beer adds to the spontaneity of the print [1976, 10–11].

Janibeth Johnson shared her thoughts with me about the four-day Montréal workshop. Johnson was a student of respected puppet master Frank W. Ballard, creator of the innovative puppet program at the University of Connecticut which still flourishes today. Johnson had always been fascinated by miniatures and always attracted to the interplay of light and shadow in photographic images. She was introduced to the art of shadow puppetry when she had the opportunity to participate in the first groundbreaking puppetry class at the University of Connecticut, offered in the fall of 1967. She was introduced to Reiniger's art at that time through her shadow puppetry book and one of her films. After viewing the film, Johnson remembered, "To me, she was shadow puppetry on film." In Ballard's class, Johnson created her first shadow puppets, a series of snakes made in different shadow styles from contrasting materials. One of Ballard's objectives was to present a wide range of puppet styles and techniques to educate his students, and he encouraged his students to develop their own specialized styles of puppets in what was very accurately called "the puppet laboratory."

Johnson's first foray into shadow puppetry was serendipitously followed by her being assigned the design of the Tit Willow shadow sequence in the 1968 University of

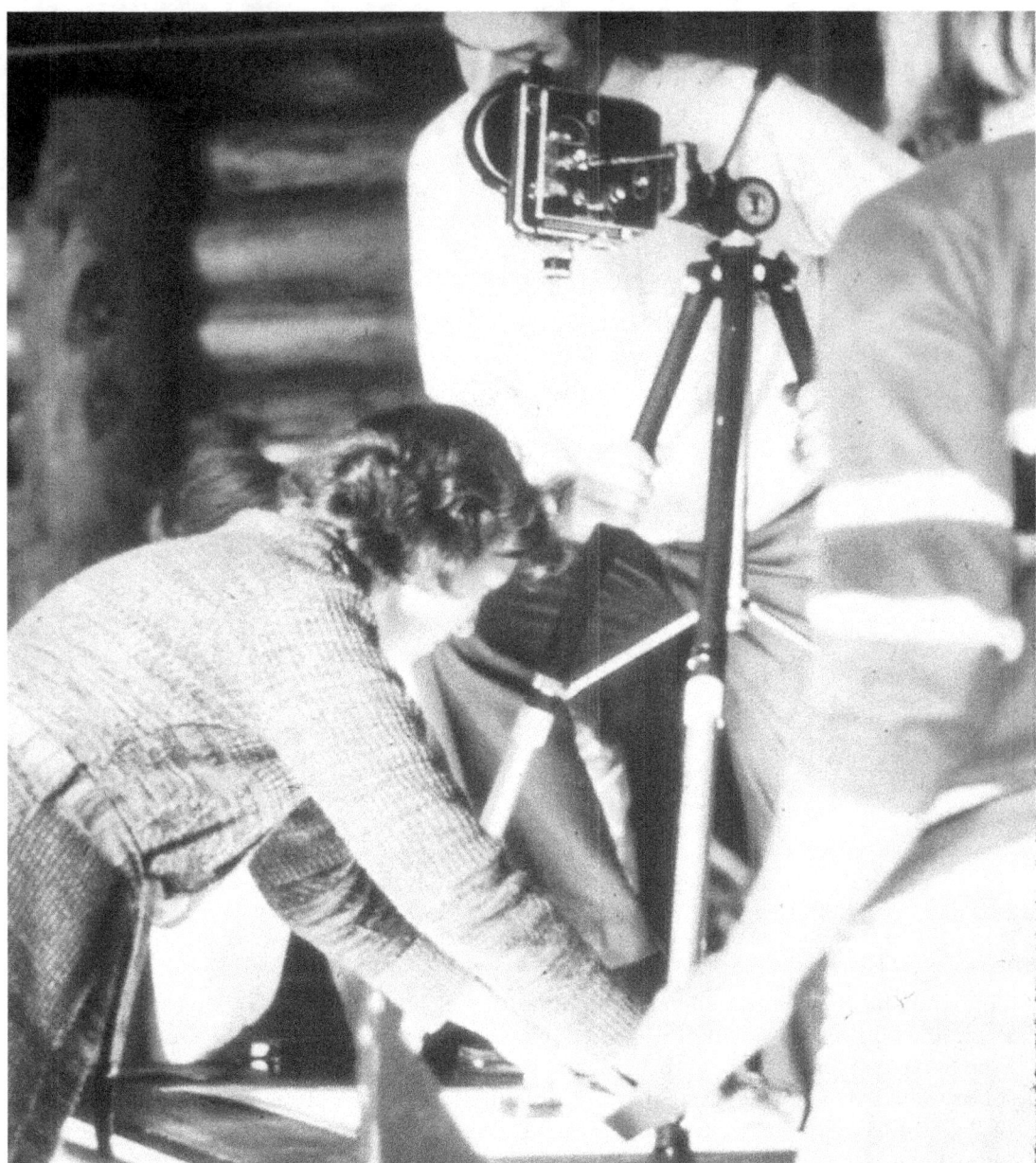

Pat Martin (left) and Gordon Martin (center) set up the camera to record the silhouette animation during the 1976 workshop (courtesy Janibeth Johnson).

Connecticut production of Gilbert and Sullivan's *The Mikado*. Johnson soon became the principal designer-director for all shadow sequences for Ballard's subsequent puppet operas and other major productions at the University of Connecticut. Reiniger's book were never far from Johnson's side for inspiration and edification.

After the then-new technology of overhead projectors became available through the education department, Johnson expanded her knowledge of shadow puppetry from traditional upright shadow figures to the innovative overhead shadow puppetry techniques that became her hallmark. She became known internationally as *the* expert on overhead shadow puppetry.

Johnson wrote an instructional manual entitled *Shadow Puppetry on the Overhead Projector* and taught many workshops including some at National Puppetry Festivals. Johnson's other major contribution to puppetry was as co-founder of the Ballard Institute and Museum of Puppetry, which grew from a traveling exhibit to a brick-and-mortar cornerstone at the University of Connecticut.

Johnson developed her overhead shadow expertise in a trial-by-fire process, experimenting with various materials: glass stain paints, theater lighting gels, chiffon and net fabrics, wax paper. She also discovered the wonders of multiplane levels to give her shows depth. She explained, "I would go away and work on my own to develop techniques, then I'd bring the results back to the puppet lab and try it out in front of my colleagues. I had the advantage of working both alone and within the community of my fellow puppeteers to develop a project, then eventually I would present the finished product before a live audience." In her art presented "live" before an audience, she utilized many cinematic techniques including the cross-fade, the close-up, the long shot and even a long moving panorama that was painted on glass and moved past the overhead projector plate. This panorama was part of the opening "morning" sequence in 1973's *Peer Gynt* production and was remembered by many audience members years after as the highlight of the show. Johnson often said that one of her biggest compliments was when her live-action figures and scenic effects were assumed to be film by viewers, even though they were being done live. Johnson's most treasured moment with the University of Connecticut company was when her work was recognized and she was honored, as shadow director-designer, with top billing and equal credit alongside the director and choreographer of 1975's *Kismet* production. She still remembers the moment that a grinning Frank W. Ballard presented her with a copy of the finished playbill-program with her name emblazoned in prominent letters as a reward for her creative work.

Johnson once worked with a colleague, Sascha Block Gardiner, on a stop-action shadow film called *The Robot Blues*. Johnson handled the puppet figures while Gardiner photographed. She remembers this as an isolating, painstaking, tedious experience which she therefore never repeated (preferring the live reaction of the crowd in a theater setting). But it gave her more admiration and respect for Reiniger's achievements.

After years of absorbing Reiniger's work, Johnson was surprised to learn that Reiniger was going to lecture in Boston ("I was astonished to realize that she was still alive!"). Johnson could not wait to attend the Boston lecture with a group of friends and she was not disappointed. In fact, she was blown away by Reiniger's lively sense of humor, which filled the auditorium with laughter and life, and she never forgot the experience.

Johnson attended Reiniger's Montreal workshop during Johnson's busiest year in puppetry, 1976. Johnson's friend and colleague Shirley Roman encouraged her to speak with the lady animator and Johnson eventually showed Reiniger her own silhouettes via photographs. She was gratified that Reiniger recognized the strong kinship that Johnson's images shared with her own work. "I was proud that she saw the similarities, because Lotte Reiniger was definitely one of my idols and a major influence on my work" (Johnson email to author, October 4, 2015).

Germany once more beckoned for Reiniger to share her expertise for a program about cartoons from the 1920s and '30s for the non-profit broadcasting station in 1975 and then she went on another German lecture tour, this time to cinemas playing her films (Happ, 2004, 106). At a festival in Istanbul, she spoke about her experience in silhouette films and shadow puppetry (Happ, 2004, 100). Once she returned to Canada in 1976, she went on another round of lectures and began discussions with Gordon Martin to make another film for Media and Education. Reiniger gave a few lectures at American and Canadian schools to film and animation students. 3D animation and related computer effects were in their infancy and experimentation with the new technology took place mostly at universities, privately held companies and a few Hollywood studios.

Reiniger still used her old-fashioned tricktisch and puppets to animate, so the new technology was overwhelming to her but also awe-inspiring. She was just as surprised that film and animation students would be interested in what she had to say.

> I had the funniest experiences. There was a college movie series at the film schools in America and Canada.... One of the teachers had seen me [lecture] and then invited me [to her college]. There the technical set-up, cameras, was the best of the best and the most expensive, and the students are sitting there, with everything around them that they could possibly want and I thought, "My God, my God, what should I tell these students?" Everyone there knew ten times more than I knew then, and the longer they showed me around, the more meek I became. And I thought I wouldn't have any success there with my primitive silhouettes, I told them then that I came from the prehistoric times of film, I didn't have everything that they had now. But they were totally spellbound by my things, and later a teacher said to me, "Just what did you do? They're all coming to me and telling me, 'Can't we work like Ms. Reiniger does?'" They also make lovely films that are technically perfect, but they leave one feeling completely cold [qt. in Happ, 2004, 100–01].

Reiniger may have doubted the impact her films had on her audiences, but many future "magic makers" would owe some of their own creativity to her.

Despite the tiring travel between two continents, Gordon Martin worked his wonders once more on Reiniger and through Media and Education, produced her penultimate film *The Rose and the Ring*. Based on William Makepeace Thackeray's satirical story, the film took over three years to complete (it was finally shot over six months in the summer of 1978) and she used black silhouette puppets on colored backgrounds.

Once more Pat Martin was her assistant, working on the storyboards and constructing minor characters. Martin observed how much Reiniger cared about her craft:

> Lotte had developed a very close relationship to the figures, with whom she worked and firmly believed that they had be to be treated like old friends with respect. At one of the many workshops she carried out, a young student who was unhappy with his figure had thrown it into the recycling bin. Not only did she scold him, but she made it clear to the entire group that all of the figures needed to be treated with feeling. Without this mindset, one becomes nothing more than an average animator, who moves lifeless objects [qt. in Happ, 2004, 101].

Martin also commented on Reiniger's careful writing and animation method:

> Lotte always works from a story she likes. She writes a very rough script, and then makes first-draft figures. The color sets were put together like a mosaic, with Scotch tape holding the little pieces of cutout acetate gels used for theater lighting. For the actual filming, this background was covered with pieces of frost that softens colors and also makes it possible to move the figures over the surface without catching onto the little pieces [qt. in Starr, 1980, 18–19].

The 24-minute-long *Rose and the Ring* debuted in 1979, but Reiniger didn't see it until it was shown at a film festival in July 1980 in New Barnet (Happ, 2004, 101). It's a satire about aristocracy and purported definitions of beauty told using theatrical tropes of mistaken identity, magical artifacts, fairy or divine intervention, missing royalty and more romantic entanglements than a Shakespeare comedy.

In August 1977, after a visit to Renoir in Los Angeles, Reiniger was a guest at the 38th National Festival of the Puppeteers of America, held at California Polytechnic Uni-

22nd Annual American Film Festival honoring Reiniger held on May 25, 1980, and three postcards with silhouette reproductions of *The Rose and the Ring* characters (courtesy Gordon Martin and Paul Gelder).

versity (Polus, 1978, 28). It was a special occasion for her. Betty Polus, former shadow puppetry consultant for the Puppeteers of America, described the event:

> A joyful reunion was held between Lotte and some dozen of her student-puppeteers who had studied with her in Canada during the past year. Lotte generously held two sessions at the Festival detailing her silhouette film technique; was guest of honor at a "Meet Lotte Reiniger" hour; shared her films during two nights of films (her students' films were also presented); and freely gave of her afternoons to individuals seeking additional knowledge. The Puppeteers of America were able to treat Lotte to the performances of other world-renowned puppeteers whose work she had only seen in photographs before. The high spot for Lotte was the Balinese Shadow [sic] performance by Larry Reed. She had only seen one performance previously ... in Berlin during the 1930s [1978, 28].

Reiniger wasn't always teaching or animating during her many trips. Paul Gelder wrote, "In her 80th year she made one of several return trips to North American and confronted her first cowboy at the Calgary rodeo. She even got herself a cowboy hat...," one of the prime symbols associated with the North American culture (1981).

Throughout the last decade of her life, Reiniger made many new friends in different countries, but she had one of the closest friendships with Alfred and Helga Happ, who were shadow puppeteers. They visited Reiniger at the Abbey Arts Centre and persuaded her to attend a shadow puppet seminar in Dettenhausen from October 26 to November 1, 1978 (Happ, 2004, 107). Many famous shadow puppeteers attended, Reiniger shared her shadow puppet techniques, and her films were shown as she provided commentary about the political, economic and personal details when she made them (Happ, 2004, 107). At the shadow puppet seminar, Alfred Happ and Werner Biedermann of the München Stadtmuseum decided to celebrate Reiniger's eightieth birthday with a career retrospective in 1979. It was held at the museum along with an exhibition of her figures, designs and backgrounds from her shadow films. They also displayed puppets and shadow theaters she used for shadow plays (Happ, 2004, 107). Reiniger performed her *Die siebzehn*

Kühe (*The Seventeen Cows*) with Happ at the exhibition (Happ, 2004, 107). After the conference, Reiniger said, "People asked me about my process and asked if I would like to do something less boring. But it isn't boring at all, it is tremendously exciting, one will never be done with it" (qt. in Happ, 2004, 107)

One of the best eightieth birthday gifts she received was the Iron Cross of Merit, bestowed upon her by the Federal Republic of Germany (Happ, 2004, 108). Some time later, Queen Elizabeth II honored Reiniger for her work as an activist for the arts. Reiniger loved living in England and was gratified that her work was held in high esteem there (Happ, 2004, 108).

During 1980 and 1981, the full extent of travel and age took its toll on Reiniger and she began to slow down (Happ, 2004, 108). Reiniger described herself to her journalist friend Paul Gelder as an old battlehorse: "When I hear the trumpet I'm off," and she plodded on (1981). From March 4 to 29, 1980, a retrospective was held at an old synagogue in Essen where her iconic tricktisch (on loan from the Düsseldorf museum) was displayed and the German premiere of *The Rose and the Ring* took place afterwards at the Oberhausener Short Film Festival. She had planned to attend the American Film Festival in New York, but remained at home due to exhaustion (Happ, 2004, 109). In her honor, the festival had a discussion panel attended by Pat Martin, Richard Kaplan, Diana Bryant, Grant Munro and others who were influenced by Reiniger's work. According to attendee Cecile Starr, Munro described how Reiniger influenced animators in the 1940s and said that he visited Reiniger in England and she gave him a silhouette camel puppet with red and black legs. He thought the different colored legs were to remind Reiniger which legs to shoot in the foreground and background. Martin added that Reiniger made silhouettes out of any material she could get her hands and scissors on (Starr, 1980, 19).

> The last member of the Festival panel, Diana Bryan, is a cutout, silhouette artist whose work appears frequently in *The New York Times* and other publications. When she first saw stills from Lotte Reiniger's films, she was thrilled to see how expression, caricature, emotion and movement were distilled in images that were clearer, less confused than those of anyone else she had seen. "She can reduce everything to its simplest terms," Ms. Bryant said, "and the movement in her films is so superb that after the first few seconds you forget that you're looking at flat paper. You see dancers whirling around as if they're three-dimensional. She can create an illusion even with the gesture of one finger. I would like to think that my work someday will achieve some of that potential for greatness that Lotte Reiniger achieved even when she was very, very young." Kaplan also mentioned Reiniger's bad habit: "Lotte said that when people criticized her chain smoking. She often said it saved her life, because she ran out of material … [she'd light a] cigarette and [take a drag], enjoyed it" ["Reiniger with Starr and others," 1978].

Her friend Paul Gelder visited her shortly before her death. "I last saw her in September 1980, just before she returned to Germany, in failing health, for more lectures and a holiday. Death was mentioned. 'I have had my fill of life. I have been very lucky and I am ready,' she told me. There was no hint of pessimism. The Reiniger radiance still shone through her eyes" (1981).

Reiniger traveled to Dettenhausen and spent time with the Happ family to recover and they celebrated her birthday on June 2 with her old friend Else Wasmuth (Happ, 2004, 109). Reiniger loved Dettenhausen's natural beauty and took many walks in the area. Reiniger was asked to illustrate a book to raise funds for the renovation of a local evangelical church. The church gave Reiniger free rein to choose the story and she was more than happy to agree. She decided on Hans Christian Andersen's *The Little Mermaid* and with the same vigor as the Mozart silhouette illustrations, she researched the ocean and drew pencil sketches of her ideas. Reiniger was particularly fastidious with the mermaid's shape. Once she was satisfied with her designs, she finished the silhouette cutouts in a few days. When she presented the book in November 1980, she said, "If you do things that you like, you have to stand behind it with all your soul." She also repeated her commitment to fairytales: "To be ashamed of fairytales is an outright folly. I believe more in fairy tales than I do newspapers" (qt. in Happ, 2004, 110).

Reiniger attended several more film festivals, but her health was failing and she knew it was time to leave the Abbey Arts Centre and England. She informed Paul Gelder, "I had a full life. I was very happy and I'm ready" (qt. in Happ, 2004, 110). She returned to Dettenhausen and she remained with the Happ family for many months.

After her final move to Germany, her schedule was still packed. It included a visit to the Düsseldorf Filmmuseum and a visit to her old tricktisch. Earlier in 1980, the former director of the Düsseldorf Stadtmuseum Hartmut W. Redottée wanted to preserve Reiniger's legacy:

> I was keen on getting her animation table for our museum At the beginning of 1980, I called her and asked if she was making any films. "No," she said, she was very weak at the time. "No, the table is all in bits up in my bedroom and that's probably the way it will stay." As discreetly as possible, I told her we would be most honored to have the table for the museum. Then she said in her usual nonchalant way, "You can have it. I shouldn't imagine I'll be working on it again." Then we arranged a price. I think she was pleased with what we paid for it.
>
> At the time she was living in New Barnet in North London. I ordered the transport, flew over to London, and spent a delightful day with her. At 5:00 the people rang at the door to pick up the table. Lotte was standing in the hall near the door watching them take it away. She suddenly looked so sad and said, "Adieu. Now it really is the end of my work."
>
> I felt a stab in my heart and thought to myself, "God, what have I done?" Then I said quite spontaneously, "Lotte we're making an exhibition in Dusseldorf in autumn. We'll assemble the table, you can come to Dusseldorf and make a film on it." Then she said philosophically, "Well, let's see." But we did it. In September 1980, we installed the table for an exhibition we put in Dusseldorf at the Museum ... with the things we had purchased from her back in London. And she worked for ten days in front of a highly interested and enthusiastic audience, something which demands immense concentration. The real meaning of professionalism was brought out to me. She sat at the table, clapped her hands, and said, "Right, let's get to work" [qt. in Raganelli, 1999].

Her last film was the short *Düsselchen und die vier Jahreszeiten* (*Düsselchen and the Four Seasons*), about a little boy's adventures through the changing seasons. It premiered at the museum on September 1, 1981; Reiniger died before the film's premiere. She did, however, view the final product. Redottée remembered,

> When she saw the film, she perked up enormously and said, "I don't have to be ashamed. I first thought I'd blown the whole thing and you all were just comforting me on the telephone." She looked at the three-minute film at least ten times over and said, "I was cheating there a little bit, but that was pretty good." She was once again the old professional, reliving her old art. For me, it was an uplifting moment. We were most honored to have produced her last film [qt. in Raganelli, 1999].

From that point, Reiniger decided to make one last move to Germany and she had a pleasant retirement with the Happ family. Alfred Happ recounted what happened that led to Reiniger living with them:

> She came to visit us again one day and after three weeks, I'll never forget the evening, my wife said, "Lotte, how long are you staying this time? Do you have such long holidays?" And she said, "Children, I'm here for good this time." Well to be quite frank, we weren't absolutely enamored about that, we were shocked. But I must be honest, we had often said to her, "Lotte, if it gets difficult don't hesitate to come." She lived alone in London and her friends came by to see how she was, but she wasn't

looked after permanently. Well, the situation had arisen, we accepted it, and she stayed [qt. in Raganelli, 1999].

Reiniger enjoyed living with the Happs and she created and performed a shadow play featuring animal tales for Katharina Happ on her tenth birthday. She also practiced for weeks to perfect the shadow play *Father Christmas's Mistake* from a song she translated into German for the holiday season (Happ, 2004, 110–11). She had sent the Happs the shadow puppets from *Father Christmas's Mistake* earlier, with a note reading: "To the courageous shadow-players" (Marschall *et al.*, 2012). She left the Happs and lived in Karolinenstift in Tübingen from December 1980 to the spring of 1981, when she suffered a small stroke and returned to live with the Happs. During the day, she enjoyed sitting by a window, "drawing what she saw: the church tower, the old wash house in the parish garden, the trees all around," and sometimes she would attempt to cut them from paper (Happ, 2004, 111). In the evenings, she listened to Mozart and Bach records. Beside her on a table were photographs of her husband and Renoir (Happ, 2004, 111).

Helga and Alfred Happ and Else Wasmuth were worried about Reiniger's estate and they approached her to discuss it. On May 8, 1981, she named the three her heirs with the condition that they use her artistic estate to create either a foundation or museum (Happ, 2004, 112). She had a second massive stroke in mid–May, leaving her paralyzed and unable to leave her bed. Reiniger's health kept declining and after many terrible weeks, she passed away on the morning of June 19, 1981. Alfred Happ recounted that on her final night she smoked a cigarette, didn't finish it, and then drank a glass of red wine (Raganelli, 1999). A funeral notice was sent to Reiniger's friends and family throughout the world accented by a screenshot from *Harlekin* of Columbine weeping for her beloved. The note reads:

> Lotte Reiniger a wonderful person and a great artist is dead. In the twenties she was already famous for her silhouette-films and her scissor-cuts. She was creative until the last months. Last summer she illustrated the story of H. Chr. Andersen "The little Sea-maid" and in the beginning of September 1980 she animated a short silhouette-film about the four seasons. Then she removed to Tübingen. Christmas time she had a stroke and her right side was lame. Since she could not cut out anything, her will to live was broken. Not broken was her great kindness and great attention. The last weeks she spent with the Happ-family. Together we heard much Mozart-music. She was amused about the many birthday-greetings from all over the world. She bore the time in great patience and courage. Many people she made happy by her art. We mourn for Lotte and we believe that the joy she formed in many films has immortalized Lotte.

Obituaries were printed in papers across the world. She had written a short poem, "Little sailing boat, carry once more my Carl and me" with a cutout of a little boat with Carl Koch sitting on one end and her on the other. The Happs placed it in the obituary notice (Marschall *et al.*, 2012).

While her death didn't have the same reach as Walt Disney or Jim Henson, it was felt in the animation and puppetry communities where she did pioneering work in both mediums. Reiniger was one of the first women in animation and puppetry to pioneer techniques still in use today. When she died, part of that original cinematic magic left with her. She once said this about her fame: "Yes, I didn't even know that I was so famous" (Happ, 2004, 108).

Obituaries grind a life down to basic facts and dates. Perhaps the most heartfelt obituary I read came from her fellow puppeteer Jan Bussell; it captures the minute and larger aspects of her spirit. While Reiniger referred to herself as a "well-upholstered old trouper" and "a primitive cave-man artist," humorously humble all the way to the end, Bussell was more poetic:

BERLINER GEDENKTAFEL

»Ich glaube mehr an Märchen als an Zeitungen« (1935)
Geburtshaus von
LOTTE REINIGER
2. 6. 1899 – 19. 6. 1981
Pionierin des Trickfilms
Zwischen 1923 und 1926 schuf sie den ersten langen
Animationsfilm der Filmgeschichte
Vorwiegend nach Märchen- und Opern-Motiven gestaltete sie
zahlreiche Silhouettenfilme und Scherenschnitte
Sie verließ Deutschland 1935, kehrte noch vor Kriegsende
nach Berlin zurück und lebte ab 1949 in England

KPM

Gefördert durch die GASAG Berliner Gaswerke Aktiengesellschaft

The city of Berlin erected a plaque outside her birthplace on 11 Knesebeckstraßein in the Charlottenburg district. The plaque reads: *"I believe more in fairytales than I do newspapers." / Birthplace of Lotte Reiniger / 6.2.1899–6.19.1981 / Pioneer of Animated films. Between 1923 and 1926 she created the first feature-length animation film in history / She created many fairytales and operas films mainly using silhouettes she designed / She left Germany in 1935, returned to Berlin before the war's end, and lived onward in England from 1949.*

[I]t is as a great human being, a true citizen of the world, that we remember her, as much as a great artist. She possessed the most extraordinary charisma and in particular a wonderful power to charm and inspire young people. She gave workshops in many countries and has disciples and admirers all over the world. She never lost her German accent and her English was sometimes rather difficult to follow literally, but her bubbling enthusiasm always brought the meaning through....

Lotte had an extraordinary gift of putting in small details—untidy shoelaces, the thickness of a belt, a ring on a finger, a lock of hair which gave character and life to her figures. Her art was instinctive, intuitive, springing from minute observation and a marvelous sense of design. Just as she knew which details would tell, so she knew which to leave out. She was very fond of including a checked floor in her designs. If you look at these closely, you find they are far from correct in perspective. And yet, seen as a whole, as part of the overall design, each square is perfectly placed to give one's eye satisfaction. No mathematical accuracy for her. She worked with passionate exactitude to her emotions [1981].

Under the careful supervision of the Happ family, Reiniger was laid to rest in the Dettenhausen cemetery next to her husband (his ashes were buried with her). A funeral service was held on July 4, 1981, presided over by Pastor Alfred Happ. It celebrated her life, accomplishments and the many people she had touched. Her friends Louis Hagen, Olive and Peter Gellhorn, Else Wasmuth and Gordon Martin traveled thousands of miles to visit her in the final days: (Happ, 2004, 111). Nancy L. Staub attended the service and said:

Her friend Pastor Alfred Happ conducted a lovely simple ceremony. A small brass band played a few melodies to celebrate the joyousness of her life which overshadowed the sorrow of our loss.

After the services, we gathered in the place where Lotte Reiniger had conducted her last workshops. Several relatives, friends and colleagues, including Albrecht Roser for UNIMA, praised not only her achievements as a puppet animator but her warm and generous nature. Excerpts of her films were screened and left all of us with a deep sense of gratitude for her gifts to the world [1981, 17].

In his delicate turn of phrase, Renoir couldn't have bestowed a higher honor on Reiniger than to compare her with her favorite composer. I came across this Renoir quote about Reiniger in a letter he wrote to Cecile Starr:

Lotte Reiniger is more above most of the animators. An animated film is too often the result of a crowd of wonderful technicians but I prefer the work of an artist who works with a small crew and has a chance to express himself. This is true of Lotte Reiniger. She is an artist and her work would be as good if instead of working with film, she had been a painter or a musician. Her art is definitely the expression of the traditional Austria. She is not an Austrian [sic] but artistically I have to see her as a visual expression of Mozart's music. I wish a film could be shot showing her hands during the making of one of her pictures. Her fingers clasping her only tool, scissors, make me think of a graceful classical dancer. I have no stories to tell about her. She is of herself a fascinating story (September 2, 1975).

The next quote also comes from Renoir, he once more uses Mozart as a metaphor but adds a bit more glamour; it is widely used to describe Reiniger. Supposedly he said it at age 84 when asked about first meeting Reiniger. It is perhaps the best way to explain who she was: "What do you say if you find yourself suddenly in the presence of Mozart? Especially if this Mozart is a discerning woman, slightly plump and chatting like a magpie. A sentence came to my lips, but I did not dare to pronounce it. This sentence was 'You have fairy hands.' This was no flattery, it was simply a statement of fact. She creates miracles... (qt. in Gelder, 1981).

Reiniger's death was a loss for the animation and puppetry communities, although her filmography remains behind as her legacy. Despite all the films, puppet shows, drawings and silhouettes she cut, she fell into relative obscurity although she continued to have dedicated fans. Louis Hagen, Jr. still distributed her films through Primrose Productions, until Christel Strobel assumed the role as agent. Louis Hagen, Sr. advised his son not to involve himself financially with Reiniger, but Jr. said, "Lotte's films are translated into eight or ten different languages all over the world, so it was worthwhile in the end. But it took about 20 years [for them to be financially successful for me]" (qt. in Raganelli, 1999).

For years, Reiniger's films were viewed regularly in every country except the U.S. Due to copyright and distribution laws, it was difficult to obtain and view Reiniger's films (Carmen Education Associates distributed the films in North America [Polus, 1978, 29]). Any time her films were shown in the U.S., it was an exciting event for the lucky attendees. Even Canada and Mexico were treated more liberally to silhouette film showings on television.

An unfortunate circumstance of early cinema is that many of the films are gone. Reels were thrown away or stored in studio basements when their usefulness had passed. Conservation efforts came later when movies moved from a flash-in-the-pan sensation to a serious art form. Even worse than the lack of dedicated archives is celluloid deterioration. Early movies were made on film which decays. When exposed to average room temperature over an extended period, celluloid becomes brittle. Most of the earliest films were not stored properly, so they disintegrated into dust.

Many groundbreaking films are forever labeled as lost films, unless by some miracle, a copy appears in an archive, private library or studio vault. Quirino Cristiani's filmography falls under the lost film umbrella; his films burned in a fire (celluloid also happens to be highly flammable). Special effects pioneer George Méliès' film library of about 520 films was deemed lost. The French Army confiscated his prints, melted them down and turned them into shoe heels for the World War I war effort. In a fit of rage, he burned his negatives when his studio went out of business. Two hundred of his films survive thanks to the U.S. Library of Congress and private collections; they cemented Méliès' status in film history. A complete print of Fritz Lang's science fiction thriller *Metropolis* doesn't exist, but prints with extra footage have appeared in archives.

Due to the Battle of Berlin, Reiniger's original *Prinzen Achmed* negative was destroyed along with many of her other early films. For a period, she and Koch deemed these films lost, but intact copies were found outside Germany. Louis Hagen, Jr. led the first recovery of her films to pad the Primrose Productions library and others followed after her death. Her first silhouette film, 1919's *Das Ornament des verliebten Herzens,* was believed to have disappeared: Reiniger said in Bastiancich's 1981 interview, "It was sold almost immediately, in the U.S., for quite a high price, but I believe it is now lost" (1992/1981, 9). A 35mm print was owned by a film collector who also had a lab and film stock company; he more than likely purchased the print from the Institut für Kulturforschung (Lorent email to author, April 26, 2016). The print was eventually donated to the George Eastman Museum archives in Rochester, New York. The film was tinted an amber color and it was restored in 2000. No one in Europe was aware of this film until the restoration (Mebold, 2008, 15). The Deutsches Filminstitut (DIF) has the largest collection of Reiniger's work, followed by the British Film Institute (BFI). Other repositories that contain her films are the German Federal Film Archives, Danish Film Institute, Netherlands Film Museum, Deutsches Kinemathek Museum for Film and Television and the German National Archives.

Die Abenteuer des Prinzen Achmed survives thanks to the British Film Institute housing a copy. The only surviving *Prinzen Achmed* print ended up at the BFI due to the efforts of the National Film Archive. The Film Society was disbanded in 1939 due to the looming war, which resulted in the National Film Archive accessing their collection on July 1, 1942. In fear of bombings, nitrate film reels were sent out of London. Among these reels was a copy of *Prinzen Achmed* and thus was preserved Reiniger's most popular contribution to animation history (Stewart email to author, February 4, 2016). Partnering with the Deutsches Filminstitut (DIF), the BFI began restoring the film to its original glory in 1998.

Michael Schurig of the DIF was involved with the restoration. "We found a copy in England. It was already coloured with the colour we've restored it to. It was sort of an export copy, which meant between the scenes ... there'd be four or five blank frames with inked-in instructions as to how a given scene was to be coloured ... and the film copies were colored precisely in that way" (qt. in Raganelli, 1999).

The original negative had backgrounds that been hand-tinted in vibrant colors to contrast with the silhouette puppets' blackness, but Reiniger's coloring work was destroyed in the bombing. In 1926, a *Prinzen Achmed* art book was published, containing 32 full-page film stills. Moritz observed, "[The plates show] how much detail has been lost from the backgrounds in many scenes" (1996b, 51). The BFI's export copy did contain notes within the reel about how to color the film, but as the process to color films varied from country to country it is impossible to replicate the original. While the DIF and BFI were able to follow the instructions on how to color the export print, Reiniger's handiwork from the original is forever lost. The *Prinzen Achmed* reel would be accessed in 1949 to make a duplicate negative, in order to make copies for other archives (Stewart email to author, January 25, 2016).[5] The copies that exist now are the closest approximation to the original 1926 showing and Reiniger approved later restorations.

When Milestone Films released the DVD in 2001, an English translation of the restoration was provided with the press kit:

> There is no original German version of *Die Abenteuer des Prinzen Achmed* and no (camera) negative has been preserved. The oldest known material is housed at the National Film and Television Archive (NFTVA) at the British Film Institute: a colored nitrate positive on Agfa film stock containing edited English intertitles on Kodak and Pathe material from the years 1925–1927. This is not a screening copy, but rather base material for making new copies with added handwritten instructions concerning the coloring of the inserted lengths of white film.
>
> In order to safeguard this supposedly first-generation positive (hence from the camera negative) the NFTVA had three dupe-negatives made in 1949, 1955 and 1969. All the safeguarding material was in black-and-white and varies partly in lengths. The black-and-white dupe- negatives for safeguarding purposes were used as the base for all later copying activities, for example for the 16mm version from the eighties.
>
> For this restoration project, the colored nitrate copy was used as the basis for the first time. During viewing at the National Film and TV Archive in Berkhamsted the colored nitrate positive proved to be an optimum basis for a new restoration. Technically, the condition of the copy is good; the perforation is largely undamaged. The only apparent irreparable damage are light spots in the material and, owing to the earlier customary polishing, scratches and consequently particles of dust which have penetrated the emulsion of the film material.
>
> The colors amber, red, blue, green, yellow and a straw color used in the opening title are in excellent condition. There was no color plan for the restoration on which the assessment of color in a separate sequence could be found. Only by use of the handwritten instructions on the nitrate copy could the coloring be made in a manner that would correspond with an original copy.
>
> The censorship cards from the Bundesarchiv-Filmarchiv were used for the intertitles. The film copies available contained no original German title, but an English translation. The new restored version follows the censorship card of 15 January 1926 in regard to the titles and all 124 intertitles. The new linking titles produced by Trickstudio Wilk in Berlin are regarding typeface and the decoration of the background—grafted onto the original nitrate copy. The coloring of the titles was definitely copied from this copy. The intertitles which were not available for the English version, but which can be found on the censorship cards, were filled in but not colored. The arrangement of the acts also follows the censorship cards.
>
> Luckily it emerged that the complete score by Wolfgang Zeller was preserved in the Library of Congress[6] in Washington. It numbers among the very few remaining original compositions for silent films. The illustrations of scenes pasted on the score seem to confirm the order of acts and scenes.
>
> The total length of the restoration amounted to 1,770 meters. The copying work was carried out by "L'Immagine Ritrovata" in Bologna. Following the Desmet procedure, a colored 35mm screening copy was made from the black-and-white dupe negative, into which the new linking titles were edited [qt. in Pidhajny, 2001].

Determining how to restore Wolfgang Zeller's *Prinzen Achmed* score was another matter. When restoring old films, technicians run into the issues of finding original score sheets, composer notes and any sort of communication on how to present the piece. John Bishop wrote, "[T]he biggest problem with these [silent movie] scores from an academic perspective: their general lack of communicative editorial apparatus regarding written cues, synch points, and the decisions made in adapting the material. Handled with more transparency, this could have been a boon for scholars…" (2013, 185). Fortunately, Zeller's musical scores did remain: "Finally, as bears endless repeating to students of film music, nearly *all* silent-film music was intrinsically variable, performance-based phenomenon dependent upon the musical resources present at the theater in which the film was screened" (Bishop, 2013, 185).

Lotte Reiniger was also a pioneer in theatrical soundtracks. She hired Wolfgang Zeller to compose an original score for *Die Abenteuer des Prinzen Achmed*, which he reportedly wasn't compensated for but it did help propel his career. Cover of the original film score (courtesy the Detusches Filminstitut).

While the DIF retains a copy of Zeller's original score, the restoration soundtrack is not an exact copy of how it first heard in 1926. It is a good estimation of how the audience heard *Prinzen Achmed*'s score, but the original piece will forever be lost to history. Bruno Edera included an entry on Lotte Reiniger in his book *Full Length Animated Feature Films*. The entry is rife with mistakes: Reiniger never worked at UFA and a new version of *Prinzen Achmed* wasn't made in 1954. But it does shed some light on the film's restoration and showing: "[W]ith the help of.... Primrose Films, London, and the British Film Institute a new version [restored] of *Prince Ahmed* was made in 1954, following the instructions of Lotte Reiniger herself, and was shown on television in six episodes. This version was hand-coloured and scored with new music by Freddie Phillips, as W. Zeller's score had been only an accompaniment to the original film" (1977, 27). The restored 1954 edition couldn't recreate the original soundtrack, because it was scored for a large orchestra and the newer recordings for the DVDs only require a few musicians (Bastiancich, 1992/1981, 11). Modern showings of *Prinzen Achmed* are presented in a manner to recreate the original 1926 showing with a full orchestra.

The BFI treats the only remaining copy of *Prinzen Achmed* like gold, for in the world of animation Reiniger's film is priceless: one of the few examples of pre–Disney animation, European animation, and early feature film. Housed in a cold storage vault at the BFI Master Film Storage in Warwickshire, it remains one of the BFI's greatest treasures.[7]

Due to the efforts of the, Tübingen Stadtmuseum, Düsseldorf Stadtmuseum, Deutsches Filminstitut and the British Film Institute, Reiniger's works survive. Museums are cultural archives that display past and present examples of humanity's creations, but there has always been a problem getting people to acknowledge that animation and comic books are art. (As one of the oldest art forms in the world, puppetry is highly respected by historians and museums.) Animation and comic books, direct representations of pop culture, have always had a controversial place in sophisticated art and literature.

The 1950s pop art movement made aspects of popular culture part of the haute couture art world (with influences still visible today) and allowed the "strange art sensibilities" of Roy Lichtenstein, Andy Warhol, Jeff Coons and Jean-Michel Basquiat to test the definition of avant-garde. (Ironically, when pop art took hold, Frederic Wertham was spouting how comics were corrupting youth. The medium is still stigmatized.) It is very easy to demonstrate how these pop culture mediums are, in fact, art. The argument wasn't so easy to prove in animation's early days, until Walt Disney stood up as its champion.

Early experimental and avant-garde animators were termed artists in their day, but as opinions on animation changed, they were regarded more as filmmakers than animators. Reiniger represented a conundrum: although regarded as a filmmaker, her films represented a traditional folk art and the plots were fairytales. It was easy to brush her work away in terms of a kitschy folk craft and more adaptations of tired fairytales. When *Prinzen Achmed* premiered in 1926, Werner Dütsch commented on the film, but in a more general statement he said that art, like Reiniger's, needs "to abstain from this world's sordidness" as the majority of people lack the ability to understand it (p. 57). Dütsch is correct that most people fail to recognize art or at least the beauty in their midst due to preconceived notions. He also made the pejorative comment that Reiniger's silhouettes were "cute."

Some viewed Reiniger's films as boring, repetitious fairytales with shadowy figures, but as years passed the consensus pushed her into the world of high art for her unique skills and imagination. When Walt Disney started championing animation as an art in the U.S., his ideas along with his cartoons were imported to Europe. Disney's actions indirectly kept interest in Reiniger's film alive due to both drawing on the same source material and animation medium, but Reiniger was a pure European invention and could be a symbol of pride when and where she was pulled out of the archives.

While Walt Disney's motive was to bring animation into the world of high art, it was a publicity move. The biggest problem animation and other pop media faced: "Elite culture is assumed to be more complex, more innovative, and more individualistic that middle and lower class popular culture.... According to this hierarchy, a descent into the middle and lower classes yields culture that is increasingly simplistic, formulaic and collectively based" (Mikulak, 1996, 111). Animation is the offspring of mass media and consumption, evolving from the art of puppetry and the even more scandalous literature, comic books. As a direct descendent of mass media, animation's wide availability loses its appeal to the elite, high art culture, but accepting animation as an art form falls under the post-modernism and Dada schools (if one must assign the terms).

Animation is art and it crosses the line into fine art depending on the content and quality of the work as well as the audience's opinion. Douglas Brode created a metaphor that compares Walt Disney and his studio (and other animation studios):

> The more perceptive journalists of the 1930s and 1940s described him as "Leonardo da Disney" and "a twentieth-century Michelangelo," while "his bustling studio was compared to that of Rembrandt." It matters little that during the Renaissance every major artist was augmented by a coterie of apprentices, many of whom dabbed color onto canvas and cathedral walls. Such a then-accepted means of producing work hardly dims the truth: Da Vinci and Buonarroti were the geniuses behind everything recalled today by their names. This holds true for Leonardo da Disney, the twentieth century's Michelangelo [2004, xvii].

All Golden Age animation studios were modern renditions of classical art studios, where defining symbols of western culture were made. As society has changed, the artistic mediums, such as film, have changed with it and artists in newer mediums created more art that is a better representative for a larger population than mediums restricted to the high art definition. Diana Crane wrote *The Production of Culture: Media and the Urban Arts*, in which she discussed how the thought that elite art and pop culture are on separate spectrums is not only an outmoded thought pattern, but, "She finds that mass media ... reach audiences that are much larger and more heterogeneous than any reached by nineteenth century culture. Instead of distinguishing among audience members by blas, these media increasingly target people on the basis of lifestyle choices ... the hierarchy's assumptions by demonstrating that avant-gardes, which ... attract relatively small audiences, exist in all forms of culture and not merely those labeled in high art" (Mikulak, 1996, 112).

Disney's cartoons were and are viewed by audiences of every ethnic background and socio-economic level, much more than the latest sculpture installation at an exclusive gallery. His legacy has a wide-reaching impact on general audiences, but he knew that in order to have the broadest impact beyond cartoon fans, he had to appeal to the elitist groups.

Among Disney's many champions was art critic Dorothy Garfly, who wrote for the *Philadelphia Public Ledger* in 1932, "It is amazing that ... painters still cling tenaciously to the concept of the particular field as a narrow area bounded by four sides of canvas. Thousands of them are seriously working away day in, day out, turning quasi-reproductions of nature with less imagination and less genuine emotional feeling than is brought to the reproduction by a skillful manipulation of a camera." She said she believed that cartoons exhibited more life and beauty: "As a result we have witnessed the birth of an American art, something that has yet to be given us in the realm of paint." Perhaps her most astute observation was: "The reason why art has suffered a steady popular alienation may be found in its gradual and sometimes precipitate retreat from life, and its wanderings on the borderlands of the psychopathic. The art of the animated cartoon is as healthy as that of so many of our modernists is sickly."

Garfly said that art had disappeared from general society and was replaced with an unhealthy version, but that Walt Disney and his cartoons restored art to a healthier mentality with a widespread appeal like the great composers and artists of history. The broad and "healthy" appeal earned him many respected fans and friends in the elitist communities. Many were invited to his Burbank studio to observe the animation process and view how static artwork came alive on screen. "Perhaps Disney's interest in raising the cultural *niveau* of animation was merely a response to the enhanced cultural capital of Hollywood. For now, there were many exiled European intellectuals in Los Angeles: artists, writers and critics who had fled Nazi Germany or the Soviet Union and hoped to find a living or handout in California with its thriving culture industries" (Leslie, 2002, 163). Mexican fresco artist and muralist, Diego Rivera was among these many famous art friends and he once praised Disney in a short essay, "Mickey Mouse and the American Art":

> If we look at the characteristics of the animated cartoons which are shown in the movies, we find them to be of the purest and most definitive graphic style, of the greatest efficacy as social products, drawings joyous and simple that make the masses of tired men and women rest, make the children laugh till they are weary and ready for sleep and will let the grown-ups rest undisturbed.
>
> Not [sic] the style, the standardization of the drawings of details, the infinite variety of the groupings, as in the painted friezes of the Egyptian and the earthenware vases of the Greeks! And with all that, the added quality of motion!
>
> ... And the esthetes of the day will find that Mickey Mouse was one of the genuine heroes of American Art in the first half of the 20th Century ... [Rivera, 1932, 53–54].

Art historian, cartoonist and Disney fan Gary Apgar studied Walt Disney and Mickey Mouse's adventures as an international pop culture icons in *Mickey Mouse: Emblem of the American Spirit*. In the chapter "In the Temple of High Art," he documents how the Mouse entered the legendary world and in effect changed it. The first physical emergence of Disney in high art society was in Thomas Benton's *The Arts of Life in America*, a cycle of eight murals commissioned by the Whitney Museum of American Art (2015, 192). Mickey is painted into the mural *Political Business and Intellectual Ballyhoo* as the new "American art," which would start a cavalcade of modern artists trying their hand at their own renditions of the Mouse.

Yet it wasn't enough to only appear in high art; Disney wanted his studio's own artwork to be on display. In order to have animation recognized as art, Disney needed to bring animation to the heart of high art: museums. Apgar includes a quote from *Notes on the Art of Mickey Mouse* from the College Art Association that "no one was more surprised than Mr. Disney when the College Art Association invited him to lend a collection of his original Mickey Mouse and Silly Symphonies drawings to form a circuit exhibition of leading museums and colleges" (2015, 207). Disney might have been surprised at first, but he quickly turned the museum exhibits into a marketing ploy and a demonstration of how animation fit into the art pantheon. The "surprised outlook" reflects how Disney played up an aspect that he might not know anything about art, despite the intense studies he and his animators went through when they needed inspiration for features:

> [A]fter receiving honorary degrees from Harvard and Yale, Disney responded to the questions, "What is art?" by asking, "How should I know? Why should anybody be interested in what I think about art?" To another interviewer the following year he answered, "Art? You birds write about it, maybe you can tell me. I looked up the definition once, but I've forgotten what it is. I'm no art lover!"

Yet Disney was willing to express definite preferences for utilitarian craftsmanship. "I think someone who makes a bed with good lines, in which you can sleep comfortably, is more of an artist than the one who paints a picture which gives you a nightmare" [Mikulak, 1996, 117].

The first museum exhibit was held in early 1933 at the Kennedy Galleries in New York City.

> The New York show was just the first stop in this ambitious traveling exhibition. The Art Institute of Chicago would be the next (and most prestigious) of some 45 venues planned for a tour that ultimately included, among other host institutions, the Albright Gallery (Buffalo), the Evansville (Indiana), Temple of Fine Arts, Currier Gallery in Manchester, New Hampshire, the Milwaukee Art Institute, Portland (Oregon) Museum, Toledo Museum of Art, Brooks Memorial Art Gallery (Memphis) and the Washington County Museum of Fine Arts (Hagerstown, Maryland) [Apgar, 2015, 207].

Museum visitors were treated to a "behind the scenes" glimpse of the Disney creative process rarely seen outside Hollywood and the occasional documentary featurette. Another reason was to make use of the stacks of finished cels, conceptual art and other pieces gathering dust around the studio. Once a project was finished, studios had little use for the cels and production artwork. While these are now considered memorabilia, back in the Golden Age studios burned or threw them away. Chuck Jones recounted how Disneyland visitors received free cels as souvenirs in the year the park opened (1999, 273). The Disney studio scoured their holdings and supplied the museum exhibits with the best cels, conceptual art, photos and even specialty paintings. The animation studios later realized the potential fortune in cels and production art when they were being sold on secondary markets. The studios, by way of the Disney approach, developed an art trade and opened a new market for distinguished "cartoon collectors" later on (none of the exhibit art was for sale):

> In contrast to the museum, the Disney marketing program stressed the art's cult value as collectibles over their exhibition value as components of Disney films. Disney had co-opted techniques employed in the elite urban fine art galleries that prized art "for the few." ... This meant altering the art so it was more easily displayable as portraiture and creating scarcity out of ubiquity. Disney's announcement makes clear that, "although 475,000 paintings were photographed during the making of *Snow White*, only about 7000 of the most suitable will be marketed. All others ... have been destroyed" [Mikulak, 1996, 125].

Disney animation art would later be commercially available at several galleries in 1938: Julien Levy Gallery, Charles Sessler Gallery, Phillips Memorial Gallery, Leicester Gallery and Albert Roullier Art Galleries. The studio would make an exclusive arrangement with the Courvoisier Galleries to sell Disney art (Apgar, 2015, 214). The hunger for an original piece of Disney history hasn't abated and fans shell out huge sums for limited edition art. "Peyton Boswell ... suggests about a later gallery showing of *Fantasia* art, 'It's a good bet to predict the growth of a cult of Disney collectors, possibly along the lines of the Currier & Ives lovers, who today think nothing of trading the price of an automobile for a colored lithograph that once sold for 20 cents'" (Mikulak, 1996, 125).

There were two touring Disney exhibits and there wasn't a precise catalog of items within them, because "every four months, [Disney] supplies 40 new items from his current movie releases" for the shows, which were so popular that "the association's director of exhibits believes it will be necessary to keep one show available 'till kingdom come'" (Apgar, 2015, 207–08).

The Disney exhibits toured the country and were showcased at respected museums, giving the public the opportunity to see and begin to associate Disney animation with fine art, working on the common conception that if an item is displayed in a museum it is meant be awed and revered.

"During the 1930s and early 1940s, museum exhibits increasingly demonstrated how Disney animation defied the simplistic hierarchy of high art and low art despite their investment in aspects of the traditional cultural hierarchy" (Mikulak, 1996, 126). It was a brilliant move for the public to support the animation high art cause and the traveling museum exhibits put an inkling in high art society, along with support from Disney's cast of famous art friends and fans, that animation was, in fact, the new American art if not the finest example of it.

While Walt Disney built the foundation that has led animation to be regarded as "fine and true art," Reiniger's silhouette animation has always fallen into this category given her association with Weimar cinema and the silhouette's up and down history as an art form. For any animated film, story always remains the key component, while animation serves as conveyance method in which the story is told. Silhouettes are flat and static creations that only spring to life when transformed into puppets with jointed appendages. They appear to many as rudimentary in their locomotion compared to Disney's traditional cel art, but it is these differences that cause animation to be high art. A painting can take any form using any medium from canvas or wood as a backing with watercolors to decoupage for the artist's renderings. Animation is as versatile if not more than a painting given the central idea "the illusion of life," which can be interpreted as an expression of emotion and sound *a la* Oskar Fischinger's films, a mouse's adventures or a saucy revisualization of *Carmen*.

Walt Disney developed a fast friendship with the Museum of Modern Art and the museum further cemented his relationship with high art.[8] In 1932, the founding director Alfred H. Barr set the groundwork for MoMA's film library, hiring Iris Barry as the film curator. Barry was one of the founding members of the Film Society of London as well as a film critic for *The Spectator* and *The Daily Mail*. She championed film as one of the finest examples of twentieth century artistic media and established the first U.S. film archive. Also a Disney fan, she said, "Nothing more joyous or more genuinely American than the Disney cartoons has ever reached the screen.... Their simplicity, their tremendous gusto and defiant disrespectfulness at once caught the public fancy and steadily maintained it, despite some few flights into artiness and sentimentality in the longer experimental features" (qt. in Mikulak, 1996, 123). At the tenth anniversary of the Museum of Modern Art (May 10, 1939), the film library's president John Hay Whitney said, "I feel that modern art is not confined to painting and sculpture. The liveliest visual art of the twentieth is the motion picture" (MoMA Archives, 39.1 A/B). This modus operandi justified Barry's acquisition of Hollywood, foreign and experimental films and even the first Disney cartoons into the library:

> An additional impetus to seek out Hollywood films came from Film Library president John Hay Whitney's financial investments and personal connections in the industry. His letter of introduction and funds made possible a late summer dinner party that Mary Pickford threw in 1935 to let Iris Barry and her husband lobby for donations to start the Film Library. Walt Disney was among the attendees whom they solicited. He immediately accommodated their requests for prints of a number of his films as well as production art showing the animation process. By 1936, the Museum included the early Mickey Mouse cartoons *Plane Crazy* (1928) and *Steamboat Willie* (1928) in their circulating film programs devoted to American silent film and the birth of the talkies, respectively [Mikulak, 1996, 122].

9. Fine Art and Resurgent Praise

Also in 1936, Barry included *Steamboat Willie* in a program alongside *The Jazz Singer* and *All Quiet on the Western Front* "illustrating the development of cinematography" (Apgar, 2015, 212). It was a start to future exhibits of Disney's art, an inclusion of a *Snow White* cel in the collection, and multiple viewings over the years of Disney's cartoons.

Mikulak wrote, "Iris Barry's program notes give a wide-ranging account of animation's forerunners, influences and developments, which culminated in the Disney studio's aesthetic exploitation of the new possibilities of technological in synchronized sound and color" (1996, 122). From her tenure at the Film Society of London, Barry was aware of Lotte Reiniger and *Prinzen Achmed*—it was a very popular film, but from my own research at MoMA I didn't discover any record of her attempting to acquire the film. I did discover that MoMA had some publicity stills from *Prinzen Achmed*, but none of the departments were interested in them and they have since been lost.

Walt Disney would be added to MoMA's board of trustees in 1944. At the tenth anniversary celebration, Disney was asked to make a speech that answered why animation, not simply motion pictures, are an integral part of modern culture and high art:

> It was only four years ago that there was considerable talk about the real need for this film library and tonight it's an accomplished fact. My congratulations! I believe that at the time it was said what a profound tragedy it would be if the record of motion pictures was lost to posterity. Tragic to posterity or tragic to us? For the human critter just naturally can't swallow the thought of himself and his life's work passing into oblivion completely.
>
> I understand that's why those kings of Egypt built their tombs and pyramids to last forever. And the fascination of the past has drawn millions to the pyramids for a look. But think of how much more interesting if we had motion picture records of the actual building of the pyramids. If we could see and hear those old kings buried and how exciting it would be to watch Nero fiddling while Rome burned.
>
> Well, our film library will be on the right side of the ledger there. Think of the knowledge we'll give posterity. The way we talk and dress and act and the ladies' hats especially. And perhaps a thousand years from now or some far time when our world is ruled by tolerance and reason, posterity will delve into these old film archives of today and see great cities ruled by gangsters; see the insane savagery of war; and perhaps the world will be so changed that our tragedies will seem strange, unbelievable, incredible, and that will make posterity feel superior. A very pleasant feeling, another gift from us.
>
> At the very least, our film library will have contributed an accurate human record of a few years in the time of man. The history of us as recorded in the history of motion pictures [MoMA Archives, 39.1 A/B].

As with the Disney revisionist actions, Walt Disney's drive to have animation recognized within the fine art community was more for his studio's benefit than any of his competitors. Not only did his efforts succeed, but they also strengthened his association with animation and dominance in the animation industry. Despite these negative impacts for other animators, the very fact that he established animation as a respected medium in art culture outweighs the negatives. While there isn't any doubt that Reiniger was a superb scherenschnitte artist and animator, Disney's actions opened the door for her career to explored in the same manner as Disney and other animation giants. In fact, it was probably due to Disney's efforts that MoMA had a Warner Brothers exhibit…

> … in September 1985, when Warners became the first animation studio to be given a full-scale retrospective by New York's Museum of Modern Art. For four and a half months, the ultra-prestigious MoMA opened some of its august gallery space to drawings of stuttering pigs and libidinous skunks, and on weekends showed films with titles like *Wabbit Twouble*. Most of the time, the screenings drew turn-away crowds; often as not, the cartoons elicited—in addition to the predictable laughter—applause both after and *before* they emblazoned the screen [Schneider, 1990 p. 19].

Cartoon artwork and films were shown at MoMA many times throughout the twentieth century well before 1985, so it wasn't the first studio. Cecile Starr built on Disney's wishes to see animation regarded well within art circles and she hoped that other animated works would reap the same benefits, which they did to a degree:

> I can remember my first visits to the Museum of Modern Art in New York City some decades ago, when a small handful of people, gawking and perplexed, could be found at the Museum's handful of bewildering Picassos. In contrast, on a recent visit to that enlarged, jam-packed museum, I heard a loud voice call out excitedly to his companions: "Hey, look, a whole room of Picassos!" It seems inevitable to me that some day, in some elegant new hi-tech museum, someone will holler out in recognition and affection: "Hey, look, a whole room of Fischingers!"—or Len Lyes—or any of the great artist animators of our century. They are the undiscovered treasures of our time [Starr, 1987, 11].

Disney's importance to the animation industry and artistic world inspired fans to further explore the medium and discover hidden treasures, like Reiniger, that would otherwise remain buried in archives. The fact that Reiniger made an animated film before Walt Disney is a symbol of pride for Germany and due to Disney's popularity, Reiniger's associates were determined to preserve her legacy not just for posterity but as a demonstration of alternate animation methods and of scherenschnitte art. Let's not forget that Reiniger is one of the more positive aspects of German culture to emerge from the twentieth century.

Despite being part of popular culture, Reiniger was never officially recognized within pop culture as Disney art has been. Reiniger's career has been preserved and reinvigorated by the high art world as an example of how animation can be used to make more "artistic" films that fall outside Disney's sphere of influence. She is lauded as an example of how there is more potential in animation than creating repetitive fairytale plots (Reiniger is cited as a truer adaptation of the Grimms' stories) and talking-singing animals.

Reiniger's modern, small yet strong popularity is spurred by Disney's own. Animation fans seek other animation with solid story and beautiful art that can't be substituted by cheap, mass-produced cartoons. Reiniger's silhouette films fulfill that desire with their beauty, simplicity and complete otherness … at least until the next Disney movie premieres.

10

Lotte's Legacy

One question I continued to ask as I researched this book: Why was Reiniger forgotten and why wasn't more written about her in animation scholarship? The reliable William Moritz echoes my question:

> Such a distinguished biography—and a filmography of more than 70 films—begs the question of why Lotte Reiniger remains rather undervalued. Despite the occasional nod to her has having made one feature-length film before Walt Disney (when indeed she made two), most critics today still tacitly assume that silhouettes constitute a secondary or inferior form of animation, so that Disney's cartoon *Snow White* counts as a real first feature [1996b, 42].

The obvious answer would be a combination of her gender, nationality, independence as an artist, and her choice to use silhouette animation. Yet there seemed to be a less evident reason for the footnoted and one-sentence coverage. When undertaking the research for this book, I encountered many people who were excited about the mere mention of Lotte Reiniger and were eager to help me document her life and career. From these encounters, I noticed a pattern but didn't think much of it beyond the normal repeat of information that turns up in research. I didn't think an answer would come to me at all, until one day during the research on World War II animation, and after a conversation with CalArts animation professor Maureen Furniss, it occurred to me in a "Eureka!" moment. Pierre Jouvanceau summed up some of my thoughts in his prologue:

> Almost 80 years after [*Prinzen Achmed*] it is still shown regularly in many cinematheques. It is quoted in most histories of the cinema, even those which for the most part spurn animation. It is analysed in symposia, dissected in universities. But *Prince Achmed*, while it has guaranteed Lotte Reiniger her place in history, has eclipsed most of her other work.... Over the years, *Prince Achmed* has become a museum piece and the whole of silhouette animation, too often thought of in terms of this film alone, is generally seen as dated, obsolete, even dead [2004, 11].

Reiniger's films are far from obsolete or dead. Jouvanceau notes that *Prinzen Achmed* is mentioned in most cinematic histories and "analyzed in symposia, dissected in universities"—but that is why she has been forgotten. Reiniger fell out of popular culture or by some standards has never been a part of popular culture as she never belonged to any overt group. Therefore, she has been regulated to only the world of academic recourse, which isn't the best commercial way to advertise to the masses. Rachel Palfreyman writes: "[T]he neglect is in part due to the difficulty of contextualising Reiniger combined with her technical virtuosity which sees her regulated to 'craft' rather than art" (2011, 6). I don't support Palfreyman's idea that Reiniger's work is considered a "craft" over cinematic film, as my research only yielded evidence that Reiniger is considered a cinematic artist. I do agree that the trouble categorizing Reiniger's work has seen her relegated to high art and only high art, with the lofty asterisk that she animated a feature film before Disney. It is quite paradoxical as most of animation's history rests in pop culture: for one of the animation pioneers to not even cross over is astonishing. Even Cristiani's political satire animated films were consumed by general audiences and voyaged into pop culture for their brief existence.

In the early part of their career, Reiniger and Koch were very successful and did entertain the public, but it was due to the Weimar culture's hunger for new and experimental films that complimented the day's intellectual art movements. World War II had considerable impact, forcing her to flee and concentrate on basic survival rather than artistic development. Her postwar Primrose Productions resurgence was remarkable and her film output increased, but these silhouette fairytale films were primarily shown to children and Reiniger was condemned to that niche market. After Koch's death, she withdrew from animation and thusly really any chance for her to enter the pop culture arena. Puppetry is an artistic medium that straddles the fine line between pop culture and high art. When Reiniger made shadow puppetry, her main focus in the 1960s and '70s, her shows had limited performances, very few were recorded, and she stuck with a niche audience: children.

Pop culture's influence is the reason why many celebrities and historical figures are still remembered when they should have faded from the modern consciousness. When it comes to animation's relevance in pop culture, Walt Disney and his company have had a big influences. That's one of the main reasons why animation is such a popular art medium. Reiniger was never part of the group even at the height of her popularity with *Prinzen Achmed* and her Primrose Productions films. Jouvanceau once more writes a poignant description about this thought:

> Reiniger's strength was her base halfway between series animation, then widely distributed and appealing to mass audiences, and the German avant-garde cinema, born as the intellectual and visual response of local artists to the American model. It was the mid-way positioning that brought Reiniger her success—it was how, without working it out in advance, she was able to "reconcile" the upholders of a modern cinematography closely linked to visual innovation with the defenders of a narrative and figurative tradition which was doubtless favoured by far larger audiences. But it also brought isolation. Unclassifiable thanks to this apparently paradoxical duality of influence and also to her constancy in continuing to use a technique already deemed outdated—but admired for the same reasons–Reiniger found herself marginalised from mainstream cinema history, a strange and unusual personality who could not be labeled or classified within the important movements of the period [2004, 41–42].

Reiniger never received mainstream attention, because she simply was never part of a mass media or cultural phenomenon. "Reiniger's contemporaries, such as Renoir and Brecht, were critically acclaimed and their discourse positions have been secured. However, not everyone has seen a French art film or play, but most people have seen an animated film" (K.V. Taylor, 2011, 120). Audiences usually *only* view animated films that are made by a known studios, associated with a popular franchise, or to keep children entertained. Older films, unless they are associated with a known studio, go unwatched, except by fans who seek them out. That is not to say that Reiniger wasn't in the public eye; she just wasn't to the same extent as her contemporaries. She and Koch operated on the outskirts or within the shadows of popular culture. Suffice to say they preferred it that way. It allowed them to nestle within their own silhouetted world, free of the demands of an opinionated studio or focus group.

In *7 Minutes: The Life and Death of the American Animated Cartoon,* Norman M. Klein wrote an intriguing yet idiomatic argument about how animation is a living historic document that supports why Reiniger occupies a unique place in animation history. His approach is from an academic stance yet he uses popular media consumption to explain their eminent longevity while still retaining the ethos of the past. Klein stressed that he doesn't want people to take his idea in the context of "how animation fits into the historiography" (frankly there are already a lot of books and essays on that subject), but rather as how cartoons affect how people remember events (1993, 106). As Reiniger was never with a definable group, arguably she can't be placed within the usual historiography but she can be observed as a person who resides within her lifetime's zeitgeist, yet outside, bringing back my "outside looking in" metaphor. It fits into how animation also inhabits an entertainment niche outside the popular realm of socially acceptable media, while at the same time she is outside the commonly accepted animation types, i.e., traditional, CGI, puppet stop-motion. Through Reiniger's silhouette films, audiences remember how one woman viewed an idealized world in the twentieth century and used cinematic animation as her medium to capture it.

> After 1934, the decline of print as the defining medium for audiences can be traced very clearly, in background layout, animation technology and technique. The cartoon literally reveals a shift in paradigm, very coherently. It documents precisely when audiences turn from print-driven entertainment to cinema-driven entertainment. [Then in the 1950s,] cartoons respond to new consumer industries like television.
>
> ... What does the cartoon as evidence tell us about the history of media? It tells us that media must be studied by the evidence of how an audience remembers (entertainment, leisure, personal details, history, politics). At one point, much of this memory was left to print, then to film, now to video. But the record in cartoons warns us to be cautious in our carbon dating. According to the cartoon "evidence," it takes quite a long while for a cycle like that. Despite the popularity of film, the '20s were still very much a print era. Only in the late '30s is there clear cartoon evidence that movies have begun to replace the way memories are stored by an audience [Klein, 1993, 107].

Reiniger offers her audience an alternate way to remember the early twentieth century instead of the usual Disney, Warner Brothers, Van Buren, Walter Lantz or MGM cartoons. Hers is a reflection of the old, European imagination interpreted through the reasonably new cinematic art.

> Why are cartoons such useful documents in this matter? ... [A]nimation must be guided by changes in perception more directly than any other area of mass culture I know, except perhaps advertising.... The world that cartoons turn upside down must be perceptually in tune very directly with a specific year. For example, audiences today still love Second World War cartoons, though we may fail to get all the gags about rationing or whether a trip is necessary. Something in the way cartoon humor was assembled simply operates as its own code. That does not mean that humor is the international language. *Quite* the opposite. It means that humor must be lodged inside its moment to be funny [Klein, 1993, 107].

Reiniger doesn't operate on the principle of humor for her silhouette films. Klein's idea that "humor must be lodged inside a moment" to generate laughter can be interpreted as establishing an emotional connection with the audience. To make her connection, Reiniger relies on the language of fairytales and how the same stories resonate from one generation to another; they are lodged within her films to communicate her idea of beauty and take on the stories. Klein also answers the question about why people continue to laugh or in regard to Reiniger latch onto her fairytales:

> I believe they laugh because the humanity of the cartoon is coordinated in subtle ways: gestures, turns of phrase, characterization, they all operate so well together. The notion that Disney features are timeless has tended to obscure the crucial modernity that makes cartoons funny. They are their own brand of ethnic correlative. Cartoons are timeless because they look—and feel—like the year they were made. They are the upside-down version of entertainment and consumer rituals popular that season. As historical documents, they are priceless journeys into the signified [Klein, 1993, 107].

Or they are priceless windows into the past that offer glimpses of how people interpreted the world, but rather than depicting static art on paper or another medium, it is via "living" film.

Marginalized works, like Reiniger's, are the favorite of academics due to their obscurity, making them perfect topics to discuss how they uphold this art movement or were meant to convey this message by over-analyzing the work to find the hidden meaning within each word or every placement of a shadow puppet.

There have been several informative and well-produced documentaries on Reiniger, including *Lotte Reiniger: Homage to the Inventor of the Silhouette Film* by Katja Raganelli and *Lotte Reiniger: Tanz der Schatten* by Susanne Marschall, Rada Bieberstein and Kurt Schneider. None reflected on Reiniger's place within animation history, except when it was related to silhouette animation and the discrepancy of *Prinzen Achmed* being the first animated film. *Tanz der Schatten* features interviews with Michel Ocelot and Hannes Rall, but not with any other animators. None of the documentaries even address her importance in shadow puppetry's history. Other scholars have made connections to animation; Taylor notes how Henry Selick and Ben Hibon[1] were inspired by Reiniger's style and Jouvanceau describes Reiniger's impact on silhouette animation and says she is usually regarded as the only silhouette animator. Reiniger has had a bigger impact on the modern animation industry that extends beyond silhouettes and shadow. Reiniger's biggest advocate in the U.S. was film historian Cecile Starr; during her teaching days, she showed *Prinzen Achmed* to her students at Bennington College in Vermont. "Their reaction? 'They're terribly impressed with [Reiniger's] career,' she said. 'When [they discover it was made in] 1926, they are definitely overwhelmed by it and by the idea that a woman made it'" (qt. in Liebenson, 2001). Many contemporary animators use her animation techniques, style and storytelling methods to inspire their own works. No one has ever asked them how Reiniger shaped their careers, until now. At the beginning of cinematic film history, Lotte Reiniger and Carl Koch were at the height of technological advances and experimental with the animated film. During the filming of *Prinzen Achmed*, Bartosch and Ruttmann (especially the former) received high praise for their experimentation in animated special effects, but Reiniger deserves her own credit for her curiosity about exploring a fledgling medium. Reiniger's sense of humor had her downplay her involvement with technological development as she grew older, saying she was more interested in the paper cutting and story development, but she was just as eager to try the newest technology. "Whatever she said on the subject, Lotte Reiniger was actually first off the mark to bring her animation stand certain improvements" (Jouvanceau, 2004, p. 114). Koch helped her implement changes and invented his own to better the silhouette animation process.

Throughout her career, Reiniger credited her husband with most of the advances, including the multiplane camera, although that should be left in her wheelhouse as she constantly sought to improve her tricktisch. It becomes a question of personality about

Reiniger and her relation to technology. In her early career, she displayed a great drive to experiment and learn new technologies. In her "Moving Silhouettes," she wrote with an amicable competitive spirit:

> A world of experimental variety was thrown open [for film]; but by exploitation of the technical resources and the artistic possibilities of this new medium, the film developed to such an extent that it now looks back ungratefully and rather with scorn on the good old days—the basis of its glory. I regard this as rather unjust. However, such are the penalties of evolution. Artists and commercial people constantly try—sometimes working together, but more often opposing each other—to discover new means to bring fresh life and further development to the new art [1936, 14].

Reiniger never pitted herself against her fellow animators, but she did believe her silhouette animation process was superior to the popular cel animation.

She could even arguably assert that silhouette animation was superior in the animation industry's early days, since other animators were experimenting with processes and trying to refine them so animation could be easier to manufacture. Reiniger's animation style was extremely simple: she needed her silhouette puppets, tricktisch and a camera, then all she had to do was point and click. She could make an entire film with Koch's help.

After *Prinzen Achmed*'s 1926 release, the animation industry hit its biggest development stage and it was due to Walt Disney. Stephen Cavalier summed up the state of the animation industry at the time and what Disney did:

> By 1928 animation had enough blueprints to work for both commercial, technical and artistic successes. European abstract animations such as Oskar Fischinger, Walther Ruttmann, Viking Eggeling, Fernand Léger and Hans Richter had pioneered animation as high art, but the American Winsor McCay had shown that mainstream cartoons could also be beautifully crafted and of fine quality. American producers of animation like James Stuart Blackton, Otto Messmer, Pat Sullivan, Raoul Barré, Earl Hurd, the Fleischer brothers, Paul Terry and John Randolph Bray, and to a lesser extent on the other side of the Atlantic, Charles-Emile Reynaud, Émile Cohl, Ladislaw Starewicz, Arthur Melbourne-Cooper, George Studdy and Lotte Reiniger had created cartoons that could be funny, entertaining and commercially successful, while developing and applying technical systems that moved the process toward something practical and sustainable. It just needed someone to pull the best of these artistic and commercial ideas together: step forward, Walt Disney [2011, 96].

Walt Disney would continue to develop the animation medium up until his death in 1966 and his studio continues with animation innovation (although it went through a dry spell from his death to the late 1980s). He even asserted in 1956, "I kind of like to think it was the nicest thing I ever did for this business when I realized that it was not like the old art of painting and things, that it was a new art. That it was a mass production for survival…. Of course, the industry was set up that way … before I came along. But I think I organized more mass production things than had ever been used in the industry before" (qt. in Barrier, 2007, 81).

When Koch and Reiniger were forced to return to Germany to take care of Reiniger's ailing mother, they used silhouette animation as a refuge from the bombs and death outside. Silhouette animation was a comfort to both husband and wife and when the war ended, her creative ambitions weren't thwarted but they did change. Walt Disney was interested in industrializing animation for profit and to further his idea of art, but Reiniger and other animators were more interested in pursuing animation for art's sake alone. She very much adhered to Winsor McCay's aesthetic views on animation, although she wasn't opposed to industrial animation and she did make it her trade. McCay said, "Animation should be an art, that is how I conceived it, but as I see it, what you fellows have done with it is make it a trade" (qt. in Cavalier, 2011, 64).

As Reiniger believed that her films were art, she never had a character who went on serial adventures or could be mass-merchandised. Each film was a singular piece of art that stood on its own and reflected a traditional yet new storytelling approach. In other words, Reiniger never created a franchise. Franchises are one of the prime ways that animation projects are funded, because they have the potential to generate huge profits for years. Walt Disney didn't invent the franchise formula, but he perfected it and the formula continues to work to this day, although tweaks have had to be made to take into account audiences' consumption habits with new technology. Taylor spun her own take on this idea, by noting that *Prinzen Achmed* with its lack of famous actors "damaged its critical reception and limited its popular appeal" (2011, 26). Taylor was referring to the live action movie stars that had massive fan followings and inspired their own franchises (2011, 26). Fan followings play a huge part in determining an animation property's future in whether or not it can be transformed into a profitable franchise. If a property becomes popular, companies seek to develop it further with more movies and TV shows as it achieves longevity. All of Reiniger's films are stand-alone pieces (there are some that revolve around the common theme of opera or *commedia dell'arte*, but aren't connected beyond that) without recurring sequels. Her films never developed into a franchise and while she does have a fan following, it never gained traction.

After World War II and during her 1970s world tour, her method of silhouette animation became very "old school" and aspiring animators viewed her as a grand dame of the medium. When Reiniger hit her career highpoint for animation production with Primrose Productions during the 1950s, her animation habits were well ingrained into her methodology. Coté quoted her: "I like my old puppets best: they're used to moving around on their own. Their joints are broken in when they're old, so they take up their natural positions more easily" (1954, 16). She didn't want to change nor did she need to, because she was comfortable with the familiarity and where it had taken her career.

Jouvanceau describes this period as "an abandonment of ambitious projects in favour of a more regular and sometimes sterile output and saw a return to more traditional equipment and a renunciation of her previous experimentation" (2004, 114). He fails to recognize that Reiniger was at the height of her artistic accomplishment and she was under a strict deadline to deliver silhouette films for a television series. Experimentation wasn't a luxury she could afford. Reiniger refined her technique during this period using the technology she knew. As technology improved, however, and the animation process became more streamlined, she didn't want to update her own techniques. She was more in line with John Lasseter's approach to animation and technology: "The art challenges the technology, and the technology inspires the art" (Price, 2008).

Her animation technique had remained the same, thus she became a master silhouette animator. In her earlier days, she was challenged by the medium and was inspired to animate all manner of ideas. As she came in her autumnal years, she trusted the technology to help her create silhouette films and while they were artworks, she eventually reached a point when the technology was no longer a challenge. She embodied a wish that Chuck Jones expressed in an interview:

> I do wish people would ... explore a discipline once they've discovered it, and not jump from discipline to discipline.... When you come right down to it, isn't it true that one artist is identifiable by what he contributes to other artists, and not at all what the public thinks of him? Every artist of any importance, and that includes writers and musicians, is a person from whom other artists can glean something to use in the following generations. If Beethoven had written a symphony, then turned

around and tried to do jazz, we should never have understood anything about him. People should stay with what they do, and then it would be useful to all of us [qt. in Lewell, 1982, 141].

Koch died in 1963 when Reiniger was in her early sixties. Reiniger attributed much of her career's success to her collaboration with her husband, which is one of the reasons she quit animating but also another justification to remain stagnant. As a sign of grief, keeping close to her tried and true silhouette animation process, she kept her husband close. She might have viewed progressing with her animation career with new techniques as dishonoring his memory. Reiniger, however, really just lost the desire to carry on animating, because Koch wasn't by her side. Reiniger was also a senior citizen by the time it became optional for her to shake-up her animation process. It is difficult for people to learn new processes as they age and is not always a feasible course. While Reiniger was interested in new technology, she didn't want to learn it. She preferred her own methods and found it superior, if not comforting, compared to modern animation processes.

"For the contributors to the animation column of the monthly magazine *Fluide glacial*, Lotte Reiniger's death offered the chance to take a public stand against the chorus of praise in the press, from *The Times* to *Le Monde*, and say bluntly that these 'feeble stories of love between princes and princesses, such as *Aucassin et Nicolette*, and *The Adventures of Prince Ahmerd* [sic], were 'animated like jumpy grasshoppers'" (qt. in Jouvanceau, 2004, 122). Another critic angrily wrote, "The worst thing is that, during the course of her life, Reininger [sic] made at least 50 films, and it's 80 times the same thing" (qt. in Jouvanceau, 2004, 207)

Critics quick to judge silhouette animation are the same ones who are quick to call animation a genre rather than a medium. Early silhouette animation is "primitive" due to the lack of development in that specific form of animation, and also because most silhouette films were made during a more primitive technological time. All early films, animation and live action, are primitive compared to the latest CGI spectacle to grace the silver screen.

In his Walt Disney biography *The Animated Man*, Michael Barrier chronicled how Walt sought to improve his studio's animation quality. He was practically driven to replicate the human form as perfectly as possible. Barrier quoted a 1937 article that Walt Disney is said to have written, "Mickey Mouse Presents," where "he articulated his growing ambitions for animation invoking 'caricature' as his goal" (2007, 132). Disney wrote,

> While we have improved greatly in our handling of human figures it will be many years before we can draw them convincingly as we can animals.... The audience knows exactly how a human character looks and acts [and] therefore accepts our caricatured interpretations of animals without reservation. Some day our medium will produce great artists capable of portraying all emotions through the human figure. But it will still be the art of caricature and not a mere imitation of great acting on stage or screen [qt. in Barrier, 2007, 132].

Barrier follows up this quote with an interview with Disney conducted by Douglas W. Churchill of the *New York Times* in March 1938, in the wake of *Snow White*'s success. Barrier notes, "Disney again used the crucial phrase 'a caricature of life'" (Barrier, 2007, 132). He also included this quote:

> Our most important aim is to develop definite personalities in our cartoon characters. We don't want them to be just shadows, for merely as moving figures they would provoke no emotional response from the public. Nor do we want them to parallel or assume the aspects of human beings or human actions. We invest them with life by endowing them with human weaknesses which we exaggerate in a humorous way. Rather than a caricature of individuals, our work is a caricature of life [qt. in Barrier, 2007, 132].

Following these two quotes, Barrier wrote that "'caricature' has a parasitic sound," although I find the term as a less serious art form (similar to how cartoon has a juvenile association) (Barrier, 2007, 132). The "caricature of life" would eventually transform into the more poetic phrase "illusion of life" dubbed by Ollie Johnston and Frank Thomas. Disney quotes explain the evolution of the medium through the Golden Age and mirror Reiniger's own attempts to make her own silhouettes not mere black husks on the screen, but with a glimpse of life interpreted through her puppets. For Disney, his glimpse of life was projected through ink and paint on celluloid sheets.

Barrier further cements the differences between Reiniger and Disney by invoking, coincidentally, Jean Renoir. "[Walt Disney] was working his way through the artificial elements of animation ... so as to emerge with an art form that was unmistakably artificial, did not turn its back on animation's fundamental characteristics, but still had the breadth and impact of those rare live-action films—Jean Renoir's, say—that had fully captured life on film" (Barrier, 2007, 132). Renoir is one of the pillars of French cinema, if not global cinema, with his films that challenged social conventions and revealed the horrors of World War I. His films are described as thought-provoking reflections on the human condition in the early twentieth century. Although real-life drama inspired his work, they were all fake yet they still captured life on film.

Renoir's quote about his friend Reiniger is the most popular blurb used to publicize her work: "She had fairy hands." The French director was keen to comment on life using the cinema's artificial magic, and when viewing *Prinzen Achmed* he was carried away by the fantasy world Reiniger created with a pair of scissors and cardboard. To Renoir, Reiniger's animation was pure magic. Although he knew it was artificial trickery, it captured the same real-life emotions as his own films. As the careers of Reiniger and Disney progressed, their grasp on human movement and emotion improved to the point where they truly represented the illusion life.

Chuck Jones is the Gene Kelly of animation while Walt Disney is the Fred Astaire; Jones found several ways to one-up Disney in the industry. He took the beautiful "illusion of life" quote from Johnston and Thomas and made it better, this fitting into how Reiniger, Disney and other animators actually replicated life: "The great wonder of animation is not the illusion of life but of life itself" (C. Jones, 1999, 263).

Cecile Starr and I have noted that while Reiniger never felt held back due to her gender, she was withheld due to financial constraints. Starr wrote, "[G]reat sums were spent on films of little or no imagination while so little was available for the films she wanted to make" (Starr, 1980, 19). The origin of this resentment comes from the 1936 article "Moving Silhouettes." Reiniger ended the article about music and synchronized puppet movements with a comment concerning how each musical score presented its own set of problems,

> [A]nd this is perhaps good, for without it I certainly could not help feeling a certain amount of bitterness towards an industry that fails to appreciate the hard work put into the creation of a silhouette film—after all an artistic achievement—yet is always ready to squander money on things of little importance [1936a, 18].

Reiniger was a kind woman with a type of self-deprecating humor that was more humbleness than anything. She was 37 when she wrote that piece, still young, but old enough to be aware of the film industry's attitude of profit over art.

The quote is one of the few examples that negative feelings existed within her, but it is a sentiment expressed by all animators, puppeteers and artists. Take out the term "silhouette film" and insert any art form and Reiniger's sentence sums up all artists' feelings. Reiniger's critics say she did the same thing over and over again, but this quote is evidence she wanted to experiment more and possibly even make another silhouette feature. Her biggest obstacles were funding (a problem all artists suffer) and the outbreak of World War II. If Germany had remained peaceful and without Nazi ideology, Reiniger might have had the chance to animate another silhouette feature film, grow her studio, and maybe even test new technology while her curiosity was still ignited. It is even possible that Germany could have been an European animation powerhouse with Reiniger as a possible leader, if not founder, had other Germans desired to compete with Disney Studios and raised funds.

The animation industry primarily exists to generate money, just like any branch of entertainment. The bigger animation studios (Walt Disney/Pixar, DreamWorks, Blue Sky, Laika, Aardman, Studio Ghibli and more) are at the top; independent studios and animators on the bottom. The bigger studios receive funding with promises to return the investment plus more with a hit feature film or TV series that could become a popular franchise complete with merchandising. While many of the films from these studios are hits, others fail to impress audiences and return the investment. One wonders how some ideas were ever green-lit, while other, better ideas were left on the drawing table. The independent studios and animators want to make films that resonate with audiences and contribute to the art world but, as Reiniger wrote, money is hard to come by and squandered somewhere else. It has always been the case for any artist trying to make a career. Think about Leonardo da Vinci's many unfinished projects and attempts to find a patron. Nowadays, however, there is more opportunity for animators, puppeteers and artists to get their work "out there"; the harder part is getting noticed now.

* * *

I have wondered many times what would have happened had Lotte Reiniger and Walt Disney met. Would the event been as grand as Quirino Cristiani's recollections and would Disney have offered Reiniger a job? Or would it have been subtler like his interaction Tezuka with Disney expressing his admiration for the lady animator? The animation industry was too small for Disney not to have heard about Reiniger and he might have even watched some of her films as he did to keep tabs on industry developments and seeking inspiration.

Reiniger would have presented him with a silhouette as a gift. I assume it would have been of Mickey Mouse or even a portrait of Disney. They might have discussed their various techniques, vested interests in fairytales, projects they each wished to work on, and Reiniger would have assuredly inserted her wicked humor in some part of the conversation. I doubt she would have accepted a job from him as she preferred her own methods of animation over a studio schedule.

When comparing their careers, one can easily find the surface parallels with their shared love of fairytales, telling intricate and fabulous stories, and wanting their films to astonish and entertain. The beginning of their careers also bears similarities in the rudimentary ways both animators clawed their way to the top of the animation industry in their respective countries. Beyond their individual starts and other subtle details, the pair lack any career commonalities. Walt Disney never commented on Lotte Reiniger, so I can't make inferences about what Disney thought of her. Reiniger, however, spoke about Walt Disney and his animation on the rare occasion.

Alfio Bastiancich's 1980 interview with Reiniger includes this short Q&A:

BASTIANCICH: What do you think of Disney?
REINIGER: His films are technically perfect: too perfect [1980/1992, 15].

Given the knowledge that she was frustrated that films with subpar stories and animation techniques were funded over her own films, Reiniger's response is blunt and humorous. It could easily be said that she despised Disney, but such a statement would be the furthest thing from the truth. She visited California in 1974 and toured the Walt Disney Studios. Happ included this Reiniger quote about that visit that elaborates on the Bastiancich response and includes the Disney animators' impressions:

> In my humble opinion, the early movies of [Disney] are really extraordinary but he got himself such a tremendous [film production] factory, that he had to focus so much on the commercial aspect and that he had to distribute work to so many people, that he basically disappeared. In the first movies you can find a personal spiritedness and his personal genius, but in the other films there is a little bit too much colour.... I do this with a free hand [improvise]. I had to demonstrate [this improvisation] to them [the Disney animators] and then they were awestruck [qt. in Happ, 2004, 99–100].

Reiniger expressed her admiration for Disney movies and apparently enjoyed *Snow White*. What she noticed about Disney's work as his studio grew bigger and bigger is an attribute that many people notice when a company or project becomes too big: lack of the original message or purpose. In other words, she felt there was less of Disney's personal touch on his latter animated films.

I don't know how familiar Reiniger was with the Walt Disney Studios' operations and its animation process. She was aware how traditional cel animation worked, but did she know that Disney personally stopped drawing his cartoons when the studio grew? He felt his talents were better used to direct and guide the animators on the proper way to make a film. The popular illusion, however, is that Disney drew for the animated films and very few people realize how early in his company's history he stopped. It is possible that Reiniger believed this common misconception along with many others and it would explain why she so strongly believed there was so little of him in his studio's movies after *Snow White*.

Reiniger was never a smug individual. But as Richard Bradshaw mentioned, even though she epitomized self-deprecating humor, she was extremely confident in her skills. If Reiniger said she was capable of handling a project, she would do it. She knew her strengths and weaknesses and wasn't afraid to stress her talents when the situation required it. Knowing that she maintained a healthy self-esteem, perhaps Reiniger felt a sense of superiority that she was able to intimately connect with each of her films

Reiniger during a candid moment, 1976 (photo by Lois Segal).

and work on the project start to finish, thereby inserting her own genius and temperament into the film. "These silhouette films will never challenge the popularity of the Disney cartoon film; but, within their clearly prescribed limitations, they are assured of fame. Not the least part of their fascination is caused by the fact that their production is almost entirely a one-woman show" (White, 1939, 48).

Disney cartoons rely on striking color, using the best and newest techniques, and detailed characters, while Reiniger used simple black silhouettes, limited color and an refined stop-motion animation process. Due to her reliance on perfecting the silhouette technique and a "less is more" mentality, she had an artistic advantage.

> While Walt Disney's name will stand for the early phase of animated and coloured cartoons with all degrees of fantasy and sophistication, Lotte Reiniger will surely be remembered for the artistic exploitation of the silhouette. As the Disney cartoon escaped from the cardboard flatness of silhouette, it gained pictorial fullness at the expense of a peculiar charm depending on simplicity and economy of means. It is an essential quality of the trick film or animated cartoon to be to some extent stylized and formal, because it relies on the trick mechanism as well as the creative touch of the artist. There is a danger in the complicated organization of the later Walt Disney films: In escaping largely from the mechanical restrictions of making and operating innumerable figures and parts of figures that must be photographed in succession, it begins to lose its proper character and to vie with the film picture of living actors. The stylized formality of the animated cartoon could be artistically used by Lotte Reiniger because she was an expert silhouette cutter whose best work gains rather than suffers by relying on the black shade [Mégroz, 1949, 115].

Intrinsically, neither cel nor silhouette animation is the superior form just as neither Reiniger or Disney is the superior animator. Both coped with the hardships of the industry: Reiniger felt it as she encountered limited funding and Disney dealt with the problems running a huge studio. Both met with the same criticisms about their chosen profession, as Disney described in this often quoted story:

> Disney recalled in 1956 that when he was on the train to California in 1923 … he fell into conversation with some fellow passengers and told them that he made animated cartoons. "It was like saying 'I sweep up the latrines' or something, you know." As he acknowledged, those anonymous skeptics meant nothing to him; but remembering them contributed to the satisfaction he felt at the success of *Snow White* [Barrier, 2007, 132].

Reiniger has entered the animation pantheon as someone who can't be duplicated, almost to the same awe-inspiring level as Walt Disney and other Golden Age legends. It is the modern animators who are throwbacks to legends like Reiniger, because just like her they realize that "the silhouette film never stops focusing on the human figure, and seeks to get as close to it as possible. It finds its own special compensations…" for the modern 3D tricks and the strict black surface (Jouvanceau, 2004, 181). "The silhouette cinema will seek to achieve the same effect by tricks of composition that are all its own" (Jouvanceau, 2004, 181). With this legendary status, she has inspired more modern-day animators to try their hand at silhouette animation, use her techniques, and evolve it into a new form. As Eric Walter White wrote in *Walking Shadows*:

> [T]he trick film in its original form will remain one of the purest manifestations of the cinema, and there is no doubt that a century hence (if the films have not perished by then) the best work of Walt Disney and Lotte Reiniger will be looked upon as primitives in the same way as the present generation looks on the paintings of [William] Byrd and [Claudio] Monteverdi [White, 1931, 31].

11

Influence and Adaptation

A common question all artists are asked is, "Who do you make your films for?" Reiniger's answer:

> I am very droll and when I tell a story, people gladly listen to me. Why shouldn't they watch what I narrate in pictures? ... It appears that the films that had the most success were the ones in which I moved myself into my innermost self, for example *Papageno* with the Mozart music, because I could do that best. I always brought what I could do best [Happ, 2004, 112].

Reiniger's shadowy legacy has attracted a following within the animation and puppetry communities. Her work inspires many talented artists on a frequent basis as her pioneering role in animation is discovered. Her fans admire what she accomplished long before computers came to the modern animator's aid. According to Jayne Pilling:

> The passage of time also affects perceptions, even the way we interpret what we see. I am sure I am not the only teacher who has had difficulty convincing students that a scene in a film they have singled out for praise in terms of its use of a particular computer effect was in fact done by hand, the old-fashioned paint on paper and cel way. Since they have never worked that way, they simply can't see it. A whole generation who have never used anything other than digital cameras might now require an introduction to the physical properties of old-fashioned celluloid film stock, in order to grasp how scratching on film works as an animation technique. Nowadays, regardless of any actual animation skill, just about anyone can make an animated film with nothing but a computer, some software, maybe a scanner and a drawing tablet, on very little money [Pilling, 2011, 1–2].

Reiniger's silhouette films, storytelling methods and artistic style have been adapted by these new animators and evolved into the next phase of the animation industry. Frank Thomas ended his article "Can Classic Disney Animation Be Duplicated on the Computer?" with:

> Ultimately the breakthrough in the use of endearing characters generated by computers ... will be something new and vital, something probably as different from classic animation as the very successful Muppets have been. But the new characters, whoever they are, will only find public acceptance if they will entertain, and communicate, and involve the audience. They must have appeal and good acting and appear to think. They must use the same principles that have prevailed in the theater for over 2000 years. The only real question now is, who will be the first to do it? [1984, 25].[1]

Allow me to reword Thomas' question in relation to Reiniger: "Who are the modern animators who are influenced by her and how is she reflected in their work?" The wonderful answer is that not only do they adhere to Thomas' requirements, but they have set their own standards for the industry that many find as inspiring as they find Reiniger and her silhouettes: Brenda Chapman, Jorge Gutiérrez, William Joyce, Michel Ocelot, Henry Selick, Rebecca Sugar and Nora Twomey.[2]

These animators' careers remind me of an Art Babbitt quote: "Today we are only beginning—just walking—as far as animation is concerned—we really are not animators yet, nor have we realized the possibilities in animation" (qt. in Hahn & Miller-Zarneke, 2015, 52). This is an observation on how the medium is only on the cusp of being explored. He said it in an interview with Dr. Boris Morkovin, who did a ten-part lecture series at the Disney Studios about humor. "The great majority of the crew felt that Morkovin was a blowhard with no real experience who taught the obvious in a condescending way" (Hahn & Miller-Zarneke, 2015, 278). Putting aside the context, Babbitt expressed that animation medium has a long way go before animators have realized the truest extent of its capabilities. Animation has traveled from ink and paint drawings to startling realism with computers.

Rather than making animated movies and shorts as realistic as possible, animators are instead interested in expressing art over realism. There is a recent tendency in animated films, "the practice of filmmakers who, knowingly or not, strive to differentiate their work from traditional imagery, be that Reiniger-style silhouettes or eighteenth century cutouts. Relatively speaking, this aesthetic concept is to Lotte Reiniger's what, in drawn animation, the famous UPA style was to the Disney school: the refusal of an ever-greater realism in favour of a simpler image" (Jouvanceau, 2004, 80). They use the new, advanced technology to augment their personal styles, and for inspiration they are turning to the past, including the works of silhouette animation. Reiniger-inspired German animator Hannes Rall observed, "[Reiniger] always remains up to date, a counterpart to the digital flood of images, the overwhelming variety of realism, photorealism, texture. There are very many animators returning to her reduced style and applying it in their art" (qt. in Marschall, 2013).

Academy Award-winning director-writer-artist Brenda Chapman (*The Prince of Egypt*, 1998; *Brave*, 2012) looks to Reiniger as a symbol of self-expression and wonders about past what-ifs[3]:

> The thing about Lotte is that she was the first—before Walt. She created a feature film that was so beautiful, unique and riveting and I just wish that she'd had the marketing machine behind her film that Disney had. That could have made a huge difference in getting women into the field of animation much earlier, as well as opening up different styles of animation to the public. I didn't discover her until I was already working at Disney. That discovery just blew me away. I wish I had seen *The Adventures of Prince Achmed* when I was a child. I wonder how Lotte's work would have influenced my own vision. As an adult, she inspired me to put myself into my work. I wish I could have met her [Chapman, email to the author, February 18, 2016].

Chapman's views echo many of her fellow animators who find a unique personality behind Reiniger's dark silhouettes that exemplifies how an artist can use animation to express any sort of idea and how personal such projects can be.

Nora Twomey is from Ireland's Cartoon Saloon, an animation studio that focuses on combining the aesthetics of older art and storytelling methods with new techniques to create gorgeous films and shorts. She was co-director of *The Secret of Kells* (2009) and head of story for *Song of the Sea* (2014). While seeking inspiration for her own cutout animated film…

> The first film of hers I came across was *Cinderella*. I had been desperately trawling the net for anything that could inform the cutout styled sequences I'd planned for my film. I'd been scrolling and clicking for hours but then I stopped. The strength and beauty of Lotte Reiniger's film made me stop. She drew me in, revealing a portion of the screen; the silhouette of a sad young Cinderella,

another; two wicked stepsisters teasing a caged bird and lastly a horrid stepmother poking a stick at Cinderella, forcing her to scrub the floor.

The flow of storytelling, the transitions from scene to scene, the ingenuity with which she made the most of the limitations of her craft were and are truly inspiring. May she finally get the credit she deserves; animation's very own Cinderella [Twomey email to the author, April 11, 2016].

Both Chapman and Twomey's reflections mirror Reiniger's 1929 *Lebende Schatten*, in that these two modern animators seek to bring to light new forms of expression via animation, yet they are at the mercy of funding, though they continue to pursue their visions:

The most beautiful is the uncharted of the entire realm. Through the work one new possibility reveals itself after the other. Unfortunately very few artists concern themselves with this new territory of expression. The reasons are obvious. First, the work is too expensive. The material, the technical equipment, costs a lot of money. An individual can't afford that. The industry today, however, does not have much of an inclination to care for animation as independent form. It uses usually only the most obvious effects, usually for the purposes of advertisement. Independent work is rare. Americans put the biggest allocation with the most gorgeous grotesques of Felix the Cat and Oswald the Lucky Rabbit, whose wide success shows that in pure animation lies great financial possibilities. Also the great interest in my work confirms my resolution, to eke out further positions in this unexplored field of human expression in the hope that every new result helps film to exploit one of the most promising fields [1969/1929, 5].

Twomey's words explain how Reiniger is not only an inspiration for making lovely films, but also proves that her animation techniques are still in use in an age where it seems everything is animated by computers.

When Jorge Gutiérrez, director of the beautiful el Día de los Muertos fable *The Book of Life* (2014), was growing up in Mexico City, he was privileged to view Reiniger's work on the channel Canal Once. Canal Once played cartoons and movies from all around the world and they included a show dedicated to her silhouette films. The first of her works he watched was *Papageno*. When he later attended CalArts, head of the Experimental Animation program Jules Engel (a former Disney and UPA animator) showed him *Prinzen Achmed*. Gutiérrez said, "The strong use of staging and gorgeous silhouettes were mesmerizing. I think every animation designer owes a lot to her."

Gutiérrez's first animated short was a cutout film called *Loteria*. "I love to stage scenes with very clear silhouettes in any medium I work, especially in CG and it's because of her." He carried his love for silhouettes into *The Book of Life* and borrowed an old animation technique from Reiniger. The characters in the computer animated film are designed to resemble marionettes with jointed hinges and each has a carefully rendered hand-made appearance for the textures. While the marionette characters are used in a "story within a story framework" similar to *1001 Arabian Nights*, they and the story framework are an indirect homage to Reiniger. Gutiérrez stated, "There are actually some characters in the film, like the cowardly soldiers, that were designed and rigged to be cutout type puppets. We could only shoot them from one angle, which made them really unique." Reiniger's techniques might be old-fashioned in the modern sense of animation, but her tricks are still useful even in computer animation.

Gutiérrez sees elements of Reiniger's works in modern animation programs, proving how the early animation techniques continue to shape the industry and even dissolving Thomas' fears that "those darn computers" would never have the same effect as hand-drawn animation. Gutiérrez believes that Reiniger "is incredibly influential. If you look at all the Flash, Harmony and After Effect animation out there, it's basically digital silhouette animation. The principles are exactly the same but Lotte did it first!" (email to author, July 23, 2015).

Reiniger's influence extends beyond cinematic animation to TV. Rebecca Sugar, creator and director of *Steven Universe*, shared her experience with Reiniger's body of work. For *Steven Universe*, Sugar used a style that mixed aspects of Japanese anime (notably *Revolutionary Girl Utena* and *Sailor Moon*), John Kricfalusi and Bob Camps' *Ren and Stimpy*, and trace of amounts of Looney Tunes and Charles Schulz. The show renders a gentle style that delivers quick action and strong characters, but among the other influences is Reiniger. Sugar's first exposure to Reiniger was when she attended the School of Visual Arts and during her animation history class she watched *Prinzen Achmed*.

> I was blown away. I was surprised that a film so important to animation history, using techniques that would inspire so many animators from that time on, could still feel so completely unique and original almost a century later. Nothing has really touched or topped the aesthetic she was able to achieve, in my opinion.

Sugar also shared a lovely description of Reiniger's silhouette animation:

> The mix of the simplicity and complexity of her cutouts is what really inspires me about Lotte Reiniger's work. She is able to create so much character with the body language of her silhouettes, and under the details, the shapes are so simple and clear. It's incredibly elegant and efficient. The compositions too. You're left with the sense that her compositions are dazzlingly complex. But they're very simple, clear and decisive. It's absolutely masterful design.

Sugar scatters bits of Reiniger's work through the *Steven Universe* episodes; she and her team made a special episode, based on silhouette animation and Reiniger's art style. Called "The Answer," this episode featured a flashback from one of the main characters, Garnet, and in the flashback the characters and backgrounds are rendered like Reiniger's silhouette puppets. Despite being hand-drawn, these silhouette figures could have been cut by Reiniger's own hand. The backgrounds especially mirror one of Reiniger's most beautiful scenes, including the colors: when Prince first sees the fairy Peri Banu and spies on her while she bathes. Sugar said:

> A lot of *Steven Universe* crew members are hugely inspired by Lotte Reiniger's work, and we all wanted to pay homage to her in the episode "The Answer." We knew we wanted the episode to be heavily stylized. We wanted it to feel like a truly classic fairytale, powerful and simple and timeless! Ian Jones-Quartey did the initial concept drawings, with crowds of silhouetted Gems surrounding Ruby and Sapphire. The episode was storyboarded by Lamar Abrams and Katie Mitroff. We tried to pull our favorite things from every powerful animated fairy tale interpretation, but it really starts and ends with Lotte Reiniger. We tried for silhouettes at the beginning, and powerful compositions both simple and lush for the ending.

Sugar also revealed why she thinks Reiniger and her work was overlooked. Keeping in line with Twomey, Chapman and Gutiérrez, she knows that silhouette animation isn't quite dead yet:

> I've seen *The Adventures of Prince Achmed* labeled as "German," without mention of Lotte Reiniger's name, which seems absolutely bizarre to me. I feel extremely lucky to have learned about her in school. It seems like a huge oversight not to include her in any and every book about animation history, not only because she was a pioneer, but because she was so incredibly prolific. I think shadow animation does have a future. I think as long as her films exist and continue to be as beautiful as they are, which they of course will, and with more recognition for her work, animators are going to continue to want to follow in her footsteps. Personally I'm dying for another chance to reference her technique, though I think her work is truly incomparable! [Sugar email to author, February 22, 2016].

Academy Award-winning director, producer, animator, and writer William Joyce is a Lotte Reiniger fan and, in my opinion, is outmatched by few. His filmography includes *Rise of the Guardians* (2012), *Meet the Robinsons* (2007), *Epic* (2013) and *The Fantastic Flying Books of Mr. Morris Lessmore* (2011). He has intensely studied her animated works along with Weimar cinema. Joyce's style can only be described as a futuristic rendering of Atomic Age aesthetics with a crisper and more varied color palette. Despite the differences in Weimar cinema's art movements and his modernistic postwar leanings, he delivered a tribute to Fritz Lang and *Metropolis* with his educational and adorable *The Numberlys*, both a picture book and an animated short. Silhouettes and shadows slip into his work not as physical representations, but as inspirations for how he can improve his work at Moonbot Studios.

> I first saw *The Adventures of Prince Achmed*, that was the only film of Lotte's I had seen for a while, and I think it was on Turner Classic Movies.... I thought, "This is the coolest thing I have ever seen!" I was blown away by it. Not long after that, I was working at Pixar and I visited an arthouse theater in Berkeley where they projected a restored version of *Prince Achmed* with a 20-piece orchestra to play the score to go along with it. It was an amazing print. Any of the prints I have seen since, on DVD or broadcast on television, they don't have half the vibrancy or delicacy of shadow and tone that I saw in Berkeley. It was so beautiful. I felt like it was the most waking dream film experience I have ever had. When it ended, the place was packed to standing room only, everyone cheered for ten minutes or it felt like it because it was one of the most beautiful things imaginable.

Joyce was learning how to direct an animated film at the time of the viewing and he was amazed that so many of the things Reiniger did, especially with *Prinzen Achmed*, countered what he had learned about animation. He related that he had been told many times "the eyes are the soul of an animated character," because that is where the emotion and performance is generated. After watching *Prinzen Achmed*, he was astounded he felt the same immediacy from elegant, subtle black silhouettes as he would have with a fully painted character. "It taught me you can be more subtle with your animation, especially with your faces. There is so much chattiness in today's animated movies and you can tell stories with no words [sic] and black silhouettes. You know what the characters are feeling and it is amazing."

Joyce observed that at the beginning of any medium, people are extremely experimental and "get away with so much crazy stuff. That continues to hold up today, but wouldn't get made today." Of special note are early American pioneers Ub Iwerks, the Fleischer brothers and of course Disney's early Mickey Mouse cartoons. Even more impressive, in his opinion, is the fact that Reiniger worked with the best, most ambitious filmmakers of her time. He attributed the scarcity of distribution and the rarity of good prints of her films to her obscurity.

Joyce loves the silhouette animation style so much he adapted Edgar Allan Poe's "The Cask of Amontillado" into a short film and featured many of the same graceful cutout movements of Reiniger's puppets with the same mysterious quality. Joyce said, "Lotte Reiniger is getting cool again and it's not just creative people, it's also audiences. If it's in the right context, you can make large, mass audiences dig silhouette animation" (interview with author, March 3, 2016).

All of these prior animators work in either traditional or computer animation, but Reiniger was a stop-motion animator. One of the finest stop-motion animators in the world is Henry Selick, who improved animation's genre reach in the west with 1993's *The Nightmare Before Christmas* (he also changed how people view the yuletide as well). He is a Reiniger fan. Selick directed *James and the Giant Peach* (1996) and *Coraline* (2009).

Selick first encountered Reiniger's films in front of the TV. He grew up in the late 1950s in the New Jersey suburbs, where he watched the local low-budget New York kiddie shows broadcast from the Empire State Building. A favorite was *Merrytoon Circus*, originally *Terrytoon Circus*, hosted by ringmaster Claude Kirchner. He remembered, "They showed a lot of old, often unusual cartoons (probably because they were inexpensive), which included portions of Lotte Reiniger's *Adventures of Prince Achmed* and bits of her other films."[4]

He notes the "jumpy grasshopper movement," but Selick enjoyed that trait:

> They were—and remain—pure magic, filled with twitchy but elegant life and mystery. The look and motion and design and stories were nothing like the Mickey Mouse, Bugs Bunny, Tom and Jerry and Gerald McBoing Boing shorts I saw in the '50s and '60s. Being silhouette, her characters invited my imagination to fill in what couldn't be seen in their faces and clothes, making her work more memorable for me. Lotte's work struck me as powerfully as the two other major animation filmmakers from my childhood: Ray Harryhausen with *7th Voyage of Sinbad* and *Jason and the Argonauts* and Disney with "Night on Bald Mountain" and "The Sorcerer's Apprentice" from *Fantasia* (both shown on TV in Disney Halloween specials).

Although Selick never used silhouette animation, he is experienced with cutout animation as a direct result of viewing Reiniger's films.

> While I've never done pure silhouette cutout animation, I've done lots of cutout work including the dream sequence in *James and the Giant Peach* and one section of my short film *Slow Bob in the Lower Dimensions* as well as other shorts and a music video. Her work influenced my thoughts on how characters might move, showing me the stretch and squash of American cartoons might be fine, but there were other, more elegant ways to bring something to life. I've animated scissors in both "the office nightmare" sequence from the cult cutout feature *Twice Upon a Time* and, again, *Slow Bob in the Lower Dimensions*. I'm certain I got that idea from Lotte's *Cinderella*, which feature animated scissors snipping out characters that come to life.

Selick notes that there aren't any recent successes with silhouette animation as investors are keen to put their money into popular fads rather than a film popular 80 years ago. He points out, "Anything is possible with a great story, design, production and means of distribution, especially for a short film. But doing a feature-length silhouette animated film would be nearly impossible…. Certainly, a section of a feature film, live action or animated, might be done in silhouette animation."

On the subject about why Reiniger has been overlooked within animation history:

> Honestly, I think most people are just unaware of Lotte Reiniger and her work. When I took my first animation class at Syracuse University in 1974, we viewed films from all over the world including brilliant shorts from the Canadian Film Board and puppet films from Eastern Europe. Not once did the instructor, Bruce MacCurdy, show us any of Lotte's films. Maybe they weren't available or there was no easy way to access them? I don't think her work has been overlooked because it's considered less important than others, it's mainly ignorance [Selick email to author, March 29, 2016].

The only downside about Reiniger being the premier silhouette animator is that "her fame has likewise totally overshadowed the other directors who, throughout the 20th century, have tried their hand at this very distinctive genre" (Jouvanceau, 2004, 11). There are many other animators who experimented with the medium since she started in films with Paul Wegener. Charles Armstrong animated the first silhouette short in 1909, *The Sporting Mice.* Interestingly, *Romeo and Juliet* (1917), reputedly the first stop-motion film, was made by a woman, Helena Smith Dayton. During World War I, Bray

Production was the most productive studio in the U.S. Founder J.R. Bray financed a series of silhouette films titled *Silhouette Fantasies* through independent animator C. Allen Gilbert in 1915 and '16. Tony Sarg, one of the foremost U.S. puppeteers in the twentieth century, made his only known excursion into film with Major Herbert Dawley. Dawley and Sarg animated used silhouette cutouts for a series called *Tony Sarg's Almanac* (1921–23), which used silhouette cutouts. Only the first three titles are known to us: *The First Circus, The Tooth Carpenter* and *Why They Love Cavemen*. Moritz revealed how one of Reiniger's contemporaries drifted into silhouette animation: "Lotte Reiniger's *Prince Achmed* screened in May 1926 to rave reviews. This film ... must have inspired Oskar [Fischinger] to make his own silhouette animation," so in 1927 he made *Spiritual Connections* and *Noah's Ark* (Moritz, 2004, 17). Japanese animator Noburo Ofuji developed his own form of silhouette animation and began his career with chiyogami animation (the Japanese version of cutout animation), which requires cutting out paper in various recognizable shapes, assembling them into a human and then using the stop-motion process to record them on film (Sano, 2013, 88). In the 1920s, he made the silhouette films *Kujira* (*The Whale*, 1927) and *Kokka Kimigayo* (*National Anthem: Kimigayo*, 1931). Chiyogami was respected, but strict Japanese works were seen as inferior to the American cartoon imports. Within the Japanese animation industry, animators were urged to make their work more Japanese, but no one was able to find it within the medium (Sano, 2013, 89–92). Ofuji remarked, "I think there are storylines in Japan that use uniquely Japanese gags, but since we watch American cartoons, there are constant feelings of sadness in Japanese cartoons, so I have gotten stuck in a rut and haven't made animation for just about a year now" (qt. in Sano, 2013, 92).

Sensing the need to find the correct style for his work, Ofuji returned to the silhouette animation from the 1920s. He made the switch because shadow puppetry had a long, beloved history in Japan and due to the floundering attitudes towards U.S. animation (Sano, 2013, 93). "In any case, Ofuji's repeated changes in direction clearly demonstrated [that] Japanese animation continued to grope for a sense of direction while floating in limbo between American- and Japanese-centric orientations" (Sano, 2013, 94). Ofuji's method: "These papers were then manipulated and filmed on different levels of glass plates, techniques similar to those used by Lotte Reiniger" (Cavalier, 2011, 93). He made *Mareoki kaisen* (*Sea Battle of Malaya*, 1943) and many other silhouette films, including a remake of *Kujira* with color in 1952. Akiko Sano noted in her essay on Ofuji that the Japanese were aware of 1920s silhouette animation and used it in the same avant-garde manner (2011, 93). Recent DVD editions of early Japanese silent animated films have revealed not only the usual Hollywood influences, seen in almost any country's animation from that period, but a great many exquisite silhouette-animation films, suggesting that in its time, Reiniger's work had more of an impact there than elsewhere (Pilling, 2011, 9).

If there was ever a true heir to Lotte Reiniger, it is French animator Michel Ocelot with a rich filmography of traditional, computer and silhouette animation. He directed *Kirikou et la sorcière* (*Krikou and the Sorceress*, 1998; its success in Europe is said to be comparable to *The Lion King* in the U.S.), *Azur et Asmar* (2006) and the beautiful silhouette films *Princes et princesses* (2000) and *Les Contes de la nuit* (*Tales of the Night*, 2011). For his own silhouette films, he relies on the fairytale genre, but he writes his own tales vs. adapting well-known ones. According to Ocelot, "With silhouettes you can create fairytales that are very touching, very unusual.... They are far from conventional. I wanted to rediscover that purity and intensity" (qt. in Marschall, 2013; Ocelot email to author, November 24, 2014).

The purity and intensity Ocelot sought is evident in the careful consideration he generates with his original stories and concentrating on making his characters believable and identifiable. This puts him in the same vein as Reiniger, but rather than copying her, Ocelot stands on his own. In an interview with Christine Gudin, Ocelot said:

> I don't like adaptations. I think it's very bad to make an adaptation. Perhaps, what I make is very bad, but I don't make adaptations.... On the other hand I have my own stories to tell. I am inspired by those roughly told anonymous tales, which are often poorly composed. I vamp the tales of folklore, and I make out of them what I want. I utilize them like ore from a mine, and I try to make jewels out of them. But I don't at all respect the ore of the miners. I think those people told tales in their time. Today, it's me who's the storyteller, and I do what I want with the heritage. I cite whatever has inspired me, but they are my tales. They are my guts, my heart, and all the rest [qt. in Zipes, 2011, 7].

He found it quite amusing how he came to be associated with Reiniger after audiences viewed his *Les Trois Inventeurs* (*The Three Inventors*, 1979), a white silhouette film (the delicate paper cutouts resemble lace doilies):

> I worked in Lotte Reiniger's style long before I knew her. But mostly in white paper. I'd make decorations, little presents. I'd also use the doilies that cakes are put on. They would be white silhouettes made of little pieces of paper that had been nicely cut out with the lacy effect of baker's doilies. I showed this film at an international festival in Canada and someone called out: "A male Lotte Reiniger." So I discovered I was the reincarnation of Lotte Reiniger [qt. in Marschall et al., 2012].

Ocelot explained that he didn't animate *Les Trois Inventeurs* in the back-lit manner as Reiniger. His silhouettes are bas-relief and are side-lit sculptures. Ocelot said, "The puppets of *Les Trois Inventeurs* came naturally, without thinking about Lotte Reiniger, whose films I had never seen." As he had never viewed her films, Ocelot was inspired by other sources and he sees her methods as a little old-fashioned:

> As for the black silhouettes, I had many inspirations: delicate illustrations from the 18th to the 19th centuries, lovely cutouts from Swiss folk art, the shadow theater of Le Chat Noir.... When I say "I felt she was archaïc," it is not to lower her merit, which is great. It is just that, since the 1920s animation had a lot of progress and storytelling must always be improved. But I had no intention of doing any silhouette animation.
> What brought me to this technique was workshops for children. I thought, "It was good enough for children." I did not know what her technique was, but it wasn't was no mystery for me, flat puppets with hinges, which the kids understood very well. In one week the kids did such brilliant footage that I understood the potential of this technique and decided to use it. It had two seductions: I enjoyed the strong stylisation, the strong graphics it demanded, and it was the fastest and cheapest of all animation techniques—and I had no money at that time. I was very happy doing the eight tales of *Ciné Si*, which had later on a cinema release under the title of *Princes et Princesses*. And years after, although I had access to correct, normal budgets, I started again, because I simply love this image. I did ten new fairy tales, using computers this time, which were released under two different titles, sometimes *Dragons et Princesses* sometimes *Les Contes de la Nuit*.

As for his own future, Ocelot plans on continuing using black silhouettes. The only director actively (as of writing this book in 2016) working in this medium, he says, "Will black silhouettes be popular again? I don't know, but what I know is that I shall do more of them, and this time going back to black paper and scissors, and frame by frame animation. It is more enjoyable, and it is faster" (email to author, February 24, 2014).

It is hard to imagine animation with its own "old masters" along the lines of renowned names in painting and sculpture, because in the grand time scheme it is still a young art. Old masters maintain their fame due to their extraordinary artistic ability, curious histories, and achievements that rocked their chosen profession's foundation. New artists in these fields keep turning back to old masters for inspiration and to discover the old masters' techniques so they can incorporate it in their own work. Lotte Reiniger is an old master of animation along with many of the other animators discussed throughout this book. Very much like other old master animators, who continue to be reborn through new animators' work, her presence is keener than thought among the current animation industry and will continue to grow as more aspiring artists discover her.

Even in her golden years, Reiniger never wasted a chance to show her humor (photo by Lois Segal).

Afterword

My goal with this book was to discover who Lotte Reiniger was, why she was forgotten, and if more of her films existed other than *Die Abenteuer des Prinzen Achmed*. As I learned more about her, I understood more about an artist's journey and the passion that drives one to create, despite hardships along the way. It is not an easy path, but the reward comes from the act of creation and the final end product. For artists, the saying "Life is more about the journey than the final destination" doesn't ring true. It is through the final destination or end result of a work, that an artist can gain a perspective about how far they have come, reflect on what they created, and ultimately decide where to head next.

Reiniger tried to reach perfection in her art. Interviewed in 1976, she still didn't think she had attained it ("Lotte Reiniger Recording"). Reiniger was a champion of two under-appreciated art forms—puppetry and animation. Her legacy asserts the validity and the versatility of both mediums. The biggest problem for silhouettes in the future won't be audiences uninterested in dark figures on a screen; rather it will be securing the finances to make these works.

Reiniger only wrote one book in her lifetime that serves as both an autobiography and an instruction manual on shadow puppetry and silhouette animation (photo by Lois Segal).

I can't end this book on the fairytale ending line, "And they lived happily ever after" because I don't know what the future holds and happily ever after is more subjective than the opener "once upon a time." I can only predict that animators and puppeteers will continue to experiment with different forms of their mediums, including silhouettes and shadows, as technology changes and it becomes easier for them to make their chosen art.

Afterword

Lotte Reiniger has passed into our imaginations as a fairytale creature, perhaps even the Queen of Silhouettes and Shadows. From her silhouette stylings, she indulged herself as well as us. Her goal was to alleviate tension and share a bit of joy, but she did better than that because she gave us animated art.

It is better to end this book, "And they lived through happiness and perils as they began to create…"

Appendix I: Filmography

1916

Rübezahls Hochzeit (Rumpelstilskin's Wedding)
Die schöne Prinzessin von China (The Beautiful Chinese Princess)

1918

Apokalypse (Apocalypse)
Der Rattenfänger von Hameln (The Pied Piper of Hameln)

1919

Das Ornament des verliebten Herzens (The Ornament of the Loving Heart)

1920

Der verlorene Schatten (The Lost Shadow)
Amor und das standhafte Liebespaar (Cupid and the Steadfast Lovers)
Geheimnis der Marquise (The Marquise's Secret)
Die Barcarole (The Barcarole)

1921

Der fliegende Koffer (The Flying Suitcase)
Der Stern von Bethlehem (The Star of Bethlehem)

1922

Aschenputtel (Cinderella)
Dornröschen (Sleeping Beauty)

1923

Reiniger made a shadow puppet falcon sequence for Fritz Lang's Die Niebelungen.

1923–26

Die Abenteuer des Prinzen Achmed (The Adventures of Prince Achmed)

1927

Heut' tanzt Mariette (Today Marietta Dances)

1928

Doktor Dolittle und seine Tiere (Dr. Dolittle and His Animals)
Der scheintote Chinese (The Seemingly-Dead Chinaman)

1929

Die Jagd nach dem Glück (The Pursuit of Happiness)

1930

Zehn Minuten Mozart (10 Minutes of Mozart)

1931

Harlekin (Harlequin)

1932

Sissi

1933

Don Quixote
Carmen

1934

Das rollende Rad (The Rolling Wheel)
Der Graf von Carabas (Puss-in-Boots)
Das gestohlene Herz (The Stolen Heart)

1935

Der Kleine Schornsteinfeger (The Little Chimney Sweep)
Galathea
Papageno

1936
The King's Breakfast

1937
The Tocher
La Marseillaise

1939
Dream Circus
L'Elisir d'Amore

1944
Die goldene Gans (The Golden Goose)

1949
Greetings Telegram
Post Early for Christmas
Radio License

1950
Wool Ballet
Other films for the Crown Film Unit

1951
Mary's Birthday

1953
Aladdin
The Magic Horse
Snow White and Rose Red

1954
The Three Wishes
The Grasshopper and the Ant
The Gallant Little Tailor
The Sleeping Beauty
The Frog Prince
Caliph Stork
Cinderella

1955
Hansel and Gretel
Thumbelina
Jack and the Beanstalk

1956
The Star of Bethlehem

1957
Helen La Belle

1958
The Knight in the Seraglio aka A Knight in the Harem

1960
The Pied Piper of Hamelin

1961
The Frog Prince

1962
Wee Sandy

1963
Cinderella

1975
Aucassin and Nicolette

1979
The Rose and the Ring

1981
Düsselchen und die vier Jahreszeiten (Düsselchen and the Four Seasons)

Appendix II: Works Written by Reiniger

Reiniger, L. (1929). "Lebende Schatten."

Reiniger, L. (1934, December 31). "Deutsche Schaffende: Pläne und Wünsche, Fülle des Strebens, Reichtum an Können!" *Film-Kurier*.

Reiniger, L. (1936). "Moving Silhouettes." *Film Art*, 3, 14–18.

Reiniger, L. (1936) "Film as Ballet." *Life and Letters To-Day*, 157–163.

Reiniger, L. (1936, Spring). "Scissors Make Films." *Sight and Sound*.

Reiniger, L. (195?). *Cinderella: A Lotte Reiniger Story-Play*. London: Hutchinson.

Reiniger, L. (195?). *The Magic Horse: A Lotte Reiniger Story-Play*. London: Hutchinson.

Reiniger, L. (195?). *Puss in Boots: A Lotte Reiniger Story-Play*. London: Hutchinson.

Reiniger, L. (195?). *The Sleeping Beauty: A Lotte Reiniger Story-Play*. London: Hutchinson.

Reiniger, L. (1970). *Shadow Theatres and Shadow Films*. London: Batsford.

Reiniger, L. (1970b). "The Adventures of Prince Achmed, or What May Happen to Somebody Trying to Make a Full Length Cartoon in 1926." *Silent Picture*, 8, 2–4.

Reiniger, L. (1975). *Shadow Puppets, Shadow Theatres, and Shadow Films*. Boston: Plays, Inc.

Chapter Notes

Chapter 2

1. The only print of this film exists in the Deutsches Filminstitut archives.
2. Andersen would also delight himself and his fans with his own scherenschnitte.
3. Modern perceptions of animation as a medium also run parallel to the ruination of comic books by Frederic Wertham, i.e., meant for children and are a phase children will grow out of. Wertham wanted to ban (and in some cases literally burn) comics altogether.
4. There are many translations of this conversation. I felt that William Mortiz represented my ideas best.
5. K.V. Taylor is referring to animation as a "genre," when it is actually a medium. Reiniger, however, worked in more than one medium: puppetry and animation.

Chapter 3

1. Steven Bingen affirms that Warner only used this line as a joke and that his daughter Barbara said that he screened all the Warner Brothers cartoons at home for the amusement of his family (2014, 108).
2. Reminds one of the Utah teapot, a standard reference for 3D computer models.
3. White also describes how Walt Disney simplified the animation process using celluloid and making characters with flexible limbs.
4. When Walt Disney began his animation career at Film Ad in 1920, he used cutout animation and also shot the films as negatives (Barrier, 2007, 25–26). Without knowing it, Reiniger, Cristiani and Disney used the same animation styles.
5. An example of art snobbery is the great Pierre Brassau, who had four paintings exhibited at a Swedish gallery. After critics showered compliments on him, it was revealed that he was actually Peter, a chimpanzee from the Borås Djurpark zoo (Boese, 2015).

Chapter 4

1. Jack Warner sold all the 400 Looney Tunes and Merrie Melodies cartoons from 1948 and earlier for $3000 each. It compares little to the fortune these cartoons have since amassed (Thomas, 1990, 212).
2. Upon seeing *Snow White and the Seven Dwarfs*, Leon Schlesinger said "with his usual amazing grace: 'I need a feature cartoon like I need two assholes'" (C. Jones, 1999, 74). He would not make his own feature film to compete with Disney.
3. Stokowski was managed by Michael Myerberg, who fell in love with animation after viewing *Fantasia*. Myerberg "concluded that there must be a better way to do this kind of film" (McPharlin, 1969, 570). Myerberg, Stokowski and puppeteer Lou Bunin collaborated on a stop-motion puppet film in 1942 that would adapt Wagner's 14-hour Ring Cycle. Universal was going to produce until they learned Hitler was a Wagner fan and pulled the plug (Priebe, 2011). He produced 1954's puppet film *Hansel and Gretel*, released by RKO not long after that studio lost its Disney distribution contract (Beck, 2005, 103).
4. Eric Walter White wrote that Zeller's score was performed live until the reels were synchronized to sound in 1931 in the U.S. (1931, 28).
5. I omitted illustrated storybooks as these were an entirely separate realm.
6. It was quite the eye-opener when I read how Cinderella's step-sisters cut off parts of their feet to fit inside the shoe, the little mermaid died at the end, the evil queen in Snow White danced in fiery red iron shoes, and Rapunzel's prince was blinded by thorns. I was spared Bluebeard.
7. *Silverlock* by John Myers Myers, 1949.
8. "The first principle was 'Story Is King,' by which we meant that we would let nothing—not the technology, not the merchandising possibilities—get in the way of our story" (Catmull & Wallace, 2014, 66).
9. Such as the first black princess in *The Princess and the Frog*; *Enchanted*, which pokes fun at the formula, albeit remaining the same; and *Frozen*, which trades the true love romance for sisterly affection. Also in the mid 2010s, Disney is venturing into making live action adaptations of its animated classics, including *Maleficent, Cinderella, Beauty and the Beast* and *The Jungle Book*.

Chapter 5

1. There are two silhouette characters that resemble Sigmund Freud and Adolf Hitler at the end and they

argue over a window. Hitler wants it closed and Freud wants it open. Did the closed window represent Hitler's political views and Freud's openness the opposition? While this probably wasn't a political comment and a coincidence, it does make one wonder if some message is buried within this segment. In the end, the train makes a sudden stop and throws Hitler on Freud.

2. A new soundtrack was cut for *Dr. Dolittle* in 1970 and the intertitles were removed. The newer soundtrack is a better accompaniment to the movie, but the film loses part of its uniqueness without the intertitles.

3. Strasser was the first of Reiniger's avant-garde friends to leave Germany (Mebold, 2008, 20)

4. *Dr. Dolittle* was synchronized to a score by Philip Braham in 1930 (White, 1931, 28).

5. For an extensive look at Disney's development with the multiplane camera, check out John Canemaker's book *The Lost Notebook: Herman Schultheis and the Secrets of Walt Disney's Movie Magic*. It contains many behind-the-scenes photographs and information not included in previous publications.

6. Iwerks and Disney respected each other as colleagues. While other animation historians hint at animosity between the pair, Ub's granddaughter Leslie Iwerks told a different story in the biography she wrote with John Kenworthy, *The Hand Behind the Mouse*. Leslie and her co-author felt the relationship was best described by Leonard Maltin, "I think they had a great working relationship because they sparked each other—they fed off each other in a very effective way—so that without Ub, Walt probably couldn't have done some of the things he did and without Walt, Ub's inventions wouldn't have been put to good use" (qt. in Iwerks and Kenworthy, 2001, 230).

7. Disney Animation abandoned the multiplane camera after *Lady and the Tramp* (1955) because it was expensive to operate. It was taken back out in the 1980s for *The Black Cauldron* but no one remembered how to work it (Sito, 2013, 225)

8. Logically the Disney Company would want to raise Walt to the status of god, perhaps in a manner comparable to how the Japanese refer to Osamu Tezuka as the "god of manga." Manga is Japanese for comic book. While Tezuka is called a comic book god, his animation work shaped the modern anime industry (he was inspired by Walt Disney's cartoons as he developed his own style). It is apt to also call him the "god of anime." Tezuka is revered in Japanese culture on the same scale as Walt Disney is in America. If not for the Judeo-Christian population within the U.S., perhaps Walt Disney would be labeled the "god of American animation."

9. Walt Disney testified before the House Un-American Activities Committee in 1947.

10. As of writing this book, I conducted a basic Google search using the term "first animated movie" and the first search result was a Wikipedia article on *Snow White and the Seven Dwarfs*.

Chapter 6

1. This is best documented in *The Rape of Europa* by Lynn H. Nicholas, the documentary of the same name distributed by Menemsha Films, and *The Monuments Men* by Robert M. Edsel and Bret Witter. The Hollywood film based on Edsel and Witter's book relies too much on inaccurate and unnecessary drama.

2. *Carmen, Dr. Dolittle, Papageno, Harlekin* and *Prinzen Achmed* were Reiniger's favorite films that she made (Happ, 2004, 42).

3. Had Reiniger met Walt Disney, she probably would have cut a silhouette for him.

4. Cristiani owned a laboratory in Buenos Aires that he ran with his sons. He added subtitles to Hollywood movies and others, and experimented with animation (Zucchelli, 2010).

5. Tezuka's most famous work is the anime *Tetsuwan Atom* (*Mighty Atom*), or *Astro Boy* for U.S. viewers.

6. Grierson possibly created the first viral GIF, when he noticed that Hitler raised his leg high when he stepped backwards. He looped the footage to make it look like Hitler was jigging. It was distributed across Canada and played over and over again on newsreels. It made Hitler look foolish and silly (Selwyn-Holmes, 2011).

7. Pierre Lestringuez wrote several screenplays for Renoir in the 1920s.

8. This was later rectified and correctly noted by Alfred Happ, Evamarie Blattner, Christel Strobel and other Reiniger scholars.

9. It was actually 1935.

10. Another translation of this quote was used to introduce readers to Art Spiegelman's Pulitzer Prize-winning graphic novel *Maus: A Survivor's Tale Vol. II*. Spiegelman depicted Jews as mice in the graphic novel.

11. Perhaps an inspiration for Spiegelman?

12. The Palestinian al-Aqsa TV station aired a show, *Tomorrow's Pioneers*, that used the same concept to indoctrinate children with a hate for the Jews and Israel: Mickey Mouse lookalike Farfour taught children a poem, "Rafah sings 'Oh, oh.' Its answer is an AK-47." Farfour was later killed by Israel (NBC News, 2007; Oliver, 2007). Walt's daughter Diane said, [qm]Of course I feel personal about Mickey Mouse, but it could be Barney as well" (Oliver, 2007).

13. When *Snow White* premiered in Baltimore, there was a riot as fans tried to enter the Hippodrome cinema. The police had to be at the theater for the film's entire first week and "the throng at one time was out of control for four hours" (Smoodin, 2012, 85). For the most part, animation fans are well-behaved, although they do get excited at conventions.

14. Marc Eliot's book *Dark Prince of Hollywood* questioned Disney's birth parents and stated he was actually born in Spain to an unwed mother. Disney did wonder if he was adopted, but all records and his resemblance to his parents and brothers is proof otherwise. (He inherited his father's straight sloped nose

and his mother's eyes. His nephew Roy E. Disney bore a striking resemblance to him in later years.)

15. Politics and origins aside, as a first attempt at an animated cartoon, *Armer Hansi* isn't that bad.

16. Vladek Spiegelman, Art Spiegelman's father, was imprisoned in Dachau and survived.

17. Similar to *Armer Hansi*, it would have been interesting to see what the final product would have been like.

18. Giesen and Storm share a story how Fieber in the early 1970s wanted to save money on animation, so he contacted a Japanese cartoon director. "[The director] bowed and then fluently cited a poem by Heinrich Heine in German language. I couldn't have done that." It was Isao Takahata, Hayao Miyazaki's partner. However, Fieber and Takahata never worked together, because studio officials were afraid characters might be drawn to look too Asian (2012, 109).

19. I interpret how Reiniger's films are feminist pieces and how shadow puppetry helped her cope with Koch's death in later chapters. These are my interpretations, however.

20. Concurrently an exhibit was held that showcased proper German art idealizing the Nazi lifestyle. The Degenerate Art exhibit had more visitors.

Chapter 7

1. In 1948 and '49, author H.W. Whanslaw visited Reiniger at her studio and interviewed her for his book *Shadow Play*. That book was inspired Richard Bradshaw to pursue puppetry.

2. He would also marry Norwegian painter Annie Mie and have two daughters. He died on August 17, 2000. As for Büdi's parents, they fled Germany in 1941 via the Trans-Siberian Railroad.

3. Politically incorrect representations of ethnic Africans, Asians, Jews and other people is a popular topic amongst animation scholars, especially with depictions in Disney, Warner Brothers and MGM cartoons.

4. The swan boat-swing is a bit much as are the dancing girls bedecked in pink costumes.

5. This is part of a small collection of Lotte Reiniger silhouettes located at the Getty Research Institute. Twelve other silhouettes consisting of *commedia dell-'arte* characters, including Columbine, Harlequin, and Pantaloon, were apparently made for someone named Ervald, as they were inscribed with a 1959 New Year's greeting and signed by Koch and Reiniger.

Chapter 8

1. Happ also includes this description in his own book, I conclude, for the same reason.

2. Muppet fans might recognize Bradshaw's shadow puppets as a featured guest performer on *The Muppet Show* episode 122 with Ethel Merman. A mouse, a hippopotamus and an ostrich play on a tightrope and slide, and hilarity ensues.

3. Currell cites Blackham's book *Shadow Puppets* (Barrie & Rockliff, 1960) with the latter portion of the quote, but I couldn't find it in there. Credit is still given to both authors.

4. Sarg moved to New York, launched a modern puppet movement, established a production company and shaped the foundation for modern American puppetry. He also performed his own version of *The Rose and the Ring* (Bell, 2002, 89–90).

5. Holman predicted that "the 'Hollywood factory' of producing extravagant films for huge profits is rapidly dying." He also thought directors would be regarded more as artists and the traditional puppet films would be considered more "serious art" than entertainment (1975, 46). CGI action films made for eye candy and children's entertainment say otherwise.

Chapter 9

1. Ann Hogarth and Jan Bussell comment that Reiniger's shadow Nativity play had an elephant and palfrey (1985, 125).

2. Walt Disney and Ub Iwerks read Edwin G. Lutz's *Animated Cartoons: How They Are Made, Their Origin and Development* to teach themselves animation.

3. Subsequent editions of *Shadow Theatres and Shadow Films* contain the same text and information.

4. I remember viewing Reiniger's *Jack and the Beanstalk* and *The Gallant Little Tailor* in elementary school as well as in preschool in the late twentieth century.

5. Jez Stewart of the BFI proposed an intriguing thought that Reiniger's *Die Abenteuer des Prinzen Achmed* was never lost as film archivists were aware of its importance. He wrote, "Was her film any different than any other silent cinema film—or rather any other masterpiece of silent cinema? Their importance was understood on their release, they were preserved, and they are rereleased on new formats or with a new lick of paint every decade or so to capture a few new hearts and minds, or refresh the relationship with old friends" (Stewart email to author, 25 Jan. 2016).

6. I was surprised the Library of Congress had Zeller's original film score, because my research indicated that the DIF had Zeller's papers as well as the scores for *Prinzen Achmed*. When I queried the Library of Congress, I was told they had housed Zeller's score for the film on behalf of MoMA until the New York museum requested it back. As the DIF mentioned, they contacted the Library of Congress for the original score to use in the restoration; perhaps the DIF was allotted a copy or one was discovered in Zeller's papers post-restoration. As of this book's writing, MoMA and the DIF both house copies.

7. For the purposes of this book, I asked the BFI to send me a photo of *Prinzen Achmed*'s storage container as it would be cool for readers to see (pun intended). Removing any film canister from cold storage must follow a strict protocol to preserve the film's integrity, and due to *Prinzen Achmed*'s fragile nature it wasn't possible. In hindsight, it would have been horrible if

my request caused accidental harm to the only remaining original negative. Best to leave it on ice (pun intended again).

8. Disney helped MoMA get out of a bind in World War II, when the museum was accused of being too focused on European art. MoMA's relationship with Disney helped prove their American loyalty. After all, what is more American than Mickey Mouse? (Mikulak, 1996, 121)

Chapter 10

1. Hibon animated "The Tale of the Three Brothers" in *Harry Potter and the Deathly Hallows, Part 1*.

Chapter 11

1. Frank Thomas and Ollie Johnston eventually came around to computer animation and were later immortalized as caricatures in a crowd scene in Pixar's *The Incredibles*, spouting, "There's no school like the old school."

2. In no particular order of importance, except alphabetical.

3. Much like myself when it comes to Lotte Reiniger's career.

4. Selick wrote, "In doing a little research on Claude Kirchner, I found he was born in Rostock, Germany, moving to the United States in 1925. It's possible he saw some of Lotte's earliest films as a child in Germany, perhaps suggested having them on his show."

Bibliography

Adams, D. (2002). *The Salmon of Doubt: Hitchhiking the Galaxy One Last Time.* New York: Harmony Books.

Adams, S. (2013, December 17). "The Dead Hand of Walt Disney: Harlan Ellison Reviews 'Saving Mr. Banks.'" Retrieved from http://blogs.indiewire.com/criticwire/the-dead-hand-of-walt-disney-harlan-ellison-reviews-saving-mr-banks.

"'Adventures of Prince Achmed' Discovered in Paris Two Years Ago." (1931, February 12). *The Harvard Crimson.* Retrieved from http://www.thecrimson.com/article/1931/2/12/adventures-of-prince-achmed-discovered-in/.

Allan, R. (1999). *Walt Disney and Europe: European Influences on the Animated Feature Films of Walt Disney.* Bloomington: Indiana University Press.

Andersen, H. C., J. Hersholt, N. Daniel, and A. Disl (2013). *The Fairy Tales of Hans Christian Andersen.* Hohenzollernring, Köln, Germany: Taschen Gmbh.

Andrew Lang's Fairy Books. (N.D.). Retrieved from http://www.mythfolklore.net/andrewlang/blue.htm.

Apgar, G. (2014). *A Mickey Mouse Reader.* Jackson: University of Mississippi.

Apgar, G. (2015). *Mickey Mouse: Emblem of the American Spirit.* San Francisco: The Walt Disney Family Foundation Press.

Arnheim, R. (1928, December 24). "Lotte Reinigers Schattenfilme." *Die Weltbuhne.* Nr. 52. (p. 961). In Reiniger, L. (1969). *Lotte Reiniger: Eine Dokumentation.* (p. 5) Berlin: Deutsche Kinemathek.

Arnheim, R. (1997). *Film Essays and Criticism.* Madison: University of Wisconsin Press.

"Art Nouveau Movement, Artists and Major Works." (2016). *The Art Story.* Retrieved from http://www.theartstory.org/movement-art-nouveau.htm.

Ashoff, B. (1980/1981). *Die Frau Hinter den Schatten.* In Reiniger, L. (2008). Lotte-Reiniger-Gesamtausgabe. Berlin: Absolut-Medien.

Ballard, F., and L. C. Schubert (1974). "We Love You, Lotte Reiniger!" *The Puppetry Journal,* 26(1), 39–42.

Barrier, J. M. (1999). *Hollywood Cartoons: American Animation in Its Golden Age.* New York: Oxford University Press.

Barrier, J. M. (2007). *The Animated Man: A Life of Walt Disney.* Berkeley: University of California Press.

Barrier, M. (2015, October 5). "What's New Archives: October 2015." Retrieved from http://www.michaelbarrier.com/home page/whatsnewarchivesoct15.html.

Barrier, M., and B. Spicer (2003, December 14). "An Interview with Chuck Jones." Retrieved from http://www.michaelbarrier.com/Funnyworld/Jones/interview_chuck_jones.htm.

Bastiancich, A. (1981). Lotte Reiniger. In Pilling, J., and British Film Institute. (1992) *Women and Animation: A Compendium.* London: British Film Institute.

"Bauhaus Movement, Artists and Major Works." (2016). *The Art Story.* 2016. Retrieved from http://www.theartstory.org/movement-bauhaus.htm.

Beck, J. (2005). *The Animated Movie Guide.* Chicago: Chicago Review.

Beck, J. (2015, March 29). "Cartoon Terms" [E-mail to the author].

Beck, J. (2015, April 1). "Jerry Beck for Toon-In Talk" [Telephone interview].

Beck, J. (2015, May 8). "Is This a Chuck Jones Quote?" [E-mail to the author].

Beckman, H. (1974, Summer). "Animated Women." *Animation Kit,* 40, 42.

Beckerman, H. (2003). *Animation: The Whole Story.* New York: Allworth Press.

Bell, J., and Detroit Institute of Arts. (2000). *Strings, Hands, Shadows: A Modern Puppet History.* Detroit, MI: Detroit Institute of Arts.

Bendazzi, G. (1999). *Cartoons: One Hundred Years of Cinema Animation.* Bloomington: Indiana University Press.

Bendazzi, G. (2008). *Quirino Cristiani, Pionero del Cine de Animación: Dos Veces el Océano*. Buenos Aires: Ediciones de la Flor.

Beyfuss, E., and A. Kossowsky (1924). *Das Kulturfilmbuch*. Berlin: C.P. Chryselius.

Bingen, S., and M. Wanamaker (2014). *Warner Bros: Hollywood's Ultimate Backlot*. Lanham, MD: Taylor Trade Publishing.

Bishop, D. (2013). "German Film Scores from the Silent Era." *Notes* 70(1), 180–186.

Blackham, O. (1960). *Shadow Puppets*. New York: Harper & Brothers.

Blakeston, O. (1962). *The Queen's Mate*. Lowestoft, UK: Scorpion Press.

Blattner, E., P. Colombo, S. Kissane, Irish Museum of Modern Art (Kilmainham, Dublin, Ireland), İstanbul Modern, and Mouseio Benakē (2008). *In Praise of Shadows*. Milano: Charta.

Blattner, E., K. Wiegmann, L. Reiniger, et al. (2010). *Lotte Reiniger: "Born with Enchanting Hands": Three Silhouette Sequels*. Tübingen: Wasmuth.

Blumenthal, E. (2005). *Puppetry: A World History*. New York: Harry N. Abrams.

Bock, H.-M., and T. Bergfelder (2009). *The Concise Cinegraph: Encyclopedia of German Cinema*. New York: Berghahn Books.

Boese, A. (2015). "Pierre Brassau, Monkey Artist." Retrieved from http://hoaxes.org/archive/permalink/pierre_brassau_monkey_artist.

Borowsky, K., and L. Reiniger (1982). *Und Schon Geht Sie auf die Reise: Annas 1. Lebensjahr 72 Gedichte*. Tübingen: Heliopolis.

Brode, D. (2004). *From Walt to Woodstock: How Disney Created the Counterculture*. Austin: University of Texas Press.

Bulik, M. (2014). "1930: Mickey Mouse, Censored." Retrieved from http://www.nytimes.com/timesinsider/2014/09/26/1930-mickey-mouse-censored/?_r=0.

Burg, K. (n.d.). "Disney Rejection Letter, 1938." Retrieved from https://www.flickr.com/photos/polaroid/632255233.

Burlingame, J. (2000). *Sound and Vision: 60 Years of Motion Picture Soundtracks*. New York: Billboard.

Bussell, J. (1981). "Lotte Reiniger: In Memoriam." *Animations: A Review of Puppets and Related Theatre* 4(6).

Canemaker, J. (1994, July 10). "Life Before Mickey." *The New York Times*, 14–16.

Canemaker, J. (2000, May/June). "Un Disney." 54(3), 95–99.

Canemaker, J., and H. Schultheis (2014). *The Lost Notebook: Herman Schultheis and the Secrets of Walt Disney's Movie Magic*. San Francisco: The Walt Disney Family Foundation Press.

Catmull, E. E., and A. Wallace (2014). *Creativity, Inc.* New York: Random House.

Cavalier, S. (2011). *The World History of Animation*. Berkeley: University of California Press.

Clevderdon, D. (1985, September 17). "Obituary of Mr. Eric White." *The Times*. Nr. 62245.

Colt, S., T. Jennings, M. Zwonitzer, O Platt, J. Neuburger, M. Dugas, J. Baynard, et al. PBS Distribution (Firm). (2015). *American Experience: Walt Disney*.

Coté, G. (1954, October). "Flatland Fairytales." *Film*, 16–18.

Cowan, M. J. (2013). "The Ambivalence of Ornament: Silhoutte Advertisements in Print and Film in Early Twentieth-Century Germany." *Art History*, 362013, 784–809.

Crafton, D. (1982). *Before Mickey: The Animated Film, 1898-1928*. Cambridge, MA: MIT Press.

Crafton, D. (2013). *Shadow of a Mouse*. Berkeley: University of California Press.

Currell, D. (1999). *Puppets and Puppet Theatre*. Wiltshire [England]: Crowood Press. D23. (n.d.). "Disney Legends: Bill Garity." Retrieved from https://d23.com/walt-disney-legend-bill-garity/.

Davidson, G. (1959). *Ballet Stories for Young People*. London: Cassell.

Davis, J. R. (1996). "Ballet on British Television: Christian Simpson, Producer, 1949–1959—Divine or Diabolic?." *Dance Chronicle* 19:1, 17–92.

Davison, A. (2004). *Hollywood Theory, Non-Hollywood Practice: Cinema Soundtracks in the 1980s and 1990s*. Aldershot, Hants, England: Ashgate.

Deitch, G. (2005). "Gene Deitch's Definition of Animation." Retrieved from http://www.cartoonbrew.com/old-brew/deitchs-definition-786.html.

Deitch, G. (2015, March 21). "Animation—What the Heck Is It?" Retrieved from http://blogs.indiewire.com/animationscoop/animation-what-the-heck-is-it-20150321.

Denslow, P.K. "What Is Animation and Who Needs to Know? An Essay on Definitions." Pilling, J., and Society of Animation Studies. (1997). *A Reader in Animation Studies* (pp. 1–4). London: J. Libbey.

Deutsches Filmmuseum. (1999). "Restaurierungsbericht: Die Abenteuer des Prinzen Achmed" [Pamphlet]. Frankfurt: Deutsches Filmmuseum.

Disney, W. E. (1940). *U.S. Patent No. Us2201689*. Washington, D.C.: U.S. Patent and Trademark Office.

Doherty, T. P. (2013). *Hollywood and Hitler, 1933–1939*. New York: Columbia University Press.

The Dream Doll. (2016). American Film Institute: Catalog of Feature Films. Retrieved from http://www.afi.com/members/catalog/DetailView.aspx?s=1&Movie=14523.

Dütsch, W. (1926). "Bemerkungen zur Postion der Zeitgenössichen Kritken." In Reiniger, L. (1969). *Lotte Reiniger: Eine Dokumentation*. (pp. 57–58) Berlin: Deutsche Kinemathek.

Ealy, C. (1999, November 3). "Japan's 'Princess Mononoke' and Disney Films Are Worlds Apart." *The Dallas Morning News*.

Eckes, A. E., and T. W. Zeiler (2003). *Globalization and the American Century*. Cambridge: Cambridge University Press.

Edera, B. (1977). *Full Length Animated Feature Films*. New York: Hastings House.

Egan, D. (2012, June 12). "Five Women Animators Who Shook Up the Industry." Retrieved from http://www.smithsonianmag.com/arts-culture/five-women-animators-who-shook-up-the-industry-120442836/?no-ist.

Eliot, M. (1993). *Walt Disney: Hollywood's Dark Prince: A Biography*. Secaucus, N.J: Carol Pub. Group.

Fahr-Becker, G. (2004). *Art Nouveau*. Köln: Könemann.

Falk, K. (2016, March 17). "Puppeteer Quote" [E-mail to the author].

Feild, R. D. (1942). *The Art of Walt Disney*. New York: Macmillan.

Fessenden, M. (2014, November 26). "Lemmings Do Not Explode or Throw Themselves Off Cliffs." Retrieved from http://www.smithsonianmag.com/smart-news/lemmings-do-not-explode-or-throw-themselves-cliffs-180953475/?no-ist.

Fifth Avenue Playhouse (1942). *Surrealist and Fantastic Film Festival Film Festival*. Theater program detailing the movies playing at the festival.

Film-Kurier. (1931). "You Can See Mickey Mouse Dancing." In G. Apgar (Ed.), *A Mickey Mouse Reader* (pp. 35–36). Jackson: University Press of Mississippi.

Film Portal. (n.d.). "Lotte Reiniger." Retrieved from http://www.filmportal.de/person/lottereiniger_c94c9327f5cc4ce8ac33debaf05e27e0.

Finch, C. (1981). *Of Muppets & Men: The Making of the Muppet Show*. New York: Muppet Press/Knopf.

Finch, C. (1993). *Jim Henson: The Works*. New York: Random House.

Finkielman, J. (2004). *The Film Industry in Argentina: An Illustrated Cultural History*. Jefferson, NC: McFarland.

Fogg, A. (2007). *The Film Society 1925–1939: A Guide to the Collections* (S. Parker and I. O'Sullivan, Eds.) In *British Film Institute*. Retrieved from http://www.bfi.org.uk/sites/bfi.org.uk/files/downloads/bfi-the-film-society-1925-1939-a-guide-to-collections.pdf.

Forbes, Edward W. "Report of the Fogg Art Museum, 1926–27." *Annual Report (Fogg Art Museum) 1926/1927* (1926): 1–15.

Foster, G. A., K. Jacobs, and A. L. Unterburger (1998). *Women Filmmakers & Their Films*. Detroit: St. James Press.

Freud, Sigmund. (1900). "Interpretation of Dreams." *Classics in the History of Psychology*. Christopher D. Green. Retrieved from http://psychclassics.yorku.ca/Freud/Dreams/dreams.pdf.

Friedman, J. (2016, January 2). "Disney Strike" [E-mail to the author].

Furniss, M. (2007). *Animation—Art and Industry: A Reader*. London: John Libbey Cinema and Animation.

Galle. (2003). *RIAS Berlin Und Berliner Rundfunk 1945–1949*. Münster: Lit.

Gelder. (1981, June 25). "Lotte Reiniger, Cut Out for Fame." *Barnet Press*, 1–2.

Giesen, R., and J. P. Storm (2012). *Animation Under the Swastika: A History of Trickfilm in Nazi Germany, 1933–1945*. Jefferson, NC: McFarland.

Grafly, D. (1932). "Animated Cartoon Gives the World an American Art." *Public Ledger*.

Grafly, D. (1932). "Disney Has Debut in Art Circles." *Public Ledger*.

Graham, J. (1965, June 23). "The Cup of Sorrow in Every Woman's Life." *The Ladies' Home Journal*, 68–70.

Graity, W. E. (1940). *U.S. Patent No. Us2198006*. Washington, D.C.: U.S. Patent and Trademark Office.

Green, R. L., and L. Reiniger (1975). *King Arthur and His Knights of the Round Table*. London: Puffin.

Gritten, D. (2009, January 28). "Bolt—Interview with Director John Lasseter." Retrieved from http://www.telegraph.co.uk/culture/film/4371064/Bolt-interview-with-director-John-Lasseter.html.

Haase, D. (July 22, 2004). "The Arabian Nights, Visual Culture, and Early German Cinema." *Fabula* 45, 261–274.

Hahn, D., and T. Miller-Zarneke (2015). *Before Ever After: The Lost Lectures of Walt Disney's Animation Studio*. Los Angeles; New York: Disney Editions.

Hake, S. (2002). *German National Cinema*. London: Routledge.

Halas, J., and R. Manvell (1976). *The Technique of Film Animation*. London: Focal Press.

Hall, M. (1931, February 27). "The Adventures of Prince Achmed." *New York Times*.

Happ, Alfred, and Lotte Reiniger. *Lotte Reiniger: 1899–1981: Schöpferin einer Neuen Silhouettenkunst*. Tübingen: Kulturamt, 2004. Print.

Harryhausen, R., and T. Dalton (2008). *A Century of Stop Motion Animation: From Méliès to Aardman*. New York: Watson-Guptill Publications.

Heine, H. "Surlalune Fairy Tales: Fairy Tale Quotations." (2007, July 2). Retrieved from http://www.surlalunefairytales.com/introduction/quotes.html.

Heller, S. (2016, April 1). "Fifth Avenue Surrealism." Retrieved from http://www.printmag.com/daily-heller/fifth-avenue-surrealism/.

Henson, J., and Frank Oz. Films for the Humanities and Sciences (Firm), and WNET (Television station: New York). (1994). "The World of Jim Henson." New York: Thirteen/WNET.

Hiller, M. (6 Jan. 1924). "Der Silhouettenfilm." *Der Kinematograph*. Nr. 881. In Reiniger, L. (1969). *Lotte Reiniger: Eine Dokumentation*. (pp. 7–8) Berlin: Deutsche Kinemathek.

Hoedeman, Co. (2015, December 7). "Lotte Reiniger 1" [E-mail to the author].

Hoedeman, Co. (2015, December 10). "Lotte Reiniger 2" [E-mail to the author].

Hoedeman, Co. (2016, February 7). "Lotte Reiniger 3" [E-mail to the author].

Hogarth, A., and J. Bussell (1985). *Fanfare for Puppets!* Newton Abbot, Devon, UK: David & Charles.

Hochstetter, G., and L. Reiniger (1919). *Venus in Seide: Ein Neues Liebesbrevier*. Berlin: Eysler.

Holman, L. B. (1975). *Puppet Animation in the Cinema: History and Technique*. South Brunswick: A.S. Barnes.

Hopf, C. (2007). *Papercutting: Tips, Tools, and Techniques for Learning the Craft*. Mechanicsburg, PA: Stackpole Books.

Isaacs, J. (1971). *Ein Scherenschnittfilm Entsteht. Lotte Reiniger bei der Arbeit*. In Reiniger, L. (2008). Lotte-Reiniger-Gesamtausgabe. Berlin: Absolut-Medien.

Isaacs, J., and L. Hagen (1964/1965) *Lotte Reinigers Kunst*. In Reiniger, L. (2008). Lotte-Reiniger-Gesamtausgabe. Berlin: Absolut-Medien.

Iwerks, L., and J. D. Kenworthy (2001). "The Hand Behind the Mouse." New York: Disney Editions.

Johnson, J. (2015, October 4). "When I Met Lotte Reiniger" [Telephone interview].

Jones, B. J. (2013). *Jim Henson: The Biography*. New York: Ballantine Books.

Jones, C. (1999). *Chuck Amuck*. New York: Farrar Straus Giroux.

Jouvanceau, P., and J. Roda (1980). "L Était une Fois une Grande Dame du Cinéma. Lotte Reiniger." *Banc-Titre*, (13).

Jouvanceau. (2004). *Le Film de Silhouettes* (The Silhouette Film). Genova: Le Mani.

Joyce, W. (2016, March 11) "William Joyce Loves Lotte Reiniger" [Telephone interview].

Kaufman, J. B. (June 01, 1993). "Before Snow White." *Film History* 5:2, 158–175.

Kaufman, J. B. (2012). *The Fairest One of All: The Making of Walt Disney's Snow White and the Seven Dwarfs*. San Francisco: Walt Disney Family Foundation Press.

Keefer, C. (2016, April 12). "Cecile Starr" [E-mail to the author].

Kelly, G., S. Donen, A. Green, B. Comden, A. Freed, D. O'Connor, D. Reynolds, Turner Entertainment Co. (2002). *Singin' in the Rain*. Burbank, CA: Warner Home Video.

Kemp. (2003). "Bfi Screenonline: Reiniger, Lotte (1899–1981) Biography." Retrieved from http://www.screenonline.org.uk/people/id/528134/.

Kenny, C. (2015, March 9). "The Debate Over the Term 'Anime' Is Pointless." Retrieved from http://blogs.indiewire.com/animationscoop/the-debate-over-the-term-anime-is-pointless-20150309.

Klein, N. M. (1993). *Seven Minutes: The Life and Death of the American Animated Cartoon*. London: Verso.

Knight, M. (2014, January 13). "Toons of the Orient 3: East Steals West." Retrieved from http://cartoonresearch.com/index.php/toons-of-the-orient-3-east-steals-west/.

Korkis, J. (2014, February 26). "Debunking Meryl Streep, Part Two." Retrieved from https://www.mouseplanet.com/10606/Debunking_Meryl_Streep_Part_Two.

Kotlarz, I. "Working Against the Grain: Women in Animation." (pp. 101–104) In Cook, P., and Dodd (1993). *Women and Film: A Sight and Sound Reader*.

Kracauer, S. (1947). *From Caligari to Hitler: A Psychological History of the German Film*. Princeton, N.J.: Princeton University Press.

Kraszna-Krausz, A. (1928, December 6). "A Fairy-Tale Film." *Close Up*, 52–58.

Kreimeier, K. (1999). *The Ufa Story: A History of Germany's Greatest Film Company, 1918–1945*. Berkeley: University of California Press.

Krüger, H. (1920). *Das Loch im Vorhang: Licht- und Schattenbilder aus dem Deutschen Theater*. Berlin: Dr. Lysler.

Kubersky, S. (2014, January 7). "Fact-Checking Saving Mr. Banks with Disney Historian Jim Korkis." Retrieved from http://www.orlandoweekly.com/orlando/fact-checking-saving-mr-banks-with-disney-historian-jim-korkis/Content?oid=2240838.

La Monica, R. (2006, January 25). "Disney Buys Pixar." Retrieved from http://money.cnn.com/2006/01/24/news/companies/disney_pixar_deal/.

Lang, A. (1990). *The Blue Fairy Book*. Champaign, IL: Project Gutenberg.

Lange, A. (2015, August 28). "Inside the Persistent Boys Club of Animation." Retrieved from http://www.buzzfeed.com/arianelange/creative-work-in-connection-with-preparing-the-cartoons#.vdw7VD6qK.

Lawson, V. (2006). *Mary Poppins, She Wrote: The Life of P.L. Travers*. New York: Simon & Schuster.

Lee, N., and K. Madej (2012). *Disney Stories: Getting to Digital*. New York: Springer.

Leeuwen, R., U. Marzolph, and H. Wassouf (2004). *The Arabian Nights Encyclopedia: Vol. 1*. Santa Barbara, CA. [u.a.: ABC-CLIO.

Leslie, E. (2002). *Hollywood Flatlands*. London: Verso.

Lewell, J. (1982). "The Art of Chuck Jones." In M. Furniss (Ed.) (2007), *Animation: Art and Industry* (pp. 131–144). London: John Libbey Cinema and Animation.

Lewell, J. (2004). "The Live Wire: Margaret J. Winkler and Animation History." In M. Furniss (Ed.) (2007), *Animation: Art and Industry* (pp. 105–110). London: John Libbey Cinema and Animation.

Liebenson, D. (2001, December 10). "Dazzling Gem of Animation Rediscovered." *Los Angeles Times*. Retrieved from http://articles.latimes.com/2001/dec/10/entertainment/et-liebenson10.

Littmann, E. (1921). *Die Erzählungen aus den Tausendundein Nächten: 1*. Leipzig: Insel-Verlag.

Littmann, E. (1923). *Die Erzählungen aus den Tausendundein Nächten: 2*. Wiesbaden: Insel-Verl.

Littmann, E. (1924). *Die Erzählungen aus den Tausendundein Nächten: 3*. Wiesbaden: Insel-Verl.

Littmann, E. (1925). *Die Erzählungen aus den Tausendundein Nächten: 4*. Wiesbaden: Insel-Verl.

Littmann, E. (1927). *Die Erzählungen aus den Tausendundein Nächten: 5*. Wiesbaden: Insel-Verl.

Littmann, E. (1928). *Die Erzählungen aus den Tausendundein Nächten: 6*. Wiesbaden: Insel-Verl.

Lofting, H., L. Reiniger, and E. L. Jacobsohn (1930). *Der Böse Gutsherr und die Guten Tiere*. Berlin-Grunewald: Williams & Co. Verlag G.M.B.H.

Lorent. S. (2016, 26 April). "Lotte Reiniger's Film at George Eastman House" [email to author].

[Lotte Reiniger's Dr. Dolittle]. (1929, February). *Close Up*, 4(2), 97.

"Lotte Reiniger Recording." Interview. *Hugh M. Hefner Moving Image Archive*. USC School of Cinematic Arts, N.D. Web. Recorded in 1976.

Lustberg, J. (Writer), and J. Crowell (Director). (2015). *Behind the Magic: Snow White* [Television Broadcast]. ABC.

Maltin, L. (1987). *Of Mice and Magic: A History of American Animated Cartoons*. New York: New American Library.

Manson, R. (1942, January 16). "Going Out Tonight?" *The New York Post*, 14.

Marschall, S., R. Bieberstein, and K. Schneider (2012). *Lotte Reiniger—Tanz der Schatten*. Berlin: Absolut Medien.

Marzolph, U. (2016, January 20). "German Arabian Nights" [E-mail to the author].

McFadyean, M. (2000, September 21). "Louis Hagen: Wartime Torture Failed to Dim His Creative Lust for Life." *The Guardian*. Retrieved from http://www.theguardian.com/news/2000/sep/22/guardianobituaries.filmnews.

McPharlin, P., and M. B. McPharlin (1969). *The Puppet Theatre in America: A History, 1524–1948*. Boston: Plays, Inc.

Mégroz, R. L. (1949). *Profile Art Through the Ages: A Study of the Use and Significance of Profile and Silhouette from the Stone Age to Puppet Films*. New York: Philosophical Library.

Mebold, A. (2008). [Linear notes]. In "Doktor Dolittle & Archivschätze" [DVD] in Reiniger, L. (2008). *Lotte-Reiniger-Gesamtausgabe*. Berlin: Absolut-Medien.

Merritt, R. (2005). "Lost on Pleasure Islands: Storytelling in Disney's Silly Symphonies." *Film Quarterly*, 59, 1, 4–17.

Mikulak, B. (1997). "Mickey Meets Mondrian: Cartoons Enter the Museum of Modern Art." *Cinema Journal*, 36, 3, 56–72. Millhauser, S. (1999). *Little Kingdoms*. London: Phoenix.

Mörike, E. (1800). *Mondscheingärten: Gedichte*. Gütersloh?: Bertelsmann.

Moritz, W. (1992) "Resistance and Subversion in Animated Films of the Nazi Era: The Case of Hans Fischerkoesen." In Pilling, J., and Society of Animation Studies. (1997). *A Reader in Animation Studies*. (pp. 228–240) London: J. Libbey.

Moritz, W. (1996a). "Lotte Reiniger." Animation World Magazine, 1, 6–23.

Mortiz, W. (1996b) "Some Critical Perspectives on Lotte Reiniger." *Animation World Magazine*, 5, 40–51.

Moritz, W. (2004). *Optical Poetry: The Life and Work of Oskar Fischinger*. Bloomington: Indiana University Press.

Museum of Modern Art Archives, NY. Collection PI. Series Folder: 11.B.2023.

NBC News. (2007). "Mickey Mouse Double 'Martyred' on Hamas TV." Retrieved from http://www.nbcnews.com/id/19509117/ns/world_news-mideast_n_africa/t/mickey-mouse-double-martyred-hamas-tv/#.VslHqzYshcY.

Newsom, J. (July 01, 1980). "A Sound Idea" Music for Animated Films." *The Quarterly Journal of the Library of Congress* 37, 279–309.

Nicolella, H., and J. T. Soister (2012). *Many Selves: The Horror and Fantasy Films of Paul Wegener*. Duncan, OK: BearManor Media.

Ocelot, M. (2014, November 24). "Michel Ocelot on Lotte Reiniger" [E-mail to the author].

Oliver, M. (2007, May 09). "Palestinian TV Uses Mickey Mouse to Promote Resistance." Retrieved from http://www.theguardian.com/world/2007/may/09/usa.israel.

Osmond, A. (2010). *100 Animated Feature Films*. New York: Palgrave Macmillan, on behalf of the British Film Institute, 2010.

Otten, K., and L. Koch-Reiniger (1949). *Der Ewige Esel: Eine Jugenderzählung*. Zürich: Atlantis.

The Oxford American Dictionary and Thesaurus: With Language Guide. (2003). New York: Oxford University Press.

Palfreyman, Rachel. "Life and Death in the Shadows: Lotte Reiniger's Die Abenteuer des Prinzen Ahmed." *German Life and Letters* 64.1 (2010): 6–18.

Pallant, C. (2011). *Demystifying Disney: A History of Disney Feature Animation*. London: Continuum International.

Parrill, W. (2006). *European Silent Films on Video: A Critical Guide*. Jefferson, NC: McFarland.

Peet, B. (1989). *Bill Peet: An Autobiography*. Boston: Houghton Mifflin Company.

Pettigrew, N. (1999). *The Stop-Motion Filmography: A Critical Guide to 297 Features Using Puppet Animation*. Jefferson, NC: McFarland.

Pidhajny, C. R. (2001). *Milestone Films the Adventures of Prince Achmed Press Kit* [Pamphlet]. Harrington Park, NJ: Milestone Films. www.milestonefilms.com.

Pilling, J., and British Film Institute. (1992). *Women and Animation: A Compendium*. London: British Film Institute, Exhibition & Distribution Division.

Pilling, J., and Society of Animation Studies. (1997). *A Reader in Animation Studies*. London: J. Libbey.

Pilling, J. (2011). "Historical Milestones: Who Gets to Tell Whose Stories? (Or ... the Dilemmas of Programming...)." In *Tricky Women: AnimationsfilmKUnst von Frauen*, ed. by Birgitt Wagner and Waltraud Grausgruber. Marburg, Germany: Schüren.

Pliny the Elder. (1855). *The Natural History* (J. Bostock, Trans.). Retrieved from http://www.perseus.tufts.edu/hopper/text?doc=Perseus:text:1999.02.0137.

Polus, B. (1978). "Lotte Reiniger, Guest Star, P of A." *A Propos*, Spring (14), 28–29.

Price, D. A. (2008, November 11). "Art Challenging Technology." Retrieved from http://www.pixartouchbook.com/blog/2008/11/11/art-challenging-technology.html.

Priebe, K. A. (2011, January 20). "The Advanced Art of Stop-Motion Animation: History of Stop-Motion Feature Films: Part 1." Retrieved from http://www.awn.com/animationworld/advanced-art-stop-motion-animation-history-stop-motion-feature-films-part-1.

Purschke, H. R. (1957). *The Puppet Theatre in Germany*. Darmstadt: Neue Darmstädter Verlagsanstalt.

Raganelli, K. (Director). (2001). *Lotte Reiniger: Homage to the Inventor of the Silhouette Film* [Motion picture on DVD]. In *Die Abenteuer des Prinzen Achmed: Adventures of Prince Achmed*. United States: Milestone Film & Video.

Ratner, M. (2006). "In the Shadows." *Art on Paper*, January/February, 44–49.

"Reiniger with Starr and Others, 1978." [MP3]. (1978). Cecile Starr. Recording of Lotte Reiniger Tribute in New York City, 1978. Cecile Starr Papers, Columbia University.

Reiniger, L., K.-P. Beyer, W. Zeller, Deutsches Filmmuseum Frankfurt am Main, British Film Institute, Comenius Films, Oscilloscope Laboratories (Firm). (2011). *Die Abenteuer des Prinzen Achmed: Adventures of Prince Achmed*. United States: Milestone Film & Video.

Reiniger, L. (1926). "Lotte Reiniger's Introduction to the Adventures of Prince Achmed." In Pidhajny, C. R. (2001). *Milestone Films the Adventures of Prince Achmed Press Kit* [Pamphlet]. Harrington Park, NJ: Milestone Films.

Reiniger, L. (1929). "Lebende Schatten." In Reiniger, L. (1969). *Lotte Reiniger: Eine Dokumentation*. (pp. 8–9) Berlin: Deutsche Kinemathek.

Reiniger, L. (1934, December 31). "Deutsche Schaffende: Pläne Und Wünsche, Fülle des Strebens, Reichtum an Können!" *Film-Kurier*.

Reiniger, L. (1936a). "Moving Silhouettes." *Film Art*, 3, 14–18.

Reiniger, L. (1936b) "Film as Ballet." *Life and Letters To-Day*, 157–163.

Reiniger, L. (1936, Spring). "Scissors Make Films." *Sight and Sound*.

Reiniger, L. (195?). *Cinderella: A Lotte Reiniger Story-Play*. London: Hutchinson.

Reiniger, L. (195?). *The Magic Horse: A Lotte Reiniger Story-Play*. London: Hutchinson.

Reiniger, L. (195?). *Puss in Boots: A Lotte Reiniger Story-Play*. London: Hutchinson.

Reiniger, L. (195?). *The Sleeping Beauty: A Lotte Reiniger Story-Play*. London: Hutchinson.

Reiniger, L. (1969). *Lotte Reiniger: Eine Dokumentation*. Berlin: Deutsche Kinemathek.

Reiniger, L. (1970a). *Shadow Theatres and Shadow Films*. London: Batsford.

Reiniger, L. (1970b). "The Adventures of Prince Achmed, or What May Happen to Somebody Trying to Make a Full Length Cartoon in 1926." *Silent Picture*, 8, 2–4.

Reiniger, L. (1975). *Shadow Puppets, Shadow Theatres, and Shadow Films*. Boston: Plays, Inc.

Reiniger, L., and L. Da (1999). *Die Hochzeit des Figaro*. Tübingen: Universitätsstadt Tübingen, Kulturamt.

Reiniger, L. (2008). *Lotte-Reiniger-Gesamtausgabe.* Berlin: Absolut-Medien.

Renoir, J. (1974). *My Life and My Films.* New York: Atheneum.

Renoir, J. (1975, September 2). Letter to Cecile Starr. Cecile Starr Papers, Columbia University.

Rich, C. (1993). *The Book of Paper Cutting: A Complete Guide to All the Techniques with More Than 100 Project Ideas.* New York: Sterling Pub. Co.

Richter, H., and D. Britt (1997). *Dada, Art and Anti-Art.* New York: Thames and Hudson.

Rivera, D. (1932). "Mickey Mouse and the American Art." In G. Apgar (Ed.) (2014), *A Mickey Mouse Reader* (pp. 53–54). Jackson: University Press of Mississippi.

Roman, S. (1974). "Close Up: Lotte Reiniger." *The Puppetry Guild of Greater New York Newsletter,* 11(5).

Roman, S. (1976). "Lotte Reiniger." *The Puppetry Guild of Greater New York's Newsletter,* 14(1), 8–11.

Roman, S. (1976). "The Magic of Lotte Reiniger." *The Puppetry Journal,* 28(3), 19–22.

Russell, H. (1937). "Mickey Mouse and American Art." In G. Apgar (Ed.) (2014), *A Mickey Mouse Reader* (pp. 141–145). Jackson: University Press of Mississippi.

Russett, R., and C. Starr (1988). *Experimental Animation: Origins of a New Art.* New York: Da Capo Press.

Rutherford, E. (2009). *Silhouette.* New York: Rizzoli.

Sano, A. "Chiyogami, Cartoon, Silhouette: The Transitions of Ofuji Noburo." In Masao, Y., and G. H. Tze-yue (2013). *Japanese Animation: East Asian Perspectives.* (pp. 87–97). University Press of Mississippi.

Scheffauer, H. G. (1926, July 18). "New Shadow Film Enriches the Screen: Arabian Nights' Story Lives." *The New York Times,* SM6.

Schneider, S. (1988). *That's All Folks! The Art of Warner Bros. Animation.* New York: H. Holt.

Schodt, F. L. (2007). *The Astro Boy Essays: Osamu Tezuka, Mighty Atom, and the Manga/Anime Revolution.* Berkeley, CA: Stone Bridge Press.

Schönfeld, C., and C. Finnan (2006). *Practicing Modernity: Female Creativity in the Weimar Republic.* Würzburg: Königshausen & Neumann.

Schreck, K. (2012). *Persistence of Vision* [DVD].

Schreck, K. (2016, February 12). "*The Thief and the Cobbler* Storyboards" [E-mail to the author].

Selick, H. (2016, March 29). "Henry Selick Was Inspired by Lotte Reiniger" [E-mail interview].

Selwyn-Holmes, A. (2011, June 21). "Hitler's Little Jig." Retrieved from https://iconicphotos.word press.com/tag/nazi/.

Sembach, Klaus-Jürgen. (2002). *Art Nouveau: Utopia, Reconciling the Irreconcilable.* Köln: Taschen.

Sherman, R. B. (2013). *Moose: Chapters from My Life.* AuthorHouseUK.

Sigall, M. (2005). *Living Life Inside the Lines: Tales from the Golden Age of Animation.* Jackson: University Press of Mississippi.

Sito, Tom. (2006). *Drawing the Line.* Lexington: University Press of Kentucky.

Sito, T. (2013). *Moving Innovation,* Cambridge, MA: MIT Press.

Small, E. S., and E. Levinson (September 1989). "Toward a Theory of Animation." *Velvet Light Trap: A Critical Journal of Film & Television,* Fall(24), 67–73.

Smith, A. (2016, February 17). "Quote." [E-mail interview].

Smith, D. "New Dimensions—Beginnings of the Disney Multiplane Camera." Solomon, C., American Film Institute, and Walter Lantz Conference on Animation. (1987). (pp. 37–49). *The Art of the Animated Image: An Anthology.* Los Angeles: American Film Institute.

Smoodin, E. L., and British Film Institute. (2012). *Snow White and the Seven Dwarfs.* London: Palgrave Macmillan on behalf of the British Film Institute.

Solomon, C. (1993). *Enchanted Drawings: The History of Animation.* New York: Knopf.

Stanton, A. (2012, February). "The Clues to a Great Story." Retrieved from https://www.ted.com/talks/andrew_stanton_the_clues_to_a_great_story?language=en.

Starr, C. (1980). Lotte Reiniger's Fabulous Film Career." *Sight Lines.* (pp. 17–19).

Starr, Cecile. "The Adventures of Prince Achmed." Lyon, C., and S. Doll (1984). *The Macmillan Dictionary of Films and Filmmakers.* (p. 12). London: Macmillan.

Starr, C. (1987). "Fine Art Animation." In M. Furniss (Ed.) (2007), *Animation: Art and Industry* (pp. 67–71). London: John Libbey Cinema and Animation.

Starr. C. (28 June, 1994). Letter to Louis Hagen. Renoir, J. (Cecile Starr Papers, Columbia University.

Starr, C. "Lotte Reiniger." In Foster, G. A., K. Jacobs, and A. L. Unterburger (1998). *Women Filmmakers & Their Films.* (pp. 349–352). Detroit: St. James Press.

Staub, N. L. (1981). "Lotte Reiniger." *A Propos,* Fall (22), 16–17.

Steffans, L. (1926, September 28). *Die Weltbühne* Nr. 39. In Reiniger, L. (1969). *Lotte Reiniger: Eine Dokumentation.* (p. 55) Berlin: Deutsche Kinemathek.

Stewart, J. (2016, January 25). "Rediscovery" [E-mail to the author].

Stewart, J. (2016, February 4). "Rediscovery 2" [E-mail to the author].

Strobel, C. (n.d.a). "Lotte Reiniger: Bio-Filmgraphie." Retrieved from http://www.lottereiniger.de/lotte_reiniger/biofilmographie.php.

Strobel, C. (n.d.b). "Silhouetten-Kurzfilme Im Zusammenhang Mit Dem Film 'Die Abenteuer des Prinzen Achmed': Der Scheintote Chinese." Retrieved from http://www.lottereiniger.de/filme/kurzfilme.php.

Strobel, C. (2008). [Linear notes]. In "Märchen und Fabeln" [DVD]. In Reiniger, L. (2008). *Lotte-Reiniger-Gesamtausgabe*. Berlin: Absolut-Medien.

Strobel, C. (2015, October 27). Buch von Lotte Reiniger [E-mail to the author].

Sugar, R. (2016, February 22). "Rebecca Sugar on Lotte Reiniger" [E-mail to the author].

"Surrealism Movement, Artists and Major Works." (2016). *The Art Story*. Retrieved from http://www.theartstory.org/movement-surrealism.htm.

Taylor, K. V. (2011). *Nationality, Gender, and Genre: The Multiple Marginalization of Lotte Reiniger*. University of South Florida.

Taylor, R. (1996). *Encyclopedia of Animation Techniques*. Philadelphia: Running Press.

Telotte, J. P. (2006). "Ub Iwerks' (Multi)Plain Cinema." *Animation*, 1(1), 9–24.

Telotte, J. P. (2008). *The Mouse Machine: Disney and Technology*. Urbana: University of Illinois Press.

Telotte, J. P. (2010). *Animating Space: From Mickey to Wall-E*. Lexington: University Press of Kentucky.

Thomas, B. (1990). *Clown Prince of Hollywood: The Antic Life and Times of Jack L. Warner*. New York: McGraw-Hill.

Thomas, F., and O. Johnston (1981). *Disney Animation: The Illusion of Life*. New York: Abbeville Press.

Thomas, F. (1984). "Can Classic Disney Animation Be Duplicated on the Computer?" *Computer Pictures*, 2(4), 20–26.

Thompson, K. (2014). "'Quick—Like a Bunny!' the Ink and Paint Machine, Female Labor and Color Production." *Animation Studies Online Journal*, 9. Retrieved from https://journal.animationstudies.org/kirsten-thompson-quick-like-a-bunny/.

Tupper, C. (2014, June 4). "A History of Women in Animation: Mothers of a Medium." Retrieved from http://www.themarysue.com/history-women-in-animation/.

Twomey, N. (2016, April 11). "Nora Twomey Cartoon Saloon" [E-mail to the author].

Von Boehn, M. (1932). *Dolls and Puppets*. London: G.G. Harrap & Company.

Vorwärts. (1926, May 9). Nr. 216. In Reiniger, L. (1969). *Lotte Reiniger: Eine Dokumentation*. (p. 53) Berlin: Deutsche Kinemathek.

Warner, M. (2012). *Stranger Magic: Charmed States and the Arabian Nights*. Cambridge, MA: Belknap Press of Harvard University Press.

Walt Disney Family Museum. (2013, November 19). "The Walt Disney Family Museum Mourns the Loss of Diane Disney Miller." Retrieved from http://www.waltdisney.org/press-room/walt-disney-family-museum-mourns-loss-diane-disney-miller.

Watanabe, Y. "The Japanese Walt Disney." In Yokota, M., and T. G. Hu (2013). *Japanese Animation: East Asian Perspectives*. (pp. 98–114). Jackson: University Press of Mississippi.

Weaver, R. T. (1931, June). "Prince Achmed and Other Animated Silhouette." *Theatre Arts Monthly*. (pp. 505–509).

Wells. (1998). *Understanding Animation*. London: Routledge.

Whanslaw, H. W. (1950). *Shadow Play*. Redhill, Surrey: W. Gardner, Darton.

White, E. W. (1931). *Walking Shadows: An Essay on Lotte Reiniger's Silhouette Films*. London: Leonard and Virginia Woolf at the Hogarth Press.

White, E. W., and L. Reiniger (1934). *Wander Birds*. Bristol: Perpetua.

White, E. W., and L. Reiniger (1936). *The Little Chimney Sweep*. Bristol, Eng: White & White.

White, E. W. (1939, January). "Lotte Reiniger and Her Art." *The Horn Book*, 15(1), pp. 45–49.

Wilson, J. K. (2011). *The Most Dangerous Man in America: Rush Limbaugh's Assault on Reason*. New York: Thomas Dunne Books.

Wizansky, N. G. (2004). "Crosscut: Handicraft and Abstraction in Weimar, Germany."

Yokota, M., and T. G. Hu (2013). *Japanese Animation: East Asian Perspectives*. Jackson: University Press of Mississippi.

Zipes, J. (2002). *The Brothers Grimm: From Enchanted Forests to the Modern World*. Houndmills, Basingstoke, Hampshire: Palgrave Macmillan.

Zipes, J. (2011). *The Enchanted Screen: The Unknown History of Fairy-Tale Films*. New York: Routledge.

Zipes, J. (1997). *Happily Ever After: Fairy Tales, Children, and the Culture Industry*. New York: Routledge.

Zipes, J., P. Greenhill, and K. Magnus-Johnston (2016). *Fairy-Tale Films Beyond Disney: International Perspectives*. New York: Routledge, 2016.

Zohn. (2010, February 5). "Coloring the Kingdom." Retrieved from http://www.vanityfair.com/culture/2010/03/disney-animation-girls-201003.

Zucchelli, G., P. M. Roig, K. Welz, S. Woods, R. Borgini, G. Bendazzi, and Caravel Animation (Firm). (2010). *Quirino Cristiani: The Mystery of the First Animated Movies*. London: The Caravel Animation.

Index

Aardman 237
Abbey Arts Centre 152, 159, 188, 203–204, 213, 215
Abduction from the Seraglio 161–162
Des Abenteuer des Prinzen Achmed 1–2, 19, 23, 30, 39, 44–45, 47, 49, 51, 92, 98, 102, 105, 108–110, 113, 122–123, 126, 141–142, 144, 147, 151–152, 154, 156–157, 159, 162, 168–169, 171, 173, 177, 202, 205–206, 219–222, 227, 229–230, 232–234, 236, 241–246, 249, 255–256
Abstract films 7, 10, 15, 19, 24, 46, 55, 58, 66, 105, 131–133, 143, 204, 233
Acciaio 56
Actualidades Valle 83–84
Adams, Douglas 197
Adventures of Baron Munchausen see *Münchhausen*
Aesop's Film Fables 97
Aladdin 1, 57, 67–72, 81, 156, 159, 169
Alexeieff, Alexander 41, 121
Alhambra 93
Alice comedies 105, 179, 195
Alice in Wonderland 50
All Creatures Great and Small 202
Les Allumettes animées 84
Alper, Mara 120, 164, 175, 208
Amor und das standhafte Liebespaar 16
Andersen, Hans Christian 16, 118, 121, 164, 206, 214, 216, 254ch2n2
Anderson, Ken 105, 106
Animation as art 222–228
Animation definition 21–27
Animation desk see Tricktisch
Animation errors 29, 37, 39, 118, 162, 180
Animation vs puppetry 196–200
Anime 24–27, 75, 124, 176–177, 243, 255
anti–Semitic 135
Die Apokalypse 7, 268
El Apóstel 1, 53, 84–86
Argentina 42, 53, 83, 86, 123
Armer Hansi 140–141, 256ch6n15&17

Armstrong, Charles 245
Arrugas 18
Art nouveau 4, 15, 40, 45–46, 112, 162, 279
"Art of Animation" 108–109
Arthurian legends 89, 149–151
Aschenputtel 17; see also Cinderella
Ashida, Iwao 131
Astro Boy see Tetsuwan Atom
Athens 124, 184–186
Atlanta Center For Puppetry Arts 3, 199
Atlantis Verlag 148, 161, 165, 184
ATV 202
Aucassin and Nicolette 28, 31, 175–176, 208, 235
Avant garde 19, 41–42, 48–49, 55, 79, 93, 105, 110, 122, 134, 136, 143–144, 154, 184, 206, 222–223, 230, 246, 255
Avatar 197
Azur et Asmar 246

Babbitt, Art 87, 241
Badener Lehrstück vom Einverständnis 95
Baker, George 125
Bakshi, Ralph 18, 178
Ball of Fire 66
Ballet 16, 33, 93, 99, 103–104, 125, 150–151, 161–162
Ballet Stories for Young People 163
Band von Gold 204
Die Barcarole 16, 45, 118
Barnyard Battle 134
Baroque 40, 207
Barr, Alfred H. 226
Barré, Raoul 233
Barry, Iris 226–227
Bartosch, Berthold 15, 39, 41, 46, 54–57, 59, 75, 92, 94–96, 121, 133, 177, 204
Basquiat, Jean-Michel 222
Battle of Berlin 67, 130, 146, 159, 202, 219
The Battle of Skagerrak 56
Bauhaus 18, 41–42, 45–48
The Beautiful Chinese Princess see *Die Schöne Prinzessin von China*
Beauty and the Beast 77, 81, 198

Beck, Jerry 18, 25, 82
The Beggar's Opera 117
La Belle et la bête see *Beauty and the Beast*
Benjamin, Walter 110, 126
Benton, Thomas 224
Berg, Alban 101
Bergeron, Bibo 142
Berlin 4–5, 14–16, 49, 55–56, 62–63, 85, 93–96, 100–101, 115–116, 121, 124, 128–129, 135, 140–141, 144, 146–147, 154, 167, 183–184, 194–195, 202, 206, 213, 217, 220
Berlin, Die Sinfonie der Grosstadt 55
Berlin Schattenspiele 146–147, 187
Berlinale 204–205
Berliner Rundfunk 146
Bertelsmann-Lesering 165
Betty Boop 131, 133, 176
BFI see British Film Institute
Bible 4, 194, 205
Biedermann, Werner 213
Bierling, Lore 56
Bird, Brad 197–198
Birmingham, England 202
Bizet, Georges 101, 115
Blair, Mary 178, 181
Blake, William 118
Blakeston, Oswell 165
Blank, Dorothy Ann 178
Blitz Wolf 131
The Blue Marble 207
Blue Sky 22, 237
Bonjour Paris 178
The Book of Kells 241
Bosko 131
Boston 205, 211
Bradshaw, Richard 113, 150, 188–189, 238, 256ch8n2
Braham, Philip 255ch5n4
Brave 241
Bray, J.R. 233, 245–246
Brecht, Bertolt 62, 92, 95, 115, 130, 204, 230
Bremenr Stadtmusikanten 137
Bresson, Henri Cartier 125
Brewer, Frances 177
Bristol 53, 121
British Film Institute 82, 219, 222, 256ch9n5

Britten, Benjamin 126
The Broken Bridge see *Le Pont Cassé*
Brüderchen und Schwesterchen 146
Bryan, Diana 206, 214
Bugs Bunny 130, 245
A Bug's Life 80
Bührman, Max 201
Bunraku puppetry 22
Burke, Richard 159
Burton, Richard 74, 75
Burton, Tim 85
Bussell, Jan 21, 148–150, 188–189, 196, 256*ch*9*n*1
Bute, Mary Ellen 41

Das Cabinet des Dr. Caligari 18, 42, 122
California Institute of Arts 179, 229, 242
Caliph Stork 154
Callihoe see Core
The Cameraman's Revenge 80
Cameron, James 197
Campos, Florencio Molina 123
Canada 24, 125, 131, 159, 193, 205–208, 211–212, 218, 247, 255*ch*6*n*6
The Cardinal 207
Carmen 98, 101, 115–116, 120, 159, 171–174, 189, 226, 255*ch*6*n*2
The Cartoonist's Nightmare 195
Case-Zwicker, Elizabeth 178
Cassell and Company 162
Catmull, Ed 78, 88
Cavalcanti, Alberto 121, 125
CGI 12, 25–26, 197–198, 231, 235, 256*ch*8*n*5
Chagall, Marc 143
Chaplin, Charlie 96, 122, 161
Chapman, Brenda 240–243
Charlottenburg 4, 146, 217
Le Chat Noir 194, 247
Le Château de sable 207
Cheap-quels 88
The Child and the Spells see *L'Enfant et les sortilèges*
Children's Television Workshop see Sesame Workshop
China 4, 7, 10, 68, 88, 95, 183–184, 187, 190–191, 193, 201
Chiyogami 246
Chomet, Sylvain 142
Chouinard, Nelbert 179
Christmas 25, 128, 134, 148, 165, 187, 216, 244
Christmas Is Coming see *Post Early for Christmas*
Churchill, Frank 102
Cinderella 17, 88, 151, 154, 156–157, 165, 169, 241–242, 245, 254*ch*4*n*9
Clausen, Jürgen 142
Cohl, Émile 84, 195, 233
Columbine 98, 100, 172, 216, 256*ch*7*n*5
Comenius Films 53–54, 63, 83
Comic books 6, 94, 124, 193, 197, 222, 254*ch*2*n*3, 255*ch*6*n*10
Commedia dell'arte 100, 125, 185, 234, 256*ch*7*n*5

Concentration camps 140, 152, 156, 186–187; see also Dachau
Confusions of a Nutzy Spy 131
Congo Jazz 131
Connecticut 208–209, 211
Les Contes de la nuit 246
"Control Device for Animation" 107
Cooney, Joan Ganz 206
Coons, Jeff 222
Coppa Mussolini 136
Coraline 245
Core 189
Corinthian Dame see Maid of Corinth
The Corsican Brothers 66
Così fan tutte 98, 204
Coventry Theatre 165
Cristiani, Quirino 1, 51, 53, 61, 84–86, 112, 122–123, 135, 196, 218, 230, 237, 254*ch*3*n*4, 255*ch*6*n*4
Crown Film Unit 147–148
CTW see Children's Television Workshop
Cupid and the Steadfast Lovers see *Amor und das standhafte Liebespaar*
Cürlis, Hans 14–15, 18, 136
Cutout animation see Silhouette animation process

Dachau 140–141, 256
Dada 41–42, 45–47, 143, 223
Daffy Duck 130–131
The Dance of Death 95
The Dancing Fleece see *Wool Ballet*
Darwin's Theory of Evolution 53, 83, 86
Däumelinchen see *Thumbelina*
David, Tissa 27, 178
Davidson, Gladys 162
Davidson, Retta 178
Davis, Marc 122–123, 179
Dawley, Herbert 246
Dayton, Helena Smith 245
DECLA 18
DEFA 141
Degenerate Art 79, 114, 136, 143–144, 191, 256*ch*6*n*20
Dessau, Paul 94, 101
Dettenhausen 213–215, 217
Deutsche Film Prize 204
Deutsche Zeichenfilm 138–141
Deutschen Institut für Puppenspiel 202
Deutsches Filminstitut 1, 58, 86, 203, 219, 221–222, 254*ch*2*n*1, 256*ch*9*n*5
Dibutrade see Core
Dickinson, Thorold 121, 124–125
Diehl, Ferdinand, and Herman 132, 196
DIF see Deutsches Filminstitut
Dillinger 50
Dinner Time 97
Disney, Edna 122
Disney, Lillian 122
Disney, Roy 51, 97, 122, 135, 198

Disney, Roy E. 222, 254*ch*6*n*14
Disney, Walt 1, 3, 11, 18, 22–23, 38, 41, 50–52, 55, 57–59, 61, 64, 76–78, 80–87, 89–91, 98, 102–112, 121–124, 130, 132–133, 135–139, 142–145, 179–181, 195, 198, 216, 222–230, 234, 236–239, 254*ch*3*n*3, 254*ch*3*n*4, 254*ch*4*n*2, 255*ch*5*n*5, 255*ch*5*n*6, 255*ch*5*n*8, 255*ch*5*n*9, 255*ch*6*n*3, 255–256*ch*6*n*14, 256*ch*9*n*2, 256*ch*9*n*8
Disney Animation Studios/Company 22–23, 26, 38–39, 41, 51–52, 64, 66, 71, 76–83, 85–89, 101, 104–105, 107–112, 122–124, 130–145, 177–182, 191, 194–195, 198, 206, 222, 225–228, 230–232, 236–238, 241–242, 244–245, 254*ch*3*n*3, 254*ch*4*n*3, 255*ch*5*n*5, 254*ch*4*n*9, 255*ch*5*n*7, 255*ch*5*n*8, 256*ch*7*n*3
Disney Brothers' Studios see Disney Animation Studios/Company
Disney Formula 76–81, 87–89, 112, 233
Disney Renaissance 12, 24, 77, 182
Disney revisionist actions 110–111, 227
Disneyfication 51, 88–89, 109
Disneyland 225
Disney's Folly 50–52, 61
Distler, Walter (Walt Disney's German "identity") 137
Dr. Dolittle und seine Tiere 93–96, 255
Doctor Who 168
Don Quixote 115, 149
Donizetti, Gaetano 127
Dornröschen 17, 137, 146; see also Sleeping Beauty
Dream Circus 125
The Dream Doll 53, 83, 85
DreamWorks 22, 237
Ducaud, Andrés de 84
Duchamp, Marcel 42
Dulac, Edmund 60, 73–74
Dumbo 58
Das dumme Gänslein 138
Düsselchen und der vier Jahrezeiten 215
Düsseldorf Stadtmuseum 20, 166, 193, 214–215, 222
DZF see Deutsche Zeichenfilm

"The Ebony Horse" 67, 72–74, 80
Edelstein, Mike 208
Eggeling, Viking 18, 41, 46, 94, 233
Egypt 29, 35, 54, 88, 92–98, 184, 191, 224, 227, 241
Ehrenarier (Honorary Aryan) 136
Einstein, Albert 10, 12, 42, 86
Einstein's Theory of Relativity 53, 83, 86
Eisler, Hanns 101
Eisner, Michael 78
L'Elisir d'amore 127

The Elixir of Love see *L'Elisir Amore*
Elizabeth II, Queen of England 214
Enchanted 254ch4n9
The Enchanted Drawing 195
L'Enfant et les sortiléges 207
Engel, Jules 242
England 10, 24, 72–73, 112, 117, 121–122, 124, 126–127, 133, 137, 147–149, 152, 156, 158, 188, 201–203, 206, 214–215, 217, 219
Entartete Art see Degenerate Art
Ernst, Max 143
Eroticism 118
Escapism 9, 44, 49, 74, 77, 132
Essanay Films 53, 83
Der Ewige Esel, Eine Jugenderzählung 148
expressionism 5, 16, 18, 41–44, 46, 49, 52, 122, 143, 148

Facts and Fantasies 125
Fairytales 1, 3–5, 7, 9–11, 13, 19, 39, 42–45, 49–50, 55, 75–81, 87–89, 91, 94, 96, 109–110, 112, 114, 117–118, 121–123, 129, 131–132, 136–137, 142–143, 147, 149, 151–154, 156, 158–159, 161–162, 168–169, 201–202, 205–206, 214, 217, 228, 230–232, 243, 246, 249
Falk, Karen 21
Falling Hare 131
Fandom 5, 20, 24, 26, 52, 55, 64, 75, 89, 92, 98, 101, 108, 110, 124, 134–136, 144, 168, 205, 218, 223–226, 226, 228, 230, 234, 240, 244–245, 255ch6n13
Fantasia 58–59, 66, 102, 107, 225, 245, 254ch4n3
Fantasia Productions 161–162
Father Christmas's Mistake see *Santa's Mistake*
Feild, Richard 64
Felix the Cat 19, 23, 52, 131, 133, 142, 179, 242
Feminazis 166–167
Feminism 46, 112–113, 166–169, 172–174, 176, 256ch6n19
Fiddlesticks with Flip the Frog 107
Fieber, Gerhard 138, 140–141, 256ch6n18
Fifth Avenue Playhouse 64–66
55 Socks 207
Figaro 204
Film Kreditbank 118
Film preservation and recovery 218–222
Filmpause 146
Finding Dory 80
Finding Nemo 80
Firth, Michael 21
Fischerkoesen, Hans 138
Fischinger, Oskar 18, 41, 46, 58–59, 94, 117, 121, 123, 132–133, 144, 204, 226, 228, 233, 246
Fisher, Bud 137
Fleischer brothers, Max and Dave 8, 23, 53, 82–83, 85, 97, 131, 178, 195, 233, 244

Die fliegende Koffer 16
Flip the Frog 107
The Flying Suitcase see *Die fliegende Koffer*
Fogg Art Museum 64
Folklore 72, 79 112, 131, 154, 247
Fontainebleau 100
Ford, Mary V. 177
The Foreign Prince see *Der fremde Fürst*
Fraggle Rock 168
France 52, 89, 95–96, 122, 125–127, 142, 177, 191, 193, 205
Franchises 74, 88, 168, 230, 234, 236
Fraser-Simon, H. 125
Freire, Dido 127
Der fremde Fürst 7
Freud, Siegfried 44, 254–255
Friedman, Jake 51
Friedman, Lillian 178
Fritz the Cat 178
Fritz the Dog 23
The Frog Prince 151, 154, 162, 165, 169, 170
Frozen 254
Frye, Sylvia 178
Fugue in D Minor 59
Der Führer's Face 130
Fürst, Leonhard 7, 144, 274
Futurism 41
FWU see Institut für Film und Bild in Wissenschaft und Unterricht

Gabin, Jean 125
Gaiman, Neil 90
Galathea 118, 120–121, 169–170, 173–174
Galland, Antoine 72–74
The Gallant Little Tailor 107, 154, 158–159, 256ch9n4
Gallopin' Gaucho 23
Gardiner, Sascha Block 211
Garity, William 105, 108, 112
Geeks 24, 26, 110
Das Geheimnis der Marquise 16, 45
Gelder, Paul 6, 16, 47, 69, 71, 164, 171, 181, 185, 213–215, 218
Gellhorn, Paul 120, 127, 147, 158, 161, 217
General Post Office 24, 125–126, 147, 153
Genscher, Hans-Dietrich 204
Gerald McBoing McBoing 245
Gert, Valeska 95
Gertie the Dinosaur 195
Die Geschichte vom wilden Jäger 149
Der gestiefelte Kate see *Der Graf von Carabas*
Das gestohlene Herz 116, 132, 144
Getty Institute 256
The Ghost of Slumber Mountain 83, 86
Gibbons, Orlando 117
Gilbert, C. Allen 246
The Girl of the Golden West see *Una Signora dell'ovest*

Glasgow 126, 165
Gliese, Rochus 6–7, 15, 96, 147, 274
Gloria Palast 63, 67, 91
Gluck, Christop Willibald 127
Glyndebourne Festival Chorus 158
Goebbels, Joseph 40, 58, 116–117, 119, 130, 132, 134–139, 141, 144
Goethe Institute 125, 206
Goldberg, Eric 51
The Golden Goose see *Die goldene Gans*
Die goldene Gans 128–129, 147, 202
Der Golem 5, 7
The Golem and the Dancing Girl 7
Good King Wenceslas 151
Goofy 130
Göring, Herman 130
GPO see General Post Office
Der Graf von Carabas 117, 120, 137, 146, 154–155
Grain Harvest 148
La Grande Illusion 125
Grant, Pauline 165, 206, 214
Graphic novels see Comic books
The Grasshopper and the Ant 154, 156, 169, 206
Grave of the Fireflies 18
Greece 6, 93, 118, 124, 149, 184, 186–187, 191–192, 224
Greeting Telegrams 148
Greve, Felix Paul 72–74
Grierson, John 24, 121, 125, 148, 196, 255ch6n6
Grimm Brothers 1, 4, 9, 17, 42–43, 72, 75, 77, 87, 121, 132, 136, 228
Gropius, Walter 45
Grotesken im Schnee 93, 254ch5n1
Groves, Olive 125
The Guardians of Childhood 244
The Guinness Book of World Records 85
Gutiérrez, Jorge 240, 242–243
Gutterer, Leopold 138

Hacivat 190–191
Haeseler, J.A. 63
Hagen, Louis 49–50, 52–54, 56–57, 92–93, 151, 154, 206, 217
Hagen, Louis, Jr. 92, 151–154, 156, 159–160, 165, 206, 218–219
Halas, John 25, 27, 33, 38, 99
Halm, Harry 93
Handel, George Friedric 117
Hanks, Tom 25, 81
Hans Trutz im Schlaraffenland 7
Hansel und Gretel 137, 154, 156, 158, 254ch4n3
Hanslick, Eduard 14–15
Happ, Alfred 9, 122, 124, 213, 215–218, 256ch8n1
Happ, Helga 116, 213–217
The Happy Prince 149–150, 188
Harding, LaVerne 178
Harlekin 98, 101, 144, 172, 185, 216, 255ch6n2, 256ch7n5

Harline, Leigh 102
Harry Potter 168, 257*ch*10*n*1
Hart, Peter 199
Harvard University 63–64, 123, 224
The Headless Horseman 107
Held, Hans 137, 139
Hellzapoppin' 66
Helvenston, Hal 106
Henning, Max 72
Henson, Jim 12, 21–22, 98, 168, 186, 198–199, 206, 216
Here and There 148
Herman and Ising 131
Herr Meets Hare 131
Hertfordshire 152
Hessling, Catherin 92, 96, 115
Heut' tanzt Mariette 93
Hibon, Ben 232, 257*ch*10*n*1
High art *see* animation as art
Himmler, Heinrich 130
Hindemith, Paul 94
Hitler, Adolf 56, 64, 66–67, 79, 114–119, 121, 123, 125, 127–129, 131–137, 139, 141, 143–145, 254*ch*4*n*3, 255*ch*6*n*6
Hitler Youth 135
Hochstetter, Gustav 15
Hodgkinson, Jo 147–148
Hoedeman, Co 207
Hoffmann, Heinrich 149
Hogarth, Ann 21, 147–150, 188–189, 196, 256*ch*9*n*1
Hogarth Puppets 21, 147–150, 187–189, 196, 201
Hollywood 11, 52, 66, 74, 76, 78, 80, 89, 104, 114, 122–123, 132, 136, 147, 172, 178–179, 212, 224–226, 246, 256*ch*8*n*5
Holocaust 141, 146, 156
Home Alone Mice 131
Homer 170
Homosexuality 95
Hotaru no Haka see *Grave of the Fireflies*
The HPO: Heavenly Post Office 126
Hubley, John 178
Huggett Family 207
Hürlimann, Martin 148, 161, 165
Hutchinson Publishing 154

I Wake Up Screaming 66
IBT *see* in-betweeners
L'Idée 94
Iger, Bob 78
The Imaginary Invalid 127
Impressionism 40
The Incredibles 257*ch*11*n*1
Ink and Paint Department 150, 162, 164, 166, 178–180, 235, 241
Insect's Aviation Week 80
Institut für Film und Bild in Wissenschaft und Unterricht 202, 204
Institut für Kulturforschung 9, 14, 31, 64, 90, 219, 277
Institute for Cultural Research *see* Institut für Kulturforschung
International Puppetry Association *see* UNIMA

La Intervención a la provincia de Buenos Aires 84
Introducing the Commonwealth 148
Irigoyen, Hipólito 84
Iron Cross of Merit 214
Irving, Ernest 125
Israel 255*ch*6*n*12
Istanbul 212
Italy 3, 56, 83, 99, 122, 125, 127–128, 130, 193, 277
It's a Small World 124
ITV Granada 164
Iwerks, Ub 8, 23, 97, 107–108, 244, 255*ch*5*n*6, 256*ch*9*n*2

Jack and the Beanstalk 158, 160, 256*ch*9*n*4
Jackson, Wilifred 98
Die Jagd nach dem Glück 96–98
Jannings, Emil 6
Japanese animation 8, 26, 63–64, 75, 90, 123–124, 130–131, 133, 136, 145, 176, 178, 180, 243, 246, 255*ch*5*n*8, 256*ch*6*n*18
Javanese puppetry 192
The Jazz Singer 23, 97, 102, 227
Jenkin, John 117
Johnson, Janibeth 31, 209–211
Johnston, Ollie 3, 12, 23–24, 236, 257*ch*11*n*1
A Jolly Good Furlough 131
Jones, Chuck 22, 103, 123, 179, 225, 234, 236
Jorinde and Joringel 151
Joyce, William 240, 244

The Kaffessackschmeisser 95
Kahlo, Frida 22
Kandinsky, Wassily 143
Kapelle, Rote 140
Kaplan, Richard 125, 152–154, 206, 214
Karagiozis 124–125, 184–186, 190–191
Karbe, Hans 141
Kardan, Alexander 17, 54, 147, 177
Karolinenstift 216
Kaskeline, Wolfgang 137, 139
Kenworthy, Janice 178
Kermit the Frog 98
King Arthur and the Knights of the Round Table 149
King Kong 82
The King's Breakfast 124, 149
Kirikou et la sorcière 246
Kleese, Debbie 208
Kleienberg, Ernst 116
Der kleine Schornsteinfeger 117–118, 120–121, 154, 159, 174
Klosterarbeiten 10
Knesebeckstraßein 4, 217
Knight in the Harem *see* Abduction from the Seraglio
Koch, Carl 14–19, 30–31, 33, 39–40, 47–49, 52–54, 56–57, 59–63, 79, 92–96, 100, 102, 114–116, 118, 120–130, 136–137, 143–149, 151–153, 158, 160–162, 177, 183–184, 187, 189, 191, 193, 201, 204, 216, 219, 230, 233; death 165–166
Kodak 220
Kora *see* Core
Kore 192
Kouichi, Junichi 8
Krämer, Otto 202
Kreisler, Fritz 115
Kriemhild's Dream 18, 55
Krüger, Helmuth 15
Kujira 246
Das Kulturfilmbuch 14, 30
Kurosawa, Akira 90
Kyoto 63

Laika 22, 237
Lang, Andrew 72–73
Lang, Fritz 18, 42, 55–56, 62, 112, 122, 219, 244
Lantz, Walter 178, 231
Lasseter, John 12, 51, 78, 88, 234
The Last Company 96
Laugh-O-Gram Studios 77, 105
Lauron, Marcellis 117
Léger, Fernand 233
Leicester 225
Leisen, Mitchell 59
Leonard and Virginia Woolf Press 100
Leonardo da Vinci 223, 237
Leslie, Hubert 164, 224
Lichtenstein, Roy 222
Lichtspiel Opus I 55
Limbaugh, Rush 166
The Lion King 1, 81, 246
The Little Chimney Sweep see *Der Kleine Schornsteinfeger*
The Little Mermaid 1, 81, 214, 254*ch*4*n*6
Littmann, Enno 72–73
Liverpool 121
Das Loch im Vorhang 15
Lofting, Hugh 93, 95
Lohengrin 119
London Film Society 96, 98, 121, 219, 226–227
Looney Tunes 22, 131, 243, 254*ch*4*n*1
Lord of the Rings 168
The Lost Shadow see *Der verlorene Schatten*
The Lost Son see *Prodigal Son*
The Lost World 80
Loteria 242
Louis Jouvet Théâtre 62
Louisiana Purchase 66
Love, Kermit 98
Lubitsch, Ernst 6–7, 74, 278
Lutz, Edwin G. 256*ch*9*n*2
Lye, Len 41, 121, 228

M 96
Mackeben, Theo 96
Madame Bovary 115
The Magic Flute see *Papageno*
The Magic Horse 154
Magritte, René 25
Mahabharata 192
Maid of Corinth 189–190, 193

Index

Majolie, Bianca 178
Maleficent 254
Malhoyt, David 208
Malkin, Michael 3, 278
Malory, Sir Thomas 149
Maltin, Leonard 111, 255*ch5n*6
Manchester 147, 225
Manchu Court 11
Manga 124, 255
Manvell, Roger 27, 33, 99
Marburg 14
Marceline, Kansas 117, 121–122
Mareoki kaisen 246
Marienbad 4
Marietta's Dancing Day see *Heut' tanzt Mariette*
Marionette 3, 13, 22 30, 77, 149, 187–188 196, 202, 242
The Marquise's Secret see *Das Geheimnis der Marquise*
La Marseillaise 125–126, 143, 193
Martin, Gordon 205–208, 210–214, 217
Martin, Pat 28, 206–207, 210, 212, 214
Marvel Comics 78
Maryland 225
Mary's Birthday 149
Masserell, Franz 94
Maus 255*ch6n*10
Mauxion Chocolate 16
McCay, Winsor 137, 195, 233
McKay, Ken 208
McLaren, Norman 24, 41, 125
McSpadden, Rae Medby 177, 180
Media and Education 208, 211–212
Meet the Robinsons 244
Méliès, Georges 45, 82, 194, 199, 219
Melodie der Welt 55
Memphis, Tenessee 225
Menken, Alan 51
Merchandising 52, 110, 135, 139, 142, 233, 236, 254
Merrytoon 245
Messmer, Otto 23, 131, 233
Metropolis 18, 42, 122, 219, 244
Mexico 218, 242
MGM 58, 77, 131, 231, 256
Michael O'Halloran 50
Michelangelo 223
Mickey Mouse 22–23, 51, 77, 98, 102, 109–110, 124, 130–131, 133–135, 137, 142, 195, 224, 226, 235, 237, 244–245, 255*ch6n*12, 257*ch9n*8
Mickey Mouse Club 135
Mickeymousing 61, 102
Miles, Celine 178
Milestone Films 220
Miller, Diane Disney 110, 180
Milne, A. A. 125
Milroy, Viviana 151–152
Ministry of Enlightenment and Propaganda 137, 141–142
Minnie Mouse 176
Mintz, Charles 23, 97, 179
Miramax 90
Miyazaki, Hayao 90–91, 256

Moberly-Holland, Sylvia 178
Modrone, Visconti Luchino di 125, 127–128
Moholy-Nagy, László 62
Molière 127
Mollas 124, 149, 184–187, 191
MoMA 226–228, 256*ch8n*6, 257*ch9n*8
Momotaro no Umiwashi 131
Momotaro: Umi no Shinpei 131
Momotaro vs. Mickey Mouse 131
Mondscheingärten: Gedichte 165
Mongols 191
Monroe, Marilyn 1
Monsters, Inc., Laugh Floor 195
Montreal 205–208, 211
Moonbot Studios 244
Moore, Tomm 142
Die Mörder sind unter uns 146
Mörike, Eduard 165
Moritz, William 5, 7, 16, 54, 58–59, 85, 93, 96, 132, 136, 143–144, 204, 219, 229, 246, 279
Morrell, Larry 102
Le Morte Darthur 149
Moss, Howard 53, 83
Motion capture technology 4, 25, 197–198
Mouse House see Disney Animation Studios/Company
Mozart, Wolfgang Amadeus 98–99, 112, 118, 161, 204–205, 215, 216, 218, 240
Multiplane camera 30, 38, 55, 82, 104, 108, 110–112, 131, 140, 191, 194, 211, 232, 255*ch5n*5
Münchhausen 77, 133
Munich 14, 55–56, 143, 202–204
Munro, Grant 206, 214
Muppet 12, 21, 78, 240, 256*ch8n*2
Murders Among Us see *Die Mörder sind unter uns*
Murnau, F.W. 122
Murski, Alexander 96
Musashino Theater 63
Music in animation 97–104
Mussolini, Benito 127–128, 130, 133, 136
Mustafa 128
Muybridge, Eadweard 137
My Lips Betray 50
"My Old Kentucky Home" 97
Myerberg, Michael 254*ch3n*3
Myers, John Myers 254*ch4n*7

Nappies 29
National Film and Television Archive 220
National Film Board of Canada 24, 205, 207
Nativity 16, 158, 256
Naturalism 157–158
Natwick, Grim 27
Nazi animation see Deutsches Zeichenfilm
Nazism 2, 9, 18, 40, 56, 77, 79, 100, 114–121, 124, 126–130, 132, 134–146, 152, 156, 167, 184, 191, 224, 236, 256, 279

NBC 255
Netherlands 219
"Neue Kinoziele" speech 13–14
Neumann, Karl 138–141
New Barnet see Abbey Arts Centre
NFB see National Film Board of Canada
NFTVA see National Film and Television Archive
Die Nibelungen 18, 55, 112, 254*ch4n*3
Nickelodeon 24–25, 182
The Nightingale and the Rose 188
The Nightmare Before Christmas 244
Nivea 16
Nixon, Michele 208
Noah's Ark 246
Norway 205
Nosferatu 96, 122
Not Without License 148
Nothing but the Truth 66
Nübrecht 14, 202
The Numberlys 244

Obituary 216
O'Brien, Willis 83, 86, 196
Ocelot, Michel 113, 142, 232, 240, 246–247
Offenbach, Jacques 161
Ofuji, Noburo 131, 246
Ohly, William 152, 159
Oishi, Ikio 131
The Old Mill 104–107
Olympia 56, 136
Ombres chinoises 143, 193
Ondine see *Undine*
1001 Arabian Nights 1, 29, 42, 44, 52, 66–67, 70–76, 79, 87, 88, 136, 173, 242
Onkel Demetrius und die fünf Freunde 147
Opera 33, 81, 95, 98–103, 112, 115–118, 125, 127, 161, 171, 174, 204, 207, 209, 217, 234
Operetta 93, 77, 115, 161
Operettas 77
Orientalism 16, 39, 44, 71–75, 186–187
Das Ornament des verliebten Herzens 15, 45, 56, 105
The Ornament of the Loving Heart see *Das Ornament des verliebten Herzens*
Orpheus 127, 188, 192
Osaka 63
Oswald the Lucky Rabbit 19, 23, 133, 242
Otaku 75
Oten, Shimokawa 8
Ottawa 207
Ottoman Empite 190–191
Out of the Inkwell 195
Oz, Frank 21

Pabst, Georg Wilhem 62, 115, 149
pacifist 55
Pál, Georg 133, 142, 196
Paleolithic Age 189

Index

Palestine 255*ch7n*12
Pantalone or Pantaloon 100, 256*ch7n*5
Pantomime 12, 165
Papageno 61, 98, 118–121, 143, 159, 206, 240, 242, 255
Papoulias, Antonis *see* Mollas
Paramount 58–59
Paris 53, 62–63, 85, 92, 94, 115, 125, 127, 129, 161, 170, 178, 193
Parker, Claire 41
Patents 84, 105, 108, 111
Peludópolis 84–85, 123
Penguin Books 150
Pepe Le Pew 144
Pepsi 124
Peri Banu 37, 67–68, 70, 72, 168–169, 171, 173, 243
Peroff, Paul 132
Persephone 192
Persepolis 18
Persia 10, 281
La Petite Marchande d'allumettes 95
Pfenninger Rudolf 61
Phenakistoscope 199
Phonofilm 97
Picasso 22, 228
Pickford, Mary 50, 226
The Pied Piper of Hamelin see Der Rattenfänger von Hameln
Pinocchio 3, 58, 107, 195
Pinschewer, Julius 16, 18, 46, 56, 118
Pixar 12, 22, 26, 78, 80, 86, 88, 236, 244, 257*ch11n*1
Plane Crazy 23
Das Plantenbuch 128
Pliny the Elder 189–190
Poe, Edgar Allan 244
Pola, Isa 128
The Polar Express 25
Politics 9, 15, 40, 84, 95, 114, 116, 128, 130, 134, 136, 143, 154, 157, 167, 172, 184, 190, 206, 213, 224, 230–231, 255*ch5n*1
Polus, Betty 213, 218
Le Pont cassé 126, 193
Pop Art 222–224
Popeye 130, 133
Post Early for Christmas 148
Potsdam 52–54, 61, 96
Powers, Pat 107
Praxinoscope 199
Presley, Elvis 135
Primrose Productions 6, 56, 69, 99, 129, 152–153, 155–160, 167, 170–171, 175, 203–204, 218–219, 222, 230, 234
Princes et princesses 246
Princess Mononoke 90–91
The Prodigal Son 193, 205
Propaganda 9, 56, 79, 116, 130–132, 134, 136–139, 141–142, 144, 282
Ptushko, Aleksandr Lukich 196
Puffin Books 149, 151
Pulcinella 125
Punch and Judy 3, 186, 195, 282

Puppetoons 133
Puppetry vs. Animation *see* Animation vs Puppetry
Pursuit of Happiness see Jagd nach dem Glück
Purzel, Brumm und Quack 137
Purzel, der Zwerg, und die Reise vom Berg 137
Purzelbaum ins Leben 141
Der Puss in Boots see Der Graf von Caracas
Pygmalion 118, 120, 169–170, 173

Quebec 205
The Queen's Mate 165
Quick macht Hochzeit 137
Quimby, Fred 58

The Rabbit of Seville 103
Raboldt, Toni 17
Rall, Hannes 232, 241
Ramayana 192
Rankin-Bass 82
rat 7–8, 117, 165
Ration Fer the Duration 131
Der Rattenfänger von Hameln 7–9, 14, 282
RCA 77, 97
Red Hot Riding Hood 176
Redottée, Hartmut W. 215
La Règle du jeu 126–127
Reinhardt, Max 5–6, 98, 104
Reiniger, Lotte: career beginnings 13–20; death 214–218; early life 4–9; lectures 5, 13, 21, 94, 118, 122, 204–206, 121–122, 205–206, 207–211, 214, 241; 1976 puppetry and animation workshop 207–211; political views 116–117, 143–145; post-*Prinzen Achmed* 90–97; *Post* War Years 146–166; puppetry 183–189, 193, 201–205; tours 204–206, 211–214; World War II years; *see also Die Abenteuer des Prinzen Achmed*; Music in animation
Rembrandt 223
Remember the Day 66
Ren and Stimpy 243
Renaissance 40, 192, 207, 223
Renoir, Jean 14, 17, 53, 63, 74, 92, 95–96, 100, 115, 124–127, 143, 147, 166, 193, 204, 208, 212, 216, 218, 230, 236, 255*ch6n*7
Revolutionary Girl Utena 243
Reyes, Luis 26–27
Reynard the Fox see Le Roman de Renard
Reynaud, Charles-Emile 233
Richter, Hans 18–19, 41–42, 46, 48, 94, 143, 233
Riefenstahl, Leni 56, 66–67, 122, 133, 136
The Ring Cycle see Die Nibelungen
Rittau, Guenther 56
The River 147
Rivera, Diego 224
Rivière, Henri 193–194

rococo 45
Roellenbleg, Heinrich 141
Das rollende Rad 116–117, 120, 131
The Rolling Wheel see Das rollende Rad
Roman, Shirley 208
Le Roman de Renard 85
romanticism 43–44
Rome 127–128, 227
Romeo and Juliet 4, 245
"Rosamunde" 63
Rosenberg, Joe 51
rotoscoping 140, 198
The Routing of the Tengu 131
Rübezahl 137
Rübezahl's Hochzeit 6–7, 14
The Rules of the Game see La Règle du Jeu
Rulffs-Künstler-Puppenbühne 117
Rumpelstiltskin's Wedding see Rübezahl's Hochzeit
Running After Luck see Jagd nach dem Glück
Russian Rhapsody 131
Ruttmann, Walter 18–19, 39, 41, 46, 54–60, 75, 92, 113, 133, 177, 204, 233

Sabotage 50
Sahlin, Don 98
Sailor Moon 243
St. Francis of Assisi 159
Saludos Amigos 123
The Sand Castle see Le Château de sable
Santa's Mistake 193
Sarg, Tony 77, 196, 246, 256*ch8n*4
satire 84, 126, 143, 168, 173, 212, 230
Scalera Film 127–128
Schauspieler Silhouetten 6, 15, 284
Scheherazade 74, 79–80, 87–88
Der scheintote Chinese 95
Scherenschnitte 1, 4–5, 10–11, 15–16, 46, 95, 113, 165, 168, 183, 194, 199, 204, 227–228, 249, 254*ch2n*2
Schiffbauerdamm Theater 147
Schlesinger, Leon 178, 254
Der Schneemann 138
Schneeweisschen 136; *see also* Snow White and the Seven Dwarfs
Schnuff, der Nieser 141, 143, 145
Schobert, Walter 16, 86, 203, 205
Schoenberg, Arnold 101
Die schöne Prinzessin von China 7
Schonger, Hubert 136
Schubbe, Jens 60
Schulz, Charles 243
Schulz, Elsbeth 146, 187
Schulz-Boysen, Libertas 140
Scott, Marilyn 208
Scott, Retta 178
Scrap Happy Daffy 131
Secret Agent 131
Seeber, Guide 14
Seel, Louis 137–139
The Seemingly Dead Chinaman see Der scheintote Chinese

Seitaro, Kitayama 8
Selby, Kelly 177
Selck, Bea 178
Selick, Henry 22, 36–37, 85, 196, 198, 207, 232, 240, 244–245, 257
Séraphin, Dominique 126, 193–194
Sergeant Snafu 131
services 11, 64, 115, 125, 137, 218
Sesame Street 168, 206
Sesame Workshop 206
Sewell, Hazel 178
sex 21, 135, 166; sexual 1, 73, 75, 178, 284
sexuality 44, 80
shades 191–192
Shadow puppetry 183–200
Shadow Theaters and Shadow Films 8, 54, 203
Shahrazad *see* Scherezade
Sheets, Millard 179
Sherman, Richard 140
Sherman, Robert B. 140, 145
Sicyon *see* Core
Siegfried 18
Sigall, Martha 179–180
Signora 100
Una Signora dell'ovest 127
Silesia 4
Silhouette, Étienne 11
Silhouette animation process 27–40
Silhouette Fantasies 246
Silhouette history 11, 189–193
Silly Symphonies 61, 77, 102, 224
Silver Dolphin *see* Venetian Silver Dolphin
Silverlock 81, 254ch4n7
Simpson, Christian 150, 158
Sin dejar rastros 1, 53, 84–85, 284
Singin' in the Rain 52
Sinkin' in the Bathtub 131
Sissi 115
Sleeping Beauty 5–6, 17, 137, 146, 150, 154, 156, 169, 284; *see also* Dornröschen
Smith, Dave 105
Smith, Dot 180
Smith, Paul J. 102
Snow White and Rose Red 154
Snow White and the Seven Dwarfs 1, 12, 22–23, 50–51, 53, 76–78, 80–83, 85–87, 89, 91, 94, 102, 104, 107, 121–122, 132–137, 141–142, 154, 178–180, 225, 227, 229, 235, 238, 239, 252, 254ch4n2, 254ch4n6, 255ch5n10, 256ch6n13
The Snowman *see* Der Schneeman
socialism 9, 136, 143, 285
Société Française des Films Artistiques 63
Soil Science 148
Song Car Toons 97
Song of the Cloud Forest 168
Songs of Experience 118
Sound in animation *see* music in animation
South Park: Bigger, Longer, and Uncut 18
Spiegelman, Art 255–256

Spiritual Constructions 204
Stanton, Andrew 80–81
Stanzell, Grace 178
The Star of Bethlehem 16, 33, 158
Star Trek 168
Star Wars 78, 168
Starevich, Ladislas 77, 83, 85, 94, 132, 196, 233
Starr, Cecile 15, 29, 41, 48, 56–57, 83, 91, 94, 126, 153–154, 167, 206, 212, 214, 218, 228, 232, 236
Staub, Nancy L. 217
Staudte, Wolfgang 146
Steamboat Willie 23, 98, 105, 226–227
Steven Universe 243
Stewart, Jez 220, 256ch9n5
Stokowski, Leopold 58–59, 254ch4n3
The Stolen Heart *see* Das gestohlene Herz
Stop-motion animation 1, 3, 8, 21–23, 27–28, 31, 36, 38, 53–54, 81, 83–85, 93, 103–104, 107, 133, 142–143, 157, 161–162, 183, 189, 196–197, 199–200, 207, 231, 238, 244, 246, 254ch4n3
Stordel, Kurt 137, 139
The Story of Mrs. Tubbs 95
The Story of the Seventeen Cows 201, 213
Storyboards 33–35 37–39, 212, 243
Stössel, Rudolf 202
Strasser, Alex 93, 96, 255ch5n3
Stravinsky, Igor 94, 125
Strobel, Christel 16, 55, 95, 124, 167, 172, 218, 255ch6n8
Struwwelpeter 149
Stuart Blackton, James 195, 233
Der Student von Prag 5, 7, 14, 115
Studio Ghibli 22, 90, 237
Subculture 24, 110
Sugar, Rebecca 240, 243
Sullivan, Pat 23, 50, 179, 233
Sullivan's Travels 179
Svankmajer, Jan 196
The Swan Lake 158, 162
Switzerland 4, 55, 1

Taborda, Diógenes 84
Takahata, Isao 256ch6n18
"The Tale of the Magic Horse" *see* "The Ebony Horse"
Tales of the Night *see* Les Contes de la nuit
Tamura, Calvin 208
Tanaka, Yoshitsugu 131
Taro's Monster Hunt 131
Tartar, Maria 51
The Tempest 4, 286
Ten Minutes of Mozart *see* Zehn Minuten Mozart
Termite Terrace 22
Terry, Paul 98, 131, 233
Terrytoon 245
Das Testament des Dr. Mabuse 96
Tetsuwan Atom 124
Tezuka, Osamu 8, 123–124, 131, 255, 286

Thackeray, William Makepeace 212
"The Tale of the Second Qalandar" 67, 77
Thirteen Men and a Girl *see* The Last Company
Thomas, Ollie 3, 12, 24, 111, 123, 236, 240, 242, 257ch11n1
Thompson, Ruthie 178, 180
The Thousand and One Nights *see* 1001 Arabian Nights
The Three Caballeros 123
Three Orphan Kittens 106
The Three Wishes 154
Threepenny Opera 95
Thumbelina 118, 154–155, 169
Tobias Knopp, Abenteuer eines Junggesellen 141
Toccata 59
The Tocher 126
Tojo, Hideki 130
Tokyo Musashino Theater 63
Tom and Jerry 130, 245
Tony Sarg's Almanac 246
Tosca 127
The Toy Parade 107
Toy Story 81
Toynbee Hall Theatre Club 127
The Treachery of Images 25
tricktisch 30–33, 40, 56–57, 100, 103–105, 107–108, 153, 161, 166, 187, 207, 212, 214–215, 232–233
Trip to the Moon 201
Triumph des Willens 56
Trnka, Jiri 143, 196
Les Trois Inventeurs 247
Trümmerfilm 146
Tübingen Stadtmuseum 1, 17, 20, 33–34, 86, 119, 222
Turck, Walter 54, 177
Turkey 10, 187, 190–191, 205
Turtle Talk with Crush 195
Twelfth Night 4
Two-Faced Woman 66
Twomey, Nora 142, 240, 242–243

UFA 7, 15, 18, 42, 49, 56, 62–63, 85, 91, 96, 128, 132–133, 137, 221, 287
Ulrich, Laurel Thatcher 166
Ultra Film Berlin 132
Uncle Demetrius and the Five Friends *see* Onkel Demetrius und die fünf Freunde
Undine 162, 164, 201
Unicorn Theatre for Children 201
UNIMA 202, 218
Union 115, 130, 134, 202, 224
Union Internationale de la Marionnette *see* UNIMA
UPA 27, 241–242

Valentino, Rudolph 135
Valle, Federico 83–84
Van Buren 97, 231
van Gogh, Vincent 22
Venetian Silver Dolphin 158
Venice 128, 136, 154

Venus in Seide 15
Der verlorene Schatten 15–16
Versailles 9, 287
Die verwitterte Melodie 138
Victoria and Albert Museum 121, 187, 201
Victory Through Airpower 131
Voinov, Nikolai 61
Volksbuehne 62
von Harbou, Thea 62
von Stroheim, Erich 125

Waffenschmied, Otto 132
Wagner, Fritz Arno 96, 254
Wagner, Richard 254*ch4n*3; *see also* The Ring Cycle
Waldman, Myron 131
Walker, Kara 113
Walking Shadows 28, 100, 140, 239, 241
WALL-E 80
Walt Disney World 195
Waltz with Bashir 18, 96
The Wander Birds 116
Warfield, Emma Louise 208
Warhol, Andy 222
Warner Brothers 22–23, 38–40, 82, 97, 103, 178, 180, 195, 227, 231, 254*ch3n*1, 256*ch7n*3
Wasmuth, Else, and Günther 202, 214, 216–217
Weather Beaten Melody see *Die verwitterte Melodie*
Wee Sandy 165
Wegener, Paul 5–9, 13–16, 19, 27, 55, 128, 165, 183, 199, 245, 288
Weill, Kurt 101
Weimar cinema 12, 16, 19, 40–42, 44, 46, 49, 52, 54, 63, 74–75, 80, 95, 101, 112, 114, 123, 133–134, 154, 167, 226, 230, 244
Wertham, Frederic 222, 254*ch2n*3
What's Opera, Doc? 103
White, Eric Walter 28, 53, 98, 100, 116–118, 121, 124, 126, 148, 184, 196, 239, 254*ch4n*3
Whitney, John Hay 226
Wilde, Oscar 188
Williams, Richard 38
Winkler, Margaret J. 179
The Wise Jackal 201
With, Karl 62
The Wizard of Oz 77
Women in animation industry 153, 176–182
Woody Woodpecker 178
Wool Ballet 148

World War II 114, 123–145
World War II animation 114–145
World War II cartoons *see* World War II animation
Wright, Basil 121
Wu Ti/Di, Emperor 190

Yankee Doodle Mouse 131
Der Yoghi 7
Young, Cy 107
Young, Paul 142
Yueh Lung Shadow Theatre 208

Die Zauberflöte see *Papageno*
Zehn Minuten Mozart 61, 98–99, 102–103, 213
Zeller, Wolfgang 60, 62–63, 98, 102, 220–222, 254*ch4n*4, 256*ch8n*6
Zelnick, Friedrich 93
Zemeckis, Robert 25
Zipes, Jack 51, 76, 78–81, 87–89, 109
Zucchelli, Gabriele 85, 123

www.ingramcontent.com/pod-product-compliance
Lightning Source LLC
Chambersburg PA
CBHW081544300426
44116CB00015B/2749